Reluctant Landscapes

Reluctant Landscapes

Historical Anthropologies of Political Experience in Siin, Senegal

FRANÇOIS G. RICHARD

The University of Chicago Press   Chicago and London

The University of Chicago Press, Chicago 60637
The University of Chicago Press, Ltd., London
© 2018 by The University of Chicago
All rights reserved. No part of this book may be used or reproduced in any manner whatsoever without written permission, except in the case of brief quotations in critical articles and reviews. For more information, contact the University of Chicago Press, 1427 E. 60th St., Chicago, IL 60637.
Published 2018
Printed in the United States of America

27 26 25 24 23 22 21 20 19 18 1 2 3 4 5

ISBN-13: 978-0-226-25240-7 (cloth)
ISBN-13: 978-0-226-25254-4 (paper)
ISBN-13: 978-0-226-25268-1 (e-book)
DOI: https://doi.org/10.7208/chicago/9780226252681.001.0001

Library of Congress Cataloging-in-Publication Data

Names: Richard, François G., 1976– author.
Title: Reluctant landscapes : historical anthropologies of political experience in Siin, Senegal / François G. Richard.
Description: Chicago ; London : The University of Chicago Press, 2018. | Includes bibliographical references and index.
Identifiers: LCCN 2017060713 | ISBN 9780226252407 (cloth : alk. paper) | ISBN 9780226252544 (pbk. : alk. paper) | ISBN 9780226252681 (e-book)
Subjects: LCSH: Sine-Saloum (Senegal)—Politics and government. | Sine-Saloum (Senegal)—History.
Classification: LCC DT549.9.S55 R53 2018 | DDC 966.3—dc23
LC record available at https://lccn.loc.gov/2017060713

♾ This paper meets the requirements of ANSI/NISO Z39.48-1992 (Permanence of Paper).

Contents

Acknowledgments

I began the research presented in this book over fifteen years ago, and I have incurred countless debts to myriad people across three continents.

First and foremost, this work would not have been possible without the hospitality of the communities in Siin whose homes and lives I have shared over the years, and whose generosity I can never repay. I am particularly thankful to Jo and Marie Ndour, Paul Ndour and Augustin Faye (Ndiongolor), Yaay Faye (Diakhao), Mr. Ngom (Diofior), Aloise Diouf (Fatick), the late Pascal Thiaw and Alice Faye (Nguénième), Abdoulaye Faye and Fat Bintou Sarr (Tattaguine), Édouard and Hélène Diagne, and the families of Abdoulaye Faye and Antoine Diouf (Diohine), Fatou Sidibé, Roki Ndiaye and Fatou Diara (Keur Samba Dia), Maliam Sagne (Mbissel), and Aida Paye and Monique Maillet (Dakar). And to the many Siin residents whose stories have found their way into this book and whose kindness has contributed to making the Siin my second home. *Njoko njaal a paax*!

I am deeply indebted to my Senegalese colleagues for living up to the ethics of *teranga*, for countless thoughtful discussions, and for the world of help and wisdom they have offered me over the years: Ibrahima Thiaw, Ndèye Sokhna Guèye (who left us too soon), Hamady Bocoum, Alioune Dème, Tapha Sall, Massamba Lame, Moussa Niang, Adama Guèye, Abdoulaye Camara, and the late Brahim Diop. I am particularly thankful to Thiaw for having taught me so much about Senegal's past, for his role in shaping the interpretations proposed in this book, and for being a model of scholarship, ethical integrity, and friendship. I am looking forward to more projects and conversations together.

I am grateful to *waa IFAN*, and for the lively conversations we've had around the tables of the Archaeology Laboratory in Dakar. Many thanks to Seydou Camara for running a tight ship for so many years, and to Adama Athié for succeeding him so expertly. I owe much to the master's and doctoral students from the Université de Dakar–Cheikh Anta Diop and the Université de Kankan (Rep. of Guinée), who have accompanied me to the field since 2002: Amadou Oury Bah, Ousseynou Badiane Aliou Badji, Boukhane Camara, Kélétigui Doukouré, Mboussiriou Diallo, Mor Faye, and Idrissa Sall were part of the original wave associated with my dissertation project. Mor's assistance and insights were invaluable. The six subsequent seasons of fieldwork included Djidéré Baldé, Aida Boye, Absatou Dia, Cheikh Diakham, Fodé Diakho, Fatoumata Diatta, Hadi Diatta, Mamoudou Diallo, Mbass Diallo, Pape Laity Diop, Michel Waly Diouf, Madické Guèye, Safiatou Mbaye, Oumy Ndiaye, Sidy Ndour, Khady Siwaré, Tidiane Sow, Amadou Thiam, and Youssou Touré. I am also grateful to Modou Traoré, whose help and good spirits in Diohine were priceless.

I extend a round of thanks to Frédéric Chauvet, Sandrine Deschamps, and Aissata Ndiaye for their help with the 2003 fieldwork, and especially to Sandrine for our energizing conversations. I am glad that the dialogue has endured over the years. I also thank the group of US-based students who participated in the 2008 and 2009 summer field school, especially Rebecca Aguilar, Agatha Baluh, Paul Diegert, Tian Tian Cai, Kristina Guild-Douglass, Sophie Exdell, Petra Johnson, and Ruby Wilson. And to Emma Wingfield, Julia Haines, and Stephanie O'Brien for their help in 2011 and 2013. I rejoice that some have chosen to pursue their own academic paths in Africa.

This book has unfolded in dialogue with a diverse cast of scholars, to the beat of their suggestions, critiques, and encouragements. At the University of Chicago, I have learned immensely from current and former colleagues: Hussein Agrama, Ralph Austen, Jennifer Cole, Jean and John Comaroff, Shannon Dawdy, Mickey Dietler, Judy Farquhar, Kesha Fikes, Ray Fogelson, Cécile Fromont, Rachel Jean-Baptiste, Alan Kolata, Kathy Morrison, Nancy Munn, Emily Osborn, Stephan Palmié, Adam T. Smith, and Alice Yao. I am grateful to the gifted doctoral students, current and former, I've had the chance to work with over the years and who have kindly commented on my work: Adela Amaral, Joe Bonni, Jamie Countryman, Lauren Coyle, Kate Franklin, Geneviève Godbout, Chris Grant, Matthew Knisley, Bryce Lowry, Kate McHarry, Johanna Pacyga, Jason

Ramsey, Matt Reilly, Theo Rose, Haeden Stewart, Mudit Trivedi, Estefanía Vidal-Montero, and Brian Wilson. I'm especially thankful to Brian, Kate, Matthew, Bryce, Johanna, Haeden, and Chris for all the help they've provided in the field. I look forward to reading their books and dissertations in the near future.

My work has also unfolded in dialogue with scholars at other institutions in the United States and Europe, who have influenced my thinking about African history, archaeology, landscape, and the workings of colonialism: Doug Armstrong, Bettina Arnold, Robin Beck, Rob Blunt, Hans Buechler, Fred Cooper, Zoe Crossland, Nic David, Chris DeCorse, Jason De León, Cyr Descamps, Mamadou Diouf, Tarek el Haik, Jeff Fleisher, Sev Fowles, Dennis Galvan, Laurence Garenne-Marot, Cameron Gokee, Alfredo Gonzalez-Ruibal, Gastón Gordillo, Rémi Hadad, Mark Hauser, Rosemary Joyce, Webb Keane, Marty Klein, Adria LaViolette, Mark Leone, Matt Liebmann, Amanda Logan, Kevin MacDonald, Scott MacEachern, Sue and Rod McIntosh, Lynn Meskell, Don Mitchell, J. Cameron Monroe, Neil Norman, Akin Ogundiran, Bertell Ollman, Deborah Pellow, Jean Polet, Sandra Rozental, Peter Schmidt, Sudipta Sen, Monica Smith, Ann Stahl, Linz Weiss, LouAnn Wurst, and Steph Wynne-Jones. I am uniquely indebted to Ann Stahl, whose thoughts and seminal research pervade almost every page of this book.

Institutionally, I am grateful for the assistance provided by the Institut Fondamental d'Afrique Noire (IFAN) in Dakar, the Musée Théodore Monod d'Arts Africains, the Séminaire Saint-Joseph de Ngazobil, and the remarkably helpful staffs of the Archives Nationales du Sénégal (ANS), Archives Nationales Françaises, Section Outre-Mer (ANSOM), and the Archives de la Congrégation du Saint-Esprit (ACSE). The research presented here has been funded through grants from the graduate school, Anthropology Department, and Maxwell School of Citizenship and Public Affairs at Syracuse University; support from the Anthropology Department, Social Sciences Division, Committee of African Studies, France Chicago Center, and Adolph and Marion Lichtstern Fund at the University of Chicago; and research grants from the Wenner-Gren Foundation (Gr. 7001) and National Science Foundation (BCS-0244774, BCS-1015989, BCS-1219499). I am also grateful for the fellowship at the Franke Institute for the Humanities, during which the first half of this book was written.

I feel very fortunate to have worked with the University of Chicago Press. I'm uniquely thankful to David Brent for believing in this project as a work of historical anthropology, and to Priya Nelson for expertly taking up David's editorial mantle. Both have been extraordinarily patient, flexible, supportive, and insightful. Many thanks also to the press's reviewers (one of whom turned out to be Ann Stahl), whose suggestions vastly improved the original manuscript. And to Christine Schwab and Carol McGillivray for their work on production and copyediting, and to Marta Steele for her wonderful index.

Finally, I'd like to thank my family: my mother, Catherine; my father, Jean-Claude; my stepfather, Frank; and my brother Julien and his wife Jenni, for their unwavering support over the years, and for providing humorous, caring respite from academia. My grandparents, who missed the completion of this book by decades, continue to inspire me. Last but not least, thanks to *mi esposa* for her poetic eye, our mutual love of small things, her endless little stories, and making sure I never take myself too seriously.

Portions of chapter 3 were published in "'The very embodiment of the black peasant?' Archaeology, history, and the making of the Seereer of Siin (Senegal)," in F. G. Richard and K. MacDonald (eds.), *Ethnic Ambiguity and the African Past: Materiality, History, and the Shaping of Cultural Identities* (Walnut Creek, CA: Left Coast Press, 2015), reproduced with permission from Taylor and Francis. Parts of chapter 5 have appeared in "The African state in theory: Thoughts on political landscapes and the limits of rule in Senegal (and elsewhere)," in S. Wynne-Jones and J. Fleisher (eds.), *Theory in Africa, Africa in Theory: Locating Meaning in Archaeology* (New York: Routledge, 2015), reproduced with permission from Taylor and Francis. Portions of chapter 7 can be found in "Recharting Atlantic encounters: Object trajectories and histories of value in the Siin (Senegal) and Senegambia," *Archaeological Dialogues* 17(1): 1–27 (2010), reproduced with permission from Cambridge University Press. Sections of chapters 7 and 8 were previously presented in "Hesitant geographies of power: The materiality of colonial rule in the Siin (Senegal), 1850–1960," *Journal of Social Archaeology* 13(1): 54–79 (2013), copyright © 2012 by François G. Richard, reprinted by permission of SAGE Publications; and "The politics of absence: The longue durée of state–peasant interactions in the Siin (Senegal), 1850s–1930s," in F. G. Richard (ed.), *Materializing Colonial Encounters: Archaeologies of African Experience* (New York: Springer, 2015), © Springer Science+Business Media New York 2015, reproduced with permission from Springer.

Note on Orthography

In the spelling and transliteration of Wolof and Seereer terms, I have followed the orthographic and phonetic conventions presented in J.-P. Diouf, *Dictionnaire Wolof-Français et Français-Wolof* (Paris: Karthala, 2003). Vowels are pronounced as in Spanish. Consonants should also be read as in Romance languages (e.g., *r*'s are rolled; *ñ* is identical to *ny*; *x* is meant to be read like the Spanish *jota*; *j* is pronounced as in *jam* and *g* as in *great*). *C* should be read *ch*. A doubling of letters denotes when native speakers lengthen vowel or consonant sounds. For the sake of convenience and fluidity, I have omitted glottal stops, tonic accents, and other diacritical marks in Seereer words. I have similarly simplified matters of pluralization. Unlike English, Seereer and Wolof do not express the plural by adding a terminal letter to the word. In Seereer, plurals generally entail a morphological transformation of the word (e.g., *fangool* [spirit shrine] is pluralized as *pangool*), while in Wolof the plural is marked by a set of articles that vary with the noun class (e.g., *caabi ji* [the key] becomes *caabi yi* [keys]). To avoid confusion in the text, I use the singular word root, accompanied by relevant verbal forms, to express both singular and plural (e.g., "the *ceddo* [slave warrior] is" or "the *ceddo* are," depending on context).

I use this phonetic system to transliterate all terms (proper names, kingdoms, historic provinces, ethnic groups), *except* the names of villages and towns, for which I retain the French spelling. Note, also, that I have not altered transliterations of local terms when quoting from archival records or historical scholarship. For example, the word "Seereer" shows the largest orthographic range and is variously spelled in primary and secondary sources as "Serer," "Sereer," "Sérer," "Sérère," and so forth.

All translations from foreign languages are mine unless indicated otherwise.

Prologue: Opening Frames, Orientations

Must we unfold the ancient drama and the epic?
Go to Mbissel, go to Fa'oy; Recite the rosary of sanctuaries
That marks out the Great Way
Retrace the steps of the Royal Road and meditate over the Way of the Cross
And Glory
Your High Priests will answer: Way of the Blood!

L. S. SENGHOR, "LE MESSAGE"[1]

October 1848. Shortly after arriving in the small trading village of Joal on the coast of Senegal, Father Gallais embarked on the first of what would become many trips to Diakhao, the capital of the kingdom of Siin. The small Catholic mission of Joal had been founded nine months before, attracted by the prospects of conversion among the Seereer, Siin's largest population, reputed for their animism and staunch resistance to the incursions of Islam. The mission, however, was established without the permission of the Siin ruler, without much backing from the French colonial administration, and had very little support within the village. Problems erupted almost immediately. The priests' presence raised fierce suspicion from local residents, especially elders, who contested the sincerity of the mission's evangelical motives. Then came the royal envoys and the countless vexations the priests endured at their hands. Many times, the king's strongmen descended upon the mission to collect the payments of liquor, gunpowder, and textiles normally expected of French traders, resorting to the persuasion of weapons when the fathers proved insufficiently cooperative. Tensions reached their zenith in June, when the missionaries hoisted up the frame of a small wooden church. Traveling fast, the news triggered a vigorous response from Joal residents and neighboring villages, which joined forces to block the construction. After months of pourparlers, the village governor's continued insistence that the chapel should be built of straw, like all architecture in the region, prompted Gallais's quest for a higher ruling before the king himself.[2]

Gallais's journey to the capital was crowned with success. During his audience with King Amat Juuf, the priest was granted royal benediction to preach "the law of Issa [Jesus]" and the right to build as many huts as he saw fit, including a wooden chapel, thus overturning the earlier decree. Shrouded in royal authority, Gallais returned to Joal triumphant, a triumph that would prove fleeting. The king's orders notwithstanding, the small chapel remained the object of loud objections. Many villagers believed the small structure would house "an arsenal or a bunker, [to be] outfitted with one hundred cannons." Building efforts were seen as a violation of the village's autonomy, an illegitimate act of seizure, and were met with popular ire, volleys of stones, sabotage, and the threat of arson.[3] While the chapel was eventually completed, the missionaries' struggles endured and spread to other missions established nearby. Seereer villagers kept complaining about the fathers' encroachment and rightfulness of their activities, and periodic embassies had to be sent to Diakhao to reclaim concessions that had been made and repealed, and to renegotiate the terms of the missionaries' presence in Siin: their rights to build and convert, to land and security, and the gifts and customs that would cement it all. By 1851, as political conflicts in the region intensified, diplomacy gave way to the realities of harassment, military raids, and violence, and the missionaries around Joal evacuated, not to return until ten years later.[4]

September 16, 2003. In an op-ed published in Senegal's daily newspaper *Walfadjri*, Pépin Joseph Faye, a schoolteacher in the Fatick region, penned, with heartfelt frustration, his dismay at the country's most recent ministerial reshuffle. How is it, he wondered, that not a single member of the newly appointed cabinet hailed from the Seereer community, even though the latter made up the country's third largest ethnic group? This historic omission, Mr. Faye opined, was a shameful dismissal of the nearly 15 percent of Senegalese who considered themselves to be Seereer, adding to an anthology of grievances about the marginalization of the Seereer from Senegal's public culture. Most troubling of all to him, however, was not the latest episode of governmental neglect per se but its implications. For, in denying the Seereer a seat at the table of political representation, were not the president and prime minister also denying them full-fledged membership in the national community?[5] And, in doing so, were they not calling into question the very institutions of the republic and its tradition of democracy since the time of independence?

Mr. Faye's *j'accuse* disputes the very foundations of the nation, citizenship, governance, and ethnicity in contemporary Senegal—questions that have long animated political debates in the country and that acquired particular salience during the regime of president Abdoulaye Wade.[6] The letter draws liberally from the mood of disenfranchisement that has rippled across Senegal's rural world since the early 1980s, a symptom of the "peasant malaise" that settled in the wake of a confluence of circumstances: the state's gradual withdrawal from rural life, the sinking reality of austerity measures imposed by structural adjustment programs, declining world agricultural prices, rising domestic costs of living, and the flight of public and private investment to the country's largest cities.[7] Yet, in Faye's words, the cabinet change also unveiled invisible features of Senegalese politics, and displaced the causes of political inequity between city and country to the charged terrain of identity and difference. In this, the opinion piece provides a pointed illustration of the anxiety among the Seereer community about its position within the space of the nation. Echoed in Faye's indictment is a condition of acute disenchantment commonly found in the Siin province and among its farming populations: the feeling of being left out of state programs, a sentiment of political alienation, a sense of disempowerment when it comes to controlling history, culture, and language as they show signs of erosion in the tumble of Senegal's particular brand of modernity. Whether or not these perceptions are entirely valid, they capture in glimpses the expression of a collective imaginary rooted in rural Siin, a Seereer political commentary on the state and political life in Senegal, which concurrently exposes salient lines of force across the country and a twitchy feeling of belonging to the nation.

July 26, 2007. During his first official visit to sub-Saharan Africa, newly elected French president Nicolas Sarkozy traveled to the prestigious Université Cheikh Anta Diop in Dakar to deliver a much-heralded speech to an auditorium brimming with students, professors, and journalists.

Targeting Africa's youth as its primary public, the allocution offered a Delphic meditation on the continent's troubled engagement with the world. Gazing into the mirror of history at the Medusa of Africa's future, Sarkozy searched the past for causes, diagnoses, and answers to today's ailments. While acknowledging the crimes of the slave trade and colonialism, and the fractious bonds they forged between Africa and Europe, the French president also reminded the audience that Europe's sins did not absolve Africans from blame; in fact, somewhat tastelessly, the speech devoted long passages to the continent's errancies and responsibilities for its own woes.[8] "Africa's tragedy," he declared,

> is that the African man has failed to enter far enough into history. The African peasant, who, for millennia, has lived with the seasons, whose living objective is to be in harmony with nature, knows only of the eternal repetition of time marked by an endless recurrence of the same gestures and same words.
>
> In this *imaginaire*, where everything always repeats itself, there is room neither for human adventure, nor for the idea of progress.
>
> In this universe where nature rules all, [the African] man escapes the anxiety of history that haunts the modern man, but he stands immobile in an immutable order where everything is already preordained.
>
> Never does man launch toward the future. Never does it come to his mind to exit repetition and invent a destiny for himself.
>
> This is . . . Africa's problem. Africa's challenge is to enter into history further, [and] draw from it the energy, the strength, the desire, the willingness to listen and espouse its own history.
>
> Africa's problem is to stop repeating and turning over endlessly; it is to emancipate itself from the myth of eternal return; it is to come to terms with the fact that the Golden Age it keeps mourning will not come back because it never existed.

Sarkozy exhorted young Africans to leave the entrenchments of myth and tradition and join the world, to give themselves over to globalization instead of fearing it. Such openness, he argued, would provide the foundation for a new partnership, where French benevolence and African aspirations of modernity would fructify to usher in the continent's twenty-first-century Renaissance.

As it drew to a close, the controversial speech collected meager applause from a crowd sunken in disbelief. The stupefaction almost as soon gave way to outrage: first, in the rumble of conversations among those in attendance, then, the next day, in the denunciations of national and international media, and, finally, in the flurry of academic reactions that emerged in the allocution's aftermath and whose echoes still resonate today. True, the speech's lyrical flourishes did not fall completely flat, but the passions it fanned were less those of persuasion than incensement. Commentators, lay and expert, took redemptive pleasure in dismantling the shortcomings of Sarkozy's journey into ethnophilosophy: its gaucherie and paternalist tone, its neocolonialism smuggled under the banner of friendship and frank conversation, its offensive contraposition of African emotion/tradition/isolationism and European reason/modernity/cosmopolitanism, its hypocrisy, its fanciful rendering of history's heritages more indebted to a passé brand of ethnology than sober diagnosis.[9] Perhaps most vexing of all was the fact that Sarkozy's admonitions were made in the name of an Africa in which no Africans, in Dakar or beyond, could recognize themselves. In a feat of sublime irony, the speech castigates Africans for being lured by the fetish spell of an invented golden age, when, in fact, this mythical past that Africans supposedly worship and the sister idea of a static, pure Africa unspoiled by outside contact are themselves fetishes of the European imagination, allegories come to life.[10]

For all of its wrongheadedness, however, one cannot deny that the Dakar speech hit a sensitive nerve: a bundle of buried traumas, violent memories, and unresolved histories were exposed in its evocation of the slave trade and colonialism. As many have argued, these moments of originary suffering, through the play of repression, internalization, diffraction, and troubled remembrance, have deeply haunted African historical consciousness and subjectivities. The ghost of their presence, like a watermark, continues to inhabit postcolonial milieus and how Africans imagine and understand themselves in a changing present.[11] By posing the question of Africa's relationship to itself and to the world, the speech forced the recollection of a raw wounded past. Yet, by framing it in the alien idioms of culpability and alterity, it also prompted a momentary loss of recognition, forcing an audience held verbally hostage to ask itself, "Who am I in reality?"[12]

In different ways, these vignettes capture salient themes in the historical experience of Siin, a small province in west-central Senegal, over the past five hundred years. While involving multiple actors, texts, and contexts, they all implicate deep claims to history, politics, and identity located within geographies at once imagined and concrete, both local and global. In doing so, these episodes touch on three central motifs of this book. First, as Catholic missionaries learned the hard way, the material world is not an innocent stage, free to be roamed or shared by all.[13] Space *matters*, and, because it does, it is a primary arena for the working out of political life and power relations. In Siin, as in many other places, landscapes—as meaningful, culturally constructed milieus—have historically been the loci of particular social investments. As such, there is often a material or spatial dimension to political statements, actions, and conflicts, and the material world frequently serves as a suite of targets, stakes, or media for different games of power.

Second, over the course of their history, Seereer communities in Siin have cultivated an ambivalent relationship toward state institutions and centralized modes of government. On one level, Faye's lament joined a rumble of angry voices frustrated with the controversial regime of President Wade and its perceived abuses of power. More significantly, it also stands at the tip of a much deeper, if less studied, history of tensions driving peasants' engagement with precolonial, colonial, and postcolonial forms of rule.[14] These long-term interactions conditioned the nature of political experience in Siin over time and influenced the possibilities available to local communities.

Lastly, as with other regions of Africa, Siin's past and present cannot be understood without the Atlantic trade and colonialism. Historical destinies in the region were bent by the throng of corrosive events, forces, and effects unleashed by these two moments. Visions of Siin's history are also pigmented by the discourses that have colored historical understanding of Africa's encounter with global processes over the past 150 years. Nicolas Sarkozy's speech is a good reminder that representations born in the crucible of colonial thought—images of the continent as a land of radical difference, left out by modernity—continue to circulate widely in the public sphere and inform popular views of Africa and international policy toward it.[15] Concerns over Africa's relation to world history, however, are not confined to lay conversation but the object of ardent debate in contemporary scholarship as well. There, too, the emotional, moral, and political weight of slavery and colonialism have inflected the course of discussions, and residents of the ivory tower remain as conflicted as ever, as the plays and plots, actors and agencies, causalities and casualties of these historical dramas continue to be determined, weighed, and argued over.

Weaving these elements together, this book essays a history of political life and experience in Siin, one seeking to elucidate the relationships between space, cultural practice, formations of power, and global processes associated with European expansion, roughly from the 1500s to the beginning of the twentieth century. One of the book's main arguments is that historical encounters between village communities, successive regimes of rule, and political economy in Siin have been waged on material terrains and mediated by spatial relations binding people, objects, and landscapes. One consequence is that the complex interactions between Siin's populations and larger-scale political and commercial forces imparted shape to local material worlds—how African actors read, inhabited, and experienced their changing surroundings. Another implication, in turn, is that material landscapes at various points in time also structured the outcome of power relations and political histories in the region, as regional conditions evolved from the Atlantic era to the colonial period.

This book, then, is a study of the making and remaking of "political landscapes" in Siin, of the operation of power and political practice through space.[16] Part of this narrative rests in understanding how, over time, sovereign authority, structures of governance, and the political projects of elites were constituted in and through landscapes—namely, how precolonial and colonial regimes sought to mobilize or transform cultural topographies to institute effective government, legitimize rulership, and ensure the compliance of their subjects. In this spirit, the volume marshals a diverse spectrum of sources to trace the social arrangements, practices, and ideas that have organized the Siin landscape over the past four hundred years and guided political relations between different historical actors. One of my objectives is to gain a clearer sense of the distinctive logics and foundations of power at play in Siin's past and how they were expressed, channeled, and materialized in space. Conversely, it is crucial to note that political worlds are not just the playground of the powerful but constructed in dialogue with those they seek to subjugate or control. A fuller understanding of African political landscapes, then, must also examine their fashioning from the standpoint of nonelites and lend attention to how political sovereignty was accepted, maintained, or contested at the level of village communities. After all, the blueprints of power are never realized entirely as planned, and their effects can take unintended turns when meeting the test of practice. Political programs and decisions also face obstacles when they challenge entrenched cultural practice among their constituencies or trespass over the bounds of what collectivities understand legitimate order to be—think of the popular unrest over the building of the Joal chapel, even after the king authorized it. Like political culture, political landscapes cannot be (re)made out of whole cloth. The material world is not endlessly malleable, and, in Siin, the crafting of consent often implied working with what was already concretely in place: grassroots social, economic, and religious institutions orchestrating the distribution and management of people, land, labor, property, and resources, and finding spatial expression in a patchwork of villages, fields, gardens, religious shrines, and spiritual places. In other words, power does not diffuse in a straight line across space; rather, political projects encounter adversities in the form of social geographies, which modify the course of their application.

The political landscapes created in these interactions thus embody different projects and relations, which variably complement, coexist with, or contradict each other. Rather than being opposed to each other as domination is to resistance, the courses of action of peasants and elites were inextricably entwined. Commoners' modes of being could entrench and perpetuate political regimes, just as they could upset or actively resist the coordinates of stately order. These different possibilities were nurtured in the same historical sociology of power. In fact, one of the arguments I make in the course of this book is that in the Siin social arrangements and their projection in space have historically acted as material constraints on the operation of sovereign power. Siin's reluctant landscapes, as I call them, offer a way to theorize the particular articulation of space, politics, and culture in the region after the fifteenth century. Which is to say that they help us understand the distinctive ambiguity of state power in this part of Senegambia, and account for the skepticism that Seereer communities displayed toward centralized government and global market forces.

One difficulty in accounting for past political life in Siin, beyond lapses in documentation, is that its foundations were doubly dynamic. The relationship between states and subjects mutated over time, and political fields were redrawn with the institutionalization of new balances of power. At the same time, the conditions of political experience in Siin became bound to the tides of a globalizing political economy. While Senegambia had long been connected to the Mediterranean and Islamic worlds, the opening of Atlantic commerce, Pandora's box–like, kindled the voracious energies of merchant capitalism, colonialism, and imperialism, which noosed the societies of Africa, Europe, and the Americas into each other's histories.[17] During the seventeenth and eighteenth centuries, the establishment of European trading posts and settlements on Senegambian coasts, the introduction of trade goods and firearms into local economies and the forceful extraction of enslaved bodies, and the growing meddling of French and British interests with interkingdom politics violently altered political geometries in Siin. Likewise, in the nineteenth century, the interruption of the slave trade, its replacement with commercial crop cultivation, France's annexation of Senegalese kingdoms, and the gradual colonial infiltration of African ways of life profoundly affected the political liberties and prospects of different social classes in Siin. The task, of course, is to determine precisely how, to what extent, and with what effects internal and external forces pressed on Siin's populations and sculpted their political landscapes.

Recomposing Siin's political pasts is in many ways about unwinding the convolutions of processes, events, and experiences. As Rolph Trouillot reminds us, however, what happened in the past is not faithfully recorded in memories, texts, and artifacts; rather, past realities are always refracted to posterity through the cracked mirror of images, ideologies, and representations.[18] Trouillot's compelling point is that what we call history is a palimpsest of *both* lived experiences *and* the fragmentary ways in which these experiences are remembered and narrated, and that the study of history must attend to both these dimensions. For example, just as Siin's landscapes have been chiseled by *historical processes* like Atlantic commerce, precolonial statecraft, French colonialism, and world capitalism, the transcription of this history has been influenced by what these processes as *questions* or *categories* have come to mean and do for different schools of thought. In point of fact, the Atlantic system, the state, colonialism, and capitalism are influential referents that have lorded over historical writing in Senegal, providing critical lodestars for the interpretation of historical pathways in the region. As we will see in chapter 2, while these perspectives have advanced our knowledge of Senegambian history, they have tended to locate the capacity to make history in global processes and polities, and placed more limited attention to other aspects of historical experience. Still incompletely written, for instance, is the narrative of how people at the local level unevenly translated the swirl of forces stretching beyond their immediate control and awareness and absorbed them into the fabric of their lives.

If the Siin has been somewhat less studied than its northerly neighbors, existing scholarship has provided robust foundations for the present study. The best corpus of academic research on the region has examined political and economic history during the colonial period and Seereer agriculture and cultural ecology after independence. The political landscape prior to French colonization has received less consistent academic attention and has often been treated as part of synthetic accounts analyzing the political transformation during the Atlantic era in northern Senegambia. My work is profoundly indebted to these strands of research, even as it takes them in different directions and tries to scribble new lines in pages already composed. The pathbreaking geographic analyses of Jean Pélissier and research teams working under the mantle of the Office de la Recherche Scientifique et Technique d'Outre-Mer (ORSTOM) from the 1950s onward have provided invaluable ethnographic inspiration for my reading of Seereer cultural space, land-management practices, and landscape occupation. Martin Klein and Mohamed Mbodj have written definitive accounts of political and economic reconfigurations in Siin from the mid-1850s to the 1930s. More recently, these studies have been enriched by the insightful work of political scientist Dennis Galvan, which examines cultural memory in Siin and the tradition of syncretic practices crafted by Seereer peasants to accommodate and subvert the legal shadow of the colonial and postcolonial states during the twentieth century.

My attempt, in what follows, is not solely to stitch together the distinct knowledges that these bodies of literature have generated but also to interweave their respective epistemologies, theoretical vantages, and methodologies to cast Siin's political past in a different light. Conceptually, I adopt French geographers' interest in questions of space, spatial practice, and territory but use historical and archival research to bring greater temporal depth to the analysis of cultural space and investigate the roots of contemporary landscapes in a broadening world of exchanges during the Atlantic era. I also expand on geographic conceptualizations of Seereer landscapes in terms of *cultural traditions* by taking a cue from Galvan's work and placing the question of *state power* and *politics* squarely at the heart of peasant cultural and spatial production. While drawing heavily on historical studies of Siin's colonial past, I seek to push their analysis of regional political culture into the Atlantic period and reexamine Seereer colonial experiences through the lens of spatiality and materiality.

Like these various works, however, I maintain a close focus on peasantries and popular experiences. The word *peasant* has both practical and analytical value. As used in French geography and recent African history, it refers to agriculturalists who control their land and labor, are organized in kin-oriented households working to meet subsistence needs, who channel part of their production to a political elite either directly or through state power, and who articulate with broader political economy partially on their terms. In this sense, the term perfectly captures the character of politics, work, and life in rural places like Siin. It also places an identity, albeit loose, on rural landscapes' often anonymous contours. Lastly, it locates villagers in political fields where their ability to mobilize land and labor—and control social reproduction—grants them a degree of autonomy vis-à-vis ruling classes and an active role in rural politics. Peasant lives, necessarily, are political lives. On account of this dynamism, the peasant communities I describe were and are neither static nor harmonious but processual formations: internally diverse, dissolving and recombining, and historically responsive.[19]

Beyond the specifics of Siin's history, the turn to landscapes and material worlds also offers a point of engagement with the compass of Senegambian historiography writ large. Using oral memory and documentary records, historical scholarship has often recounted the Atlantic history of African societies between the Senegal and Gambia Rivers from the standpoint of states, dynastic traditions, and world-system dynamics. This perspectival framing has captured a certain scale of historical interactions, but it has afforded more limited insights into the subtle transactions of power and culture operating below the polity and on which kingdom-level politics were built. My interest, thus, lies in rural communities, the peasants and commoners whose modest actions and mundane lives are often edited out of historical archives and whose imprints on the course of regional history feature faintly in historical accounts. By contrast, landscapes have grown over time as the products of aggregate human actions, and they stand as partial transcripts of the activities and subjectivities that went into their making, including those of peasant actors. They thus provide us with unique access to the silent underside of global encounters in Atlantic Senegambia.

Finally, if a concern for materiality distinguishes this account from previous studies of Siin, the book also differs from earlier histories with respect to its methodological commitments. While much of the evidential fabric for my arguments rests on original research in archival repositories in France and Senegal, as well as published historical accounts, ethnographic materials, and oral traditions, when possible, I have also tried to supplement conventional sources with existing archaeological information. Material vestiges have not systematically featured in recountings of Siin's history, in part because they had not really been consistently studied or identified until quite recently.[20] While still in its infancy in the Siin region, archaeological work nevertheless trains our eye on those fleeting strands of community experience—the material intimacies tying people to objects and places—that generally escaped the purview of firsthand observers in the historical past and that of collective memory, whose respective concerns were often directed elsewhere. Additionally, an archaeological perspective mindful of other archives affords glimpses of history's many textures and tempos, alloying the plane of deep temporalities that is often the playground of archaeology with the quicker pulse of happenings, actions, and decisions recorded in textual documents. The resulting vantage can accommodate the play of events and contingencies and the waves, cycles, and structures of the *longue durée* that enfold past and present; more critically, it can help to suss out how different regimes of time interlocked to bear upon Seereer political experiences. My original hope for this book was to write an archaeological history of Siin, pieced together from the fragmentary remains of settlement vestiges, pottery sherds, and other material relics.[21] This formulation failed to take into account serious empirical resistances in Siin, where archaeological pictures are still barely etched out, and do not yet lend themselves to monographic synthesis. While such a project must be postponed for now, I found alternative motivation for this book in the recognition that, between the capable lines of historical scholarship in Siin, many aspects of social history remain to be plumbed, especially during the Atlantic period. I was also comforted by the fact that, despite its limitations, Siin's nascent archaeology stood in fertile tension with other sources and could be productively confronted with texts, maps, and oral memory to foster new questions, outline new directions of inquiry, provoke new readings of old situations, and shake conventional reason. Throughout the book, I have systematically tried to cross-examine different types of sources and avoid historical leapfrogging by comparing evidence created ostensibly at the same time.[22] These precautions notwithstanding, my account is composite and pragmatic by necessity. Part of the historical craft demands a certain conceptual openness to the possibility of surprise, and, consequently, I often followed the lead of sources to particular clues or salient questions at the expense of others. Analytical strategies have also been complicated by a certain unevenness across evidential terrains, where not all classes of information are equally reliable, detailed, or available for all periods. In this light, while seeking to elucidate the character of political landscapes, I have sometimes had to draw rather exclusively on one or another kind of evidence when others were lacking, patchy, or poorly suited to addressing the questions at hand.

In some quarters, this hybrid mélange of theory, methods, and evidence might be identified as historical archaeology. I would prefer to see the latter as a species of historical anthropology—here, a mode of anthropological inquiry driven by historical concerns and firmly committed to deciphering local articulations of cultural forms, power, and representations, as populations around the world were increasingly brought into the gravitational fields of capitalism, colonialism, imperialism, and globalization.[23] Recast as a subset of historical anthropology, archaeology acquires salience not simply as a set of techniques or the study of buried remains (though it certainly involves those dimensions) but also as a particular *sensibility* to the material world, a way of seeing and thinking materiality.[24] In this optic, teasing out the relationships between past people and their material worlds need not exclusively or principally rely on material artifacts but can also flow from the inspection of written testimonies, ethnographic accounts, oral traditions, or extant built environments seen through an archaeological looking glass—or, indeed, an engagement with the archaeological record from the standpoint of texts, memories, and images.

Architecture of the Volume

Divided into four parts, the book consists of eight chapters and a conclusion. Each chapter centers on a conceptual problem within Siin's history: landscape, history, ethnicity, ethnography, tradition, the Atlantic system, the state, exchange, colonialism, and the postcolony. In each chapter, I use context and theory to elucidate (and complicate) each other.

Part 1 lays out the conceptual scaffold of the book, tackling the interrelated questions of materiality, politics, and history. Chapter 1 opens with an ethnographic look at Siin's rural landscapes and the political marginalization that the province has suffered since independence. Moving away from ideas of space as map, physical setting, or background to human dealings, I build on people's relationship to their agrarian milieu to develop a theory of political landscape. This approach centers on three premises:

Landscapes are inherently anachronistic; they juxtapose the remains of many historical times at once, making it possible to track the traces different histories left on them.

Landscapes are inclusive. They conserve material traces of elite and nonelite communities alike. Political worlds are not the sole province of the powerful but contrarian terrains constructed in dialogue with those the powerful seek to control.

Landscapes are chancy; that is, they are not completely amenable to political rule and human engineering. This unpredictability confers a certain reluctance to Siin's landscapes, in that they sometimes get in the way of power, resisting the wills and testing the designs of political actors.

For these reasons, landscapes open a unique, long-term window onto material wranglings over sovereignty and autonomy in coastal Senegal.

Chapter 2 addresses the question of global history in Senegal and suggests, following David Scott, that we reframe its "problem-space." Instead of foregrounding the agencies of state, capital, and colony, I suggest we interrogate their limits through the lens of landscape, with an eye for minor-key stories of resilience, dissidence, and complicity that slice across the plane of global events and reintroduce a sense of unpredictability in the making of Atlantic Africa. As we do so, it is important to remember that landscapes' recalcitrance is not just material but also archival: landscapes do not amount to a complete vision of the past. Instead, they articulate what I call an epistemology of fragments. As we track landscapes' fragmentary expressions across various sources—and move dialectically between patchy archives—we gain an appreciation of the incompleteness and messiness of Atlantic histories. In this sense, landscapes offer a promise of historical humility. To be sure, material ruins can make vanished pasts visible and reanimate some of their ghosts. Yet, equally often, they point to the difficulties of historical understanding and raise more caveats than answers. In doing so, they caution us against the seductions of holistic reconstructions of history and alert us to the productivity of never quite getting the whole story.

Part 2 reflects on the perceptions that have informed scholarship on the Siin and Seereer people—namely their deep-time identity and cultural conservatism—and offers a critical analysis of the work of "tradition." Chapter 3 takes on the historical limits of ethnicity, a public secret whose avoidance does a great deal of political work in Senegal. It confronts multiple sources to question established histories of Seereerness and the applicability of ethnicity to past settings. Specifically, I argue that, far from making up a primeval entity, the Seereer label was constructed over time in relation to other social groups and consolidated relatively recently as a primary mode of identification. If it came to condense the cultural substance of Siin residents, its authenticity also embodies a history of alterity and difference. Chapter 4 addresses the questions of peasantries and tradition in colonial ethnography. Although the Seereer have been portrayed as timeless farmers, a close reading of ethnographic archives, attentive to shared and dissonant discourses, shows that images of typical peasants greatly underestimate the dynamism of rural culture. The chapter examines how colonial observers (and postcolonial ones as well, to some extent) constructed static portraits of Seereer farmers that speak as much to imperial desires and anxieties as to the social existence of people in Siin. Key to these discursive productions was the crystallization of Seereer farmers as creatures of their natural milieu. Landscape here serves as a visual technology of colonial power, which assisted the primitivization of rural Africans, while camouflaging evidence to the contrary. These two chapters together suggest that models of Seereer identity and depictions of their cultural practices may not fully describe the colonial and precolonial pasts. Rather, they view tradition as a labile mode of engagement with outside forces of change.

Part 3 combines archaeological, archival, and oral sources to revisit key motifs in the historiography of the Atlantic trade in Senegambia. Chapter 5 targets the problem of the state and performs a genealogy of the trope of the predatory kingdom, which has structured the literature on Atlantic West Africa. Where scholarship has often viewed centralized kingdoms as coeval with the whole field of politics and assumed their sovereign control over matters of space and place, I suggest that rural landscapes were more fractious political terrains, shaped by peasant ambivalences about sovereignty. In effect, I show the obstacles to centralization embedded in Siin's material world, itself the medium of grassroots social, political, and spiritual institutions. Siin's rulers had to confront their inability to fully manage an unruly rural geography. Effective governance depended on conciliating peasant structures of authority, which were implicated in the construction of state power. Landscapes, then, were as much a *constraint* on royal power as a canvas for its legitimation. Even as monarchies were growing stronger during the eighteenth and nineteenth centuries, they remained tensely bound to village institutions. In lieu of a narrative of state predation, the Siin polity remained highly fluid throughout the Atlantic era, oscillating between episodes of relative centralization and relative autonomy at its periphery. This is a story of statecraft and centralization as *process*, born by shifting histories of communities and landscape occupation. It is also a prelude to the political present, mapping the historical roots of Seereer sentiments of suspicion toward sovereign authority in the turbulences of the Atlantic era.

The resilience of Siin's cultural landscapes also extended to object worlds, as examined in chapter 6. While Atlantic commerce is often associated with the stagnation or destruction of African economies, artifact assemblages suggest a more complex scenario. In effect, the cultural life of trade goods in Senegal illuminates facets of oceanic commerce other than the trade in slaves and reveals complex strategies of appropriation, creative transformation, and consumption. The chapter places emphasis on practices of composition and ideas of wealth rooted in relations binding persons, things, and skills, which shaped understandings of value and steered the popular reception (or rejection) of foreign commodities. One surprising trend emerging from the analysis is that the Atlantic era seems to have presided over a democratization of African consumption, as peasants were enabled to bypass sumptuary restrictions to access a greater world of goods.

Part 4 follows the tribulations of Siin's reluctant landscapes into the colonial era, showing that the French administration faced problems with Siin's mosaic geography of power similar to the problems faced by its indigenous predecessors. Chapter 7 revisits the problems of colonialism and the colonial state by analyzing the brittle foundations of French power in rural Senegal and the deeply contested history of colonial rule in the Siin. Picking up on the discussion of state forms and political landscape begun in earlier chapters, I argue that rural milieus offer clues about the materiality of colonial rule, more specifically, about the logics of colonial government, and the conduits and channels through which French officials sought to manage colonized subjects. Peanut cash cropping is important to this story, and the material networks of commerce and habits it set in motion developed into central vectors of colonial transformation. In tandem with colonial ethnographies, rural assemblages also hint at the anxieties and epistemic confusion inhabiting the early days of colonial rule, as well as obstacles to its implementation. Siin's colonial countryside thus emerges as a hesitant and nervous geography of power, whose outcomes were disputed, partial, and not quite foreseeable. Chapter 8 expands this analysis with an examination of the lived experience of colonialism—namely, how Siin villagers negotiated, complied with, and elided colonial government. Shortages of human (and other) resources compelled the colonial administration to graft itself onto local institutions, a politics of absence that gave peasant communities ample room to rework colonial policies and reconfigured space in unexpected ways. This period prolongs Siin's record of cultural entrepreneurialism, recombinant geographies, and recomposed traditions, yet it also witnesses significant ruptures in landholding, kinship orientations, and capacities for self-sufficiency that prefigure the conditions of peasant malaise after independence.

The realities of contested sovereignty and the dialectics of state presence/absence also extend to postcolonial Senegal. Since independence, the state's involvement in Siin has tacked between intrusiveness and benign neglect, which has propped up some social projects while bringing about economic decay. The conclusion examines the consequences of these long histories of power for our thinking about tradition and how it has featured both in narratives of national modernity in Senegal and in our thinking about Siin's past in relation to the present. Writing the history of Senegal's margins unpacks some of the tensions inhabiting narratives of the nation. Just as contemporary discourses of Siin's primitivism gloss over the region's deep integration into regional histories, it seems that, in reimagining itself along Wolof and Muslim lines, Senegal represses its own fascination with tradition. Likewise, I suggest that reinscribing the Siin (and other parts of rural Africa) in long histories of power that connect precolonial, colonial, and postcolonial times can generate more robust understandings of the predicaments and possibilities that peasant communities experience today. It may also, perhaps, help to anticipate broad directions for the political futures of African countrysides.

PART ONE

Framing Perspectives

We could, without much exaggeration . . . assimilate Senghor's country [e.g., Siin] to a "poetic terroir." Its singular geography, its situation of culture on the margins, the homogeneity of its peasant population essentially composed of "people of the word" make the region a cultural entity that is other, politically unmarked, where poetic speech . . . unfolds in all the activities of life, to the whim of the pertinent significations of ecological time. A. FAYE, "SENGHOR EN PERSPECTIVE DANS LE CHAMP LITTÉRAIRE SEEREER"[1]

Geography can be deceptive. Take any map of Senegal, and it will show, with minor slippages of perspective and proportion, roughly the same assemblage of dots, lines, and intervals sprayed across landforms accented in green and brown. One's eyes drift to the Cap Vert peninsula on the left of the map, lured by the arabesques of Dakar's urban tangle. From the capital city, an arborescent road network ramifies across the territory in gradations of density, its spindly tendrils growing thinner as they press inland. The mesh is closer-knit, more vascular in the vast crescent plain opening at the back of Dakar; there, segments of asphalt interweave, firmly cinching the region to the orbit of the capital's influence. This immediate hinterland is home to the province of Siin—in cartographic view, a small polygon loosely draped around the towns of Joal, Diourbel, Gossas, and Ndangane—that sits less than 130 kilometers from Dakar (figure 1). A slanted road grid, now boasting a highway, veins through the province and places it a mere four or five hours away from the capital by public transportation and almost half that amount by private car.

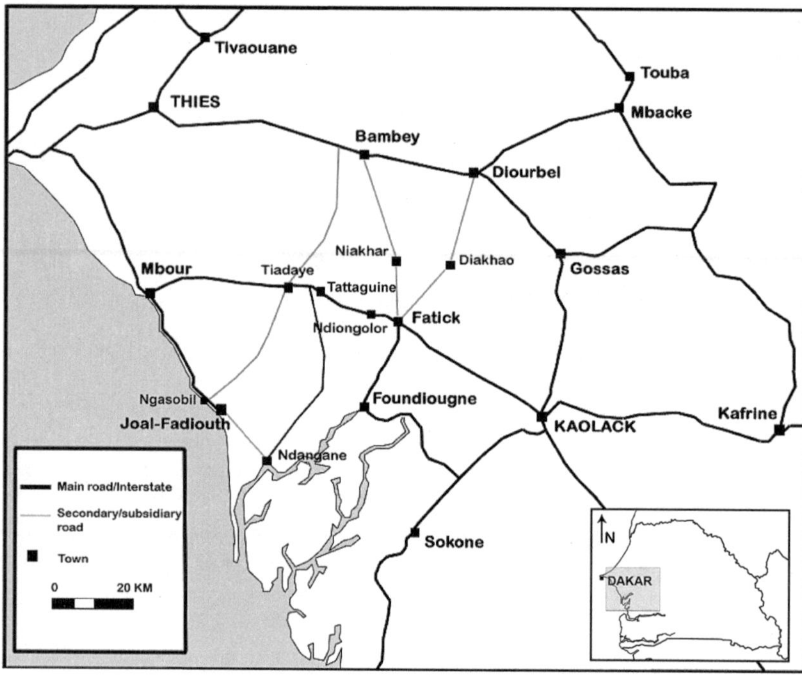

1 The Siin region of Senegal

Maps are useful, obviously. In projecting space onto the abstract plane of Cartesian geometry, they conjure up certain sets of perspectives—of extension, distance, position, and relation—that elude the naked eye. Cartographic grids define a plane of commensuration, an absolute foundation that can subsume myriad subjective coordinates and recode them into objective depictions of the world. The trade-off is that, in making certain things visible, maps occlude others. Aseptic surfaces, sanitized distances, and neat geometric lines not only flatten a rugged topography of social experience but also smooth out the grooves and faults of history and evacuate the games of power driving the politics of visual representation.[2] That said, the power of geographic images is not limitless, and their seeming honesty cannot quite spirit away what Gregory terms a certain "cartographic anxiety." Much indeed simmers between the lines of represented forms. Maps do not literally paper over the lived world. They act like translucent overlays that distort but also refract in blurry light the contested geographies seething below their façades.[3]

Returning to the map of Senegal, the fact of Siin's closeness to the country's center of gravity is an optical trick, a partial fantasy; it tells a story of objective proximity that clouds the fragile integration of the province into the "geo-body" of the nation.[4] Closer to the ground, Siin remains surprisingly estranged from Senegal's economic and administrative nuclei—a distance forged in the cauldron of historical circumstances and ossified in the historical, ethnic, and political imaginaries cultivated by the Senegal state. Until recently, Siin's peripheralization was most visible in the region's crumbling infrastructure, public works, and rural development initiatives.

Between 2002 and 2004, as I was conducting my doctoral fieldwork, the major thoroughfares that serviced the region and linked it to the country's largest towns (Dakar, Kaolack, and Touba) were monuments of decrepitude, pockmarked by crater-sized potholes and makeshift repairs, with deep fissures gashing the asphalt at regular intervals. While the main stretches of road have been rebuilt since 2004, maintenance and development have bypassed smaller axes, such as those leaving Joal or Fatick, despite the considerable traffic they support. This neglect has had disastrous consequences for the communities of the Saalum estuary, whose economy revolves around tourism and marine resources and depends on effective transportation systems.[5] More tragically, because of their poor condition, these roadsides are the scenes of frequent accidents, littered with the carcasses of *car rapides*, the ubiquitous overcrowded minibuses that carry the bulk of passenger traffic in Senegal. The secondary untarred road network is not much better, a target of frequent complaints by travelers. Lateritic routes are constantly eroded by the passage of cars and trucks. Many are also prone to flooding and unusable during the rainy season, creating enormous travel delays and requiring much ingenuity on the part of local commuters to reach their destinations. Today and in 2003 alike, one is often better served by the subsidiary dirt-road system. While scraggly and unruly, rural trails extend gossamer-like across the countryside, providing an expedient traveling medium, if not always hassle-free. It is not unusual for rural roads to morph into imaginary highways, as they are reclaimed by vegetation, crops, or waterlogged marshes, or unexpectedly empty into thick blankets of sand.

Fifteen years ago, many villages along the road network remained off the grid. Such was the case with Ndiongolor, for instance, where I resided for several months, a mere six kilometers from Fatick, the regional capital. In many of these villages, particularly those straying off the main roads, water had to be hand-drawn from nearby wells, and mechanical pumps seemed a distant luxury. In some areas, cars were rare enough that they would garner the children's undivided attention. While the electrical grid has been extended to numerous communities since, the energy crisis afflicting Senegal in the last decade has brought chronic power shortages lasting for days on end. The Siin was the last region in Senegal without a bone fide hospital, and it was not until 2007, after many false starts, that a partially operational structure was opened, despite the acute medical needs of rural people living in endemic poverty. While improving, the provision of health and educational services remains precarious (Siin has one of the country's lowest levels of formal schooling, well below the national average), and schools and dispensaries remain few and far between in many areas still.[6]

The material conditions of Siin's marginalization also frame local imaginings about the failures of postcolonial governance. Siin residents rake through the neglected ruins of improvident governmental programs in search of signs, clues, and scraps of evidence to explain the bleak circumstances of contemporary life. Conversations often focus on deciphering the opaque mechanisms of state bureaucracy and governmental machinery to expose the lines of force orienting everyday politics. Local actors often craft elaborate theories of state power, as they debate the relationship between sovereignty and autonomy, the nature of the government's obligations toward its citizenries, as well as the legitimacy of postcolonial institutions.[7] Note the resonances with Mr. Faye's angry words in the prologue.

In Seereer communities across the Siin, these commentaries often betray deep suspicion about the Senegalese government. During my fieldwork, this crisis of faith was expressed in the form of frequent diatribes toward the regime of President Wade (r. 2000–2012), its pro-urban orientations, and its failure to make good on promises of economic improvement in rural areas. Senegal's *malaise agricole*, however, is not new. The Senegalese state was once centrally involved in the agricultural sector, but, since 1979, pressed by the World Bank, International Monetary Fund, and foreign creditors, it has withdrawn from the countryside in dramatic fashion and embraced a market-driven policy placing the burden of improved productivity on peasants themselves.[8] For the past thirty years, ruralists have been living in a state of generalized crisis, sparked by disastrous agricultural campaigns, sinking world agricultural prices, and the lifting of agricultural subsidies (on fertilizer, seedlings, credits, mechanical equipment, and prices). Even recent government efforts to promote subsistence crop production, despite reasonable success, were met with criticism by many of the people I talked to in 2009.[9] This is, in part, because other material nuisances—the escalating costs of living, access to potable water, energy shortages—show few signs of subsiding, thus fanning the local economy of rumor and resentment in new and intensified ways. In the summer of 2009, for instance, the high incidence of power outages in the Joal area ignited a powder keg of conspiracy scenarios that decoded electricity cutoffs as punitive measures enacted by the president's coalition party against regions and municipalities that had voted in support of the opposition.[10]

As demonstrated by Galvan's research in northern Siin, remembrances of times past often feature centrally in Seereer reflections on the political present.[11] Facing incessant reminders of the peasant world's gradual excision from Senegal's elite- and urban-oriented politics, the drying up of benefits once rushing through clientelist networks, and the anemic influence of the common man over the conduct of national politics, local actors have tended to find retrospective solace in the land of memory.[12] Frustration with the shortcomings of the welfare state has encouraged the development of nostalgic passions that adopt a number of forms. Some have reinvented the precolonial era as a golden age, compared to the dark age of modern times, where revered customary structures and the old monarchical regime stand in opposition to the reviled postcolonial state. For others, the colonial state offered a stability and predictability that seem preferable to the precariousness of postcolonial futures. And, to an increasing number of people, the political cosmology of Sufi Islam—its spiritual order and rewards of salvation—trumps the broken promises of secular government. A strong current of revisionism runs through this prism of positions, and the specific visions of the past and modes of authority they invoke are often colored by anachronisms, historical liberties, and idealizations. Regardless, these historical discourses all share a common impulse in reinvesting traditional institutions with moral credibility, authenticity, and trust, while revoking these qualities from the vilified postcolonial regime.

That historical memory has swung to the center of Seereer conversations on contemporary governance is not exactly surprising. First, because the past suffuses the Seereer social milieu, pooling in corners and crannies, dyeing every square inch of land, welling up in the words of elders and those in the know. As a consequence, contested claims to history and memory are heavily implicated in the fabric of Seereer politics, agency, and modes of belonging. Second, many feel that the local past is under assault and gradually slipping away in a Senegal where relevance speaks in the idiom of urban modernity and global aspirations. Functioning all at once as critique, ontology, epistemology, and analysis, then, the "workshopping of history" becomes how many social actors choose to grasp and stabilize the instabilities of a changing world.[13]

Siin's awkward position in the nation's political geography can be regarded as the structural offshoot of what Momar-Coumba Diop and Mamadou Diouf have called the Islamo-Wolof model. This model refers to the long-term processes of political peripheralization and cultural exclusion that have shaped Senegal since the opening of the Atlantic frontier. Over the past five hundred years, through the play of chance and design, Senegal's interactions with the world economy have increasingly privileged coastal areas dominated by Wolof populations; these areas, in turn, have become the political-economic hub of the country and center of gravity of national sensibilities. These material processes have been articulated and legitimated in a broader discourse, which accords a preponderant place to Islam, the Wolof language, and urban lifestyle in the national imagination, while downplaying the importance of the pre-Muslim past, non-Wolof groups, and rural settings in national narratives. As a result, culturally stigmatized and economically sidelined groups like the Seereer of Siin, or Joola of Casamance, have been pushed to the margins of Senegal's imagined community. Another consequence has been the rewriting of the history of the République as a tale of Wolof and Muslim achievement, focusing on the will for self-determination and resistance to the forces of colonialism, a process assisted by state cultural politics in the postindependence era.[14]

In his recent examination of Senegal's history, Mamadou Diouf urges us to offset accounts of the Islamo-Wolof past with alternative visions of history produced at the periphery of Wolof hegemony.[15] He makes the important point that Senegal's past is an ensemble of pluralities sharing a common, if uneven, field of historical experience. As such, it cannot be adequately captured without reference to that of its peripheries, which were fundamentally implicated in the making of Senegal's political geography and were thus integral components of the country's history and modernity. Margins, then, are important because they *supplement* ways of seeing and thinking from the center.[16] Denoting an absence at the core of centrist narratives, they supply something that is missing *and* something additional, and in the same stroke estrange the center from itself and destabilize the images it supports. Interstitial spaces (frontiers, peripheries, margins) are zones where the past takes on a different look. Because their political realities often are in a state of *becoming*, they are also places where historical mechanisms achieve heightened visibility. Yet, fringes do not just refract regional trajectories in crisp alternative light; they also force upon us a rethinking of the implicit truth of dominant representations, the hierarchies they convey, and the political realities they consecrate.

This is one such marginal history that I pursue in this book, one that navigates between anthropology, archaeology, and history, between the past and the present, to retrieve the distinctive qualities of Siin's past without losing sight of its participation in Senegambian history. Much as geography provides a critical overture to the "scandal of the nation," a hieroglyph of Siin's ambivalent ties to the polity today, it also offers a lens for parsing the entwinement of history, discourse, and politics in the province's deeper past.[17] For this reason, spatial concerns and material signatures ground my analysis of Siin's interactions with the rest of the world. This history of spatial experience is concerned both with structural forces and their translation into the realm of lived geographies, with "the ways in which meanings are spun around the *topoi* of different lifeworlds, threaded into social practices and woven into relations of power."[18] By rooting my reading of Senegal's global past in Siin's material world, I hope to interrogate at a number of interlocking questions. First, I seek to look anew at the course of Siin's history, the role of external forces in driving these transformations, and how political experiences in the region have been represented. Second, scaling up from the particularities of Siin's experience, I want to think about the processes that have shaped Senegambian historical geography in the past five hundred years and the manner in which they have been recounted. Finally, extending the previous query, I attempt to critically reflect on the mythical moments of Africa's modern experience—the opening of the Atlantic world, colonial subjugation, and the global movement of ideas, desires, and objects—and the categories that have propped up analysis of these seminal moments in Senegal (but in other places on the continent as well). This requires me to take up questions of identity, ethnicity, peasantry, culture, tradition, economy, and statecraft, and more abstract questions of time, agency, determination, and resistance, as African communities made their histories under the circumstances of a social milieu altered by European intervention, from the early sightings of caravels on the coast through the years of colonial rule and postindependence government.

Before getting to these issues, the next two chapters will set the ethnographic, historical, and conceptual stages for the analysis. In chapter 1, I describe Siin's contemporary landscape and the activities giving it form and content. This ethnographic canvas lays out the groundwork for a theoretical reflection on the work of landscape, especially the demands it places on politics, which will inform my interpretation of materiality, power, and history in Siin's past. I follow in chapter 2 with a discussion of the kinds of questions that have framed the study of Senegalese history and thus background the present study. Wary of assigning too much determination to the big processes of world history, I advocate a perspective concerned with material worlds, temporality, and source eclecticism—an expanded archaeological epistemology that queries the past through the lens of history's debris. Here, again, landscape's patchy archives resist and impose demands on our readings of the past, directing us to smaller, more uncertain narratives of world making in Africa.

ONE

Reluctant Landscapes

The place is unavoidable.

E. GLISSANT, *TOUT-MONDE*[1]

Mise-en-Scène: Locating the Siin

Sitting on the northern bank of the Saalum delta, the Siin lies at the heart of Senegal's old peanut basin, long the country's most productive agricultural region, which still accounts today for the bulk of national grain and commercial crop outputs. Named after the erstwhile kingdom of Siin, the province is regarded as the geographic center of the *pays seereer* (Seereer country), a loose territorial designation coinciding with the area traditionally inhabited by a number of ethnolinguistic subgroups sharing the Seereer ethnonym. In the course of this book, and unless indicated otherwise, I will use *Seereer* as shorthand for the Seereer people of Siin.

While the past three decades have witnessed considerable demographic transition and a concomitant rise in social, ethnic, and economic diversity, public discourse in Senegal continues to bundle together the Siin, Seereer peasantries, and agricultural life in a tight knot of metonymic association. Siin acquired its image of rural area par excellence during the colonial period, thanks to its flourishing agriculture. Its agrarian penchant flowed in part from geography, owing much to the region's oceanfront, and to more clement rains, better natural irrigation, and more homogeneous soils than its northern neighbors. The cornerstone of

Siin's rural economy, however, was the sophisticated agropastoral system forged over time by its Seereer populations. Through careful practices of landscape management, Seereer farmers crafted an agrarian park that supported elevated human densities, high peanut yields, and bountiful harvests. These favorable conditions breathed life into the colonial sentiment that the province was home to one of the most iconic peasant societies in francophone Africa, a perception that retains strong currency in Senegal today.

Since the 1970s, the combined blows of environmental degradation, desiccation, agricultural policies, and overexploitation have accentuated pressures on land, landholding, and natural resources and eroded the integrity of Siin's agricultural edifice.[2] Stresses on peasant existence have been further compounded by internal demographic expansion and the rise of land speculation, which have intensified problems over inheritance, conflicts between property regimes, and the fragmentation of familial estates. As subsistence farming has become ever more precarious, a growing number of villagers have turned to other activities, mostly petty trade and urban jobs. Every year, flows of seasonal and more permanent migrants crisscross the country to relocate to Dakar, Thiès, or Kaolack, or to the smaller towns and village agglomerations that have grown in and around the Siin. As in other parts of Africa, Senegal is becoming increasingly urban.[3] The Siin does not escape this phenomenon. As administrative centers, places of business, and stepping-stones to a broader geography of opportunities, towns like Fatick, Kaolack, or even the smaller Joal, which all originated as colonial *escales* (trading points), absorb a growing number of residents, pulling in people from neighboring provinces, and thus redirecting the gravity of social relations.[4] While these dramatic economic reconfigurations and pockets of urbanity are remodeling Siin's sociology and altering its spatial ecology, the region retains an indelibly rural character.

In Sahelian societies practicing rain-fed subsistence agriculture, weather regulates the tempo of daily life, binding farmers to their milieu in a relation of ecological closeness, intimacy, and savoir faire—a mode of dwelling that recursively connects the seasonal contours of the landscape to the labor and activities that constitute it.[5] During the dry season, which runs from November to May, Siin's hinterland drapes itself in a mantle of undulating dunes, mutating into a sun-scorched plain almost ethereal in its minimalism: denuded stretches of beige sand, carved into a mosaic of asymmetrical fields, speckled by knotty trees, thorny shrubs, and spectral silhouettes toiling away in the distance (figure 2). Villages seem braided into this agrarian tableau, springing here and there from the patchwork

2 *Top*, fields and gardens, village of Ndofène (photo by author, 2003); *bottom*, Island of Falia, Saalum estuary (photo by author, 2009)

of arable lands, their edges dissolving into the earth to surface again every few hundred meters and give rise to the next settlement. Moved by a residential gestalt that can best be described as constellated, Siin's habitat diffuses cloud-like across the landscape, forming a semicontinuous network of single farmsteads, hamlet clusters, and more densely concentrated hubs. When the rain goes away, agricultural operations are brought to a near halt. Able-bodied youths and adults depart for the city, leaving behind older men, married women, children; a few artisans, traders, and civil servants; relatives visiting on the weekend, and so forth. Under winter's hazy sun, rural life slows into a scene of sleepy farmsteads wrapped in blankets of smoke, awakened from their seasonal slumbers by the rattle of drums cheering public celebrations.

By contrast, in the few weeks preceding the rainy season, the pace of life picks up. This period ranks among the busiest in the agricultural calendar, and everywhere peasants can be seen pursuing their tasks with laborious industry: preparing the fields, clearing brush, or transporting wood and equipment in ox-drawn carts. Fertilizing fires fill the humid air with clouds of pungent smoke. Here and there, tufts of green—orchards and gardens—sprout from the ground, adding touches of color to the monochrome sea of sand. With the return of precipitation, the verdant shades accentuate. Depressed areas become pools of stagnant water. Activities intensify. After the first rains, residential units mobilize all working hands to plant the precious peanut crop, which still brings the majority of revenue in peasant households. Attention then shifts to other fields, where the seeds of subsistence cereals (millet, sorghum) are sown. Planting schedules are often staggered, to distribute the risk of crop failures, and they are followed by grueling weeks of hoeing, weeding, and crop monitoring to the fickle pulse of precipitation. As the cultivation season advances, fields are gradually overgrown with the scraggly tangle of peanut pods and tall stands of millet stalks, though uneven rainfall may bring unluckier outcomes. The time of harvest, which generally begins roughly three months after the first sowings, marks the last major expenditure of labor, when all participate in the collection, processing, and sorting of cash and grain crops, as well as their storage for sale or subsistence needs. A flurry of festivities concludes the cultivation period and sets the next cycle of seasons in motion.

While this picture of broad continuities in milieu, activities, and social time imparts a certain identity to the Seereer hinterland, Siin's cultural landscape is not a homogeneous canvas. Broad consistencies of social ecology cohabit with variations in landforms, spatial arrangement, and economic practices that tend to concentrate along the province's geographic margins. Siin's southern fringe, for instance, is dominated by the Saalum delta, whose two main channels, the Siin and Saalum Rivers, have historically granted distinct personalities to local ecologies.[6] The Saalum River meanders inland about 230 kilometers, past Kaolack and Kahone, before branching out into a dendritic series of small *marigots* (tidal channels). The river once defined the political border between the Siin kingdom and its powerful rival, the Saalum polity. More diminutive, the Siin River is a subsidiary of the Saalum delta, whose sinuous course once traversed the entire province and at its northernmost point grazed the border with the Bawol polity.[7] Today, all that is left of the riverbed is a desolate fluvial valley, made up of shallow *marigots* etched into the earth, where seasonal rainfall occasionally accumulates. The main trunk of the *ria* advances toilsomely to the latitude of Fatick, beyond which its water level rapidly plummets, leaving only faint impressions of a once flowing riverbed. Some elders still remember an earlier time, some sixty or seventy years ago, when now dried-up channels were flush with water and fish and formed thin ribbons scrolling far beyond the regional capital. In the early part of the colonial era, the Siin River was an active commercial axis. During the trading season, it carried a procession of watercrafts transporting peanuts and merchant goods to and from the port of Foundiougne and beyond. While these two rivers' outflow never permitted recession cultivation, their presence over time has favored higher water tables, humidity, and agricultural fertility. In contrast to the ubiquitous dry savanna grasslands, the northern bank of the Saalum valley enjoys comparatively lusher vegetation and better growing conditions than the rest of Siin. The local milieu also favors the development of salt flats (*tann*). Produced by the effects of evaporation on saline soils, infertile *tann* expanses often grace natural terraces that overlook waterlogged or tidal terrains.

South of Foundiougne, the point of confluence between the two rivers, the main arm of the Saalum opens onto an estuary, which announces the microhabitat of the Saalum Islands. Clogged by silts and earth, the delta fans out into a Byzantine network of tidal channels lined with mangrove, vegetation, and compact shell islands rising above the water (figure 2). This partially submerged environment has long housed the villages of the Seereer Niominka, fisherfolk-farmers whose activities have straddled land and sea. These activities perdure to this day, and many men are employed in the fishing industry, locally or in fishing ports further up the coast. Likewise, in the summer, as one travels by motorized pirogue across the maze of tidal corridors, it is not uncommon to see small groups of women in dugout canoes collecting oysters and other mollusks, while men make the daily journey to grain and peanut fields located on drier ground inland. As elsewhere in the Siin, however, subsistence labor is losing ground to more lucrative businesses. Local residents increasingly take advantage of the Saalum Islands' breathtaking scenery and enter the growing tourism sector, working as guides, campground managers, or hotel personnel. Another distinctive feature of the region is the nature of the human habitat. In stark contrast with Siin's interior, where settlements accrete and disseminate like mist across the countryside, villages dotting the Saalum delta, and the littoral more generally, are compact and self-contained, an anatomy of crowded dwellings veined by narrow alleyways. The small fishing village of Fadiouth exemplifies such spatial arrangement. Even in nearby Joal, which has outgrown its modest origins to become a small town in its own right, this logic of residential clustering continues to influence urban space.

If Seereer peasants have lived to the pulse of their milieu, they have also, within the compass of its constraints, endeavored to make it their own. Through a choreography of improvised acts and everyday practices staged in the *longue durée* of local ecologies, Siin's residents have landscaped the environment into a profoundly social world. Weaving together the routine gestures of agricultural work, the mundane rhythms of social organization, and shifting fields of cultural signification, they have incorporated material surrounds into the flow of their lived existence. The outcome of this practical engagement is a lived world at once objective and subjective, both natural and cultural, a meaningful terrain critical in orienting the course of social action.[8]

The distinctive aesthetic of the Seereer social habitat has long captivated outside commentators. In the early years of colonial rule, French observers were often intrigued by the Seereer countryside's manicured landscape, with its tidy fields, neat network of hedges and footpaths, and choreographed activities. Writing many years later, in a more analytical vein, cultural geographers resorted to the concept of terroir to capture how the Seereer have occupied their natural milieu and directed their activities in it. The idea of terroir—which loosely translates as "human-made, agrarian landscape"—denotes the qualities of geographic identity conferred upon a region by the combined influence of ecology, weather conditions, agricultural system, and farming technology.[9] In evoking the concept, geographers have sought to lend attention to the projection of social relations in space and the assemblages of practices put in place by the Seereer to concretely organize their milieu. An integral aspect of elucidating the Seereer *rapport à la terre*, their relationship to the land, has involved meticulous studies of Seereer landholding arrangements: modalities of access, ownership, and control of land; regimes of rights; modes of tenure; effective exploitation of land lots; and logics of development; as well as the relations of labor, kinship, production, and social reproduction underlying agricultural schemas.[10]

The idea of terroir, however, denotes more than the crystallization of social relations in space and hewing out of the landscape into a sociable world by way of human labor. Sitting at the interface of land and territory, the terroir also conjures a sense of place, a being-in-the-world that translates into a variety of subjective attachments. The crafting of linkages to milieu and its perceptible rhythms via bodily sense and activity creates a ground of collective experience, cohesion, and recognition, which plays a key role in the constitution of cultural and political identity. Most ethnohistoric and ethnographic sources concur that, historically, being Seereer has entailed an acute sense of belonging to a social geography. Until a few decades ago, a majority of Seereer defined themselves through the craft of agriculture and their organic ties to the land, which provided not only the material means of existence but also a physical connection to the cement of local histories and identities: kin, ancestors, and spiritual forces.[11]

The Siin countryside entwines the deep past (the time of myths, legends, and long ago events), a more recent history of biographies and collectivities, and the changing present into dense gnarls of temporality, scattered unevenly across its surface; as such, it makes up an elaborate topology of memory, charged with affective resonance.[12] Around villages, for instance, the assortment of land plots, cultivated patches, and cattle herds stands as a visual transcript of lineage and collective wealth, which calls up contested stories of inheritance, community formation, and disagreement with other families or the agents of the state. Beyond the theater of the visible, however, Siin's physical milieu is also the dwelling ground of myriad invisible and occult forces. Its landscape, for those who can read it, is full of ghosts and spirits, and replete with material signs pointing to their presence and intentions. While the recent explosion of Islam has reconfigured Siin's religious geography, in earlier times, the region boasted a complex pantheon of natural spirits and ancestral figures congregating around salient natural features: earthen mounds, streams and rivers, freshwater wells, imposing trees, and sacred woods. Those were generally adorned by shrines of various makeup, ranging from broken ceramic vessels and the residues of libations to upright posts covered with charms and enclosed by short palisades, to consecrate them as places of worship and supernatural potency (figure 3). Other sacred places include the tombs of famous ancestors

3 *Fangool* (spirit shrine) on archaeological site (S204) near village of Ngohé (photo by author, 2011)

and memorable characters, as well as the earthly abodes of mythical figures such as lineage or dynastic founders.[13] Oral traditions often recall the auspicious intervention of supernatural forces in the narrative of Siin's formative moments, representing the province's past as a product of the twinned actions of spirits and humans. Hence, in addition to offering signposts to the high points of Seereer history, places of memory and sites of ancestral attachment have over time provided critical coordinates for the settlement, movement, and relocation of Seereer people and communities.[14]

However, because invisible agencies are mercurial and not always pure in their intentions, not all parts of the landscape are marked out as welcoming. In fact, Siin's natural milieu abounds with negative spaces and dangerous conjunctures (roads, crossroads), where and when malevolent forces congregate, and which constrain the presence of bodies devoid of mystical competence; these can be transient boundaries imposed by certain sensitive conditions (pregnancy, young age), moments of the day (noon, dawn, moonless nights) that favor occult activities and render the landscape uncertain, or places to be avoided at all costs, such as cemeteries or untamed forests, where witches (*naq*) and the living dead (*kon paaf*) conduct their nefarious assemblies and feast on human souls.[15] Finally, the Seereer terroir is also full of words, stories, and images that emerge from the encounter with natural places and infuse them with moral significance and didactic potential. Performed in different contexts and shadowing different activities, songs, prayers, legends, and oral poetry provide so many ways of reading, teaching, and remembering, so many tales of warning and incitement to action, thus reaffirming the bonds of mutual constitution between milieu and culture.[16]

The Work of Landscape

Inherently duplicitous, the term *landscape* refers both to visual perspective and the geographical territories seized by it. Landscapes articulate nature and culture, seer and scene.

D. MOORE, *SUFFERING FOR TERRITORY: RACE, PLACE, AND POWER IN ZIMBABWE*[17]

From years of exposure to this human geography, learning its contours and poetics, I have come to find powerful resonance in the idea of *landscape* as an organizing rubric, an analytic that conjoins the intuitive sensibility of Siin's environment, vernacular modes of feeling and thinking through it, and theoretical representations of its workings. While the landscape touches on colloquial meanings of *image, view, panorama,* and *physical background,* these meanings by themselves stop short of elucidating the subtle force that the landscape exerts on people even as it appears to recede into the backdrop of deliberate actions. In fact, it may be argued that it is precisely from its understated presence, its "nearness" (in Geertz's terminology), that the landscape draws its efficacy as a social form and interpretive framework. To unriddle this indeterminacy, anthropologists, geographers, and literary theorists have looked to more relational understandings of landscape that ground aesthetics in place and space, and recognize that milieu and society not only bleed into each other but also are bound in a process of mutual fashioning. Moving beyond defining the landscape as a stage, a text to be read, or a visual genre, these perspectives are less concerned with what the landscape is or means than with understanding "what it *does,* how it works as a cultural practice."[18]

Many relational approaches to landscape start, as I do in this book, with Henri Lefèbvre's famous aphorism that "(social) space is a (social) product."[19] From this perspective, space is not an objective reality that exists prior to people; rather, it is generated in relationships between objects and subjects. In the same vein, the landscape is not an inert vessel to be furnished with people, gestures, and things, but it is *socially* and *culturally* constructed. Landscape is what happens to the physical milieu when it is transformed by human practices and mediated by subjective experience.[20] This implies very material operations like turning a stretch of idle land into a field, founding a village, building a road or a bridge, or modifying the environment through the long-term selection of trees, preferred use of plants, or excessive burning of wood fuel. Mundane or mindful, premeditated or unconscious, these engagements with geography are collective enterprises that build up over time—Lefèbvre calls the landscape an oeuvre slowly molded from the earth by history—though not all members of a social formation participate in them equally or share equal understanding of their landscape.[21] Nor are they equally invested in it or do they exercise equal mastery over it. That said, while spatial practice is an essential dimension of landscape, its fashioning is made possible by meaning-making activities that render the external world intelligible and its forms culturally legible, and thus authorize action in it; landscapes, in effect, are *lived* through the signs, codes, and representations that organize cultural terrains over time.[22] Significations here link people and land, binding together spaces, places, and practices into *assemblages* made and remade within particular histories of politics and society; these recombinant assemblages are the stuff of which landscape is made.[23]

Through the prism of landscape, history and geography interpenetrate. Space does not merely traject the passage of time, nor does it stand as a witness to the spectacle of events. A thingly archive, the landscape has a history and temporality (it is always under construction), yet it also records, incompletely, in concrete strokes of earth, wood, and stone, the various histories that went into its making (it enfolds *multiple* expressions and durations of time). This is because people never quite make their worlds from scratch. Rather, in the course of social production, they encounter variably consistent configurations of social and ecological relations materialized in space. These antecedent forms must be contended with and affect the outcome of social projects. Some will be transformed, replaced, or incorporated in the creation of new spaces and spatial practices; others will linger in landscapes in connivance or contradiction with new spatial assemblages. Consequently, different parts of the landscape change at different rates and times, and embody palimpsest historicities. In this sense, under the appearance of stasis, landscapes always inhabit several historical tenses at once.[24]

The turn to landscape also draws our attention to the recursive quality of the material world. The landscape is not a canvas pressed into shape by social forces. Rather, as Lefèbvre repeatedly reminded his readers, space is both "*work* and *product*" both a "*field of action* (offering its extension to the deployment of projects and practical intentions) and a *basis of action* (a set of places whence energies derive and whither energies are directed)."[25] This means that landscapes (and the spaces, objects, and nonhuman entities that constitute them) have *effects* that twist or resist trajectories of the social. In their inescapable concreteness, material worlds limit and delimit what human actors can do, just as they open loci of possibility for social work. This also points to the role of the natural and built environment in shaping subjectivity, as we have seen among the Seereer. In the process of engaging and transforming the concrete dimensions of their world, people are appropriated by it. In learning to orient themselves in their material surrounds, they craft forms of self-consciousness; that is, in making their worlds, social actors also make and remake *themselves*.[26] While my concern in this book is with *social* landscapes as a transcript of political histories of peasant communities, it is important to remember that aspects of Siin's rural milieu escaped the intentionality and agency of its inhabitants. As Moore remarks, "landscapes, like history, subject people to conditions not of their own choosing." They are full of elements that are not (just) human in origin, which have the capacity to mold the worldly circumstances under which actors operate.[27] In this light, in Siin and beyond, landscapes are hybrid assemblages, where livelihoods mix with crops, animal herds, ancestral spirits, impoverished soils, and (un)propitious rainfall. We cannot understand how these mixtures impact the history of peasants without acknowledging the role of nonhuman entities.

Landscapes, finally, are not just places of shared identity and worldview; rather, they are cleaved by games of power, politics, and difference.[28] This sentiment is elegantly expressed by Jacques Rancière, for instance, when he says that politics is about the "configuration of the sensible, about questions such as what is given. . . . It's about the visibilities of the places and abilities of the body in those places, . . . about the very configuration of the visible and the relation of the visible to what can be said about it . . . the partition of the sensible." Thus construed, politics hinges on arranging and rearranging landscapes, and the capacity of people to sense, perceive, and act in them.[29] If space is intrinsic to the functioning of power, however, landscapes are not just expressions of politics in space. Rather, they involve the assembly of distinct visions of regulation, authority, and order; indeed, as Adam Smith insists, "they are *political order*." For W. J. T. Mitchell, the landscape functions a bit like ideology: "it naturalizes a cultural and social construction, representing an artificial world as if it were simply given and inevitable, and it also makes that representation operational by interpellating its beholder." Landscapes are about creating certain kinds of worlds and subjecting people to their order of things. Part of the project they carry is to fashion social and political persons.[30] Indeed, the (re)building of space and place is often viewed as a prerogative of sovereignty, and an important vehicle for state practices of subjection and rulemaking.

The Chance of Space and Reluctance of Landscapes

Space is fundamental in any exercise of power.
M. FOUCAULT, *POWER*[31]

And yet, it is important to emphasize that the element of surprise, the unexpected, the other, is crucial to what space gives us. D. MASSEY, *FOR SPACE*[32]

While acknowledging that spatial production is always bound with modes of social and political authority, we should not be seduced by totalizing (and tantalizing) portrayals of the landscape, remembering that this sense of permanence and coherence is a *desired effect* of the ideological projects sustained by landscape. As we will observe repeatedly in this book, along with Lefèbvre, landscapes are first and foremost arenas of struggles, the loci of competing imaginations of legitimate political society. In Moore's words, landscapes are *entangled*: they conjoin multiple orders of space and time, "shaping a plural terrain, where no single space prevails." In the case of Siin, historically, local landscapes have been traversed by overlapping matrices of power: geographies of difference structured along the axes of age, gender, labor, kinship, and social position; regimes of rule that have jostled for sovereign control over resources, people, and territory; as well as larger ensembles of relations (capitalist political economy, the geography of empire, the nation's geo-body, regional ecologies) that have incorporated the region into wider constellations of spatial order and configured the texture of local existence. The lived landscapes that have accreted over time in Siin are the products of *contingent articulations* of these various fields of forces and their playing out in local places, rather than through structural determination at any singular level.[33]

These minglings add some nuance to landscape's relationship to polity, power, and agency, given that landscapes are commonly understood as the playground of state and capital. Mixedness imparts a subversive shadow to the medium of landscape, an underside characterized more by uncertainty than transitive efficacy. While recognizing that material settings are prime instruments of rule, it is important to recognize that they are not endlessly pliable, nor placidly hewn into transcripts of authority. We must, then, also interrogate the *limits of space* and the *holds it places on power*. Here I find common ground with recent theories of materiality that underscore what Jane Bennett calls the force of things—namely, the fact that cultural productions can be enlisted toward the pursuit of a variety of human projects, but, once objectified, they always retain some material recalcitrance; the materiality of artifacts, bodies, and places exudes a resistant intensity that partially defies attempts to control them.[34] In the same vein, a number of authors have drawn attention to the *incompleteness* of spatial worlds, to their capacity to outdo and outwit the best laid plans of appropriation, design, and regulation. They have, in other words, underscored what Massey terms the chance of space, an unpredictability that can never be fully contained by dominant orders, and that endows space with a certain capacity to act as a force unto its own.[35]

Building on this proposition, I suggest that there is a degree of political independence to the material world, a *reluctance of landscape* that recalibrates its relationship to power and sovereignty. More specifically, my argument is that landscapes do not always offer the path of least resistance to governance because cultural geographies (and the multiple spatialities they contain) sometimes constrain rather than facilitate the operation of state rule and other political institutions.[36] In coining the idea of reluctant (undisciplined, indocile) milieus, my intention is not to advance a vision of landscapes as historical actors sui generis divorced from the people that fashion them, or as cultural blueprints suspended above the heads and deeds of people caught in the thick of political building. Nor am I referring to an unchanging *habitus* of spatial resistance defying space and time. Quite differently, I want to make a cautious move away from too plastic a reading of landscapes, one that overestimates the instrumentality of space and power. Instead, I suggest that to do proper justice to the political work of landscapes and what people do through them, we need to consider their unpredictability, itself the artifact of many forces. Landscapes are reluctant *because* they are composite historical, natural, and cultural productions, and because they implicate a mix of spaces that do not necessarily cohabit seamlessly and carry effects that bear unevenly on different social actors.

Lefèbvre once intimated that the analyst of space confronts a central paradox: that "the political power which holds sway over 'men,' though it dominates the space occupied by its 'subjects,' does not control the causes and reasons that intersect within that space, each of which acts by and for itself."[37] The idea of *reluctant landscape* seeks to capture this conundrum, by acknowledging the irreducibility of material worlds to any single mode of power, while recognizing that space is never innocent, and that landscapes are formidable vehicles of politics. Taking stock of landscapes' reluctance means accounting for *both* dominant order(s) *and* the obstinate causes interrupting their horizons. It means exploring how political projects are produced and received, how they succeed and backfire—in no small part due to the ambiguities of material worlds. Indeed, it means unpacking how power moves through space yet how its articulations with landscape secrete unanticipated effects that constantly reshape political fields. Lastly, it means attending to the cultural politics of place without succumbing to the spell of human determinism, and how different groups of actors construct a common world while dislocating people as the sole agents of history.

Through the lens of reluctant landscapes, I hope to draw on the properties of Siin's cultural milieu to revisit visions of political history in Senegambia in the age of global flows. Although scholarship in Atlantic Africa has shown that some political regimes crafted political aesthetics that successfully set power in space, in other situations, inherited spatial forms got in the way of polities as they imparted material shape to their political aspirations; what is more, these defiant spaces sometimes articulated with competing projects to become the platforms for alternative political visions. Such was the case in the Siin throughout its history, where space never quite functioned as a straightforward vector of political control, order, and subjection. Indeed, Siin's landscapes may have afforded considerable peasant autonomy at the margins of the state, which acted as a long-term brake to mechanisms of political centralization. The historical terroirs carved by Siin's peasants seem to have carried moral feelings of distrust about sovereignty, a political unconscious anchored in matter that structured, and was restructured by, physical encounters with centralized authority over the past four centuries.[38]

As we shall see in the next chapter, modes of historical writing in Senegambia have featured more heavy-handed views of past political terrains dominated by the agencies of the state and global capital. A landscape approach troubles these perspectives with historical accounts anchored in materiality and temporal multiplicity. Here, as we seek to envision peasant worlds over the past five hundred years, we must confront another kind of resistance: an *archival* reluctance, stemming from the ambiguity of the landscape, not as a historical object, but as a *repository* of information about the past. Littered with the relics of epochs gone by, historical landscapes are a fitful archive, which shines a flickering light on the past. Far from a detriment, however, this partiality can be harnessed to reframe our understanding of Africa's Atlantic past and write narratives of global encounters that take greater account of history's limitations.

TWO

Writing Senegambian Political Pasts

These three fundamental elements of slavery, colonization, and apartheid are said to serve as a unifying center of Africans' desire to know themselves, to recapture their destiny (*sovereignty*), and to belong to themselves in the world (*autonomy*). A. MBEMBE, "AFRICAN MODES OF SELF-WRITING"[1]

Some years ago, Achille Mbembe remarked that African history has been written under the ruling signs of the (Atlantic) slave trade and colonialism and that these events (as historical processes and discursive fields) have overseen the narration of African modes of identity in the past and present. By inscribing Africa at the heart of *world history*, these historical moments simultaneously incorporated the continent into a particular *story of the world*. This singular story, which is at once universal and yet profoundly rooted in European thought, is that of global modernity and its self-propelling expansion. Whether organized through the rubrics of core-and-periphery, market logics, or anticapitalism, its narrative adopts a wide explanatory purview that privileges worldwide connections, instrumentalities, and polarities. Reading Africa through planetary storylines has imparted distinctive shape to representations of its past; it has also made it somewhat difficult to reconcile the continent's discrepant histories with the coherence and directionality of scenarios of planetwide development.[2] As the sturdy yarns of global time outweigh the delicate threadwork of local temporalities, we are left with skewed visions of what Jean-François Bayart calls "the true historicity of African societies."[3]

My interest in this chapter is to examine how these considerations have translated to historical writings about Senegambia. How, indeed, has Senegal's turbulent encounter with the forces of capitalism and imperialism configured our understanding of its political landscapes? Echoing Mbembe's observations, I suggest that slavery and colonialism have been perceived as foundational events in the plot of Senegambia's past, constitutive moments of history making and unmaking that have had a determinant hand in shaping the course of regional development. What particularly concerns me are the histories *not represented* in this account of the past. Erasure, of course, is part of the work of history. Silences sometimes signal the footprints of historical trajectories erased by material circumstances and lost to posterity. Yet I also want to argue that some of this emptying out is conditioned by the modes of questioning that have been applied to the study of Senegal's modern past. Although Senegalese historiography counts numerous currents of thought, I contend that these different perspectives have shared an episteme. Together they partake in a common *genre* of historical writing, complete with its own narrative structure, organizing categories, and coordinates of space, time, and causality—a way of writing suited to the multiple political demands of postindependence Africa.[4] By orienting analysis toward the traumas of the slave trade and colonialism, this narrative framework has directed our gaze toward a given set of benchmarks, dynamics, and interconnections, yet it has often glanced over the quirky political forms and pathways unrecognizable to its modes of historical perception. In other words, it may have overlooked some of the distinctive dimensions of African political life over the past five hundred years.

How to write accounts of Senegalese political worlds sensitive to these muted histories? One way, I suggest, might be to rearticulate the problem-space of Senegal's global past away from the problematics of Atlantic slavery and colonial rule and toward stories of time and materiality. As examined in the previous chapter, African material worlds are cluttered with the refuse of political histories. On account of their concreteness, these traces are often fragmentary, obdurate, inarticulate. Yet, their incompleteness is precisely what makes them productive; rather than piecing together a total narrative, they outline a web of piecemeal and unexpected connections. The histories of objects, practices, and milieus preserved in landscapes capture aspects of human experience that often elude the scripts of capital and colony and exceed the temporal horizon of recorded history; in pushing back against these narratives, they provoke questions, new ways of seeing, and alternative paths to follow. This epistemology of fragments, in all of its accidental and dispersed quality, can open useful insights into the more obscure facets of Senegambian political history and thus complement prevailing portrayals of the regional past.

Historical Imaginations of Atlantic Senegambia

The very aporia of historical knowledge: a non-coincidence between facts and truth, between verification and comprehension. G. AGAMBEN, *REMNANTS OF AUSCHWITZ*[5]

Historical scholarship has long regarded Senegambia's immersion in planetwide circuits of political economy as nothing short of a sea change. Studies of Atlantic Senegambia hatched in the context of postindependence inquiries about the volume of the slave trade, which expanded into broader debates over how deleterious an impact capitalist exploitation, in its mercantile and colonial forms, had on African courses of development.[6]

In drafting the balance sheet of the region's engagement with European expansion, scholars have often converged in their perception of Atlantic commerce and colonialism as moments of unprecedented interference with African ways of life.[7] Where researchers have expressed less unison, however, is in their assessment of the nature and extent of these interruptions, and there exists a diverse spectrum of opinions regarding how detrimental Atlantic forces were and the capacity of Africans to decide their own fate. In their original form, discussions have tended gravitate around two clusters of positions. At one end, an earlier generation of historians minimized the impact of enslavement, arguing that the balance of trade systematically favored Senegambia until the nineteenth century and afforded new possibilities for economic development and political accumulation. Rather than a covert apologia for the slave trade, this research, in the words of one of its most visible figures, sought to challenge the "received wisdom . . . that Africans exported mainly slaves and received in return worthless goods such as cheap gewgaws, beads, rum, and firearms" and the implication that African societies had been stagnant and incapable of economic initiative.[8]

By contrast, a rival camp, sometimes loosely labeled the École de Dakar (Dakar School), has raised doubt about the premises framing these interpretations and marshaled wide-ranging historical evidence speaking to the destructive embrace of the Atlantic slave trade.[9] This collective of authors has equated the Atlantic era with great disruptions marked by the rise of predatory states, rampant slave-raiding, crises of production, famines, and generalized insecurity. Working through the channels of Atlantic commerce and colonial regimes, world capitalism, according to Boubacar Barry, dealt a "fatal blow to all fields of artisanal production and interregional trade," thus robbing local communities of their autonomy and chaining them in sturdy bonds of dependency with exterior markets.[10] Africans were forced into a broader process of peripheralization that relegated the continent to the margins of the world economy and stalled its development relative to other parts of the globe. One of these critics' most forceful contributions has been to underscore a trend in the centralization of political power and document the rise of local kingdoms as primary actors in the theater of Atlantic Africa. The mechanics of the oceanic trade, they argue, favored a concentration of resources, military capacities, and authority in the hands of ruling elites, which flipped the gravity of political agency from rural communities to predatory monarchies.[11]

There is little doubt that in the process of taking each other to the tribunal of truth and error, and matching interpretive point with evidential counterpoint, these authors have enriched what we know about the impact of global forces on African communities. For example, it is clear that, if the terms of trade may have broadly favored Senegambia for the first three-and-a-half centuries of Atlantic commerce, Curtin's focus on market dynamics (through the import-export-price triad) somewhat downplayed the sociopolitical costs of global forces and their long-term consequences for labor and productive capacity in the region. Concurrently, recognizing the weight of structural inequities does not imply the need to subscribe en masse to the dystopian scenarios of underdevelopment and loss sometimes invoked by the Dakar School. For the time being, however, let me set aside concerns about the accuracy of these different scenarios and draw attention instead to what they *collectively* reveal about the process of historical production in Senegal. My claim is that the terms in which historical debates in Senegambia have been conducted, the images that they have mobilized, how authors have read and invoked evidence, and the scope of analyses form the parameters of a genre of history building specific to the region. It is interesting that in waging their interpretive battles on the terrain of factuality under the watchful arbitrating of empirical evidence, authors of different persuasions have generally overlooked the common horizon of assumptions informing what they see as credible evidence, argument, and narrative—in other words, the episteme that they inhabit. In the Senegambian guild, these shared sensibilities—a combined penchant for region-wide analysis, generalization, and political and economic foci—have afforded visions of the past that have exposed salient evolutions associated with the Atlantic period, just as they have clouded other dimensions of African historical experience.

One central feature of Senegambian historiography has been its reliance on a broad regional outlook as a framing device. Studies have often adopted the Senegambia/Upper Guinea regions as their units of analysis, focusing on the string of powerful kingdoms lining the Atlantic coast and navigable waterways: the Wolof polities of Kajoor, Bawol, and Waalo, the Halpulaar kingdom of Futa Tooro, the ethnically mixed polity of Saalum, and the Mandinka principalities bordering both sides of the Gambia River.[12] This tendency partly flows from disparities in the geography of textual evidence, and, unsurprisingly, the areas most prominently featured in historical scholarship correspond to those larger kingdoms that were in frequent contact with Europeans and thus possess the densest trail of historical writings.[13] A number of these polities saw the dramatic rise of warrior aristocracies and expansion of state violence during the eighteenth century, providing a historical foundation for the models proposed by Dakar School historians. While such generalizations have been useful in outlining patterns unseen at smaller spatial and temporal scales or eluding the here-and-now grasp of historical observers, they have also entailed a number of trade-offs. Most obviously, broad-brushstroke portraits of development encompassing wide historical blocs and territorial stretches cannot account for the spectrum of idiosyncrasies that make up experience at the level of localities.[14] More subtly, the narrative focus on aristocracies and their involvement in social violence has deflected attention from other historical actors, whose responses to political-economic turbulences are poorly recorded in written archives; these silences, in turn, become the architecture of absence on which regional histories are built, as stories of militarized states and powerless peasants are scaled out to exemplify the carnage laid by Atlantic forces in northern Senegambia.

The limits of regional extrapolation have been prominently displayed in recent critiques of the predatory-state thesis, a mode of argument linking the expansion and consolidation of centralized kingdoms in West Africa to the voracious Atlantic demand for slaves. Increasingly reliant on slave production and foreign goods, these polities sustained themselves and grew wealthy from their ability to raid frontier decentralized societies and supply a continuous stream of enslaved bodies to the circuits of international slavery.[15] In addition to perpetuating an intuitive bias toward stratified polities, this interpretation is also problematic in portraying nonstate societies as defenseless, passive slave reservoirs. A closer look at Casamance or Guinea Bissau, however, shows nuanced strategies of engagement with regional states and the realities of enslavement. Not only did many of them actively resist slave raiders but others managed to exploit inland slaving networks by establishing themselves as intermediate providers and preying upon neighboring communities.[16] In more general terms, while predatory-state narratives tend to gloss the complex nuances of the broader political landscape and discount nonstate arrangements, they also partially homogenize the functioning of societies, like the Siin, that *were* organized as kingdoms but whose involvement in Atlantic commerce was more ancillary and whose internal dynamics do not quite answer to a mere logic of state centralization.

The will to generalize driving classic historical debates in Senegambia has also translated into a particular take on historical determination. Because they have been cast in the *longue durée*, an optic that smooths the rough edges of lived particularity and zooms out to align with the swing of general directions, analyses of Atlantic histories in Africa have tended to bundle transformations in different spheres of society into synthetic cause-and-effect packages. This disposition toward portmanteau thinking, pinning social, political, and economic institutions to a common trajectory of change, has also contributed to the persistence of bifurcated modes of emplotment. When documenting Africa's meeting with the hydra of global forces, authors have tended to frame their questions in terms of gainers and losers and all-or-nothing scenarios.[17] As noted above, however, it is unlikely that Atlantic dynamics had uniform social consequences that evenly spilled across all realms of social experience or that a region as vast and diverse as Senegambia could be adequately captured by single historical movements. Forcing Senegambia into sweeping stories of (in the last instance) African autonomy or powerlessness that already presume the logic of history ultimately obscures the character of once-living African communities and the quilt of historicities sewn in the wake of Atlantic contacts.

A final observation touches on the way in which scholarship of all stripes has treated the question of culture in Atlantic Senegambia. Building on a strong interest in political and economic processes, researchers have produced excellent accounts of the fraught landscape of diplomacy, warfare, state building, and commerce, which is comparatively well-documented in European writings, especially in the eighteenth century. Some exceptions aside, matters of African cultural life are seldom touched upon in the documentary record of the Atlantic period. Hence, to flesh out the cultural milieus of Atlantic interactions, scholars have often resorted to colonial ethnographies and oral traditions recorded in the late nineteenth century and later, whose information they have taken to be accurate representations of precolonial practices and institutions.[18] This juxtaposition has produced interesting outcomes. While scholars have accorded much fluency to African politics and economy, the conjuration of a vision of life as it was for an enormously capacious stretch of time (the precolonial period) leaves the impression of a relatively unmoving cultural décor against which battles take place, villages are raided, commercial dealings are conducted, and political elites strategize to accrue power and get the better hand. The foregrounding of states and aristocracies as the story's chief protagonists exacerbates this sense of stillness, as peasant societies become relegated to the penumbra of unwritten chapters or resurface in the glimmer of an afterthought (as the victims of enslavement, predation, exploitation, and famines). Hence the paradox: if the transformations introduced by the advent of global markets were so momentous, how did they not trickle into the realm of cultural institutions and traditions? Doesn't doing so consign the precolonial cultural past to a qualitatively different sphere of history barely grazed by the operation of time and congealed in collective memory? In effect, the staging of political turbulence against a conservative cultural canvas recalls the anthropological dualisms of yore that split state from society, agency from structure, history from stasis, and production from reproduction, which perhaps tells us more about our sources' partiality and about how we parse the world than about past realities.

This description does not exhaust the full range of historical thought and research on Senegambia. In fairness, recent strands of scholarship have attempted to address the limitations outlined above and sailed a more balanced course around conceptual shoals. Some authors, for instance, have supplemented regional perspectives with monographic attention to the internal dynamics of particular provinces between the eighteenth and early twentieth century. Others have produced sensitive analyses of economic developments, slavery and labor migrations, peasantries, and social order during the colonial era. And, of course, the work of geographers and sociologists has considerably clarified the cultural and agricultural organization of Wolof and Seereer communities.[19] These remarkable developments notwithstanding, researchers have not always fully managed to escape the residues of binary thinking: positing favorable terms of trade *or* negative balance sheets, agency *or* submission, autonomy *or* dependence. Nor have they avoided the tendency to write regional history from the standpoint of the better-documented (Wolof) areas, which were also the most implicated in commercial slavery and most susceptible to its disruptions. And when authors have examined—often astutely—political dynamics in smaller or more peripheral polities, culture has continued to be backgrounded as an enduring ensemble of practices, whose historicity has rarely been plumbed.[20] This is true even of geographic studies, whose attention to the changing present has been unmatched but which, in foregrounding space, have taken a relatively flat view of time and cultural transformations in the precolonial past.

Let me note here that, in raising these points, my intention is not to invalidate previous attempts to make sense of Senegambia's place in the storm of processes that have reshaped the world since the fifteenth century. Doing so would be hypocritical, given that much of this seminal research provides a robust scaffold for my own study. Nor am I questioning the horrors of Atlantic slavery, whose brutality is unassailable. Rather, my objective is to highlight certain habits of mind, immanent to the field of Senegambian scholarship and dyed into the very way we approach historical situations, the very terms we use to explore them, and the very questions we draw on to frame our inquiries. This structure of argument coalesced in the anticolonial discourses of the 1950s, 1960s, and 1970s (which came in various nationalist, pan-Africanist, dependentist, or Afro-Marxist flavors) and the debates that they sparked about Africa's past.[21] As uniquely brutal systems of exploitation, yet ones implicated in the fiber of global modernities (including African ones), the triangular trade and colonialism provided fitting cynosures for postindependence national struggles. As reverberated in the reactions to the Dakar speech, these epochal moments are also interlaced with a complex array of emotional, moral, and political feelings that span the gamut of guilt and anger, exoneration and accusation, and accountability and innocence. These positions have deeply colored the politics of the present in newly independent nations and thus contributed significantly to postcolonial academic discourse in Africa. As a result, the Atlantic trade and colonialism offered a set of plausible explanations for Africa's awkward footing in global political economy and simultaneously outlined the obstacles that needed to be overcome to foster alternatives to the present situation. In this light, the idea of history espoused by Senegambian scholarship, with its focus on regional integration and political-economic issues, has in very conscious ways functioned as a two-way mirror of sorts, its visions of the past calibrated to the moral concerns of a fragile present while nourishing the hopes of a brighter future.

If these perspectives have sought to overturn the legacies of colonial violence and representations, they have also remained bound in complicated ways to genealogies of thinking nested in the colonial library—such that scholars writing from different political convictions converge in a surprising manner with the views advocated by Nicolas Sarkozy, which stand at the edge of a long line of North Atlantic representations of otherness. These turn up in curious ways, for instance, in the treatment of cultural life and nonelite communities during the Atlantic era, which we will see bear some resemblance to colonial discourses on African peasants. More perversely perhaps, in foregrounding Atlantic markets and colonialism as the catalysts (for better or for worse) of African history, researchers have tacitly recuperated the causal structure of models of history originating elsewhere and entered into a kind of Whiggish bargain: gazing back at the impact of European expansion from the standpoint of the scars it left on the present, scholarship has reaffirmed the precedence of world history and its capacity to drive change over the rhythms and agencies pulsing through African communities. The narrative architecture of slavery, capital, and colony has rendered invisible the smaller histories and minor-key possibilities bubbling at its margins yet intrinsic to the story of global circulations.[22]

Reframing Problem-Spaces: Landscape as Dialectical Image

A landscape is the most solid appearance in which a history can declare itself.

F. INGLIS[23]

History decays into images, not into stories.

W. BENJAMIN, *THE ARCADES PROJECT*[24]

How then do we work through the conundrum that worldwide historical forces are both "indispensable and inadequate" to our reconstructions of African histories?[25] As I have proposed above, the quest for factual truth in Senegambian historical discourse is not completely satisfying in that all sides of the debate have been conducted within the same economy of concerns, according to rules of the game that have gone unchallenged. A more pertinent issue, perhaps, is the extent to which the vistas of postindependence scholarship in Senegal continue to be valid in the present and how once-relevant questions, now out of joint with the spirit of times, continue to shape how we think about the past. If some of these interrogations have run their course and have somewhat sclerosed representations of the past, I suggest that a key to keeping historical imagination critical and alive is not to pin new answers to the old haunts of the past but to pose *different questions*, which can harness the past in pursuit of new expectations about the future; in David Scott's phrasing, we need to reframe the problem-space of our conversations.[26] In the case of Senegambia, this recasting lies perhaps less in assessing the *impact* of global market forces and colonial rule and how much they actually stifled or lifted African trajectories than in charting political histories scribbled outside of those reference points.

There are many alternative histories to be unearthed in Senegal, and more than one conduit into them.[27] As regards the Siin, however, I would suggest that thinking of the past beyond the coordinates of the Atlantic trade, predatory states, and colonialism should perhaps entail thinking below these categories. In Siin, the evacuation of peasants from the past and the political present defines the parameters of relevance for historical analysis; it impels us to illuminate the context of this marginalization and what has faded out of view in the process. To do so, we must come down from the aerial view of regional and continental interactions, keep closer to the ground, and apply ourselves to sketch histories of the globe as they are brought into existence in small places like the Siin in the course of rural existence.[28] One entrée into the political past of Siin's village societies is to reconstitute the problem-space of Atlantic Africa around questions of temporality and materiality. These dimensions are good to think with because, if properly queried, they afford tangible, ground-level insights into regional pasts in a way mindful of the mundane histories of cultural and political life roping elites and subalterns together. Let me briefly consider how.

In posing the question of temporality in Senegambian history, we eschew simplified notions of history as a serial movement of changes fated to flow in the same direction and at the same rate. Instead, our awareness is trained on the fact that African pasts, as they converged with those of other societies, brought different histories and senses of time together. In Mbembe's words, Africa's dealings with the outside world are better imagined as a vast web of *entanglements*—between different rhythms of life and activity, projects of variable scope and duration, and patterns of action carrying different depths of consequence. The orders of time tied into these "knotted histories," as Chakrabarty calls them, did not equally govern local fields of practice or evenly affect its actors. Plumbing the historicity of moments of global encounter depends in large part on unpacking the nature of temporal entanglements.[29] Close attention to conditions and conjunctures helps us to parse how forces of the long and short term, in and outside of the continent, weighed on regional courses of political action. In the same breath, it also complicates our understanding of epochal processes like Atlantic capitalism and its colonial extensions as they met the sticky realities of local cultural worlds.

Temporality and materiality are bundled in inextricable ways in that different forms of history—whether fast-clipped or slow-moving, episodic or repetitive—find expression in the tangible world.[30] Like coats of patina, the times of social institutions, political orders, economic cycles, and environmental change are layered messily over rural topography, forming a palimpsest of its history. Because of the multiple temporal trajectories encased in the amber of milieu, the lens of materiality offsets the historian's perception, orienting our gaze to planes of historical experience that escape representation, discourse, and recognition. Two elements stand out with particular salience for reconstructions of African history. First, a sharpened focus on people's interactions with material things points to aspects of cultural production often ignored in textual and oral sources yet pivotal to the playing out of relations between Africa and Europe, which at their core involved traded objects and concrete outcomes (enslavement, wars, pillages, famines, to name a few). Second, the material world is often keyed to aspects of collective organization that outlast the lifetimes of individuals; social and natural environments register the imprint of long-lasting cultural and political programs and their transformation at the touch of historical forces. In this sense, materialities embody what with Chakrabarty we might call the dark side of cultural traditions—namely, those constellations of history and practice that "remain opaque to the theoretical gaze of the analyst" (because they belong in the realm of the mundane, abject, unintelligible, or nondiscursive reason) and get left out of most histories.[31] Once excavated, however, these cultural practices push back against conventional narrative wisdom and begin to point to the elsewhere and otherwise of history.

The kind of reframing proposed here plays to the strengths of a landscape perspective. Landscapes, as we saw in the previous chapter, arise at the meeting point of time, matter, and culture. In landscapes, as in Bakhtin's chronotopes, "time, as it were, thickens, takes on flesh, becomes . . . visible; likewise, space becomes charged and responsive to the movements of time, plot, and history."[32] Landscapes crystallize not just single chronotopes but *many* assemblages of space-time. In this light, they are perhaps better understood as the scenes of what Walter Benjamin called dialectical images. Inspired by his strolls through the Paris arcades, commercial spaces that had once embodied fantasies of progress and been abandoned by capital, Benjamin became fascinated with outmoded things—discarded objects, heirlooms, trash, tenements, vacant places—and their potential for a radical critique of modernity. He developed the method of dialectical imaging to capture the tensions frozen in places and things between capitalism and the counterhistories of desire, failure, and refusal interrupting it. Dialectical images are *montages* of artifacts, ruins, and spaces, then and now, that gather past and present side by side and bring out their disharmonies. So juxtaposed, these asynchronous vestiges call into question the smooth linearity of narratives of modernity, whether progressive or regressive in their tone.[33]

As a kind of archive, landscape is uniquely germane to rethinking Africa's global history, not just for its empirical virtues but also for its *rebellious epistemology*. Surely, landscapes are repositories of evidentiary clues gesturing to different ways in which the past was made, lived, and experienced, some of which antedate the advent of European contacts. Yet literal traces of Africa's past also double as *traces* in a Derridean sense, meaning, pesky reminders—if one cares to look for them—that the forward march of time is constantly obstructed, altered, or rerouted by histories that existed before or coexisted with it.[34] The relationship between these different temporal spaces is truly dialectical. The earlier, other histories are necessary to the stories of global capital and empire since they provide the turf in which global projects seek to implant themselves and embody the indigenous habits, traditions, collective practices, and resources they seek to exploit. Yet, if they are contained in these grander narratives and in some sense incorporate them in their own functioning, indigenous histories are also *excessive*: they cannot be fully enclosed by market forces and colonialism; they sometimes resist, live alongside, or temporarily opt out of them; and, consequently, they fundamentally unsettle their universalizing impulse.[35] One implication is that there is always a degree of indeterminacy to Atlantic histories, an open-endedness that is not always taken into account in historical reconstructions. By contrast, stories of practice nested in the material world abound with the *petits récits* (minor stories) of subaltern life and peasant strategies, narratives in a minor key that refuse to fall in line with the ordering schemas of Euro-modernity.

These narratives, however, are not just lying in the landscape, obvious and transparent, waiting to ensnare the poetic mind or curious analyst. Rather, they must be decrypted, sensed, composed. As Benjamin reminds us, the idea of dialectical image is best appreciated as a concrete abstraction, a way of seeing buoyed by worldly substance. Like the *petits récits* of Africa's colonial landscapes, dialectical images do not just come about; they exist as potentialities that must be brought to life by the observer's critical imagination. In other words, unpacking them presupposes a method. Benjamin's was microscopic, focused on ferreting out incongruous detail—out-of-sync image and pregnant allegory—without losing sense of the swirling world around. The method I propose is similarly concerned with the very big compressed in the small, but not exclusively. Part of this choice is empirical. Much like Benjamin's analysis was framed by the urban ecology of large European cities, mine is bound by the possibilities, constraints, and properties of Siin's rural landscapes. This entails making the best of the kind of information available in and about the landscape, some of which is episodic and some of which patterns at relatively large scales. More interpretively, the kind of problem-space reconfiguration proposed in this chapter does not entail trading the farsightedness of global narratives for a nearsighted celebration of lived experience. Rather, it necessitates tracking the nature of their entwinement—a back and forth movement attuned to the different temporal and material ensembles comprising African landscapes and perceptible at different spatial scales. To achieve this, the method I use in this book draws on the playbook of historical anthropology, a reformed historical anthropology expanded to include archaeology as one of its lenses.[36] This method is multidisciplinary, rooted in the turf of many evidential sources. It is archival, both concerned about the past and attentive to the history of sources employed to illuminate it. It is focused on temporality and materiality as a way to get at the historicity of colonial encounters, and centrally invested in unfolding the cultural mediation of politics, power, and economy, but it does not abdicate an analysis of discourse, signs, and representations.

The object of this method—its archive—is the landscape, though it is a peculiar archive: peculiar for its size, its unique materialness; peculiar for being all at once record, document, and analytical perspective; peculiar for being itself culled together from a plurality of archival repertoires. Clues of past political landscapes are in effect scattered in patches and fragments across a variety of evidential registers: written documents, oral traditions, pictorial sources, archaeological data, ethnographic materials, and geographic territory. Each archival medium has its strengths and vulnerabilities, its authors and actors, its blinders and omissions.[37] Different sources encode different accounts of experience—some within the realm of human perceptions and others beyond it, some individual and others collective, some enduring and others more fleeting, some anchored in practice, others in discourse or memory. As Ann Stahl aptly remarks, crafting richer portraits of Africa's past demands a creative juggling between multiple lines of evidence, using some sources' strengths to balance out the blind spots of others. Yet, she adds that we also must attend to the disjunctures and *productive tensions* embodied in our archives.[38] Different stories told by different archives, or different sources within the same class of materials, can potentially illuminate the contradictory social forces that shaped lives long ago and were omitted from historical narratives; the divergences they locate can also gesture to unspoken *parti pris* underwriting certain representations of the past (and the evidence on which they rest). In other words, this dance of comparison and confrontation between sources can help us to retrieve the casualties of the turbulence and loss inaugurated by the Atlantic era—namely, the strategies and pathways that once oriented African political action and slid by the wayside of recorded history, falling prey either to ideas and practices nurtured in the new global climate or to the partiality of those writing or remembering the past—and the opportunity and experimentation that accompanied them.[39]

Textual documents and oral traditions are the most frequently employed sources in Senegal, and their strengths and weaknesses as historical evidence have been extensively discussed. Lettered accounts often comment on Africa from a place of cultural distance if not one of outright prejudice, especially after the eighteenth century. This distance is sometimes literal, for while many written documents are the fruit of firsthand witnessing, others recycle descriptive information from earlier authors, sometimes recorded decades before. Whether direct or indirect, observations generally follow coastlines and fluvial channels—the axes of European presence—and pay uneven attention to African lifeworlds, preferring to focus instead on European activities. Oral traditions, by contrast, offer indigenous perspectives on local pasts spanning different historical scales, from the family to the village and from dynastic chronicles to the history of kingdoms. Its cultural sensitivity notwithstanding, oral memory often conflates disparate events and epochs into single narratives, making it difficult to subject them to cut-and-dry tests of verifiability and factuality. Despite their susceptibility to distortions, written and oral accounts afford poignant insight into the intentions, positions, meanings, and social imaginations driving historical actors and events, as well as a suite of perceptions outlooks on what happened in the past.[40]

Archaeological materials, by extension, offer an "experience-near" transcript of African orientations to the material world, which is often lacking in other archives (other than perhaps European writers' obsession with African fetishes!).[41] Archaeologists like to say that they have privileged access to the realm of daily life and embodied practices in the past. Note, however, that archaeological things relate in complex ways to the social and material forms documented by ethnographers, inviting uncertainty as to exactly what kind of histories of life and practice they reflect. In Senegal, for instance, the coarseness of artifact chronologies, counted in centuries rather than in decades for the Atlantic era, produces a lulling sense of stability within temporal periods and an impression of rupture between them. Interestingly, as I show in chapter 6, archaeologists' long, multilayered accounts of history show greater resemblance to the palimpsest narratives of oral memory than to ethnographies of practice. Hence the methodological value of mobilizing many types of sources to glimpse the faster and slower times of African history.[42]

At any rate, the relationship between materiality and representation does not fall along clean artifact/text/image divisions. In effect, what Trouillot calls the "materiality of the first moment"—the fact that "history begins with bodies and artifacts: living brains, fossils, texts, buildings"—places certain demands on history. On the one hand, it implies that the realities of what happened provide the initial scaffold for narratives and that not just any fiction can pass as history. On the other hand, it suggests that thoughts, images, and material things are implicated in each other's lives and that various archives contain traces of this interpenetration. Consequently, combing textual and oral accounts with an eye for material expressions can reveal surprising insights into how rural Africans perceived and structured their physical surroundings in the past. Or how they accommodated the avalanche of goods that yoked local object worlds to distant markets and manufacturing centers. Likewise, textual, pictorial, and oral clues can be interpolated into archaeological narratives to paint richer portrayals of the meaningful practices, political logics, and subject positions that fashioned the African Atlantic.[43] This interplay of archives transcends the explanatory framework attached to each set of sources and subjects them to more expansive reading grids.

For the purpose of this book, my archives consist of materials drawn from a variety of sources. The archaeological work is nearly all mine. It derives from seven seasons of work conducted between 2001 and 2015, though the bulk of it clusters around two large-scale surveys, the objective of which was to discover historic villages and map their temporality and distribution (figure 4).[44] The first one was carried out in 2003 near the ancient capitals of Mbissel, Ndiongolor, and Diakhao, and included limited test excavations at seven sites. This latter information, which is sparse and hard to generalize, will not feature heavily in my account.

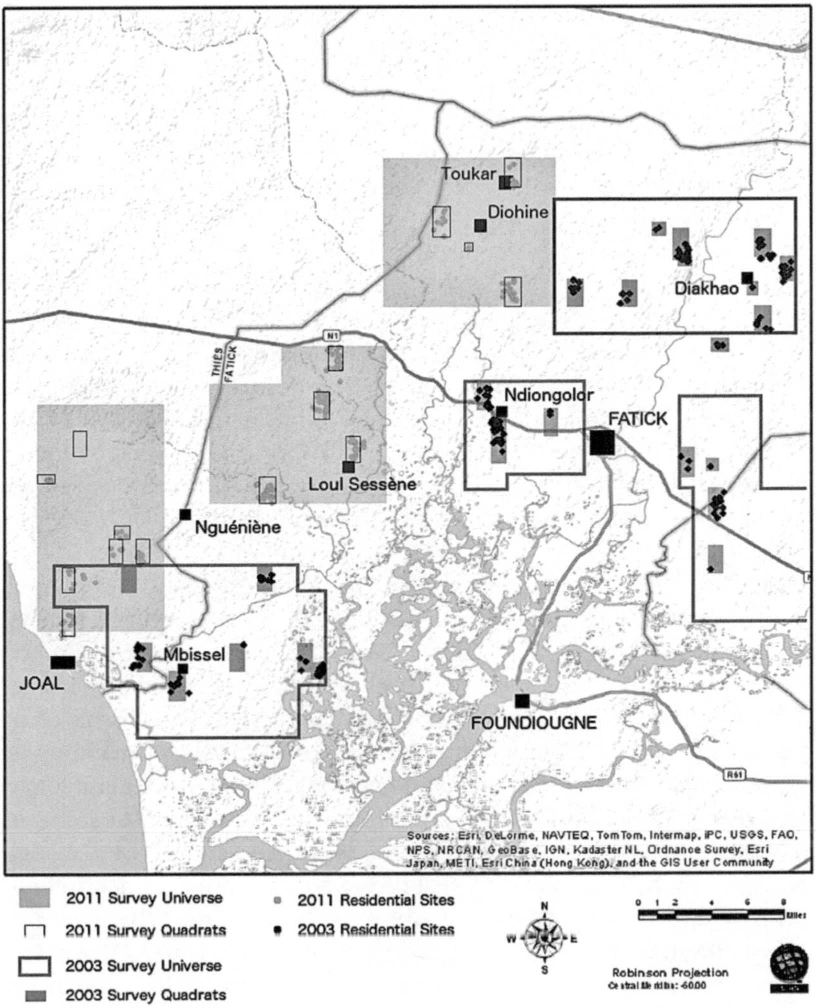

4 Regional archaeological survey in Siin, 2003–2011

This work was complemented by more recent research in 2011, which targeted previously unexamined areas of the Siin landscape, near the large villages of Nguéniène, Loul Sessène, and Toukar. I will detail these data as they become relevant in the course of the analysis. My documentary sources are more composite. Many are original—that is, the fruit of excursions in various archives over the years, mostly at the Archives d'Outre-Mer in Aix-en-Provence and the Archives Nationales du Sénégal in Dakar. Others come from historical accounts published near the time of observation and from the copious work of publication, editing, and translation of early European sources that Africanists have carried out since the 1950s. I have also drawn upon a substantial visual archive of maps, drawings, photographs, and postcards, which often combines with archaeological data in fruitful ways. Finally, perhaps less than ideally, much of the oral evidence used here is outsourced. Most of it is derived from published traditions, collected at different points in time, and compendia of village traditions. The difficulty here is that once set in writing oral traditions lose much of the fluidity, debate, and contestation that is part of the context of their performance. The publication of oral sources also tends to render authoritative that which is by nature partial. When possible, and when relevant, I have tried to lightly remedy this difficulty by summoning some of the historical memories I have collected in various villages, especially Diohine, Diakhao, and Ndiongolor.

In choosing to (re)construct past landscapes through a variety of archives, some object-based, others word-based, the perspective I propose scrambles the boundaries of history, anthropology, and archaeology.[45] It is moved by the traditional concerns, theories, and sources of historical anthropology, but its questions are also driven by an archaeological optic, attentive to different sets of material relations (including archaeological ones) and historical tempos (of both the shorter and longer view). In the process, it also conjures an expanded vision of archaeology: no longer defined just by its methods or the vestiges of buried pasts, archaeology here becomes a sensibility, a sort of "optical unconscious" calibrated to "the physiognomic aspects of visual worlds which dwell in the smallest of things, meaningful yet covert enough to find a hiding places in waking dreams."[46] This optical unconscious focuses our analytical gaze on the unsuspecting terrain of discarded artifacts, abandoned places, derelict ruins, and fragments of past lives. It magnifies the social lives of different objects, places, and milieus as they interweave with the social lives of people and enter the construction of their subjective understandings. In this view, past and present are equally archaeological. The vestiges of old villages, collections of excavated objects, historical maps, or dusty tomes of colonial correspondence can be read for clues about the Byzantine materialities coursing through global modernity, just as contemporary landscapes are full of anachronisms that serve as modest reminders of ghostly pasts dwelling in the present.

Unstitching Atlantic Histories: Toward an Epistemology of Fragments

He [photographer Eugène Atget] looked for what was unremarked, forgotten, cast adrift, and thus [his] pictures too work against the exotic, romantically sonorous names of the cities; they pump the aura out of reality like water from a sinking ship. W. BENJAMIN, "A SHORT HISTORY OF PHOTOGRAPHY"[47]

What does the history of Siin's entanglement with Europe's imperial trade networks look like through the lens of material worlds? What tempos of change, experimentation, and continuity do materialities suggest? Do they echo the narratives of disruption and state domination pieced together from the documentary record? Do they hint at other articulations between state and society? What do they uncover about the political life of village communities? How do different archives tell different stories about the colonial past they record? Why are these accounts different, and what does it tell us about the production of history? And about the categories we use to assist our reconstructions of the past?

These are some of the critical questions I ask to reorient the study of global immersions in Senegal and define the problems that guide this book. By repositioning the focus onto the terrains of materialness, historicity, and political practice, these lenses can help us to bypass certain assumptions about the nature of time, experience, and power in Africa's engagement with European nations and train our attention instead on the historicity of their construction.

Addressing these questions necessitates a kind of historical and anthropological practice that exhumes landscape archives both along and against the grain, looking for echoes and dissonances between sources and their plotlines. In truth, my intuition here is less about resolving discrepancies across different classes of evidence than exploiting their fractures.[48] My inclination, then, is to begin where the stitches suturing globalizing narratives come loose, to open gaps in their storylines and turn them into problems that can host new analyses. This critical stance is in perpetual motion: once its edge has blunted into familiar ways of seeing, telling, and thinking, the routine of questions and answers is to be undone by new inquiries aiming to unsettle standard perceptions.[49]

Perhaps because it leans more heavily on archaeology than conventional historical anthropologies, this approach adopts an archaeological poetics that not only is sensitive to object worlds, *longue durée* rhythms, and multiple spatial scales but also cultivates an appreciation of history's fractious nature. The damaged artifacts, discarded rubbish, decayed homes, and abandoned places that furnish an archaeologist's universe are patent reminders of the frailty of the past, of its selective preservation and fragmentary essence.[50] For that reason, archaeological archives introduce a promise of epistemic humility into the study of Africa's past. Not because they are the purveyors of more fulsome histories. They definitely aren't, especially relative to the evocative richness of written, oral, or visual accounts. Quite the contrary, in fact, for archaeological things are often irritating, obstinate, defiant; they stop short of combining into coherent patterns; they resist honest attempts to coax meaning out of them. Yet, this factual reticence also constitutes a point of vantage. More than just a way of looking, the archaeological imagination I have evoked also enfolds an epistemology of fragments that raises alertness to both the limits of historical knowledge and the indeterminacy of the past and harnesses the productivity of this incompleteness.

This mode of thinking finds common ground with writers like Anna Tsing, who caution against the pious search for commensurations across disparate bodies of evidence.[51] Reconciling data for coherence, she argues, patches over the disunities and multiplicities of history and culture. Attending to disharmonies in data, by contrast, entails accepting that contrary trends can and do coexist in the world and that history is better served by messy explanations than clean causality. Such sensibility to uncertainty, partiality, and fragment defines the archaeological process itself. As it rakes through the bric-à-brac of mismatched evidence, the archaeological mind pieces together mosaics that often confound historiographic benchmarks. It sketches a broad canvas of material continuities, ruptures, and trajectories that encompasses decades and centuries and leapfrogs over the minutiae of recorded events. Its slow-changing stories of pottery, trade artifacts, and village vestiges gloss long-shot visions of African traditions, community making, and social organization; they entrap long tempos of experience that don't always square with other sources. The plausible scenarios of society, economy, and politics assembled by archaeology may be suggestive, but they rarely resolve into confident narratives. At best, they shine unsteady light on relatively obscure aspects of the social life of past African societies. Archaeological histories, however, are often confined to discrete sets of artifacts—beads, bottles, or buildings—that may or may not bolster each other. Consequently, the visions they conjure are full of blank spaces, which we try to color with the assistance of other sources. Written words, spoken memories, ethnographic terrains, and discarded things combine messily, and they sometimes invite new ways of viewing the past, interpretations in the conditional that stand shy of definite answers and spark more questions and more hypotheses. Yet, this process of mixing and matching also exposes disjunctures in history-writing, which come about when different versions of the past stray too far to share the same explanatory roof or when theoretical assumptions can no longer hold together discrepancies among archives. These short circuits perform useful negative work by underlining the shortcomings of our categories and perspectives. This dialectics of patchy archives, in other words, conjures stories that tell us as much about *the past* as *what we cannot fully know about it*.

These (dis)advantages are intrinsic to the account presented in this book. While the idea of landscape provides theoretical fuel, it also channels interpretation down certain paths. My turn to landscape partly stems from methodological constraints tied to my reliance on archaeological documents. Much of the material evidence I use was collected from archaeological surveys conducted over large areas. One downside is that these materials seldom permit a detailed view of the histories of particular sites and communities. The same is true of historical writings prior to the late nineteenth century, which touch only sporadically on the specificities of life in the countryside. What these evidential landscapes lack in depth, however, they make up in breadth. Their strength is to showcase disparate pools of information from many parts of the province at many moments in time. My evidence, in other words, demands a broad analytical framework, which can accommodate various levels of resolution and integrate the eccentricities of different sets of sources.

Correlatively, evidence also partly dictates the dramatis personae of the histories examined below. With its attention to material forms and their distributions in the landscape, my account is synecdochic, perhaps mirroring the aggregative properties of Siin's archaeological record. It is centered on collective forms of experience and configurations of practice rather than historically documented groups of actors. Its primary agents are peasant communities, and the lifeworlds and assemblages of power in which they evolved. While this perspective aims to capture a broad sense of peasant location—an idea of rural commoners' relationship to the political over long time spans, of the possibilities and constraints they experienced in the progressively recontoured social fields of Atlantic Senegal—it also induces certain myopias. The villagers I conjure out of archaeological inventories cut rather normative figures, a collective of actors biased toward adult male stakeholders while underrepresenting other social actors. Clearly, peasant societies are not monochromatic entities; rather, they comprise a complex patchwork of positions structured along the lines of gender, age, occupation, wealth, kinship, lineage, ethnicity, and religion. When possible, I have tried to offset this tendency by drawing on other archives to complicate the makeup of village communities. Written, oral, and visual documents are far from perfect and rarely describe the countryside in much specificity. That said, they occasionally refer to specific villages by name, the actions of identifiable people, or events taking place in specific regions, especially after the 1850s, when colonization brought literate observers into closer proximity with rural societies, and when the volume of word-based sources began to grow at exponential rates. Whether thick or thin, these evidential threads add substance to archaeological frames, as they clear richer paths into the realms of meaning, intention, belief, and social context. While they sometimes speak past material data, they can also gesture to the cultural logics and motivations behind the systems of practice traceable in landscapes and can reveal nuances within Siin's peasant world.

In the end, and despite its sociological coarseness, the category of *peasant* remains useful for its *corrective* vistas. It promotes a vision of the past that foregrounds the lifeworld of rural commoners when Senegal's history has largely been written from the standpoint of elites. Such reframing does not mean that we ignore the other actors and projects that influenced the field of rural actions. In effect, one cannot grasp Siin's peasant societies outside of their relations to state forms, commercial systems, Muslim and Christian institutions, foreign merchants and migrant labor, ecological processes, and denizens of the spirit world. These were never external to Siin's communities but component pieces of daily existence and thus part of who local villagers were and what they became. In this respect, examining the past through the lens of local peasantries implies an engagement with indigenous kingdoms, oceanic trade, and European colonialism—but from a different perspective—and thus a reassessment of their impact on the history of nonelite actors.

The account formulated here is neither exhaustive nor definite. Rather, it revels in the certainty of its limitations, in the perverse recognition that one never *quite* gets to the bottom of historical things. Accepting the ultimate incompleteness of Africa's past is not an admission of defeat. I see it as an incitement to come to terms with the demands of history and get real with the partiality of our historical visions, imaginations, and positions. It is, by extension, a call for a more sincere empiricism, one that honors the messiness of data and acknowledges that objectivity is rooted in partial perspectives.[52] It presses us to work within the limitations of our evidence and make the best of slippery archives. More boldly, perhaps, I believe that archaeology's fragmentary reason is immensely productive. Weary of orderly stories and elegant explanations, of history with a capital *H*, it looks for motley associations across uneven bits of facts. As it tracks conjunction and dissonance between its lines of evidence, archaeology's epistemology of fragments contributes to history by both subtraction and addition. In a negative register, it raises questions of common perceptions. Poking at their a prioris through the spectrum of materiality, it proposes other directions, places, and objects for analysis, which may spur new ways of thinking about culture, history, and society between past and present. In so doing, and in a more affirmative vein, this mode of thinking keys us to *petits récits* of *isms*—globalism, capitalism, imperialism, colonialism, modernism—that trade historical totalities for a patchwork of open-ended stories, unfinished statements, partial plots, and interrupted conclusions.

Historical archaeology, as construed here, does not have a purchase on truth. It does not necessarily advance a *better* way of knowing Senegambia's past. Like other methods, its interpretive castles are founded on the quicksand of partial truths. It does, however, articulate a *different* way of thinking about history. At a time when many of the questions driving the study of Africa's past carry the dreams and dramas of an earlier generation and may have exceeded their returns, archaeology can contribute to the carving of new problem-spaces. Given its attachment to lost tangible worlds, archaeology can offer salient questions and data to reorganize the construction of Africa's global past in conversation with the continent's present. The problems of the Atlantic slave trade and colonialism cannot be ignored, as they are intrinsic to Senegambia's modernity. They need, however, to be imagined anew, for, configured as they often are in historiography, they cloak the welter of cultural histories that have entered the morphology of today's world. In concert with allied disciplines, archaeology contributes imaginative possibilities to the endless process of making and unmaking history. Working back from contemporary landscapes, it excels in dredging up histories of decay, curation, and absence—quiet legacies of a fraught past animating Senegal's political present.

PART TWO

Visions of Colonial Subjects: Imagining and Constructing the Seereer Landscape

The Serer . . . is the very model of the Black peasant.

L. GEISMAR, *RECUEIL DES COUTUMES CIVILES DES RACES DU SÉNÉGAL*[1]

One of the long-standing legacies of colonial scholarship in Africa has been the depiction of local peasantries as closed systems, sunk in the fog of customs and economic inertia. Siin cultivators are no exception. Geographer Paul Pélissier, in his monumental study of Senegalese agrarian societies, comes close to painting the Seereer as the quintessential African peasant society, referring to precolonial Siin as "the very model of egalitarian and anarchic peasantry." Linking past and present, he conjures up nostalgic evocations of a people wedded to land and cattle, industrious, environmentally conscious, fearful of ancestors and earth spirits, tradition-bound, culturally conservative, and averse to change and movement. This remarkable "geographic patriotism" is praised as the natural disposition of "a society which up to now has derived its strength and persistence from its fidelity to the past, from an essentially defensive political organization, from eminently conservative social structures."[2]

Read nearly fifty years later, these views appear out of sync with an Africanist scholarship deeply colored by the "invention of tradition" literature, and the idea of repetition without difference (or with minimal change) raises a few eyebrows. The concept of tradition as a conservative social force and as a historical explanation in its own right has been duly discredited. Numerous studies have shown that, over time, Africans have reinterpreted new and old ideas and long-standing local and imported institutions to meet changing historical circumstances. In this context, tradition has become a fertile ground of social creation and a strategic terrain of debates and contestation. Similarly, if what Europeans labeled indigenous customs were often carved out of a complex social world to suit the needs of colonial governance, the process of enframing tradition was negotiated with African actors, a negotiation that continued once categories were stabilized. Underneath the veneer of continuity, then, tradition represents a geology of changes sedimented at different rates, eroded and reworked over time. In these circumstances, it is important to track this process of sedimentation, how it interweaves with power to produce aspirations of norm and order, and understand what gives it the force of permanence.[3]

Another difficulty is the extent to which examples of typical peasants crop up across the French colonial world, which raises red flags regarding how accurately this image depicts the populations of Siin. In this light, Seereer conformity with a peasant exemplar born of the colonial imagination raises the question whether generalized concepts of African peasantry were fashioned after the peoples of Siin or the Seereer became a convenient repository for these preconceived images. More realistically, Pélissier's "Seereer peasant" reflects the outcome of a "long conversation" between French and Africans, merging lived, imported, and imagined elements, rather than a historical reality.[4]

And yet, this notion of the typical peasant cannot be just brushed off, insofar as it precipitated as a social fact conditioning outsiders' visions of the Seereer and the terms in which Siin's history has been interpreted, from colonial reports to the ethnographic and geographic work conducted in the 1960s and 1970s. In this regard, Pélissier's views on rural Africa have been critical in providing a juncture with colonial perspectives and influencing the development of later research on Siin's economy and society.[5] My aim in singling out this work is not to pillory its ethnographic achievements, which have been invaluable. Rather, my point is that while this research has been at its very best in documenting rural structures and human-landscape interactions *at the time of observation*, it has been on weaker ground when speculating about the Seereer past through the lens of tradition. In endorsing "traditional peasantries," researchers have not been sufficiently attentive to the colonial pedigree of the concept and the hidden assumptions it carries. Which is why any look at Siin's tumultuous past over the past five hundred years must first unpack this imagery and the discourses on which it builds.

This section begins such an investigation by taking a critical look at two aspects of Seereer tradition. Chapter 3 focuses on Seereer ethnicity and how it came about. Instead of presuming Seereer identity's immemorial existence, I examine the latter as a *historical* category that slowly coagulated in the context of broader Senegambian history. Chapter 4 prolongs this line of analysis by reviewing the assumptions of cultural immobility encrusted into representations of Seereerness. Turning to the colonial period, I track the emergence of models of Seereer normative culture and how discordances in ethnographic accounts paint a much more dynamic picture than suggested by Seereer peasant archetypes.

THREE

What's in a Name? Notes on the Making of Seereer Identity

Only that which has no history can be defined.

F. NIETZSCHE, *THE GENEALOGY OF MORALITY*[1]

Much has been made of the fact that ethnicity is a touchy subject in contemporary Senegal—something of a public secret, whose workings are known by all but easily articulated by none. Viewed as a divisive wedge and potentially explosive issue that might endanger the future of a young country on the eve of political independence, ethnicity was evacuated de jure from the public sphere by the engineers of the nation.[2] Today, it remains, at least in appearance, banished from political society: ethnicity is understood to embody special interest, the tyranny of custom, and irrational attachment to tradition; in other words, the obverse of the universal equivalence among citizen-subjects ensured by the Law.[3] This repulsion is also what, paradoxically, endows *l'ethnicité* with a character of near sacredness: a depth that simmers at all times below the façade of public life and rushes forth when exposed in those mundane or memorable moments fracturing the political sphere. Both hidden and in plain sight, ethnicity is a fertile site of contradictions that affirm its ambiguity in the space of the nation and the inability of the state to contain its excess.[4]

In effect, while downplayed in national political discourse, ethnicity is everywhere in modern Senegal. It is a fulcrum of social, linguistic, and moral identity, a fount of cultural pride, and an important vector of social solidarity. Cultural associations are frequently mapped along ethnic lines. Ethnic stereotypes are a staple of everyday conversations, cemented in joking relationships (*kaal* in Wolof) that tie different cultural groups with converging histories, while providing a homespun mechanism of conflict management. By contrast, ethnicity has at times taken a darker and more explosive turn, as exemplified in the conflict opposing Senegal's government to separatist movements in Casamance demanding independence (a conflict generally explained in explicitly ethnic terms) or in spates of ethnic violence directed against Mauritanians in the late 1980s.[5] In today's Senegal, the character of ethnicity's public secrecy, its hesitations and appeal, is perhaps best captured in the phenomenon of Wolofization. The latter refers to an unplanned, rhizomatic process, which marks the ascendancy of Wolof as Senegal's lingua franca and the central role it plays in the construction of Senegalese urban popular culture. Both tacitly embraced and vocally decried, the hegemony of Wolof cultural forms is rapidly reorganizing the landscape of ethnic referents in the country. Gradually loosened from its ethnic moorings, a Wolof urban zeitgeist has come to define a *national* identity articulated on the use of the Wolof language, the practice of Sufi Islam, city dwelling, and an openness to global hybridity.[6]

Imagining the Siin: Visions of the Past in the Present

Like other groups in Senegal, the Seereer have not been immune to these identitarian changes and anxieties, particularly in urban areas where the linguistic dominance of Wolof, the allure of a modern lifestyle, and tenuous contacts with the countryside (*le village*) work to distance younger people from their Seereer roots, or at least redefine what it means to be Seereer.[7] Having said this, and the shifting sands of ethnic identification notwithstanding, the Siin continues to be regarded as a bastion of Seereer identity, and the latter as a relatively stable sign (figure 5). It is seen as such by the people of Siin themselves, many of whom today identify as Seereer ethnically, culturally, and linguistically, and feel connected to the region by a long heritage of occupation and tradition, despite considerable rural exodus, cultural traffic, and the inroads of Murid Islam.[8] These views are grounded in historical memory, which traces the Seereer presence in Siin to massive migrations out of the Senegal River Valley over a thousand years ago. Oral traditions chart the Seereer expansion across Senegal and their settlement in the Siin, as they

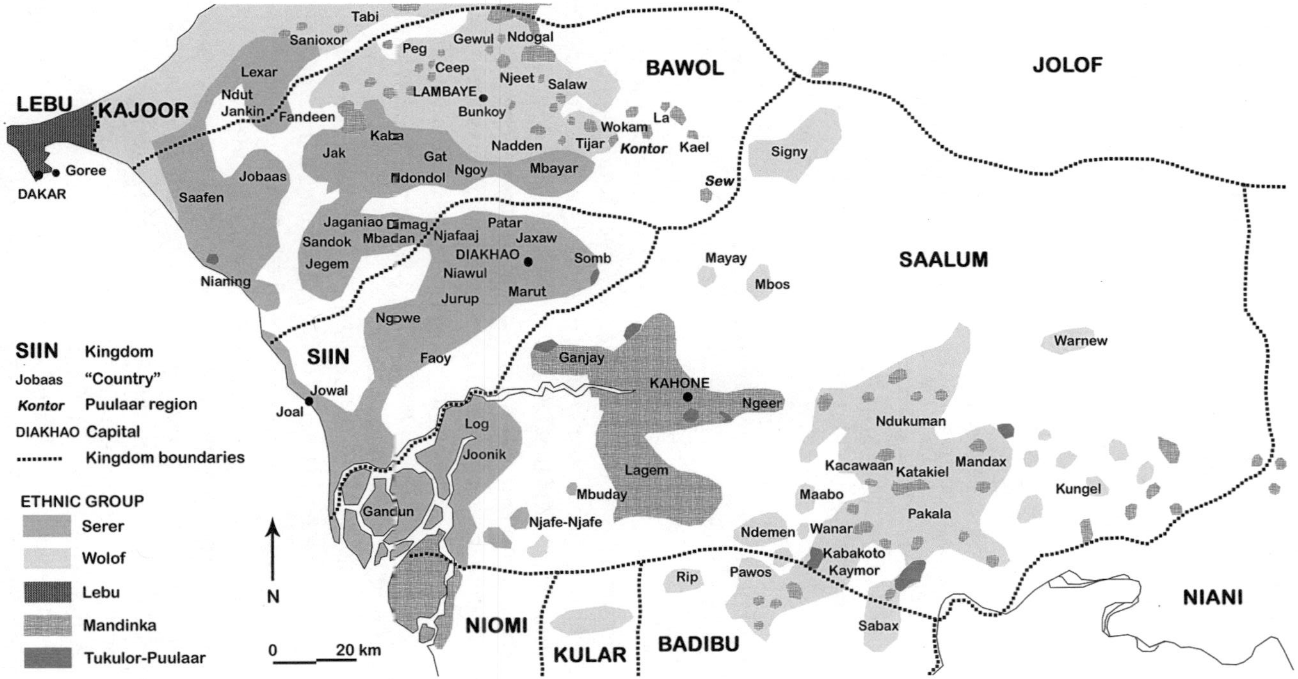

5 Distribution of contemporary ethnic grouɔs, west-central Senegal

peacefully absorbed autochthonous residents and subsequent waves of Mandinka migrants, resulting in the emergence of a small polity sometime in the mid-fourteenth century. In effect, historical sources document the existence of a Seereer kingdom at the time of early Portuguese navigations. Some argue that Seereer identity consolidated during the Atlantic era, in response to interkingdom hostilities, before effectively crystallizing with the incorporation into France's colonial empire in the 1860s.[9]

Early ethnographies describe the region as the rural area par excellence and depict the Seereer as one of the most traditional peasant populations in Africa. The colonial library abounds with images of salt-of-the-earth Seereer peasants moored to timeless customs and resistant to change (figure 6), which we will review more amply in chapter 4.[10] As a consequence, the impression of cultural longevity flowing from these different archives has encouraged historians, and archaeologists to some extent, to paint the history of Siin in the second millennium AD in resolutely Seereer colors.

The trope of Seereer backwardness has endured over the years. From colonial-period observers to postindependence writers in academic and popular discourse, Siin's ethnic and cultural singularity has been variably decried (as an obstacle to progress, modernization, and indeed, civilization), lauded (as the social cement that preserved regional political integrity in the face of global changes), or otherized (on account of being an atavistic throwback). The timeless peasant, colonial and postcolonial, premodern and antimodern, has mediated Siin's place in Senegal's national imaginary, alternating between noble savage and primitive other, as political-economic currents reshaped the country's reflections on itself.[11] What has been seldom questioned, of course, is *the nature, depth, and historical validity of Seereer identity itself.*

This chapter takes up the presumed linkages of Seereer ethnicity with long-term idioms and structures of collective identity. If the work of ethnic imagination in the Siin has generally ascribed endurance and profundity to Seereer identity, a critical engagement with the archives that have supported such conclusions seems to suggest alternative readings. In journeying along these narrative threads (which are tentative and partial rather than definitive), I wish to complicate how we have perceived of the Seereer historically, by breathing more historical life into the category *Seereer* and how it has been delimited, configured, and marked in various fields of representations over time. In other words, rather than taking the Seereer as an unproblematic object, where signifier and signified relate to each other in invariant and predictable ways, I am proposing a few thoughts

6 Postcards, early twentieth century. *Above*, "Old Serer cultivator" (Archives Nationales du Sénégal, Iconographie, no. 0810). *Overleaf*, "Cérère women" (ANS, Iconographie, no. 0801). (Both reproduced with permission from Archives du Sénégal.)

and glimpses toward an ethnography of historical production—that of Seereer identity. To do so, I bring oral traditions, documentary sources, and archaeological evidence into conversation with each other to broaden the "space of possibles" in which Seereer identity has been constructed.[12] Through this process of cross-examination, I will draw attention to points of convergence, contradiction, and divergence in their respective arguments, which index possible moments in the making of the Seereer as historical subjects and as subjects of historical discourse.

Taking a cue from the public secrecy that has colored experiences of ethnicity in contemporary Senegal, it is fair to conjecture that ambiguity is not a condition limited to the play of modern identities but one that also applied, albeit in different ways, to ethnicity in the deeper past. In this light, if the conservatism and traditionalism of Seereer culture have

6 (*continued*)

been adopted as public knowledge then my goal is to show the secret underside of this identity construct: to find in various archives moments of knowledge making during which once-existing experiences were muted and map some of the culture effects that these silences (and the absences they paper over) have generated.[13] Deconstructive exercises tend to be fated to emptiness if they fail to speak to a condition of power. For this reason, when conjuring how once-viable paths, practices, and possibilities of identity construction were left out of history, I am doing so with the purpose of recasting Seereer's relationship to the political present in new, and hopefully more dynamic, light. This entails historicizing the Seereer out of the "savage slot" to which they have been consigned by a century and a half of politics of difference.[14]

African Identities: Between Imagination and the Limits of Invention

Words wreak havoc, says Sartre, when they find a name for what had up to then been lived namelessly. P. BOURDIEU, *OUTLINE OF A THEORY OF PRACTICE*[15]

In recent years, African historical scholarship has underscored the difficulties of documenting precolonial cultural institutions and social structures across the continent. This literature has emerged largely as a critical response to the nationalist optimism of the 1960s and 1970s and the faith that an earlier generation of historians placed in oral traditions as a pristine mirror of Africa's past cultural achievements. By contrast, revisionist perspectives have painted a much bleaker portrait of historical inquiry, questioning the notion of authentic readings of the African past and the possibility of accurately reconstructing social experiences. Instead, recent trends have preferred to emphasize the hybrid, constructed nature of past narratives and the influence of colonial forces on portrayals of precolonial societies.

Earlier discussions tended to accept the deep historical existence of African cultural boundaries. Recent studies, however, have highlighted the imagined character of identities, the invention of traditions and customs, and the creation of tribes and ethnicities in the crucible of colonialism at the hand of European and African actors.[16] This perspective can be summarized as follows: "Before colonization, so the argument goes, Africans belonged simultaneously to a bewildering variety of social networks—nuclear and extended families, lineages, age sets, secret societies, village communities, diasporas, chiefdoms, states and empires. Loyalties and identities were complex, flexible and relatively amorphous, and certainly did not add up to clearly demarcated tribes living in well-defined and bounded territories."[17] As colonial authorities sought to implement their rule in newly conquered territories, they remapped existing social landscapes along new lines of demarcation that were often incongruent with indigenous modes of identification. The fluid, relational constructs and overlapping networks of precolonial times were replaced by more static political topographies featuring new social boundaries and hardened identities.[18] According to Amselle, this process led to the emergence of empty ethnic receptacles that, for the purpose of policing and social control, needed to be filled with traditions, customs, social institutions, and religious structures. The new identities found legitimation in ethnographic materials sampled by colonial administrators from local theories of politics and society. As customs were codified in writing, colonial observers consecrated a small subset of traditions at the expense of others, while creating the cultures, races, or ethnic groups they claimed to have found.[19]

By showing that modern expressions of ethnicity have histories—and turbulent ones at that—the constructivist wave has offered a salutary challenge to primordialist conceptions of cultural identity as fundamental affective bonds and a shared heritage rooted in an age-old past.[20] At the same time, however, more recent studies warn us against overstating the power of invention, particularly as waged by the colonial state. Instead, they emphasize that colonial and postcolonial identities, and the features that came to define them, were both inherited from earlier cultural modes and reassembled by European rulers, missionaries, ethnographers, African chiefs, and intellectual elites in the context of the shifting present.[21] What is more, as newly crystallized identities became interiorized by Africans, they developed a life outside of colonial representation, their contents and contours renegotiated below the plane of colonial surveillance. In this light, African ethnicities—and the customs, origin stories, and moral values they enfold—are historical processes, grounded in a repertoire of social reality, *and* processes of historical representation; they encompass at once a set of lived histories, forms of collective belonging, and political artifacts.[22]

Part of understanding how African ethnicities work historically also entails clarifying the process of identity. The concept's usefulness for purposes of history has come under scholarly doubt, which has underscored the near-oxymoronic ambiguity of identity as a foundational yet highly fluid form of consciousness. Brubaker and Cooper's trenchant critique of identity can be extended to ethnicity: both constructs are analytically weak insofar as they collapse a wide range of social processes with very different dynamics into a single category and thus smother a clear reading of how these processes actually work in social contexts. A more productive tack, they suggest, is to break down identity into a finer sociology: Who does the identifying? Does it mark sameness, connectedness, or difference? Does it represent in-group modes of identification or externally imposed categorizations, self-understanding or social location? Is it channeled in practices or representations?[23]

Taking stock of these observations, a proper historical understanding of ethnicity in Africa requires attending to social forms in their diverse expressions over time *and* their transformation as they passed into the realm of tradition, customary law, colonial annals, scholarly discourse, and popular perceptions.[24] I will attempt to do justice to both over the next two chapters, though my concern here rests with the discourses surrounding Seereer ethnicity, particularly the stories they reveal about the intersection of power and knowledge and the influence of constructed identities on later historical writing. Of course, our ability to retrace these steps is conditioned by context and evidence in crisscrossing ways: first, genealogies of ethnic practice and representation become increasingly slippery as we move into the more dimly documented past; second, sources are uneven and often distantly address matters of identity; third, there is often a great deal of incestuousness between different categories of evidence, caused by the feedback loop between different technologies of recording and remembering. Consequently, many canonical oral accounts of origins were collected during the colonial period, which configures their veracity in complicated ways; finally, and related to the previous point, our reconstructions of identity often hinge precariously on a methodological dilemma: expecting colonial writings and oral traditions recorded during that period to perform double duty in helping us study *both* social worlds before colonialism *and* the transformations wrought by colonial rule.[25] While these concerns certainly apply to the Siin, exploiting the productive tensions among and between oral, written, and material archives can help to bypass some of these empirical challenges and expose disjunctions in the narrative of deep continuity commonly ascribed to Seereer identity.

Cosaan: The Ambiguity of Origins

Although specific details may vary, stories of ethnogenesis across northern Senegambia generally regard Fuuta Tooro (Senegal River Valley) as the ethnic foundry for Senegal's major ethnolinguistic groups and the original homeland of Seereer populations. These migrations are often thought to be associated with a combination of conditions involving degrading climate, the persistent threat of nomadic groups roaming along the desert edge, and the ascent of the Islamic kingdoms of Ghana and Tekrur in the region, which would have convinced the sedentary, non-Muslim ancestral Seereer to seek a better living elsewhere.[26] Scholarship has also ascribed the Seereer migration to a series of roughly contemporary population movements that resulted in the settlement of northern Senegal, establishment of major identitarian provinces, and the formation of the first kingdoms. Historians have generally dated these events to the end of the eleventh century, corresponding with the waning of Ghana, and reckoned that the massive population waves moving across vast geographic expanses probably correspond to a more complex series of movements involving multiple routes, episodes, and logics.[27]

Narratives of origins are also evoked in other realms of Seereer cultural practice. Seereer traditions are generally punctilious in their remembrance of specific village names along the Senegal River area where ancestral figures originated, while in Fuuta Tooro, Pulaar-speaking populations attribute the archaeological vestiges of ancient villages to the Seereer before their migrations. This history of origin, cleavage, and expatriation is also evoked in the etymology of the term *Seereer*, which is generally seen as a derivative of the Pulaar word *sererabe* (to separate or to divorce) and can be interpreted as "the ones who separated." Historians of oral traditions have generally taken these clues to imply that a Seereer identity had already existed at the time of separation or had crystallized through the process of migration and that a recognizably Seereer population existed by the time it gradually spread south to southern Bawol, Siin, and Saalum.[28]

Having said this, other signs invite caution in projecting the Seereer label deep into the precolonial past and postulating the existence of an enduring Seereer social consciousness avant la lettre. The most obvious problem is that the current Seereer denomination and its colonial antecedent do not make up a single ethnicity but amalgamate seven distinct subgroups whose histories, languages, and social organizations do not always coincide (figure 7). Scholars generally distinguish between the Sérères du Nord-Ouest (Northwest Seereer), who comprise five ethnolinguistic groups that speak related languages of the Cangin family and congregate around the Thiès area, and the Seereer Singandum, themselves subdivided into subfamilies residing in the Siin, Saalum, and Jegeem (on the southern fringe of Bawol). Researchers have generally followed oral traditions in accepting a common ethnic and historic root for all Seereer groups, which could in turn explain some of the loose resemblances in social, economic, and religious organization between Cangin and Singandum speakers. At the same time, the fact that considerable cultural differences remain between different Seereer communities or that their political trajectories over the past centuries have taken very different paths

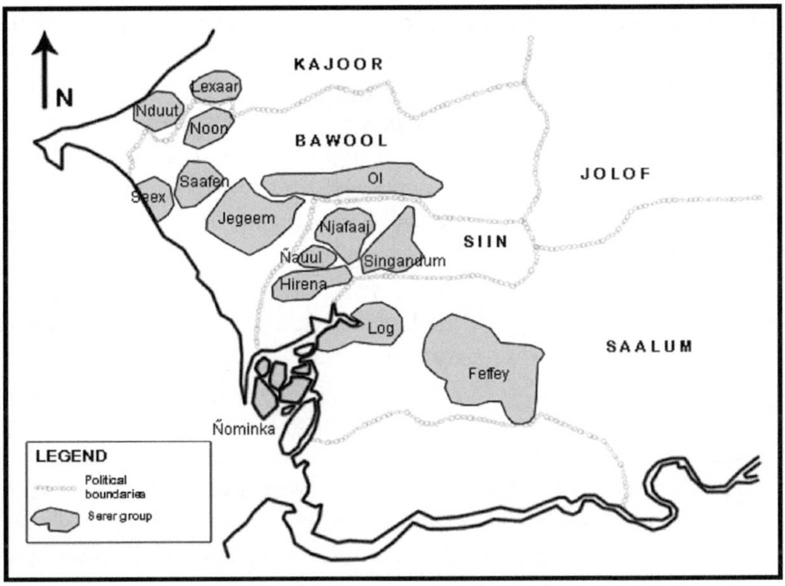

7 Seereer groups (after Pinet-Laprade, 1865)

demand that we regard scenarios of deep-time Seereer connections critically, particularly if we consider the imprint of colonial ethnography on the postulation of ethnic cultures in Senegal.[29]

A second difficulty stems from the fact that what we call today the Seereer of Siin are not a primeval entity but a historical product, shaped by centuries of cultural contact between distinct populations and the fusion of different political and cultural traditions. It is likely that, as they left the Senegal River area, original migrants came into contact and interacted with populations or polities en route to their eventual destinations. For instance, village founding narratives in Siin and on the Petite Côte frequently allude to the fact that, at the presumed time of Seereer migrations, the region was no terra nullius. Oral traditions indicate instead that the Siin was occupied by different resident populations identified as Soos and descended from earlier Soninke or Malinke migrations. These early encounters are often glossed as episodes of harmonious coexistence, peaceful assimilation, and amicable exchange, a stylistic thread recurrent in historical memory.[30] There is also a vast record of earthen tumuli, some dating to the early centuries of the first millennium AD, which attests to an earlier human presence. Both Seereer and Wolof populations attribute to the Soos the construction of the biggest tumuli (*podom* in Seereer, which they distinguish from the smaller *lomb*, which represent burials made by their own ancestors at a later time). Archaeologists have generally braided material evidence into the fabric of oral narratives, reading the apparently uninterrupted regional record of funerary tumuli as evidence that the Seereer had absorbed their Soos neighbors politically and genetically yet adopted their mortuary practices in return.[31]

The most dramatic episode of contact, however, took place in the mid-fourteenth century, when oral traditions ascribe the foundation of the Siin kingdom to an encounter between Seereer settlers and the Gelwaar, a group of Mandinka exiles originating from the empire of Kaabu, in Upper Guinea. There, again, oral traditions stress harmony, negotiation, and mutually beneficial relations between the two groups. The encounter is painted as a civil exchange, whereby the Seereer offered a home to the Gelwaar, while the latter used their political wisdom, ecumenism, and leadership to unify disparate and inchoate Seereer communities into a state. Scholars have often accepted that, in exchange for power, the Gelwaar naturally embraced the compass of Seereer culture, adopting their language, kinship organization, religion, and lifestyle.[32]

Regardless of the exact nature of these foundational encounters, we may conjecture that even if a sense of being Seereer came into existence before the Atlantic era, it was undoubtedly created and reformulated in the crucible of these cultural exchanges, making the prospect of a primordial transplant from the Fuuta Tooro quite implausible. This is compounded by the allusion in oral accounts to other salient spheres of sociality centered on lineages, matriclans, villages, lineage estates (*lamanats*), countries (*pays*), and the Siin polity itself, which call into question the primacy of ethnicity as an axis of identification.[33] Or, to put it differently, these fragmentary references may suggest that, if a sense of Seereerness existed at the time, it may have had very different connotations from what the term means for modern scholars or how it is experienced by Seereer populations today.

Concurrently, the inconclusiveness and double entendres pervading oral memory raise the possibility that the process of Seereer ethnogenesis *was* a relatively recent phenomenon, imposed or accelerated by outside forces, rather than an endogenous development or self-ascribed identity. As in other African regions, the momentous political-economic changes of the past one thousand years integrated the societies of Siin into wider networks of relations and representations, which caused likely shifts in the cartography of social boundaries.

Encounters and Refractions: Mapping Otherness

The advent of European explorations constitutes a new moment in the production of Seereer identity, inaugurating a new phase in the making of its archive. By introducing a corpus of references and observations, which can be retrieved as facts, mobilized as evidence, and bundled into narratives, this process also smuggled in new repertoires of silences.[34] These, in turn, can articulate in productive ways with the hesitations of oral traditions to spark off new thoughts and directions in the historicity of Seereer ethnicity.

Much like the oral traditions earlier examined, European reportage of African identities is not short of ambiguities, ambiguities inscribed in the tumultuous career of Senegambian ethnonyms spanning over four hundred years of textual archives. To begin at the source, early Portuguese and Venetian descriptions of coastal Senegal paint an evocative, if not always consistent, tableau of statecraft on the littoral, identifying several polities they call kingdoms. These latter were generally parsed further into distinct peoples that don't quite mesh with the ethnic identities recognized in contemporary Senegal. These differences were already perceived as early as the 1450s by explorers like Cadamosto and Gomes and in the first decade of the sixteenth century by Fernandes. These authors consistently describe the populations of northern Senegal as *Jalofs/Geloffa/Zilofi/Gyloffes*—with whom Europeans had most direct contact and who often served as translators, guides, or intermediaries—which they contrast to neighboring groups living in coastal lands between the Cape Verde Peninsula and the Gambia River, who spoke different languages and held different customs. On this stretch of the coast, European observers were faced with a more complex ethnolinguistic landscape made up of two recognizable ensembles variously labeled *Sereri/Serreos/Sercos* and *Barbazini/Barbacyns/Barbacijs*.[35] Later authors continued to use the *Sereos/Barbacins* couplet, or various declensions thereof, to characterize the non-Wolof populations of west-central Senegal. Donelha mentions the *Berbecins*, who lived in two adjacent kingdoms along the Petite Côte before arriving to the Gambia River. Sixty years later, Lemos Coelho distinguished between the *Xereos/Xercos*, who formed villages of outlaws straddling the border between Kajoor and Bawol, and the *Brebecis*, or inhabitants of the kingdom of *Berbisim*. Lemaire talks of the *Geloffes, Sereres*, and *Barbecins*. Labat's compilation makes note of the *Cereres*, who formed decentralized republics devoid of formal government and battled with the rulers of Kajoor and Bawol for their independence, while farther to the south lay the

Kingdom of Sin. Later writers continued to affix these Seereer to a condition of perpetual noble savagery, stressing their insularity, linguistic difference, and tensions with surrounding kingdoms.[36] The element jumping out most starkly from these early records is that the label *Seereer* is not extended to the Siin, the area today most closely associated with a Seereer identity, but used in reference to the areas today occupied by the Northwest Seereer.

Such consistency of reportage between authors of different backgrounds, stations, and nationalities, writing at different moments of the sixteenth and seventeenth centuries, incites caution about reifying Seereer ethnicity as a social fact of the long term in Siin. In fact, it is not until the early eighteenth century, after fully two centuries of sustained contact, that initial allusions are made of the Siin province as a Seereer area, demarcated from other kinds of Seereer strongholds to the north. By that time, the various non-Wolof groups appear to have been drawn more closely together in European accounts, and both came to be identified by the Seereer ethnonym. Early evidence of this cultural merging can be found in a manuscript map of Senegambia made by d'Anville in the 1720s (figure 8). Represented on the map is a Lake of Ceres located in the southwestern tip of Kajoor and thus corresponding with the independent Seereer communities mentioned above; yet the author also refers to the Kingdom of Barbessin as the Country of the Serres or Cereres—which constitutes one of the earliest textual mentions of the Siin as culturally Seereer.[37] This trend finds confirmation in the words of later authors, achieving its clearest expression in the writings of long-term Senegal resident Pruneau de Pommegorge, who explicitly mentions the existence of two types of Seraires. The first group, whom he visited in the vicinity of the Cap de Naze, "is called the black Seraires so as to distinguish them from other Seraires, twenty leagues below; they speak a language other than [that of] the Yolofs of the country wherein they are enclaved"; the other group, also named *Seraires*, is under the domination of a "king named *Barbefin*. . . , & whose commerce is more or less the same as in Portudal [Bawol], & and the same manner of living of its peoples."[38]

How all these groups came to be perceived as Seereer, when they once seemed to answer to separate designations, is unclear. What is undeniable is that, whether it conveyed vernacular identifications or an external commentary on local identities, the practice of referring to types of Seereer further consolidated in European writings during the nineteenth century. By the 1850s, after undergoing several transformations, the early *Sereos/Barbacins* pair had given way to the distinction between Seereer Noon (Northwest Seereer) and Seereer Siin, which found a cozy home in

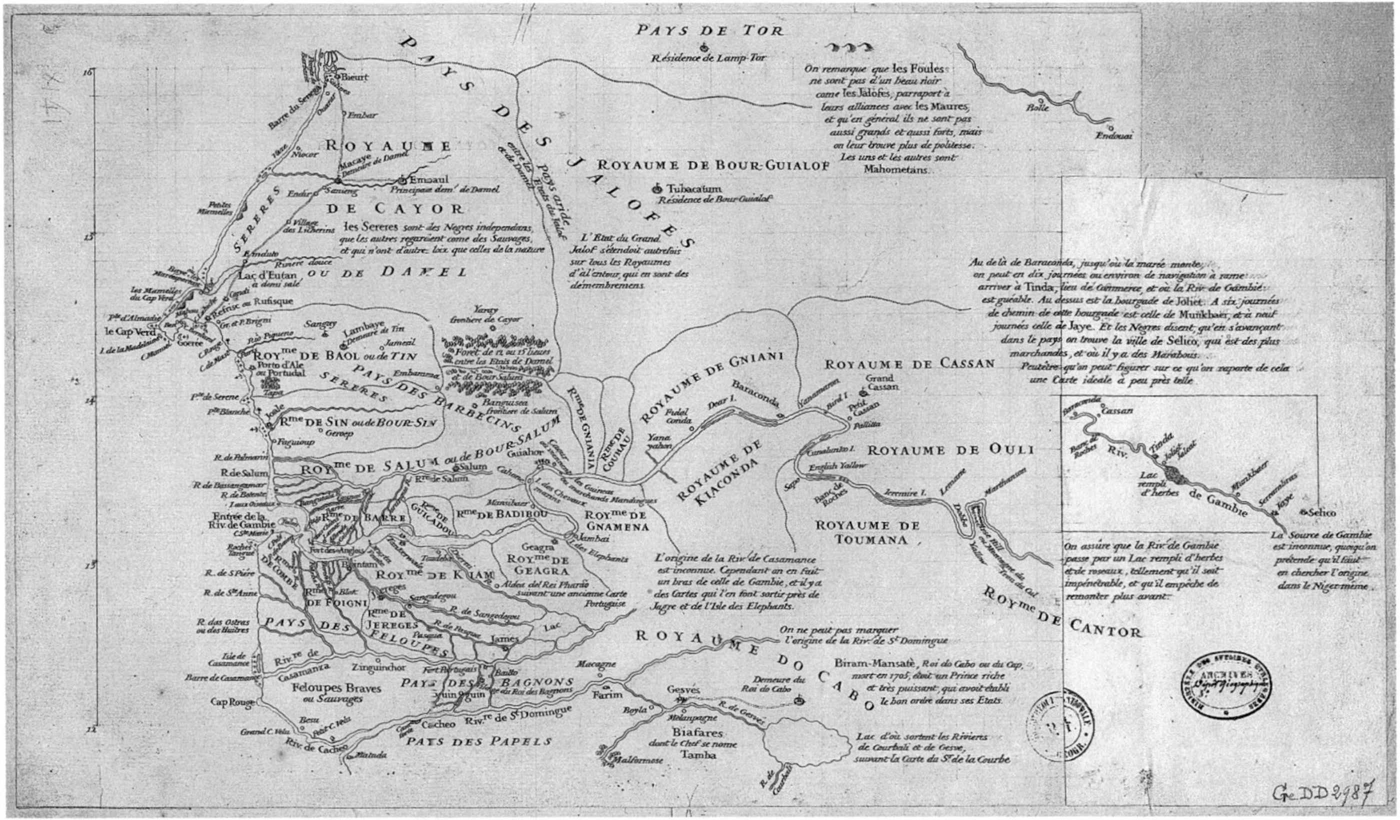

8 Manuscript map of the coast of Senegal by d'Anville, 1720s (http://gallica.bnf.fr/ark:/12148/btv1b7759805k)

the ethnic maps of colonial Senegal and continues to resonate in post-colonial taxonomies of identity.[39]

Again, how these once different peoples came to be placed under the same ethnic umbrella is obscure. This history is in part complicated by the fact that we have to reassemble its fragments through the writings of cultural outsiders, who often did not speak local languages, had superficial knowledge of the groups they purported to describe, and relied on interpreters to do so.[40] These difficulties aside, it is, of course, quite possible that the cultural and historical linkages commonly assumed between the populations of Siin and their counterparts in Bawol and Kajoor encouraged their merging into a broad Seereer ethnonym. This scenario, however, might only capture one of the many processes involved in the work of identity.[41] The coevolution and co-constitution of ethnic designations in coastal Senegal indeed point to a more opaque underside to the fashioning of Seereerness—namely, that the ascription and recognition of commonality among Seereer groups may well have its roots in alterity rather than shared culture. To put it another way, the case can be made that once-disparate societies were fixed around a *common* Seereer identity not only by the cement of cultural kinship but also, and perhaps mostly, by the *differences* separating these peoples from Wolof populations. In effect, the natural history of the Seereer ethnonym in European texts suggests that the term gradually coagulated in opposition to things Wolof, to index cultural otherness. No longer a primordial ethnicity, Seereerness, as we know it, may represent a recent relational construct underwritten by a political ideology of difference conveyed in language and establishing distance between the Wolof and their neighbors—a category that could resemble the contemporary *lakk-kat* by which Wolophones designate those who speak a foreign language.[42]

Further traces of this process of knowledge production and cultural translation linger in the etymology of the various identity labels employed in the documentary record. It is striking, for instance, that most terms used to define Seereer traditional institutions and social categories, including the word *Siin* itself, are Wolof vocables. European observers, who often knew little of African cultural and political boundaries, developed the habit of referring to peoples or polities by the name or title of their kings.[43] Following this mode of metonymic conflation, the words *Barbacin* or *Barbecin* are corruptions of the phrase *buur bu Siin* or *buur ba Siin*, which translates as king of Siin in Wolof. Likewise, the term *Noon*, which served to differentiate the Northwest Seereer from the neighboring *Iolofs* and *Barbessins*, is a Wolof word meaning enemy. The term doubtlessly conveys the tumultuous history of conflict between the egalitarian western Seereer and the predatory, centralized kingdoms of Bawol and Kajoor.[44] For all their brevity, these examples remain vivid illustrations of the role of power, language, and externality in processes of ethnogenesis. Here, refracted through a scatter of evidential clues—Wolof-centric narratives of cultural difference, their (partial) sedimentation/recombination in textual and oral archives and canonization in historical conventions—the force of experience and persuasions of discourse become entwined, with tangible implications for the definition of Seereer cultural boundaries.

Colonial Vignettes: The Content of the Form

Power, knowledge, and identity in Senegal became more inextricably interwoven in the second half of the nineteenth century in the wave of scientific expeditions, ethnographic campaigns, and military reconnaissance that preceded and followed formal colonization. Confronted with the prospect of imperial rule across a vast territory saturated with cultural unknowns, colonial authorities recognized the need to create order out of a dizzying mosaic of African peoples and customs and began to craft ethnic portraits in the service of administering and policing colonized others.[45] It is in that context that the French, with the help of ethnography, attempted to stabilize the fluid contours of Seereerness—though, ironically, stability proved to offer not so much a guarantor of authenticity but an alibi to hybridity (as we will see in chapters 7 and 8). While previous centuries of knowledge acquisition had seen a gradual sedimentation of the *form(s)* of Seereer identity, colonial ethnologists and functionaries, inspired by a new aesthetics of representation, now focused on devising images of its *content(s)* from a carousel of ethnic vignettes.

On many accounts, these reflections are partial and inadequate: descriptions are tainted by Eurocentric prejudice and abound with clichés and stereotypes; they extrapolate normative African cultures from a limited number of observations and homogenize regional patterns of difference; they mix and match cultural elements from the different Seereer subgroups into a totalizing picture of Seereer tradition; they rely on a small number of informants (generally chiefs and former political elites), whose views on indigenous history and society they helped to enshrine at the expense of many other silenced voices (women, junior men, simple farmers, professional castes). It would be impossible to separate the colonial construction of the Seereer from the administrative capacity, political intentions, and military involvement of the colonial state. Not only were colonial writings infused with ideas of social and moral progress, civilizing, and modernity, but representations of African peoples, bouncing between romanticization, vilification, and stereotypy, shifted in large measure according to the economic interests, political designs, and agendas for social reforms of French colonial officials over time.[46]

Between nascent colonial interests in the 1850s and the creation of the Siin protectorate in 1877, ethnographic knowledge of the area was mostly impressionistic, owing to its confinement to a rosary of coastal villages near Joal, while populations living further inland were poorly known. Mixing factual ignorance and military temperament, early observers such as Pinet-Laprade belabored the tyranny of Siin political rule, lamenting its stultifying effects on rural populations. Other documents blame the rampant alcoholism sweeping the Seereer states for both social degeneracy in Siin and degradation in trading relations with the French.[47] While collectively these views built up a case for greater political and commercial intervention in Siin, they brought little insight into Seereer society. Despite gaps in factual geographies, colonial observers were not shy about drawing upon cultural information gathered for the better-known Northwestern Seereer to flesh out their ethnographic portrayals of Siin. Mirroring earlier traditions of knowledge production, colonial ethnology perfected the art of distinguishing between Seereer subgroups, while indiscriminately lumping their mores, religion, and customs into one large ethnocultural unit or race, comprising a single *monde sérère* (Seereer world).[48] Again, one wonders whether, and to what extent, these representational collages influenced the received wisdom regarding a common cultural ancestry between the different Seereer groups: do they index the depth of a past whose details are lost in immemorial time, or do they paper over a laminated process of identitarian rapprochement rooted in shallower history? There, as elsewhere, we should take note that the construction of objects of knowledge (including ethnic classifications) cannot be fully divorced from the worries of the colonial state. Portrayals of the Seereer and other cultural groups existed in part to legitimize the needs and desires of Senegal's colonial government and may tell us more about the latter than about "the politics, religion, culture, agricultural practices, or even language of the people who lived in the area that came to be known as the Serer [*sic*] country."[49]

Not that all French ethnographers were blithely unaware of these manifold tensions. Bérenger-Féraud, for instance, was quite ready to accept that the Seereer had been influenced by cultural contacts with other populations, adding that "[their] lack of industry preventing sustained relations with the exterior, they confined themselves quite completely to their various respective cantons [provinces] so that each group preserved its habits, special countenances, a particular degree of blood admixture. Thus we do not find today among the Serer, either a homogeneity in kind, or an entire resemblance of mores, customs, beliefs. From one village to the next, even when only a few kilometers separate them, there are sometimes very marked differences."[50] Internal difference, however, was not what administrators wished to stress at a time when the goal was to find cultural elements that would differentiate the Seereer from their neighbors and elevate them to characteristics common to *all* the Seereer people. Ethnologists found such core features not in cultural particularism per se but in what they perceived to be its cause—namely, the Seereer disposition for conservatism and cultural isolationism. This rationale became the cornerstone of the colonial discourse on the Seereer. Thus, according to Aujas, "despite the blending, unions, alliances with neighboring tribes, the Serer constitutes today for the foreign observer a very primitive individuality which has jealousy retained its customs, beliefs, language, religion. He did not let civilization cut into him a lot. His local evolution itself has varied little throughout the centuries. There is then in him a type of humanity whose originality is undeniable."[51] From the offices in Dakar or Saint-Louis, this primitive conservatism was a crutch for the colonial imagination of the Seereer—and precisely what distinguished them from their neighbors—and consequently defined the race as a whole. Born of a bricolage of earlier motifs, this imagery both consecrated and refined the terms of Seereer alterity. The term *Seereer* continued to denote the potpourri of non-Muslim peoples hemmed in by the Wolof provinces to the north and east and the Mandinka states of the Gambia River to the south. Yet, it also became a more complex polysemous sign, a shorthand that now condensed the coordinates not only of geography and religion but those of economic, moral, and cultural proclivities as well. As ethnological binaries of hot/cold societies established gradients of indigenous difference rooted in natural inclinations, *Seereerness* hardened anew around its perceived distance from Wolof entrepreneurialism and perfectibility.[52]

While ethnologists garnered greater familiarity with the Siin during the twentieth century, theories of Seereer conservatism laid out the foundation for a more elaborate identity package centered on the image of the Seereer as farmers par excellence. Industrious, frugal, and hard-working, the Seereer's reputation as peasants was substantiated by a quasi-organic attachment to the land, perceived to be rooted in their aversion to change and migration and sanctioned by natural religion.[53] Resistance to Islam stood as one of the key symbols to which the Seereer could be tethered—despite the fact that Muslim clerics served as political advisors in precolonial Siin, that the partially Seereer province of Saalum harbors a complex history with Islam that cannot be easily fitted into that mold, and that the growing influence of Islam after World War I made such generalizations increasingly obsolete. Lastly, the Seereer were increasingly lauded as naturally peaceful traditionalists (even though they had been portrayed as fiercely independent and savage a few decades before), whose lives were organized around a collective and redistributive economy, property-sharing, kinship solidarity, and egalitarian social structures (even though the Siin and Saalum had been kingdoms, once organized along hierarchical and stratified lines). In a landscape of bounded ethnic units, the "Seereer agriculturalist" acquired significance as a counterpart to the "Ouoloff merchant, Peul herder, and Laobé woodcutter," and, in relation to the French ideas of social progress, modernization and civilization.[54] In this geography of governance, the Seereer provided a multipurpose other, whose traditional lifeways appeared at once compatible with and antithetic to colonial economic policies. For, if the colonial state was all too eager to mobilize Seereer agricultural capacities and savoir faire in the service of its nascent cash-crop economy, it could just as quickly pivot on its heels to decry the Seereer peasantry as an obstacle to development.

What we should take away from this syncopated story-behind-the-story of Seereer ethnicity is not that colonial perceptions were necessarily false or wholly made up. Rather, like tangents to a circle, they afford glimpses—and sometimes full views—that graze the arc of Seereer historical experience in different places and at different intervals. In this way, the colonial imagery of Seereer-qua-African peasants does not invalidate the fact that the historical Seereer *were* skilled cultivators whose lives *were* embedded in agricultural realities. So much indeed is documented in four hundred years of written sources that consistently corroborate the agricultural foundations of northern Senegambian economies. Where these representations are problematic is in reducing Seereer lived experience to an ethnic harlequin made up of disparate cultural elements gleaned pell-mell out of the stream of time. Once naturalized into representations and circulated in the public sphere, these cultural montages have taken the Seereer out of history, drawing a veil over the historicity of culture and identity. In the same breath, perhaps more deceptively, this imagery has also covered up the traces of its own origins in deeply polarized fields of power. Shrouded in these layers of silence, it has accommodated new power games and continues to generate truth effects whose consequences have well outlived the moment of their production. In fact, the trope of the rustic Seereer peasant forges beyond the colonial chapter. Moving into the postindependent period, it has merged and recombined with new political discourses and projects, taking an active part in fueling imaginations of the Senegalese nation and its brand of modernity. We will return to the secret life of colonial depictions of ethnicity in the next chapter, to examine the influence they have exerted over academic research on the Seereer past and interrogate the historical foundations of cultural practices and institutions held to be long-term fixtures of Seereer identity.

Identity, through a Sherd Darkly: Archaeological Interludes and Historical Caveats

Social systems, today and in the past, work at a number of levels, and it is a great mistake for archaeologists to emphasize one of those levels—the "ethnic"—at the expense of others, especially given that this may be one of the levels least suited to archaeological detection. S. A. MACEACHERN, "SCALE, STYLE, AND CULTURAL VARIATION: TECHNOLOGICAL TRADITIONS IN THE NORTHERN MANDARA MOUNTAINS"[55]

Let us pause for now, and take a step back to explore what another body of archives—archaeological evidence—tells us about issues of identity in Siin and what light they can shed on some of the questions thus far examined. Like other Africanists, archaeologists have long been involved in studying expressions of identity on the continent and have importantly contributed to reconstructions of African history in the long term. Mirroring trends in broader debates on identity, such as the ones outlined earlier, archaeologists have become skeptical of their ability to read ethnicity in the artifactual record. Instead of assuming unbroken linkages between past inventories and the ethnographic present, or between objects and identity, they have encouraged us to look at material assemblages as capturing scales of social realities that are not necessarily congruent with ethnic identities. Material patterns may be informed by logics and choices that do not neatly map onto those of living communities but vary across social arenas and historical moments.[56] The Mandara Mountains of Cameroon provide a now classic exposé of the fluidity of material culture as it cuts across ethnic lines to form axes of experience and social boundaries that often transcend contemporary ethnolinguistic realities and reflect different orders of historical experience. Consequently, archaeological traditions often present limited correspondence with existing or historic cultural groupings or linguistic territories.[57]

Rather than indiscriminately mapping contemporary imaginings of social identity onto the past or retroactively forcing archaeological objects into anachronistic categories (as archaeologists in Senegal have sometimes done), past materialities are perhaps better used to interrogate ethnicity as a foundational locus of experience. As recently argued by Adam Smith, the material world can afford unique light on past modes of historical subjectivity and the regimes of power that framed them. When contrasted with other lines of evidence, material expressions can help us examine how earlier forms of experience and identities were politically constituted over time by different social, economic, and discursive formations, and how they historically relate to the present. The key, in other words, is to use material assemblages to reclaim the historicity of identity and difference by reinscribing them in social fields shaped by history, economy, politics, and power.[58]

Unfortunately, turning to the archaeological record tends to complicate the ambiguous picture previously observed in Siin. Part of this haziness must be imputed to the preliminary nature of material information in the region. It therefore must be regarded as suggestive but liable to change with the construction of a broader comparative corpus of evidence. Partiality, however, does not prevent material culture from rubbing against other kinds of archives; it only makes the frictions more dispersed and less even. In this regard, the confrontation of sources creates knots and resistances that multiply our entry points into Seereer identity—both lived and represented—and raise provocative questions about Siin's cultural history. I want here to mobilize what we know of human occupation and commonplace artifacts to give a complementary look at the various foundational moments of Seereer identity outlined in oral traditions: the human encounters that led to the settlement of Siin by the Seereer, the consolidation of a Seereer presence, and institutional developments paving the way to the formation of a Seereer kingdom. I am interested in following the trail of different material clues over time and draw out their insights about the genesis of cultural identities in Siin. I focus specifically on settlement dynamics and ceramic assemblages, which constitute the most robust components of Siin's

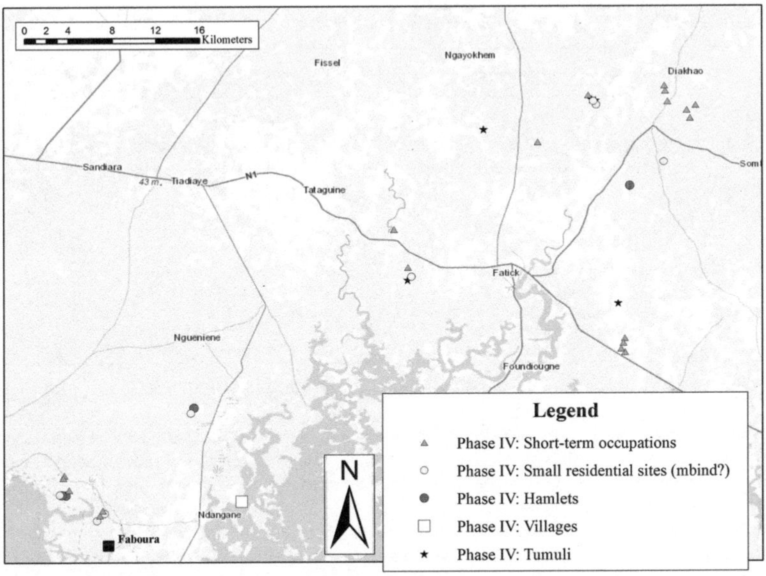

9 Siin settlement landscape, Fatick, Diakhao, and Petite Côte regions, phase IV, ca. AD 1000–1400

archaeological record, moving back and forth between these archaeological expressions and conventional representations of Seereer history.

During the first half of the second millennium AD, which collective memory associates with various waves of migration responsible for the human presence in Siin, archaeological evidence suggests relatively clear habitation patterns. This period shows a gradual increase in the number of sites, which largely consist of short-term occupations and the remains of small farmsteads (possibly no bigger than single compounds), which could indicate a level of residential movement (figure 9). Settlements tend to be established in littoral areas, with the emergence of small, ephemeral sites in the Siin interior (table 1 and figure 10). These transformations follow on the heels of an earlier phase of occupation characterized by a handful of village communities, where the bulk of the regional population might have concentrated.[59] The observable trend, then, is one toward an increasing dispersion of the social habitat, which progressively gives way to fairly small-scale, mobile communities, leaving relatively impermanent archaeological traces. When this restructuring of local landscapes began is unknown, though it probably took place sometime between AD 600 and AD 1000. Why and how these spatial processes occurred is

Table 1 2003 and 2011 surveys: Settlement types by survey region, ca. 700–1400

Survey regions	Phase III (ca. AD 700–1000)				Phase IV (ca. AD 1000–1400)			
	Short-term occupation[a]	*Mbind*[b]	Hamlet[c]	Village[d]	Short-term occupation	*Mbind*	Hamlet	Village
FAT ('03)	6				8	1		
DIA ('03)	6	2			8	3	1	
PCO ('03)	8	1	2	2	9	2	3	1
NGE ('11)	2		1	2	6	1	1	2
LOUL ('11)					16	2	1	
TUK ('11)							1	
Totals	22	3	3	4	47	9	7	3

Note: The table does not feature nonresidential sites: tumuli (S8, S65, S72, S74, S88, S91, S100, and S125) and iron scatters (S20, S22).

[a] This class of site consists of low-density, dispersed artifact scatters without visible surface features (such as mounds or structural remains). They are thought to represent the remains of small, mobile sites or brief occupations (like herding camps) leaving minimal material accumulation.

[b] These refer to those more permanent human occupations marked by distinct but limited traces of material accumulation: one or two deflated mounds with consistent artifact covers featuring material densities ranging from medium to high. They fluctuate in size due to different postdepositional histories. These sites probably represent the remains of kin residences that housed one or two families, perhaps similar to ethnographically recorded compounds (*mbind*).

[c] These residential sites are characterized by denser, larger-scale material covers. They generally feature five to ten small mounds flattened by plowing, indexing the remains of trash heaps and collapsed habitations.

[d] This class of site features high numbers of residential/rubbish mounds connected by high surface-artifact densities signaling increased intensity and permanence of human occupation. These types of deposits are often associated with baobab groves.

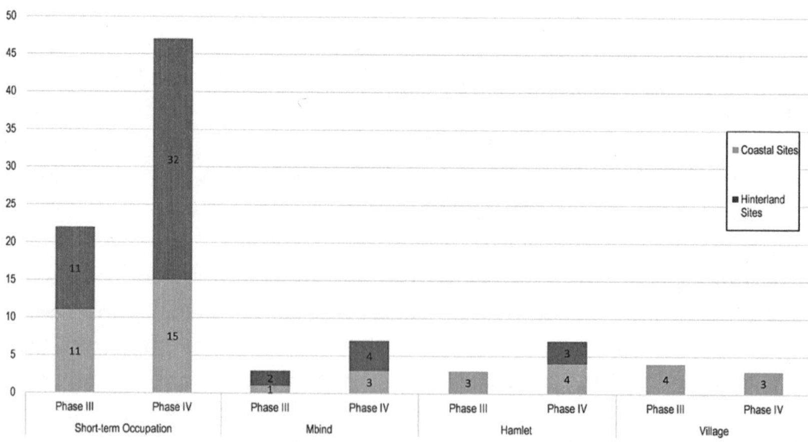

10 Phase III and IV settlements: shifts in coastal and hinterland occupations

equally obscure. In tandem, the size reduction, geographic scattering, and numerical expansion of residential sites could reflect a gradual splintering of earlier larger villages perhaps triggered by ecological necessity or political division. Concurrently, it is also possible that the new settlements were associated with the new population arrivals mentioned in oral memory.

Artifact assemblages, however, present little if any evidence of large-scale migrations, showing instead gradual changes against a background of continuities. At the turn of the first millennium AD, when it was supposedly inhabited by a homogeneous group of Soos tumulus builders, the Siin-Saalum area boasted two fairly distinct ceramic traditions betraying little affinity with each other. The first, localized along the Petite Côte and its hinterland, appears to evolve from an earlier "Neolithic" foundation with possible ties to the Cape Verde peninsula, while the second is commonly found on shell mounds in the Saalum estuary, spreading in influence along the Saalum River and its tributaries toward megalithic sites around the Gambia River and further south to Casamance (figure 11).[60] With deep anchorage in the Siin-Saalum region stretching back for centuries, these pottery traditions show sparse infusion of foreign elements that would allude to massive cultural transformations linkable to outside regions. At best, what current ceramic evidence suggests is the existence of two loosely defined and partially connected spheres of cultural interaction, though the extent and nature of these spheres and their articulation remain to be determined. Whether these assemblages reflect materialities associated with political entities, shared cultural practices and identitarian sensibilities, overlapping learning networks and manufacturing traditions, or webs of commercial circulation is unclear, making it difficult to accurately comment on the kinds of solidarities, social relations, and structures of power binding these ceramic spaces together.[61]

Before examining what these various patterns may indicate about the record of cultural interactions in the Siin, it should be recognized that regional archaeological tableaux during the pre-Atlantic era are blurred by a series of limitations. First, what we know of ceramic assemblages, particularly before AD 1000 or so, largely derives from a handful of excavated sites, which were often dug unsystematically, with little regard for the construction of ceramic chronologies. The resulting picture is impressionistic, offering a very slender window into centuries of political, economic, and cultural exchanges. Second, our reading of landscape transformations is also hamstrung by the coarse chronology of survey data. While excavated ceramics show diagnostic changes over time, surface

11 Phase III assemblages (IFAN Archaeological Collections). *Left*, vessels from site of Faboura, Petite Côte. *Right*, characteristic vessel forms from Saalum Islands.

mixing and weathering limits our ability to trace these subtle demarcations in surveyed assemblages. The fact that most pre-Atlantic sites combine features of both phases III and IV of our regional pottery sequence—a vast time span ranging from about AD 600 to the 1400s—without being specifically ascribable to either prevents finer periodizations for most of that era.[62] In turn, defining spatial patterns for an eight-hundred-year time block is bound to overlook salient cultural and historical processes that unfolded and materialized over shorter spans of time and at finer scales.

Putting aside issues of analytical resolution, it remains intriguing that although pre-Atlantic settlement histories span a period of intense human and political transformations—the Islamization of northern Senegal, vast demographic movements, ecological fluctuations, tightening linkages with Saharan economies, the foundation of state-level polities across the Senegambia—they manifest little internal change alluding to massive migrations by the Soos, Seereer, and Gelwaar, or indeed visible engagements between these different groups.[63] Nor do they appear to signal an increase in political hierarchy associated with the development of kingdoms. Certainly, we would anticipate the coarse time-scale to smudge the expression of human and political change, but it is unlikely that it would completely hide their expression—not only in spatial patterns but in ceramics as well. Perhaps, then, we can venture a few guesses to account for these disconnections between space and history—or representations of history.

Let us start with the Soos-Seereer encounter, a centerpiece of the diachronic puzzle of Seereer ethnogenesis. The absence of ceramic evidence traceable to the Soninke or Mande heartlands between the eighth and eleventh centuries AD invites skepticism vis-à-vis the historical influence, and perhaps even existence, of the mysterious Soos. As employed in oral traditions, the term is a catchall ethnic label, which glosses *any* alien population anterior to the arrival of Wolof and Seereer people. This leaves us wondering who exactly these Soos were, whether they comprised culturally homogeneous or diverse populations, and how they were organized socially and politically. When applied to the archaeological record of Siin and neighboring provinces, however, the term simply founders on the reef of ceramic variability and blurs the historical processes connecting different pottery traditions present in the region. It is likely that the mythical Soos encompass a variety of populations, different in space, time, and cultural makeup, which belies the image of cultural unity projected by the term. In effect, by associating the Soos, and subsequently the Seereer, with tumulus building, a funerary practice that stretches widely in time and space across Senegal, previous generations of scholars have not only erred in conflating pots (or vestiges) with people but also perhaps further muddied the relationship between archaeological expressions, historically recorded populations, and the political configurations in which they were embedded.[64] Rather than drawing on archaeology to produce alternative readings of the past, which can be checked against other sources and used to question local dynamics of political and cultural formation, scholars have tended to uncritically accept common historical wisdom and failed to sufficiently interrogate the assumptions underwriting conventional scenarios.

Similar suggestions can be made for subsequent cultural encounters. On one level, the absence of drastic change in settlement landscapes and material records resulting from outside intrusions might support Donald Wright's contention that the Gelwaar odyssey and other stories of Mandinka state building were narrative tropes denoting gradual political *influence* rather than physical *presence*.[65] In which case, the physical manifestations of Mande ideas would be less immediate in shaping the political landscape, while the correlates of contact and migration (in the form of ceramics, stylistic influences, trade artifacts, etc.) would be largely absent.

A related scenario could be entertained with respect to the Seereer exodus, only, in this case, we note parallels between collared vessels at the sites of Ndalane and Mbissel in Siin, Mbacké (200 km to the northeast), and phase III of the Middle Senegal Valley pottery sequence. These ceramic affinities during the AD 600–900 period might lend some credence to the myths of origin tying the two regions, even if the timing is earlier than expected.[66] The bigger problem here remains that broad resemblances separated by hundreds of kilometers without intermediary evidence provide shaky foundations for such claims. A more isolated clue of historical connections between the two areas appeared in the form of a large ankle ring showed to our archaeological team in 2002 by a resident of the village of Dioral, who had unearthed it from one of his fields several months earlier. This singular object was stylistically identical to copper artifacts retrieved along sites of the Senegal River Valley and imported from a number of manufacturing centers in the Saharo-Sahelian band.[67] Their presence in Siin denotes at least the possibility of trading relations with northern Senegal and combines with ceramic data to give limited support to scenarios of human movements out of Fuuta Tooro. It is worth noting that these artifacts can be dated by association to the AD 950–1200 period, which matches the time frame advanced for the Seereer migrations.

The ceramic assemblages that developed out of earlier traditions during the first half of the second millennium AD present a contrasting picture. While displaying internal continuities in clay properties and firing, decorative styles, and formal characteristics across the region, they also manifest unprecedented diversity in rim styles, vessel forms, and decorative techniques. One may wonder whether this homogeneity-in-diversity does not signal a culturally plural landscape becoming progressively integrated into a region-wide tradition, marked by shared and negotiated stylistic repertoires, symbolic spheres, and ceramic techniques across coresiding groups.[68] In effect, regional survey by the McIntoshes has yielded similar assemblages to the south and east, pointing to a material sphere radiating well beyond Siin's political boundaries. Possible exceptions include a handful of carved roulette designs on a minute fraction of late first millennium AD ceramic wares that *might* signal direct or indirect ties to the Mandinka region of Upper Guinea, but, while these decors make a feeble appearance on megalithic sites, they are practically absent in the Siin per se.[69]

Beyond the dubious historicity of a Soos ethnicity forming the hybrid foundation on which Seereer identity was built, material culture calls into question the accuracy of settlement narratives stylized as broad-brush migrations and their applicability to regional histories of occupation. The trope of migration in oral memory often streamlines movements of peoples as onetime, massive human displacements; populations are depicted as blocs moving en masse across the landscape toward a single terminus. Teleologically, these portrayals inject a sense of purposefulness and destiny into narratives of the deep past, while eliding the intricacies of migration, demographic shuffles, and population contact. As mentioned above, material continuities in the Siin shed skeptical light on the likelihood that settlement history involved large-scale waves of people and tectonic contact. One possible reason for the virtual absence of traces of human movements, assuming that they took place, is that migrations are often subtle and intricate historical processes that implicate numerous multidirectional movements with different tempos and extents, drawn out over long stretches of time and space. Such gradual unfolding would likely result in the dilution and mutual incorporation of different cultural assemblages over time and in their low archaeological visibility.

The related difficulty is that, because it collapses nuanced pasts into conformist storylines, historical memory often stalls into happy-ending tales of peaceful integration that effectively draw a veil over the potential contradictions, tensions, and hostility that modulated past human encounters. While short on detail and largely negative, archaeological evidence of settlement histories in Siin directs our attention to alternative corpuses of oral traditions that allow for a more turbulent and bloodstained interchange between Soos residents and Seereer migrants. One such example can be found in different accounts of the myth of Sagn Folo, which traces the debut of the Seereer in Siin. In the myth, Soos migrants precede the Seereer by one day and create a small village where they plan to spend the growing season. The Seereer arrive the next day. They are given water and shelter but refuse to live with the Soos and establish their own settlement a short distance away at Niakhar. In turn, the Soos move to a new location to create a new village. In another version, the encounter takes place at night, and both parties keep each other at bay. In this story, the dramatic emphasis is *not* placed on the seamless *entente* of first settlers and incomers, on the ritual pact tying landlords and strangers, the former extending hospitality in exchange for the latter's acceptance of the authority of residential genealogies. Instead, other narrative devices are mobilized: separation and refusal, ambivalence toward hospitality's demands, the cover of night that allows the narrator to glide over what can only be dark events, the abandonment of Sagn Folo, or the fact that the latter should not be referred to by its inauspicious name (*sagn* means "to bury" in Seereer and connotes the idea of "curse" in Wolof) but replaced by the term *njate* (meaning "the hamlet"). In other words, these narratives evoke in hushed tones and suggestive metaphors the violent conflict opposing the two peoples, shortening the painful memories of this cultural clash to a mythic night of violence. Here the blood binding the story is not that of kinship but that shed by mortal enemies.[70]

These different caveats carry significant implications for understanding the long-term historical and cultural foundations of people today referring to themselves as Seereer and the material identities that came to characterize them. In effect, many of the cultural practices and salient materialities taken to define the populations of Siin—and Seereer subjectivities by extension—during the Atlantic and colonial eras are attached to the process of biological and cultural fusion with the Soos: the adoption of tumulus construction and burial, a practice with historical correlates in the Siin (but in other areas as well), or the coagulation of such key institutions as the *lamanat* (a form of land tenure and administration) and a system of agrarian democracy, which are centrally showcased in colonial ethnographies of the Seereer (see next chapter).[71] Skepticism over the existence of Soos and the foundational moment of their encounter with the Seereer suggests the need to unhook the different links of Siin's cultural history from chains of deep-time ethnicities. By extension, it also invites further empirical explorations of the material tracery of past identity and its contextualization in histories of landscape.

Conclusions: Archaeological Genealogies of Authenticity

In casting critical light on long accepted portrayals of Seereer history, my goal has not been to deny that something called Seereer identity ever existed or to intimate that the deep affinities that Seereer people feel for their cultural heritage are misguided. The years I have spent in the Siin tell me otherwise, that Seereerness is a genuinely inhabited subjectivity, and that the senses of cohesion, location, and world-being it fosters are very real indeed, both in their inward experience and in the social solidarities they make possible. More simply, I wished to argue that the separation often implicitly drawn between authenticity and history is largely artificial and not always helpful. These terms are not mutually exclusive. Length of time is not the lynchpin of truthfulness, and forms of belonging can be redrawn or experienced differently over time without making them any less true. Perhaps more useful then, in our study of the past, is to develop a sense of *authenticity as history* or at least the need to craft better *histories of authenticity*, more sensitive to the twists and turns of its biography and the conditions in which it sediments.

This chapter has addressed these queries by confronting the different histories encoded in textual and material archives. The productive tensions arising between them point to a series of chinks in the armor of identity discourse in Senegal, which in turn can be expanded into fuller inquiries of culture's historicity. Indeed, if anything, the fragmentary notes offered above on the making of the Seereer supply a reminder that, ultimately, ethnicity is a historical product, one of many shifting constituents of individual and collective subjectivity.[72] One consequence is that assumptions of continuity should be traded for careful analyses of the *production* (social, material, discursive) of cultural categories, with an eye for consistencies as well as ruptures over time. Keeping in mind the lability of African social traditions, we should anticipate that *if* Seereerness already meaningfully existed in the sixteenth century (or before), it was probably very different from Seereer collective consciousness in the early 1900s, which, in turn, differs from today's sensibilities in Siin.

Tracking the *political constitution* of identity helps us to see where and when flexible boundaries become stabilized and categorized, just as it highlights that ethnicity is not a single entity but a cluster of related objects, each with their own histories, trajectories, and media. To do justice to these connections, it is necessary to examine past African subjectivities outside of colonial units and modern categories, but also inside them. In the context of this chapter, it has meant resolutely challenging the trope of the timeless Seereer, without ever dismissing it. To this end, I have tried to provide a few clues as to why this portrayal caught on. Echoing Walter Benjamin's notion that "truth is not a matter of exposure which destroys the secret, but a revelation that does justice to it," I have attempted to expose the allure of Seereer ethnicity in the furrows of its truth effects.[73]

I will continue to unwrap the various folds of Seereerness in the next chapter, through a closer inspection of colonial ethnography and how the savage-slotting of Seereer peasants also rested on their embeddedness, real and imagined, in a landscape of social practices. Indeed, colonial observers did not just invent the Seereer as traditional and atavistic; rather, they read this conservatism from tangible indices, like the Seereer devotion to agricultural work, ancestral lands, and local religion. In inscribing these practices into ageless nature, however, French writers also froze much of their variability and historicity, whose incongruous presence still lingers in colonial records, ready to be rediscovered.

FOUR

"The Very Model of Egalitarian and Anarchic Peasantry": Seereer Cultural Landscapes and the Ethnographic Imagination

The Seereer man is the very embodiment of the black peasant. Essentially sedentary, with little inclination toward commerce, he does not have an adventurous mind. . . . Barely does he have a sense of curiosity. Little perfectible by nature, he stands out from the other Senegalese races by his extraordinary attachment to the land. It may have been said that he lives by and for it. Thus, land-using rights are profoundly anchored into the mores of this people, which is otherwise hard-working and enjoys a profound "animal life."

M. REYNIER, "RAPPORT POLITIQUE ANNUEL" (1933)[1]

Peasant Exemplars, Ethnography, and Colonial Knowledge

This chapter provides a historical ethnography of Seereer society, which examines both cultural practices and the political forces that conditioned them in recent history. In their encounter with places, peoples, and resources, the Seereer have crafted complex forms of socioeconomic organization, which I attempt to reconstruct from oral traditions, ethnographies, and colonial accounts between 1860 and 1970. I examine what we know of Seereer social and political arrangements, human ecology, built habitat, cultural

12 Postcard, "Serer man on his donkey" (ANS, Iconographie, no. 0808; reproduced with permission from Archives du Sénégal)

economy, and religious practices during this period. If outside observers have tended to paint a Seereer world of stable norms etched in the ethnographic present (Pélissier's "model of egalitarian and anarchistic peasantry"), available sources also piece together a subtle picture of variability and change, which offsets depictions of peasant exemplars and exposes their historical roots (figure 12). We can then begin to discuss how and why traditional ways of life have transformed or persisted throughout the colonial period.

In situating Seereer social practices in the horizon of recent history, my objectives are twofold: first, I try to shore up a credible picture of the Seereer past, which, if used cautiously, can provide comparative insights for more remote and less well-documented contexts; and, second, I attempt to engage in a critical reading of the sources marshaled in the construction of this baseline. Complementing my analysis of Seereer ethnicity in the previous chapter, my aim is to examine the sensibilities that have shaped Siin's colonial library and influenced later historical writings on the region. Scholars of Senegambia have not always appreciated the extent to which their portrayals of precolonial Africa were framed by tropes inherited from the colonial mindset and inadvertently recycled earlier anachronisms, supplanting culture for history, as it were.[2] As previously argued, however, disjunctures between different archives are sites where the residue of past cultural life pushes back against discourse and where it resists entextualization. Concurrently, they are also the nodes where the noises and silences structuring ethnohistories of Siin become perceptible, where we can begin to document the emergence of colonial perceptions of rural Africa and read the historicity of cultural landscapes against the grain of colonial common sense. As Siin's corpus of colonial evidence shows, the construction of normative Seereer culture rested on the erasure of contingency in local practices, which was not lost on all colonial writers. It also rested on mobilizing the objective power of images—textual and visual—to freeze Seereer peasants into a natural landscape of apparent immutability.

Seereer Social Organization

Ethnographic studies throughout the twentieth century portray the Seereer as a bilineal society, with a dual system of descent and property devolution. Fine-grained historical ethnographies of kinship are difficult, however, because early colonial sources vary widely in their information content. They often make vague references to family organization, reflecting passing acquaintance with local institutions (figure 13).[3] Synthetic treatments of Seereer society did not emerge until the 1930s, when customary laws were codified. While social variations occur across provinces, studies highlight features broadly shared across the Siin: social identity is reckoned through both matrilineage and patrilineage, both headed by a male elder; collective property, family belongings, and management rights to land and cattle were predominantly transmitted within the matrilineage, while name, caste, social status, property (weapons, work instruments) and consumer goods acquired by the father, and land-use rights were passed through the paternal line; royalty remained the exclusive privilege of the Gelwaar matrilineage; kin groups married exogamously, but social taboos, until recently, confined castes to endogamy; modes of residence were virilocal, with a marked tendency toward patrilocality in more recent times; both lineages indifferently managed the ritual domain (places of worship, ceremonies, ministrations to ancestral spirits).[4] Authors have also emphasized, at least in earlier times, the predominance of the matrilineage, captured in the Seereer proverb *O lok yaay, teen fisu a Sinig* (It is the maternal stick that traced out the Siin).

Ethnographers have remarked on the tensions embedded in Seereer kinship and social structures—competition between maternal and paternal interests, matrilineal filiation versus virilocality, collective institutions

13 Postcard, "Serer family" (ANS, Iconographie, no. 0802; reproduced with permission from Archives du Sénégal)

versus stratified social order, to name but a few. These are generally regarded as the residue of centuries of culture contact in Siin, thus offering a window into Seereer social history, as well as an important source of cultural dynamism and adaptation over time. Certain authors like Dupire and colleagues have attempted to explain the origin of Seereer bilineal descent through migration histories, connecting, for instance, the occurrence of patrilineal estates with original (Tukulor) patrilineality in the Fuuta Tooro or tracing matrilineality to a pre-Gelwaar era dominated by Soos matriclans.[5] Such hypotheses, while enticing, remain speculative, due in part to fuzzy historical frameworks and the fact that they do not quite account for province-wide variability in bilineal arrangements. In fact, permutations of matrilineal-patrilineal principles in land tenure, inheritance, property management, labor organization, and residence seem to follow regional variations in economic activities, political geography, and history, thus attesting to the mosaic dynamism of Seereer kinship.[6] At the same time, however, matrilineal regimes have unmistakably eroded since the 1930s, a trend accelerating in the postindependence period. This decline has been observed in many domains. When compared with earlier observations, which sometimes ignore patrilineal inheritance, data from the 1960s and 1970s show a weakening of uncles' authority with a sharp increase in patrilocal residence and a growing role of the patriline in the education of children. Since the 1960s, geographers have documented a precipitous drop in matrilineal influence in land tenure, with control of matrilineal estates moving to patrilineages.[7] With roots in the bilineal tensions mentioned above, the atomization of maternal collectivity and the concomitant rise of agnatic relations have been precipitated by colonial economic reforms toward freehold property relations, individual ownership, and commodified exchange. This process was also assisted by the expansion of patriarchal religions, such as Islam and Catholicism, and fundamental land reform by the Senegalese state with the passage of the 1964 National Domain Law, which nationalized rural land and officially abolished customary land tenure institutions.[8]

Knowledge of social organization in Siin developed with French political penetration into Senegal's hinterland. Colonial reports expanded on the impressionistic treatments of Seereer society offered by seventeenth- and eighteenth-century accounts, which generally consisted of disparate mentions of sovereigns, dignitaries, and casted groups such as griots (bards, musicians), leatherworkers, and blacksmiths. From the 1850s to independence, colonial documents paint a fairly consistent picture of Siin as a stratified society, comprising a number of major social groups with uneven access to political and economic power. They distinguish between nobles, warriors, commoners, and slaves, although variation occurs in names, in internal constitution and attributions, in how these were grouped or differentiated, and whether they should be perceived as social orders, classes, or castes.[9]

Synthesizing the above information, the Seereer historically appear to have fallen into a number of broad social classes. On the eve of colonial contact, Siin was dominated politically by the nobility, which consisted of royal power holders, potential claimants to the throne, and their relatives forming a retinue of aristocratic followers. Though the highest political offices were held by the Gelwaar matrilineage, dignitaries and allies of the court, as well as nonroyal relatives (often the sons of noble men and free women), were generally entrusted with the administration of one or several villages or provinces. The *ceddo* were a class of warriors, originally recruited from the ranks of servile populations, who formed the military entourage of rulers and territorial chiefs and served as the kingdom's police and standing army. Over time, the *ceddo* diversified from a purely servile base by incorporating free nobles committed to military functions and a life of plunder. *Ceddo* warriors recognized no authority other than the king, although historical evidence shows that they developed autonomy during the eighteenth and nineteenth centuries, and bands of slave warriors frequently roamed about the countryside independently of royal orders and spread havoc in village communities.[10]

Contrasting with political and military elites, the vast majority of Seereer inhabitants belonged to a somewhat ill-defined class of commoners or free peasants (*jaambur*). The *jaambur* encompass all those who were neither nobles nor slaves. They generally engaged in a wide range of subsistence activities on land and sea: cultivation, hunting, and fishing. Most freemen were relatively isolated from the sphere of kingdom politics and referred to as *baadoole* (those without strength or lacking strength). Yet the *jaambur* also included local notables (lineage heads, land custodians, village chiefs) and ritual specialists (*saltigi*), who showed greater involvement in the circles of power. *Pad* (captives, slaves; *jaam* in Wolof) represented the servile population, subdivided into several groups socially ranked on the basis of their owner, occupation, and how they were acquired. Most notable were *ceddo*, crown, domestic, and trade slaves. House slaves were generally treated as members of their master's family and worked a plot of land, while trade slaves were often resold but could also live in their owner's concession. The dissolution of slavery enabled former slaves to slough off the stigmas of captivity by blending into their host communities and claiming belonging to the peasantry. The last major social category (*ñeeño*) denotes endogamous, hereditary casted groups, which are generally equated with socioprofessional activities and played an important part in economic life. These are further subdivided into griots (*kaul*), blacksmiths (*paal*), leatherworkers (*koora*), and woodworkers (*laybe*), who attached their services to free peasants or noble families.[11]

Political Organization of the Kingdom

Colonial sources paint the Siin as a centralized monarchy with constitutional checks wherein kingly power was balanced by "a quasi-corporatist system that granted voice to major status groups."[12] Power was vested in three political institutions—the *maad* (*buur*, in Wolof), the *jaraaf a maak*, and the *farba fa maak*—whose administration embodied the wills, decisions, and political consciousness of the aristocracy, the free peasantry (*jaambur*), and the body of slaves. These leading figures and, by extension, the major social groups they represented were united "in a state of reciprocal bondage," where "the exercise of sovereignty . . . rest[ed] on the principle of an institutionalized compromise."[13]

The *maad a Sinig* was the head of stately decision making, whose responsibility entailed declaring or calling off war, rendering justice, and mediating conflicts while ultimately ensuring the well-being and security of his subjects. His authority extended over royal lands, the slaves who worked them, and the nobility. The king was the recipient of annual taxes and customs, receiving parallel revenue from trade and the royal monopoly over salt production. He relied on a congeries of provincial governors and local functionaries, many of whom he personally appointed, who were in charge of collecting dues and duties, policing, administering the region, and ensuring the steady flow of grain to royal granaries. Locally, the king was represented by the *saaxsaax*, who exerted judicial functions and received taxes in each village, and the *jaraaf*, who were generally chosen from the lineage of the village founder and acted essentially as village heads.[14]

This centralized administration, hinging on the king's ability to select major titleholders and place representatives in each locality, may have given the *maad* a degree of political and territorial reach that neighboring rulers did not always enjoy. Moreover, unlike other regional monarchs, the *maad*'s legitimacy was strengthened by his role as Siin's foremost religious leader, whose ritual functions were essential to the reproduction of the state, socially and spiritually. Personifying both his subjects and the ancestors, the *maad* acted as the point of balance between secular and mystical forces, as a vector of continuity and order.[15] This was not the case in the Kajoor and Bawol states or the Seereer kingdom of Saalum, whose nominally Muslim kings were strictly secular leaders, and deferred to Islamic clerics on matters of religious authority.

The *maad*, however, was no absolute monarch. Rather, he can be seen as a king-in-council, whose power depended on institutions and forces that either lay beyond his direct control or operated on an equal footing with it. To start, the monarch's position was elective; he was nominated by the *jaraaf a maak*, or great *jaraaf* (spokesperson of the commoners), after consultation with a council formed by the principal heads of families and titleholders and with the *farba fa maak* (leader of the slaves). The process of royal succession suggests a distribution of power in Siin, where, in principle at least, the king's ability to govern was always partially delimited by enslaved armed forces controlled by the *farba* and the social interests of free farmers represented by the great *jaraaf*.[16]

The great *jaraaf* functioned as a prime minister of sorts, heading the royal council, advising the *maad* on political decisions, and largely governing the internal affairs of the kingdom. Confirmed by the king after recommendation from a college of freemen, once in power, the great *jaraaf* remained independent of whoever was on the throne and could only be deposed by an assembly of *jaambur*. Although he could not ascend to the throne, the great *jaraaf* could revoke the *maad* if he had fallen out of popular favor. His administration hence provided an institutional check on royal sovereignty by ensuring, in theory, that peasant interests would be heeded by power holders and cushioned from excessive aristocratic demands or random extortions by warrior bands.[17] Much like the *maad*, the great *jaraaf*'s local authority rested on a network of village representatives, including local titleholders (*jaraaf*) and another layer of grassroots notables, the *lamaan* (*yaal naay* or *yaal ndaak* in Seereer). Land custodians and rain priests, the *lamaan* coordinated agricultural activities and the management and allocation of resources. They were also empowered to settle minor affairs, lineage and familial matters, and tended to both village and ancestral shrines. These decision-making structures granted some autonomy to village communities in the conduct of local affairs and, in some instances, could afford a degree of independence from royal administrations. Traditional land authorities were incorporated into a federal system that existed in dynamic relation with the centripetal functions carried out by the state.[18] Another central political functionary was the *farba fa maak*. Although he was the chief of the slaves, the great *farba* exerted critical influence over military and foreign affairs. Despite his servile status, he could play a defining role in the administration of the kingdom, taking effective control of diplomacy and external relations when the *maad* proved too young, old, or weak to rule efficiently.

Political authority was also shared at the upper level of the Seereer state, as real power diffused among the *maad* and a number of high offices held by royal family members. The heir to the throne, called the *bi no maad* (*buumi* in Wolof), was always a potential contender for power, coalescing the political ambitions of the rival lineages from which he was often selected. To keep him at a safe distance from the capital, he was often assigned a small fief on the political frontier. The *buur jilas* was the next heir apparent, who, as another prospective challenger, was placed at the head of a peripheral province. Lastly, the *lingeer* could be either the sister, mother, or aunt of the king. She ruled over the women of the kingdom, arbitrated conflicts, and presided over cultural ceremonies and initiation rituals. She and her court resided in the village of Cupaan, and lived off the tax revenue and produce of a few dependencies. Following Seereer matrilineal sensibilities, the *lingeer* often exerted tangible influence in royal succession and political intrigues. In fact, historically, political factionalism within the nobility constituted a major source of instability built into Siin's state structures. Through matrilineal politics and patrilineal alliances, rival lineages endlessly contested the dominance of the ruling families and labored to place their claimants on the throne. These divisive dynamics were assisted by the provincial administration, which could impose federal restrictions on monarchical authority: territorial chiefs could develop alliances with various parties and acquire freedom of action; heirs to the throne used their influence to foment political intrigue; while local families often solidified their hold on political offices by controlling rules of inheritance.[19] In the end, the monarch's ability to govern depended on his ability to cater to his followers and ensure their loyalty, while conciliating competing factions and curbing the influence of rivals.

Reconstructing precolonial Seereer political organization from colonial and oral sources is in many ways a quixotic exercise. Ethnographic reports are a blend of what observers saw at the time of colonial contact, what their predecessors wrote, and what their informants remembered of traditional institutions. As a consequence, these accounts and the collective memory on which they draw tend to lump social institutions into a precolonial "as it was" epoch and construct functionalist images of political organization that resist time and change. To compound the problem of synchronicity, students of the past have held often conflicting views of how the traditional Siin state functioned in precolonial times. Early French observers decried the moral depravity of the aristocracy and slave warriors, which made a case for the necessity of colonization. By the 1930s, however, with the crumbling of the *ceddo* regime, administrators seemed more inclined to describe a harmonious balance of power among different customary institutions, which may reflect dominant historical memories at the time. Similar accents resonate in the work of postcolonial writers who, in their effort to reclaim dignity for the African past, have also viewed precolonial society as something of a golden era, marked by democratic, legitimate, and consensual political structures. Comparable tensions can be found in present-day Seereer cultural memory, which splits along competing visions of the past that variously idealize or vilify the Gelwaar state, that play up or whitewash the authority and autonomy of local customary officials.[20]

If these various strands of historical memory reveal much about the politics of remembering and representation, they also afford a peek at the Seereer social past between the lines of discourse. Specifically, they outline some of the conflicting forces that shaped the kingdom as its history acquired an increasingly inert quality in the documents and oral traditions produced during the colonial period. A general observation is that, while basic institutions may have remained relatively stable during the monarchic period, the balance of power between the various offices shifted over time. During the eighteenth and nineteenth centuries, a time of strengthened royal authority, *ceddo* warriors became more assertive, and the *maad* tightened his control over peasantries, which resulted in the decline of lamanal political power and a parallel rise in the authority of crown representatives (*jaraaf* and *saaxsaax*). It is quite possible during this time that the electoral privilege of the freemen's council was partially revoked, such that matters of kingly succession began to be decided more fully within aristocratic circles. Other signs of this power shift can be seen in oral and colonial accounts that refer to instances where the chief of slaves (great *farba*) was elected prime minister. More generally, the tensions between *jaambur* and warriors were a mainstay of colonial administrative correspondence, which reported a range of peasant responses to *ceddo* demands, from compliance (most frequently) to migration and armed resistance.[21] Still, although the trend toward political concentration and reliance on military force was real, it was not inexorable—a story we will examine in greater detail in chapter 6. Peasants may have openly contested the legitimacy of royal encroachment, yet factors pertaining to the nature of power in Siin also muddled the exercise of sovereign rule, with uneven success.

Under colonial rule, the *maad*'s authority remained palpable, as he continued to enjoy considerable popular support among Siin residents. The *maad* were generally retained as province or canton chiefs, served as political and customary advisors, and often proved effective at raising taxes and encouraging peanut production. The *maad*'s authority was buttressed by their religious functions and accoutrements of power like the maintenance of a royal court and aristocratic retinue in Diakhao, even after the institution of kingship was officially (yet not officiously) absorbed into the colonial republic in 1924.[22]

By contrast, the biggest losers in the new colonial order undoubtedly were former high-ranking officials, *ceddo*, and *lamaan*.[23] With the unraveling of the Gelwaar regime, the great *jaraaf* and great *farba* were rendered obsolete virtually overnight. While slightly longer-lived, the *ceddo*'s influence was fated to disappearance once they could no longer live off an economy of spoils. A small number of warriors sought to prolong their privileges by assisting with tax collection, but the majority rapidly joined the peasantry and ceased to exist as an independent class. Lastly, the growing importance of cash crops, commodification of land and things, and weakening of matrilineality exacted a heavy toll on lamanal authority and traditional power relations at the community level, particularly after independence.[24]

Agriculture, Land Management, and Human Ecology

Historians and geographers have long argued that Siin's agriculture has been profoundly influenced by the experiences it shares with other populations of rural northern Senegambia. Senegal's sandy soils have nurtured a certain consistency in systems of land management and distribution, farming knowledge, and technological repertoires across the region.[25] In the absence of irrigation and plowing technology, Senegalese peasants learned to accommodate the play of seasons, poor soils, irregular precipitations, and water deficiencies. Seereer farmers and their neighbors have inherited a mode of agrarian subsistence resting on rain-fed, shifting cereal cultivation, a system dominated by millet and its byproducts. Historically, they have grown two kinds of small millet adapted to light sandy soils: *mac* (*Pennisetum polystachyon*), which requires higher humus contents and *pod* (*Pennisetum gambicum*), a faster-maturing, more drought-tolerant variety that grew on the loosest, most exploited lands. The Seereer reliance on millet as a preferred food staple, as the foundation of alimentary security, even as construction material for houses, has led some authors to speak of "a veritable civilization of millet."[26]

On these regional foundations, however, Seereer groups have constructed a distinctive agricultural ecology, which has allowed them to support above-average population densities, abundant crop production, and, by most accounts, perhaps the most sophisticated agrarian system in the western Sahel. As geographers have shown, Siin's unique signature in rural production resides in a fundamental fusion of social, religious, and agropastoral realities into an agricultural system integrating fields, crops, resources, cattle, trees, villages, humans, ancestors, as well as supernatural forces. In concrete terms, Siin's rural terroir owed its special character to the integration of crops and cattle in agricultural production, the creation of an agrarian park made up of selected trees carefully preserved for their fertilizing properties, a complex system of crop rotation and systematic fallow, and particular forms of land management. These different elements combined to distinguish the Seereer peasants from their Wolof and Halpulaar neighbors to the north and Joola and Mandinka farmers to the south. This combination of resources enabled the Seereer to use the land more intensively and diversify agricultural production.[27]

Like their predecessors, colonial observers unanimously praised Seereer agricultural methods and expertise, commenting on the tidiness of their fields, the meticulous care taken in clearing and preparation, and their abundant millet yields and cotton production—though early on these remarks often seem to refer to the Northwest Seereer rather Siin residents.[28] Colonial authors repeatedly emphasized that, unlike in neighboring regions, millet fields in Siin were carefully cleared of brush and fertilized by cattle, and that the Seereer country was partitioned by a network of thornbush enclosures designed to protect crops and delimit land parcels. Later observers mention the importance of regular fallows and tree preservation in the Seereer agricultural scheme, which they contrast with Wolof farmers' generalized disregard for arboreous conservation.[29]

Although these descriptions offer few specifics on agricultural organization, they remain consistent with the geographic evidence gathered in the 1960s and 1970s, from which most current understandings of Seereer rural production derive.[30] These studies helped to document the elaborate integration of grain growing and pastoralism, which probably resembled what Siin's agricultural system looked like in the mid-nineteenth century.[31] In the 1960s, much like a century earlier, Siin's manicured landscape unfolded as an irregular grid of fields and fallow land demarcated by a dense latticework of hedges and paths. Before the peanut takeoff, Seereer agriculture was probably organized as a three-field system (figure 14). The area (*pombod*) stretching between and around habitations was permanently planted in small millet (*pod*), the preferred cereal used to commune with the ancestors. Systematic manuring, mixed with the organic detritus secreted by village activities, ensured soil fertility despite continued farming of the *pombod*. The open expanses beyond the *pombod* were partitioned into a rotating two-field system where, every year or two, the cultivation of fast millet (*mac*), which made up the bulk of Seereer diet, alternated with a fallow (*tos*) used for cattle grazing. Cotton was also cultivated in the *pombod* itself or in small fields on the periphery of concessions, while, along the coast, rice was grown by women in tidal marshes. Farming entailed modest technological requirements: well adapted to sandy soils, the tool of choice was the *iler*, a crescent-shaped blade connected to a long wooden shaft, which was used for ground-clearing, weeding, digging, planting, and harvesting.[32]

Rather than entrusting their cattle to Pulaar pastoralists and sending them to the dry prairies of the Ferlo desert for the cycle of transhumance,

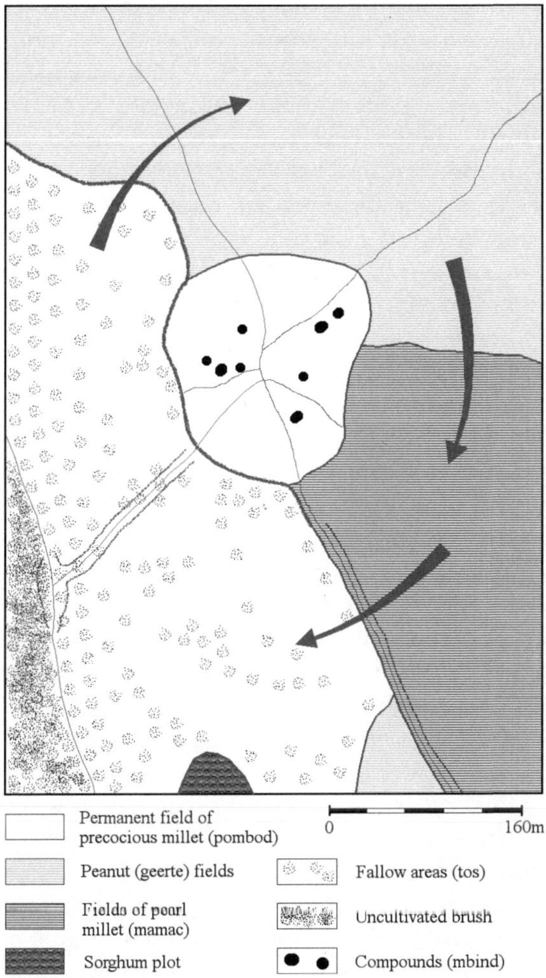

14 Schematic organization of traditional Seereer farmstead (from Pélissier, 1966)

the Seereer paired herding with systematic fallows to help regenerate soils exhausted by several seasons of millet crops. To further consolidate soil productivity, peasants complemented sedentary pasturing with an assortment of agrarian practices, including controlled burning, bush-clearing and weeding, and the intentional selection of arboreous species. In effect, strategic tree conservation gave a parklike quality to the Seereer countryside, juxtaposed with agricultural production. The cornerstone of this agrarian park was *Faidherbia albida*, a singular species that sheds its leaves before the rains begin but grows its foliage back during the dry season. This inverted vegetational cycle symbiotically meshes with soil and cattle by contributing organic matter to regenerate fields in the growing season, providing food for bovines during the dry season when plant life has practically disappeared, and helping to fix nitrogen in the soil.[33]

As ethnographers have documented, however, the management of the Seereer terroir involved more than crop scheduling and agricultural organization; it also demanded particular understandings of land access, distribution, and control, as well as knowledge of its role in Seereer memory and cultural order. Land rights were regulated through genealogical ties to the first settlers and their descendants and were reckoned in the idiom of migration histories. Dominant oral traditions generally recount episodes of village founding that unfold in a patterned, mythological progression. They depict an original encounter with the wilderness (*o kop ale*) where the first migrant chose a parcel of land on which to settle and set fire to the surrounding bush and forest to clear a vast area fit for habitation and cultivation. The original burning of the primal forest determined the rights to use and legitimately occupy the land, placing its control in the hands of the hero-founder's lineage. The burnt space delimited a fire estate (also known as a *lamanat*) overseen by the *yaal naay* (master of fire) or *lamaan*, generally the lineage's eldest man, who officiated as the manager of the land and collective resources.[34]

In time, foundation stories continue, lamanal domains began to attract new migrants looking for a place to live and grow food. *Lamaan* gave the newcomers permission to clear or cut a portion of their fire estates and granted them use rights to the land in exchange for annual gifts and payments, generally in the form of crops and alcohol. The parcel thus cleared was called a *bax*, with the *yaal bax* (master of the axe or master of cutting) as its administrator, and rights of exploitation were transmitted through the founder's lineage, so long as the descendants continued to occupy and cultivate the land while fulfilling their duties toward the *lamaan*. When the founders of the kingdom arrived in the Siin, a number of *lamanats*, variable in size and extent, seem to have been in existence, though not all land was occupied. Undomesticated stretches were found in forested areas on the periphery of the main population centers. These unexploited lands were soon claimed by the king and carved into agricultural and political estates to be distributed as rewards to allies and courtiers. Because they were delimited by the hooves of a horse, these parcels were referred to as *foxos* (hoof).

As Galvan observes, the significance of origin stories lies not in a literal reading of historical foundation but rather in the fact that they spell out "through larger-than-life metaphorical example, the parameters of rightful economic relations. These tales teach basic principles: rightful ownership or control of property is a matter of original settlement and first use, and this original title belongs not to an individual but to a lineage." These economic axioms informed the flexible, overlapping systems of rights and management that regulated the functioning of Seereer terroirs throughout most of the colonial period, despite the administration's attempts at reform.[35]

The Seereer moral economy generally evaded the grasp of colonial agents. A sentiment of confusion threads the literature on customary conceptions of land ownership. An important point of contention centered on whether one could talk of property and material possessions to describe the Seereer terroir or whether alternative notions of stewardship might be more suitable.[36] Administrator Ernest Noirot, a long-term *résident* (local administrator) of Siin-Saalum, writes of Seereer landholding practices in a late nineteenth-century reference to the inland village of Diohine:

> The soil . . . almost totally belongs to a family whose doyen representing the collectivity is in some ways the usufructuary in charge of granting other members of the family a proportional part of the rents he receives. Sovereignty does not necessarily imply property rights. Buur Siin is the sovereign of Dioïne as of the other provinces of Siin but he is not in the least its proprietor; he only receives a right in value that is represented by the land tax and presented to him by the usufructuary . . . of the soil of Dioïne.[37]

From this and later accounts, it seems that material resources such as land were not individually owned; nor did they belong to anyone. Instead, as the better-documented ethnographies of the 1930s and 1960s further show, land and cattle were a communal patrimony to be used and managed by the lineage and collectively exploited under the guardianship of the lineage head. Proper attitude toward land seemed to be one of holistic custodianship, carrying material and religious dimensions and embodied in the office of the *lamaan* (and, to some extent, the *yaal mbind*, the compound chief). The manager of the collectivity ensured the well-being of the land, both physically (by determining the allocation of land, organizing agricultural activities, enforcing crop rotation, supervising the maintenance of trees and forests) and spiritually (through tending shrines, presiding over ancestor worship, and caring for the lineage spirits inhabiting the land).[38]

As village founding narratives show, land and *lamaan* were contained in a framework of rights that regulated social relations within the terroir. Historical primacy and first-use privileges were central pillars of the Seereer moral economy that structured exchanges between landlords, land-users, and newcomers.[39] On one level, though they were free to work the fields as they chose, could not be summarily expropriated, and retained long-term access to the land, the holders of use rights remained tied to the *yaal naay* who held titles to the fire estates. In addition, the shrines of later generations of migrants were subordinated to the spirits associated with the lineage of the first settlers. On another level, origin stories also offered a metaphorical model for incorporating strangers within existing patterns of land arrangement by allowing them access to fields and resources and giving them social recognition. Staged in the fog of memory, these templates provided a flexible repertoire of cultural principles to manage the relations between resources, people, and spirits during the colonial period and probably before.[40]

As with other dimensions of Seereer social life, the Siin terroir did not escape the wave of economic changes accompanying colonial rule. The promotion of peanuts (*Arachis hypogaea*) as the centerpiece of Senegal's economy led to their inclusion into the crop cycle. Although a marginal crop at first, cultivated largely in women's gardens, peanut was progressively worked into the alternating millet-fallow rotations on the open fields surrounding the *pombod*. However, Seereer communities only begrudgingly turned their acreage to peanut cultivation and continued to focus on subsistence needs. While the adoption of peanuts and rising production levels necessitated some concessions—the substitution of cash cropping for fallows, the reduction of fallow periods, and decreased reliance on systematic manuring being the most notable—the agrarian park suffered little substantial alteration under colonialism.[41]

By the time of independence, farmers began to turn the *pombod*, once exclusively planted in millet, to peanut cultivation and lost the ability to satisfy their alimentary needs. Initial Seereer reticence toward colonial farming techniques has steadily given way to reliance on horse-drawn plows over the past decades. This limited mechanization has expanded cultivable surfaces, but agricultural overexploitation has taken a toll on soil productivity, as narrow access to chemical fertilizers has not compensated for the decline of systematic manuring. Siin's agrarian park has also suffered gravely from long-term environmental degradation.[42] While buffered by local adaptation and innovation, the commercial cultivation of peanuts radically transformed local land régimes, as was already apparent in the 1930s. As state policies during independence fostered the decline of *lamanal* institutions and maternal wealth, peanut revenues were increasingly incorporated as patrilineal goods, and cash-crop fields soon passed from the *yaal naay* into the hands of those cultivating the land, leading to the fragmentation of fire estates into small concessions controlled by fathers and their families.[43] In chapters 7 and 8, I will more fully examine these dynamics and the creative responses they engendered.

Settlement Patterns and Village Structure

Colonial discussions of the Seereer milieu were generally prefaced by references to Siin's demography and large population sizes. Nineteenth-century observers typically commented on Siin's elevated human densities and stable land occupation as features distinguishing the Seereer territories from neighboring areas. This demographic pattern was regarded as evidence of a long history of sedentary residence and a commitment to peasant terroir and tradition.[44]

We are told that, throughout the colonial period, Siin's rural panorama was dominated by small hamlets and park-villages scattered among fields and trees, a sight still prevalent today. The residential unit was the *mbind*, a small concession made up of several families organized in a compound headed by a family chief. Also called the *carré* by the French, the *mbind* generally stood as a circular cluster of huts, granaries, sheds, and walled partitions, surrounded by thornbush hedges or millet-stalk palisades. Compounds were generally built amid millet fields and stood at variable distances from each other. Cropping up among family concessions were other straw-and-reed constructions, such as mosques, churches, shops, or workshops. The rural space was veined by a web of dirt paths connecting residences to fields, wells, and water holes on the periphery of the village. Collectively, Seereer communities formed loose clustered arrangements, which, in the eyes of French observers, unfolded in anarchic designs, obeying no plan, order, or alignment.[45]

The dispersed, scattered quality of Seereer villages is a point on which all colonial observers agreed. This is well captured in Reynier's description of the Seereer habitat:

> The aspect of a Sérère village and its arrangement are curiously revealing of the taste and mood of the race: the habitations are as dispersed are they are grouped in Ouoloff villages, for example. The Sérère "carré" is implanted amidst terrains of culture and these terrains, themselves rather sizable at times, end at the limits of those of the neighboring carrés. When one traverses a Sérère village, it seems that this village is so

> to speak non-existent, so spread out is the dispersion which escapes observation. It is impossible to evaluate its importance at first sight, nor distinguish whether it counts 200 inhabitants or 1000. It reminds exactly of these immense *communes*, rounding up an infinity of minuscule hamlets, not to mention isolated habitations, that one still encounters in so many parts of France.[46]

This passage resonates with both earlier and later descriptions of the Seereer habitat, echoing for instance Noirot's late nineteenth-century testimony: "The villages [of the cultivators living in the hinterland] do not form compact agglomerations, but farms of sorts [that are] more or less distanced from each other and set up on the land cultivated by their inhabitants. Thus it is that the villages of Dioinn (from one of Dioinn's extremity to the other, there is no less than 6 kilom.), Poudaye-Toukhar, Ngoié, etc., occupy vast areas."[47]

True to the discourse of Seereer peasant conservatism, it was also a colonial habit to stress the sedentariness and stability of the Seereer habitat, generally through the trope of ethnic contrast. Just as Wolof cultural dynamism seemed apparent in the mobility of their habitat and compactness of their villages, the Seereer resistance to change was seemingly inscribed in the land as diffuse settlements and their attachment to the maternal soil.[48]

Against this background of growing homogenization of ethnographic depictions of Siin, it is noteworthy that the colonial ethnographic record is internally more nuanced and full of small, contradictory allusions to the dynamism of Siin's countryside. Once described, however, these variations were often quickly brushed aside to make room for perceptions calcifying about the conservatism of Seereer landscape.

Still, as postindependence research by geographers has pointed out, and colonial common sense to the contrary, Siin's settlements were never homogeneous in size and degrees of dispersion. Villages were perhaps better seen as points on a spatial continuum, ranging from "nebulous 'clouds' of dispersed compounds . . . to agglomerations of tightly grouped neighborhoods . . . to more stereotypical clusterings of households around central places and shared rituals."[49] In many ways, these differences reflected the dynamics of merging and splintering that shaped the social history of settlements in the region. An apparent trend in the evolution of Siin's rural habitat is that leading from dispersed village parks to larger village centers. Many of the larger village agglomerations emerged from proximate concessions (*mbind*) and hamlets gradually coming together into vast constellations of compounds stretching over several hundreds or thousands of meters, something noted by Bourgeau in the 1930s. These big villages, as they do today, generally centered around multiple nuclei, forming neighborhoods (*quartiers*) variable in size and population. These episodes of aggregation were moved by various historical forces: demographic growth, social and kinship alliances, migrations, ecological pressure, or resource exploitation. In time, larger settlements grew into bona fide centers of rural life, some even developing into *escales* (trading posts) or peanut trading centers, which attracted small traders, artisans, specialists, and clerics during the colonial period.[50]

Regional variation was also an important element of Siin patterns of settlement, as Noirot incisively noticed. If, in Siin's heartland, villages often formed large but widespread nebulae stretching farther than the eye could see, coastal settlements were by contrast much more compact and aggregated, "their huts [piled up] against one another, to such an extent that it is often difficult to circulate between them."[51] Thus, in 1823, Roger depicted Joal as a well-bounded agglomeration, made up of three distinct villages. Corre's account of his visits to Joal, Fadiouth, and Ké, all located on the Petite Côte, corroborates the impression of a more concentrated village environment along the littoral. When he traveled to Ndianda, however, a short two hours inland, Corre encountered a scattering of small huts, gathered about two islands, a landscape more reminiscent of the disseminated habitat found in Siin's interior.[52]

A different landscape also unfolded along political frontiers and near capitals. Aujas, for instance, noted that "on the marginal frontiers, there were *sangué,* that is to say wooden enclosures with frontal ditches, and *tatas,* or earthen fortifications." These works served as protection in times of war. Lastly, there were so-called *daga* villages. These were cultivation hamlets, populated exclusively by vanquished people. They were the *apanages* (feudal estates) of the *buur* (king) or his chiefs. During wartime the residents formed the king's personal guard. Unlike villages of the rural heartland, slave settlements and military outposts (*tata*) were more concentrated and smaller in size than farming communities.[53]

Seereer Cultural Economy: Domestic Production, Exchange, and Consumption Practices

Discussions of Seereer economy have generally emphasized that two systems or logics underwrote production, exchange, and consumption at the local level. They distinguish a circuit of production and consumption focused on meeting subsistence needs and a parallel circuit dedicated to the creation and accumulation of wealth for the lineage.[54] While intersecting, these two moments in the economic process operated in tension with one another because they involved different communities, with different moral interests, kin allegiances, and social spaces.

Colonial documents observe that compounds were subdivided into *ngak* (kitchens) referring to maternal huts, where submatrilineal relatives shared their meals. If the *mbind* was the unit of residence, the *ngak* was the locus of production and consumption, while the sublineage (*ndok*) was the community of accumulation. While the subsistence community was concretely localized in the kitchen, accumulation units were scattered across different concessions and villages. Clearly, Siin's economy was tightly interwoven with kinship structures and embodied the disjunctures and dynamics built into the Seereer bilineal system.[55]

Like many rural societies, the Seereer peasant economy has been predicated on a subsistence ethic and safety-first principle.[56] Because of their dependence on a precarious environment and capricious rainfalls, Seereer peasants have worked not to maximize their output but to ensure adequate, dependable grain yields and small surpluses. During most of the colonial period, Siin farmers managed a continued focus on subsistence cereal, even as peanuts occupied a growing share of the Senegalese economy. In time, however, they progressively lost their grip on the ideals of self-sufficiency. Pressured by the colonial administration, Seereer peasants conceded more ground and time to cash crops, and meeting food production requirements became impossible.

As they toiled for the reproduction of rural households, Siin peasants also worked toward accumulating a portfolio of maternal wealth. This community of goods was a sort of family insurance, which operated as a safety net to prepare for the unpredictable future facing most subsistence economies. Lineage resources also functioned as a ceremonial fund for the maintenance and reproduction of social networks and as capital invested in production. According to Gastellu's informants, the lineage was the veritable "community of interests for the Siin," and building the "wealth of the maternal hut" (*halal a ndok yaay*) was the "finality of economic activity in the Seereer milieu."[57]

These economic logics found concrete expression in the agrarian landscape as a complex system of field organization: the product of some harvests went into feeding kitchen members, while another set of fields was cultivated to shore up lineage assets.[58] Originally, millet and rice fields were devoted to self-subsistence, with cereal surpluses channeled toward amassing maternal wealth. The expansion of cash crops offered new opportunities for collective accumulation without compromising the existing subsistence economy. Agricultural production became increasingly compartmentalized, as millet farming continued to be directed toward food consumption, while the cash proceeds of peanut sales went to satisfy the immediate needs in the *ngak* (head tax, domestic purchases, credit reimbursement) before being routed toward matrilineal funds.[59] Traditionally, collective accumulation was rarely invested in production. Millet surpluses were exchanged for cattle, the most highly regarded form of wealth, generally in tandem with jewelry and cloth. Cattle have been a communal expression of economic and symbolic capital. Herds did not simply serve as emblems of the lineage's prestige and wealth. As a particularly liquid form of capital, convertible into social relations and spouses, cattle also played a pivotal role in ceremonial exchanges and the building of alliances and obligations. With the advent of modern farming techniques, collective wealth has also been progressively channeled toward the acquisition of instruments of production (carts, plows, etc.).[60]

Other spheres of Seereer production are not as well-known because they make broken appearances in historical and archival records. Several authors mention that women made pottery, but they never detail the scale, organization, or distribution of ceramic production.[61] Colonial writers are largely silent on ironworking, except for rare mentions that smiths manufactured tools and jewels, while we learn that wooden objects were acquired from Lawbe itinerant woodworkers. Slightly better documented are cotton production and textile manufacture. Households generally kept a cotton field, whose annual harvest covered the needs of the kitchen. Women spun and wove cotton yarns into *sor* (long strips of cotton cloth) that were sewn into clothes by casted artisans.[62]

In light of the dual commitment to subsistence and collective wealth, Gastellu has qualified Seereer economy as "egalitarian," taking precaution to note that this did not preclude the occurrence of competition within families or lineages. Rather, if the Seereer economy was egalitarian, it was only in the sense that equality among the members of a community was a state of mind, a model to strive for rather than a lived reality.[63] On some level, it is true that household-level redistribution, the inalienability of maternal goods, and focus on collective wealth have placed a brake on individual enrichment and exploitation. While there were obvious inequalities in village life, we also see considerable dispersal of authority and resources among different spheres and actors, at least as a tenet of the moral economy, if not in actual practice. In turn, some features of the village economy were compatible with a horizontal political structure organized around multiple loci of power.[64]

This does not imply, however, as many colonial observers were inclined to do, that until colonization the Seereer lived in autarky, largely removed from wider networks of political and economic exchange. Expanding the scale of analysis beyond the kitchen or lineage unveils salient arenas of differentiation and uneven interaction on the eve of colonial rule: conflicts between *ngak* and sublineages; inequalities between lineages; the emergence of wealthy specialist classes; the presence of a rural aristocracy with easier access to trading goods; not to mention the fact that Seereer villages were embedded in a hierarchical state structure with political power dispatched from Diakhao.[65]

Evidence of immersion in broader structures achieved glaring expression in several aspects of Seereer economy. While engaged in subsistence farming, villagers had to cultivate communal fields whose crops served to feed the king and his entourage.[66] Likewise, a commitment to self-sufficiency did not prevent the Seereer from being important precolonial suppliers of grain, who marketed their agricultural surpluses to Gorée and residents in Gambia. In fact, historically, trade and markets have complemented subsistence agriculture by permitting the acquisition of goods for collective and individual usage. Little information exists about local markets: the more provincial ones probably facilitated the barter of produce between villagers, while regional markets in Diakhao, Ndiongolor, or Diouroup afforded access to manufactured goods such as *sangara* (moonshine), knives, mass-produced cloth, glass trinkets, beads, or kola nuts, in exchange for foodstuffs, cotton, peanuts, or wood. Most scholars assert that commerce was an asymmetrical affair at the time of colonial contact (but see chapter 6), placed under the *maad*'s control, whose agents levied royal taxes on market transactions. Certain resources were also monitored based on their role in long-distance trading. Thus, because salt was an important currency in regional circuits, salt fields and their product were the objects of a royal monopoly, which was interrupted by colonial rule. Local cotton cloth was also long present in regional trading networks as a central bartering medium. Consequently, the *maad* exerted considerable control over the local textile trade, since the bulk of the production took place in village dependencies on the looms of royal slaves.[67]

Seereer consumption habits at the time of colonial contact had been shaped by centuries of interaction with European trade. One salient element of local immersion in global commerce, a feature that colonials wrote obsessively about, was the *apparently* prodigious consumption of alcohol: "according to information provided by Mr. Pichard, French Consul in Gambia . . . , no less than eighteen hundred thousand liters of trade liquor were consumed among the low-country blacks in 1863.—Consumption in 1873 rose above two million five hundred thousand liters." Authors such as Pinet-Laprade, Guy, and Carlus lamented the debilitating effects of alcohol on Seereer populations, some going so far as to foretell the extinction of the "race" because of chronic drunkenness. Others blamed French traders for having introduced one of the most condemnable traits of civilization.[68]

Certainly, the emphasis on alcoholism may have been exaggerated and used as additional fuel for the civilizing mission, but the consistency of colonial reportage suggests the reality of the phenomenon. The lack of comparative figures from other parts of Senegal prevent a critical assessment of Siin's purported alcoholic exceptionalism. Perhaps needed, also, is a more nuanced sense of regional variation: Boilat paints a ghastly picture of drunkenness in the Joal area and singles out Diakhao and its environs—the traditional *ceddo* heartland—as bastions of rampant inebriation. Corre, by contrast, writes that the residents of Fadiouth bought much liquor from French *négotiants* (wholesalers) but drank little of it, preferring instead to use it to barter with people in the interior.[69]

Crafts like pottery manufacture have persisted to this day. Others, like woodworking and textile production, have been almost entirely outstripped by foreign imports. The services that local industries once fulfilled have been partly or fully replaced by commodities obtained through international exchange. Iron tools have long been imported from elsewhere, though modern-day villages generally count one or more ironworkers who perform repairs or maintenance on metal equipment. Already in the last decade of the 1800s, cotton production was being abandoned due to the widespread availability of imported cloths. With the exception of certain handcrafted ceremonial garments, all the textiles encountered today in Siin come from the outside.[70]

Until we archaeologically unpack matters of colonial consumption in chapters 6 and 8, it bears noting that even the limited evidence presented here stands in curious contrast with how observers, even astute social scientists, saw the Siin heartland of the 1960s: "It is striking to find only few traces of these fifty years [1900–1950] of trading economy, when one draws up an inventory of the goods in a sérèr house, aside from a few tubs and cooking pots, a few dresses in chests, sometimes a few corrugated iron sheets on the roof."[71] Although commodification was certainly slow going before the 1920s, imported objects have remained consistent features of the nineteenth-century Seereer landscape. Almost a hundred years before Lericollais, in a series of sketches and descriptions of coastal houses, Corre already captured the influence of trade imports (rifles, knives, hoes, small chests) alongside locally obtained calabashes, mortars and pestles, wooden and ceramic containers, mats, and baskets, remarking that "what is least lacking are demi-johns reserved for *sangara*."[72] Though furtive, these glimpses into late nineteenth-century Seereer society raise more caveats about Seereer cultural conservatism. By accepting the validity of these assumptions for the recent and deeper pasts, scholars have underplayed the more dynamic parts of the historical picture.

Religious and Ritual Landscapes

Colonial observers were captivated very early on by what they saw as Seereer natural religion. Glossed as a primordial form of animism, to the untrained colonial eye Seereer religious practices stood in stark contrast with those of neighboring Muslim states, even when they were liberally Islamized. Early depictions are rather impressionistic, colored by colonials' green knowledge of Senegambia, the difficulty of grasping African religious concepts, and derogatory perceptions of African worldviews.

Pinet-Laprade, later echoed by Bérenger-Féraud, distinguished two gods for the Seereer: one presiding over justice and the other disposing of all the goods on Earth. Carlus added that the Seereer also practiced sun worshipping. He argued that these gods were less central to Seereer religious life than fetishes and snake spirits, which sorcerers had to appease with libations, rituals, and ceremonies. Overall, these authors saw Seereer worship as a sort of idolatrous sylvan paganism. These views held surprisingly fast in the minds of colonial administration and resurface well into the twentieth century—in the words of Aujas, for instance, who described Seereer religion as "animism paired with fetishistic beliefs."[73] To most early observers, Seereer religion remained but a relic of the primitive, pre-Islamic system of beliefs thought to have once bound all peoples across Senegambia. Animism was seen as the cornerstone of Seereer cultural conservatism, a direct determinant of the traditional social system. Most French authors also saw animism as the root of alcoholism in the Seereer country, though many were aware that excessive liquor consumption also took place in Muslim areas.[74]

The views of the French administration compare rather strangely with later accounts by doctors and scientists and by the local Catholic clergy who shared the lifestyle of Seereer populations and grew more intimate with traditional practices. A common misconception was to mistake the Seereer devotion to a pantheon of local spirits for polytheistic naturalism. Subsequent descriptions informed by missionary work present a different picture: "They believe in one god and a multitude of spirits, good and bad. They have little huts beneath which they deposit offerings to these genies. Other times, the genie must content itself with accepting these gifts at the base of a stick driven into the earth or milk libations at the foot of a baobab."[75] Contemporary writers increasingly recognized that the Seereer worshipped a supreme, creator-god (*Roog Seen*), accompanied by a constellation of spirits and ancestors (collectively referred to as *pangool*) that acted as intermediaries between human and divine authorities.[76]

Colonial authors generally struggled with defining the nature of *pangool*. They noted incredulously that spirits manifested themselves as snakes or insects, and they mocked the proliferation of fetish objects. According to Duby, "fields and villages also have their fetishes. Here it is an antique rock that superstition has enveloped, for times immemorial, with particular prestige. There, it is a tree that is the object of public veneration. . . . One frequently finds a small hut or round house, made of woven branches, covered by a conical grass roof, and isolated in the middle of a garden or millet fields; this is the hut of the *râb*, or djinn" (figure 15).[77]

Over time, it became clear that these fetishes per se were not the objects of Seereer reverence, and authors began to draw attention to what they correctly identified as the spatial dimension of Seereer spiritual life: "There are no fetishes in the sérère country; no statuettes, in wood or clay, representing gods or genies, there are only places: huts, trees, portions of bushland, devoted to worship, and, for such reason, revered, as are our chapels and our cemeteries."[78] These places generally consecrated more or less distant ancestors—"historic men, founders of cities, heroes, or large family chiefs, whose tombs were kept up by generations of admirers and that have been spiritualized by way of worship."[79] *Pangool* could also refer to earth spirits; in this case, places of worship—woods, singular trees, large rocks, small hills, tidal marshes, ponds, wells, and so on—demarcated the loci where the spirits were first encountered and where they dwelled. Given their diverse origins, *pangool* fell into several classes, forming a hierarchy rooted in how widely they were worshipped: ascending from family ancestors ministered to by household heads to compound shrines, village founders, and regional spirits, to the tombs of former kings venerated by the whole Siin population and requiring their own priests.[80]

15 Postcard, "Entrance of a Serer village, the hut of a fetish genie" (ANS, Iconographie, no. 0033; reproduced with permission from Archives du Sénégal)

Because of the *pangool*'s profound influence on the material world, it was necessary to minister to their needs and beseech their favors through food offerings. To ensure good fortune, clement rains, bountiful harvests, and ancestral blessings, people left calabashes of millet porridge by the shrines of the spirits they sought to supplicate; they also made libations of milk or trade liquor—another reminder of the entanglement of colonial objects with the Seereer cultural landscape. Combining these various threads, it is now sometimes accepted that Seereer religion was a form of ancestor worship supporting the belief in a unique god.[81]

The preponderance of ritual places of memory in Seereer life speaks to a spatialization of religion in rural landscapes. In effect, religion was tightly woven into daily activities and shaped the way in which Seereer peasants used and constructed their terroir. Tilling the fields and performing fertility rituals afforded a conduit of ancestral communion and a sense of social existence through the attachment to the land. The need to preserve one's cultivation rights, subsistence base, and obligations to ancestral shrines may have imposed a modicum of stability and some restriction on village mobility, such that the apparent permanence of Seereer settlements may have been religiously sanctioned.[82] Symbolically, this interdependence between the spiritual and the social is showcased in village founding accounts, where *pangool* feature prominently. Stories of original migration nearly always unfold under the watchful guidance of mystical forces, and oral traditions generally attribute the successful creation of a community, fire estate, or *bax* to the timely intervention of spirits.[83]

Colonial accounts also discuss funerary practices, perhaps the most visible feature of Seereer religion. Disagreements over whether each Seereer village or family had its own cemeteries, whether cemeteries formed alternative villages of the dead, or whether the Seereer had no discernible cemeteries at all probably attest to a variety of funerary practices. In effect, later assessments, dating to the late 1960s to 1970s, substantiate such variability, showing that cemeteries ranged from spotty constellations of burial mounds to smaller, variably clustered ensembles of tombs. By contrast, colonial descriptions of Seereer interment practices present a large degree of conformity, showing that the deceased was buried in a trench, capped by a straw roof, which was subsequently buried beneath a mound of sand or, in coastal areas, shell. Personal objects in the tomb accompanied the dead in the afterlife. The burial mound emplacements were demarcated by wooden stakes adorned with charms and amulets and by *canaris* (clay pots) where families performed libations. Colonial depictions show a surprising resemblance to earlier historic descriptions and archaeological examples of inhumation rituals. As mentioned previously, however, local taxonomies continue to distinguish two types of historic tombs: the massive *podom* thought to have been constructed long ago by pre-Seereer populations and the smaller *lomb* tumuli believed to have been erected by Seereer ancestors near existing or historic villages.[84]

Colonial writers held schizophrenic perceptions toward Seereer animism, praising it as an asset for peanut production or decrying it as a liability to colonial penetration. The French were content to exploit the Seereer resistance to Islam in their own battles against Muslim revolts in the 1860s and 1870s but subsequently moved toward an "indigenous policy" more tolerant of Islam.[85] Surely, colonial observers were aware that the Seereer had long been exposed to other religious influences. The Siin was surrounded by Muslim kingdoms and traversed by caravans of Muslim merchants. It had a small hybrid Christian presence on the coast made up of descendants of Luso-African communities and was in occasional contact with missionary efforts.[86] French authors, however, were inclined to emphasize the resilience of traditional Seereer religion. Corre's description of Siin's resistance to Islam and indifference to Catholicism was reiterated fifty years later by Aujas, who observed that world religions had made few inroads in the region. Admittedly, early missionary efforts proved slow going. The Catholic clergy collided with local priests and ruling authorities over doctrinal, symbolic, and political misunderstandings, tensions that were exacerbated by missionaries' aggressive and destructive tactics toward *pangool*.[87] However, resistance against missionaries and Muslim revolutionaries after 1850 was not simply a matter of differing religious worldviews but an effort to preserve the kingdom from foreign encroachment; it was a statement of political independence.

Religious change accelerated with the turn of the twentieth century. By 1910, the Siin boasted small but solid Christian enclaves (Diohine, Fadiouth, Joal) and today remains home to one of Senegal's largest Catholic communities. Islam grew in intensity after World War I, following the tracks of peanut farming. In the late 1960s, while traditional religion remained influential, Siin was overwhelmingly Muslim, and the Seereer religion and Catholicism have continued to lose ground to Islam since. These trends, however, mask a more complex reality. Again, clinging too closely to ideas of Seereer conservatism has led to the perception that religions in Siin were largely rigid, hermetic systems that ricocheted off each other like billiard balls.[88]

Historical evidence from the seventeenth century onward presents a more nuanced tableau, marked by relatively porous boundaries, mixing and borrowing, and creative adaptability within and between systems of beliefs.[89] Islam did not replace local religions wholesale but was grafted onto earlier religious structures and selectively translated into local religious repertoires. Widely documented in the colonial literature, the pragmatic incorporation of new ideas is exemplified in the generalized use of gris-gris (charms or amulets containing Koranic verses) purchased from *marabouts* (Muslim clerics) despite the overall distrust of Islam. The blending of Seereer ideas with Catholic symbols is also evident in the religious history of Joal's so-called Portuguese community. Even today, self-identified Muslims and Catholics often attend traditional ceremonies and rituals and continue to pay homage to *pangool*. In this regard, while nineteenth-century Siin religion can be described as a blend of diverse religious influences against a background of continuity, these subtle dynamics are overlooked by categorical models of tradition and its collapse at the hand of modernizing forces.[90]

Conclusion: Naturalizing the Seereer and Imaginations of Landscape

In the nineteenth-century French imagination, Siin's Seereer have been portrayed as quintessential African peasants, wedded to land, ancestors, traditions, and customs, and hostile to change and novelty. Colonial imagery, in Guigou's insightful wording, "is rife with this type of 'putting in perspective' [*mise en perspective*] based on oppositions presented as 'natural' between ethnic groups, whose mode of life and values are schematically described and contrasted one-to-one in antagonistic series."[91] In the case of Siin's people, such perspectival framing has drawn attention to those cultural traits valued as the most conservative. Naturalizing these features in the amber of timeless culture legitimated the opposition between Seereer tradition and Wolof modernism.

Landscape here played a pivotal role as a technology of colonial representation, an empirical justification for colonial imagery of Africa, and a product of the encounter between Africans and colonial aesthetics.[92] If the Seereer closeness to milieu and landscape practices represented natural signs of their incivility and resistance to progress, colonial observers also used ethnographic techniques to weave the Seereer into their physical environment and thus naturalize their position in an increasingly racialized landscape morseled out along the lines of ethnicity and custom. While sedimented through the compilation of *coutumiers* (descriptive registers of normative customs) and stiffening of ethnographic records, this process was also assisted by the use of photography, which proliferated in Senegal between 1901 and 1918 in the form of pictures and postcards of people, places, and landscapes. French ethnographic vignettes bundling ethnicity, culture, and economic activities into recognizable racial types, found compelling support in the indexical power of photographs, taken to "[freeze] the visible world on film and vouchsaf[e] its reality," and hence carry the force of wordless truth. They drew upon the implicit, innocent persuasion of visual signs and photographs to craft an "argument of images" that simultaneously entrenched the colony's moral and symbolic order and Seereer placement in its savage slot.[93] While Senegal's pre 1920 photographic corpus is varied, alternating between views of colonial infrastructure, buildings, monuments, and urban life scenes, images of the Seereer invariably depict Siin villagers as naked, covered with amulets, engaging in agricultural activities, or posing in front of mud-and-straw huts (figure 16); other common motifs include wide-angle shots of villages interspersed among Sahelian shrubs and cereal fields and pictures of fetishes and *pangool*. In these visual artifices, one finds a classic exemplar of the colonial gaze, crystallizing representations of the Seereer into allegories of African primitivity while muting the more dynamic qualities of Seereer social life—a representational economy revived in spurts in Sarkozy's Dakar speech.[94]

Parts of the colonial mythology of Seereer peasants have been recuperated by subsequent research, no doubt because it is accurate on some level to speak of a broad consistency in Seereer cultural life over time. As

16 Postcard, "Cerere man" (ANS, Iconographie, no. 0615; reproduced with permission from Archives du Sénégal)

the present chapter has attempted to show, however, there is danger in extending notions of Seereer peasant traditionalism as historical generalizations valid for both the past and present.[95] If the recent historical record attests to some stability in Seereer social structures, it also points to significant variation in land management, forms of labor, economic organization, residential patterns, kinship, and family structure in the past 150 to 200 years, offering a transcript of refashioned Seereer tradition rather than stubborn conservatism. While the colonial period marks a time of dramatic mutations for Senegambian societies, assumptions of continuity should be taken with a grain of salt for anterior contexts as well. Siin's history of contact with wider circuits of exchange and power reshaped local lifestyles, societies, and the broader economic systems in which they were embedded. What colonial writers in the mid-nineteenth century recorded as inert tradition was the outcome of centuries of interactions, syntheses, and recombinations. At the same time, the idea is not to see change and rupture everywhere. More modestly, we should keep in mind that neither change nor continuity can be taken as givens; they must be questioned and examined empirically at different points in time using the evidence at hand.[96] Placing the colonial present in historical perspective, we obtain a rich but incomplete picture of the Seereer landscape at the interface of past practices, their visible residue, and colonial depictions with roots in the Atlantic period and ties to the postindependence world. This shifting map forms a fluid baseline that can be compared with earlier lines of evidence—a point of anchorage for our dialectics of sources. As such, it creates a jumping-off point for traveling backward into the past and tracing the experiences of political communities in Siin as their histories fade into the Atlantic moment.

PART THREE

Atlantic Passages: World History and the Ambiguity of Materiality

In a report to officials of the Compagnie de Cayenne et de Guyane, general administrator of Gorée Island, Joseph Le Brasseur, depicted Senegal's political climate in the 1770s in sinister tones. Besides lamenting the dysfunctions of French commerce in the region, the document chronicled the deterioration of political relations between kingdoms and aggravation of social violence within them. At the apex of this spiraling chaos, he reckoned, sat the Saalum monarchy, where "caprice and need" determined the intensity of royal plunder and where nobilities of all ranks "[had] the right to conduct [pillages] . . . whenever they desire." He concluded that such circumstances "prove that to excite the *traite* [slave trade] in this kingdom, it suffices to dispatch a vessel and merchandises" (figure 17).[1]

Le Brasseur's reflections fit snuggly in a long catalog of like-minded observations by writers spanning the better part of the eighteenth century. They are reminiscent of Doumet, who, while in charge of Gorée Island a decade earlier, observed that the marauding that made Kajoor such an abundant supplier of captives and cattle was also the root of its degeneration. Long-term employee of the Compagnie des Indes, Pruneau de Pommegorge condemned the immorality of the slave commerce and Europeans' "criminal avidity" for transforming Africans "into ferocious beasts, [who] war among themselves and destroy each other only in order to sell their

17 "King of Barsalli [Saalum] (1732)" (Thomas Astley [ed.], *A New General Collection of Voyages and Travels* [London, 1745–1747], vol. 2, plate xxiv, facing p. 262; http://hitchcock.itc.virginia.edu/Slavery/details.php?categorynum=2&categoryName=&theRecord=5&recordCount=0)

compatriots to some barbarian masters." Similar views were reprised by later observers like British activist Thomas Clarkson, whose letters to the Count of Mirabeau decried the machinations of Moorish and European merchants—plying erratic African rulers with liquor or shiny trinkets—to provoke attacks on innocent villages and fan the flames of the slave trade. Clarkson's ghastly scenes of pillage, in turn, provided visceral support for the abolitionist denunciation of slavery in metropolitan Europe.[2]

Doumet, Le Brasseur, Pruneau de Pommegorge, and many others provide graphic eyewitness accounts of the toxic fusion of commerce and politics in Senegambia and how the "taste for human commodities" that steered the Atlantic economy jumbled up political equilibrium in Senegambian societies.[3] Along with other documentary archives—accounting records of annual slave transactions numbering in the thousands, reports of the escalation of local warfare and depredations, correspondence tracking the increasing frequency of droughts and famines—firsthand testimonies describe with grim consistency the intensifying climate of instability in eighteenth-century Senegal. As examined in chapter 2, many historians view this textual corpus as irrefutable evidence of the deleterious effects of mercantile capitalism on African economies. They argue that, by plunging the continent into a world of violence and extraction, the Atlantic trade choked industry, exchange, and initiative and set off patterns of inequality and dependence that still resonate today.

There is no disputing that the Atlantic trade system tectonically (and often negatively) impacted living conditions in Senegambia. We have seen, however, that scenarios of rupture have a tendency to assess history retrospectively; in doing so, they background historical pathways that do not lead in a direct way to today's global asymmetries.[4] By contrast, recent scholarship has given increasing consideration to stories of resilience, creative adaptation, and improvisation that belie the bold inevitability of narratives of deterioration and point to variability in Senegambian experiences. Historical documents provide clear evidence of continuities carried from pre-Atlantic times into the Atlantic era, as African institutions fused and clashed with European commerce. This shape-shifting political and economic landscape, in turn, oriented the strategies of Africans and Europeans alike. It was also dramatically recontoured as local cultural worlds and global markets grew more enmeshed. These region-wide dynamics altered the fates of coastal provinces, and, to situate my analysis of Siin's political and commercial life in the next two chapters, it is important to review key trends and departures in the making of Senegambia's Atlantic past.

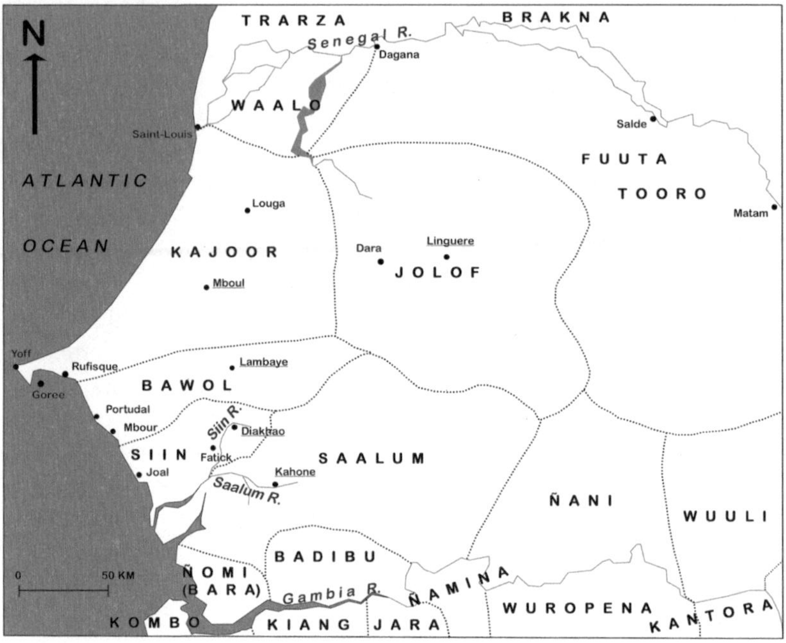

18 Principal indigenous kingdoms, northern Senegambia, nineteenth century

When Portuguese mariners first visited Senegambia in 1445, they encountered a complex political space dominated by Great Jolof, a large polity that enclosed most of today's Senegal and lorded over several tributary kingdoms (figure 18). While referred to as an empire in oral traditions, the nature of Jolof's sovereignty is opaque. Portuguese sources paint the polity as alternatively weak and strong, convulsed by internal dissent and at times overmatched by its vassals. While external accounts might have described times of heightened political trouble, another explanation is that centrifugal forces were not abnormal but part of the architecture of rule and that Jolof's political fortunes oscillated with the swing of regional conditions under different regimes—a pattern of political power that colors the history of Senegambian kingdoms. What is clearer, however, is that the region was connected to a vast sphere of economic exchanges straddling multiple cultural and ecological zones: Senegambian slaves, iron, gold, and cloth flowed to the Sahara and Mande world; the region received peppers and kola from the forest zone; manufactures, horses, and textiles arrived via desert routes; and grain and marine foodstuffs moved up and down the coast.[5]

Although the Atlantic trade was once framed as the "triumph of the caravel over the caravan," its effects on African economic exchanges were more ambiguous. One far-reaching, if gradual, consequence was the reorientation of regional economic gravities from the desert to the ocean. A more immediate one was the dislocation of Great Jolof. Landlocked, Jolof was blocked from coastal markets by its vassal states, who grew their cavalries and militaries via the maritime trade and effectively challenged its yoke. This resulted in a wave of emancipation that rippled across the region, and by the 1550s the kingdoms of Kajoor, Waalo, Bawol, Saalum, Siin, and northern Gambia had all risen to independence.[6]

However, the oceanic commerce also presented important continuities with the pre-Atlantic era, beginning with its reliance on long-standing economic structures. Historians recognized long ago that the Atlantic trade did not pioneer new exchanges but largely extended commercial patterns previously in place, especially along desert routes.[7] Nor did it bring anything that Senegambians did not already have, make, or trade. Portuguese merchants continued to supply African notables with the horses, textiles, and luxury goods they previously obtained from Moorish, Moroccan, or Juula traders. If maritime exchanges triggered increasing competition with Saharan economies, the latter continued to absorb African products, including slaves, well into the nineteenth century. What the Portuguese presence did do, however, was to enhance the scale of economic circulations, connecting people and resources in ever-expanding ways. More generally, the worlds of commercial improvisation that emerged along the coast were largely subservient to the whims and good graces of rulers and their functionaries. Europeans had not only to satisfy exacting local consumer tastes but also to pay taxes and customs to the kings' fiscal agents (*alcatis*) in exchange for protection and continued access to consumer markets.[8]

In 1600, after four decades of encroachment from French, Dutch, and English ships, Portugal relocated from Senegal to the lucrative slave markets of west-central Africa. This departure ushered in a climate of international competition, which, answering to the rise of the New World plantation complex, pushed a hitherto modest slave trade to the forefront of regional exchanges.[9] It also saw the crystallization of a new commercial order overseen by companies chartered by royal governments, which, following mercantilist principles, acted as virtual branches of European states and regulated overseas economic operations. Europeans established a string of fortified towns (*comptoirs*) on coastal islands—the Dutch on Gorée Island (1621), the British at James Island (1651) in the

Gambian estuary, and the French in Saint-Louis (1659) at the mouth of the Senegal River—connected to regional markets via small coastal outposts (*escales* or factories).[10]

While European nations battled to carve out spheres of commercial control, they were limited by a number of factors. First, commercial rivalries sparked hostilities between European *comptoirs*, a game of "musical trading posts" that saw islands pass back and forth between Dutch, French, and English hands. Holland achieved a short period of economic ascendancy in the 1660s and 1670s before being permanently ousted in 1677 by France, whose monopolistic claims over Senegal were vigorously contested by Britain during the eighteenth century.[11] Second, European nations inherited the scaffolding of cultural and commercial conventions that had constrained their predecessors' activities. They remained tangled in a tortuous commercial bureaucracy, which required them to pay taxes on traded goods and basic supplies, ply monarchs with gifts and credit, and remain dependent on African and Luso-African middlemen. Europeans could seldom guarantee their security, and their factories were often exposed to exactions from local rulers. Commercial activities were often suspended by warfare or retaliation from rulers over late payments and diplomatic disagreements.[12] Thirdly, Europeans' mercantile aspirations also suffered from their own interventionism in African affairs—what Ly called a "mercantilism of daily calculi," a divide-and-conquer policy hinged on pitting African rulers against each other in the service of trade. The goal was to incite armed conflicts and pillages to drive up slave sales, prevent the pooling of political power in the hands of single rulers, and thwart alliances between kingdoms. These stratagems often backfired, however, because African rulers proved just as adept at exploiting inter-European rivalries and because warfare could mean the suspension of trade. Moreover, the policy of fanning the flames of conflict to enhance slave revenues often impacted local food production, which directly endangered subsistence in French and British *comptoirs*.[13]

If the eighteenth century witnessed an increasing diversification of regional goods and a dramatic global expansion in the volume of the slave trade, Senegambia's economy retained much of its character. As indicated by Curtin, it remained a one-export area whose outbound trade was historically dominated by one commodity: hides and cotton cloth under the Dutch in the seventeenth century, captives between the 1680s and 1790s under the French and British, followed by the ascendance of gum until the mid-nineteenth century, and the subsequent domination of peanuts.[14] Senegambia also articulated in complex ways with the international slave trade. While a chief supplier of captives in the sixteenth century, the region never contributed more than 10 percent of total slave exports after the 1640s. If its *relative* contributions decreased over time, the proportion of slave to nonslave exports in Senegal increased between 1690 and 1790, reflecting the centrality of captives in French commerce. Year-to-year fluctuations aside, the slave trade appeared very profitable and rose during the first four decades of the eighteenth century. By contrast, absolute exports decreased steadily after 1740, never to exceed 5 percent of the total number of captives shipped to the New World.[15] These changes probably reflect commercial disruptions caused by the frequent civil wars that rattled northern Senegambia (such as those that opposed Kajoor and Bawol between 1749 and 1760), the increased use of slaves *within* Wolof kingdoms, and the growing importance of gum in the regional economy.[16] The reconfiguration of labor markets, which kept more and more captives at home and funneled them toward gum collecting, cereal production, and domestic work, anticipates the transition to "legitimate commerce" after the slave trade was abolished in 1808.[17]

There is unmistakable evidence that Senegambia's sociopolitical environment worsened as the Atlantic demand for slaves ballooned over time. The escalation of hostility between coastal kingdoms fostered an unstable landscape of violence, marked by military confrontations and slave raids, particularly along borders. European policies partly encouraged the ambient insecurity, which achieved its most gruesome expression during the British occupation of Saint-Louis, when the conflict engineered by Governor O'Hara between Moorish tribes and Waalo flooded Saint-Louis with over eight thousand captives in 1775 and 1776.[18] At the same time, the particular conditions of trade in Senegal also constrained the destructiveness of enslavement. First, Senegambia's relatively modest participation in international slavery, combined with its relatively even political field, discouraged the intense wars of conquest and enslavement observed on the Slave and Gold Coasts, and in Central Africa. Small-scale manhunts targeting a few enemy villages and smaller acts of pillage and kidnapping were often more common than massive military campaigns. Another important element, given the nature of regional enslavement, concerns the origins of coastal captives, the majority of which came from elsewhere via inland caravans. The proportion of slaves originating from the Middle Niger has been estimated at about two-thirds of total exports during the eighteenth century.[19] These dynamics in no way diminish the social impact of human predation. They do, however, indicate that between the contingencies of interkingdom conflict and the reality of smaller-scale slave hunting, some farming communities were likely more exposed to chronic insecurity, while others in more insulated provinces enjoyed better fortune and less disruption.

Another facet of the instability associated with eighteenth-century enslavement was the occurrence of endemic famines and subsistence crises. Slave raiders ransacked fields, pillaged crops and granaries, and seized cultivators, which unknitted farming routines and food-growing capacities. Insecurity also eroded traditional mechanisms of solidarity, assistance, and storage, which had once mitigated local vulnerability to droughts, natural calamities, and subsistence shortages. Food security was also intricately connected to European grain consumption. In good years, cereal was traded widely between producers and consumers, but in lean years the costs of feeding growing numbers of export slaves placed heavy pressure on food supplies. Starvation boosted slave sales, which exacerbated food crises to the paradoxical point where European merchants were either left scrambling for food or had to momentarily abandon the trade.[20]

The issues of economic loss and degradation are likewise equivocal. On the one hand, the slaves-for-weapons equation was axiomatic of the Senegambian trade, but it did not engulf all salient economic transfers in the region. Quantitative estimates show that the proportion of items like beads or textiles in total consumer imports rose steadily after the late seventeenth century, while "means of destruction"—arms and spirits—never made up more than 15 percent of imports and began to decline at the time when the slave trade reached its climax.[21] The growth of the agricultural sector further illustrates the finer linework of Senegambian commerce and its interdependences. European archives make no secret of the importance of Kajoor, Bawol, and Siin as cereal suppliers for the French colony; in fact, Senegalese millet circulated all the way to western Saharan markets. During the 1700s, grain commercialization stimulated the growth of internal slavery in Wolof states, as slaves captured near and far were increasingly absorbed into domestic farming. One likely outcome is that agricultural production increased, despite the ambient food crises. Another implication is that the food tributes extracted from farmers could be substituted for captives, especially when slave exports began to wane after the 1750s, and channeled toward the acquisition of goods of value to the state. Conversely, the food trade also allowed peasants to use their surpluses to obtain foreign products, thus complicating theories about the aristocratic monopoly over Atlantic transactions.[22]

The problem of Africa's deepening dependence on Europe is a more delicate one, assessed obliquely from export figures, given the paucity of information on African production. One gross trend over the eighteenth century is a decline in nonslave exports, suggesting the replacement of some local industries by mass-produced goods or their partial disappearance, like hides after the seventeenth century. Some sectors, however, fared better against foreign manufactures, such as iron-producing regions in eastern Senegal. If the introduction of European iron bars after 1720 propelled the demise of metallurgical centers like Galam, others like Bundu kept producing substantial amounts of iron into the 1890s.[23] Some writers have also hypothesized that the expansion of domestic slavery in the eighteenth century spurred the productivity of certain sectors, like cotton and artisanal cloth production. In fact, the threefold increase in locally made cloth in the early 1700s and its use as currency suggests strong coastal demand for cloth. Gum also benefited from the Atlantic economy, stimulated by demand in high-end textile industries like France, where gum was used to set dyes in colored fabrics. Northern Senegal's gum market expanded after the 1740s to become Europe's principal supplier, while increasingly competing with the profits of commercial slavery.[24]

The Atlantic trade reconfigured Senegal's political topography in profound ways, setting local polities on a path of centralization and militarization and spurring the surge of warrior aristocracies. After the fall of Jolof, oceanic commerce provided a material basis for the growth of state power and increasingly shaped its nature. Following the model of Lat Sukaabe Fall (r. 1695–1720), rulers rushed headlong into the slave trade to secure the means of state reproduction: they procured the goods necessary to build large corps of *ceddo* warriors, force villagers into tributary relations with the state, and coerce enemies and reward allies. At the same time, centralizing reforms also made kingdoms internally unstable. They intensified aristocratic rivalries, political factionalism, and problems of dynastic succession, which led to outbreaks of civil wars between 1750 and 1790.[25]

The Atlantic trade also inflamed political tensions already present in Senegambia—between state and village, aristocracy and peasantry, warriors and clerics. State encroachment upon the traditional rights of peasant communities is a key storyline of Atlantic Senegambia. Oral and written sources, for instance, credit Lat Sukaabe with confiscating village lands and redistributing them as political fiefs.[26] Subsequent taxation brought farmers deeper into the orbit of state sovereignty, while *ceddo* depredations disrupted the conditions of peasant existence, especially in the hinterland of Bawol, Kajoor, and Waalo, forcing communities to abandon their terroir and leaving villagers suspended between "the reign of tribute and protection and the reign of theft and arbitrary violence."[27] Alongside the rise of enslaved warriors, another important sociological transformation was the unprecedented rise of domestic slavery in Wolof, Seereer, and Pulaar kingdoms and its growing role in all economic sectors.[28] Finally, the Atlantic economy sparked a number of Islamic resistance movements, starting with the upswell of maraboutic revolts that swept northern Senegal between 1673 and 1677. Clerics rose in rebellion against the enslavement of Muslims and the actions of aristocratic slavers. While unsuccessful, these revolts widened the rift between predatory nobilities and their peasant subjects and gradually drew rural masses to Islam, which became synonymous with popular resistance to oppression. In doing so, they provided a template for later movements of religious resistance in the eighteenth and nineteenth centuries.[29]

Where does Siin stand in this mosaic tableau? While the province was an intrinsic part of Senegal's maritime economy and while accepting that it was subject to the insecurity that reorganized Atlantic Senegambia, many believe that Siin avoided the intense destruction that convulsed Wolof and Pulaar kingdoms. A commonly held explanation is that Siin's moderate involvement in the slave trade largely shielded its populations from the rampant instability of northern Senegal. The province's relative immunity to Atlantic turbulences may also derive from other integrative mechanisms. For one, historians have stressed the strong character of Siin's monarchy. The king's firm administrative control over the kingdom's provinces and his attendant ability to keep *ceddo* under check are evoked as a likely source of stability. The dynamism of Siin's sociopolitical institutions provided a second buffer. In particular, some authors view the persistence of lamanal organization in the Seereer countryside as a safeguard against royal encroachment.[30] Lastly, it is also assumed that Siin's ethnic homogeneity and religious unity curbed the eruption of social disturbance. While brief mentions of Islam in Siin can be found in some accounts, the Seereer appear to have rallied behind the local religion after the fifteenth century, and contacts with the Muslim faith do not appear to have significantly inflected Siin's historical trajectory.[31]

Siin's ambivalent situation as both a site of violence and a place skirted by its worst effects illustrates the sinuosity of historical pathways in northern Senegambia. What is interesting about these scenarios, however, is the extent to which they rest on late nineteenth-century depictions of political and social organization during the Atlantic era. As examined in the previous chapter, the ethnohistoric baseline pieced together from colonial documents cannot be assumed to hold true for earlier times. This is not to deny the idiosyncrasies of Siin's historical development. Instead, it highlights the need to investigate their nature and appreciate that Siin's uniqueness has a history. It also means recognizing that Siin's singularity did not pluck it out of the stream of Atlantic mutations but that it is itself the product of Atlantic mixtures and that the processes invoked to elucidate Atlantic changes in Siin and northern Senegal may not quite completely work.

While often told as a story of epochal rupture initiated from the outside—triumphant mercantilism, the dismantlement of native societies by the slave trade, or rocky transitions to postabolition commerce—we see that, even at a broad level, the violence of Senegambia's Atlantic past is shadowed by continuity, variability, and possibility. That global entanglements were inflected by local conditions, with different effects in different places, affirms the multistranded character of Senegalese history and asks us to consider: How did different social groups weather the effects of the Atlantic economy? What kind of social existences could they fashion in response to enslavement? And how did they seek to remake order in its wake? How was the concentration of state power mitigated by local political agencies? What economic activities unfolded parallel or transversal to the slave trade, and how were peasants integrated in them?

Extending recent arguments that scenarios of state predation do not match the histories of decentralized societies in Senegal's southern fringes, Siin provides a useful environment for revisiting the accuracy of these narratives *at the epicenter* of political centralization.[32] The province is a ripe ground of alternative political history because, unlike the aforementioned nonstate societies, it shared the political culture of Wolof and Pulaar kingdoms, the examples after which scenarios of state violence are modeled, even as its trajectory also appears to deviate from that of its neighbors. Moreover, given that Siin's postcontact history is held to be somewhat exceptional, a reassessment of its Atlantic-era past through the combined lens of archaeological, historical, and oral archives promises fresh perspective on its unique pattern of centralization, assumed cultural homogeneity, and enduring grassroots institutions. The tensions between regional conditions and local-level politics, then, give impetus to the arguments presented in chapters 6 and 7, which take on the ambiguity of Siin's state sovereignty and its articulations with grassroots spheres of power, and the incorporation of imported commodities into village societies, respectively. As we will see, villagers emerge as critical actors in the construction of power, politics, and economy in the region.

FIVE

Ambiguous Kingdoms: States, Subjects, and Spatialities of Power

The prince did not crown himself!
It is God who crowned him!
WORDS FROM ROYAL PRAISE DRUM SONG[1]

Paradoxes of Predation: Peasants and Polities in Atlantic Senegal

Published in 1943, André Villard's popular *Histoire du Sénégal* is a colonial classic that paints an exalted account of French enterprises in Africa. When the book concedes a few lines to indigenous existence before Europe, it does so with telling sobriety, imagining a Senegal where life, in the depths of history, was "more or less that of the countryside before the conquest: wealthy and revered chiefs bedecked with gold, rich in women, horses, and camels. The free men cultivate millet and vegetables, and tend to the herds. The despised castes manufacture objects and weapons. But warriors surround the great men and from time to time they pillage the harvests of enemy races or those of their own. Neither art nor techniques appear to have been very advanced. Of the great towns, only ruins, sherds, and memories remain."[2]

Not much is surprising in this diorama, which leans on a long lineage of Western renderings of African sovereignty, an imagery perfected by colonial ideologues in the early decades of French rule. Officer-ethnologists, like General Faidherbe, continually alluded to the disregard in which "negro potentates" held their subjects, in anecdotes like the following: "At the time when the slave trade was flourishing, a venerable *marabout* [Muslim cleric] from the desert came to Cayor with a resplendent horse. The Damel, or king of Cayor, wanted it at all costs. 'I asked one hundred virgin girls for it,' said the holy man. Thereupon, the *tiédo* [slave cavalry] jumped on their horses and, on Damel's order, lay waste on ten villages near Gandiole to procure the requested merchandise."[3] Whether such stories are based in fact matters less than the kind of truth they ordain—a particular vision of African politics. Faidherbe's account builds on a sturdy library of commonplaces cemented in the course of the eighteenth century—to be sure, the scenes of waste and carnage conjured by Doumet, Le Brasseur, or Pruneau de Pommegorge but also the motifs of "tyrannical ruler," "perfidious princes," and "lawless anarchy" adorning the pages of travelogues of authors like Lemaire and François de Paris as early as the 1680s. This collective of writings staged the dramatis personae of Senegal's Atlantic tragedy: the kingly despot, whether valiant or sanguinary, and its twin opposite, the body of commoners that endured the arbitrariness of sovereign power. (A third political avatar will emerge later in the figure of the [warrior-]cleric, though we will not examine it here).[4]

It would be easy to dismiss Villard and Faidherbe's historical miniatures as relics of colonial fantasia. We would, however, overlook a critical link in the chain of historical discourse in Senegambia; namely, that just as colonial writers inherited their allegories from earlier authors, these allegories, now ostensibly stripped of their ideological bearings, have permeated into subsequent scholarship and continued to frame what we know of life and society in precolonial Senegal. There is nothing inherently wrong with Atlantic worlds peopled by kings, farmers, and other social groups. What is trickier is that, in recuperating these historical images, we have also inherited certain expectations about the relationship between political classes. And, in this respect, modern accounts of Atlantic Senegal have not always significantly differed from those of colonial scholarship.

The figure of the state has been a recurrent motif in Senegambian history. Whether glossed as *kingdom* or through its metonymic extensions—sovereignty's human infrastructure of monarchs, governors, dissident princes, and slave warriors—the trope of the state has centrally organized interpretations of the regional past. This focus stems largely from oral and written archives, where matters of the state are omnipresent. Regional traditions chronicle major episodes in the history of kingdoms, starting with Njajaan Njaay, the mythical genitor of state polities in Senegambia, and trace the fates of dynastic lineages and deeds of individual monarchs. Likewise, rulers, political dignitaries, and slave soldiers are marquee protagonists in documentary archives, consistently portrayed as the movers and shakers of regional history. One byproduct of the kingly hold on politics has been the kind of state vampirism perpetuated by the large Muslim kingdoms of Kajoor, Bawol, Saalum, and Fuuta Tooro—a trajectory also attributed to the province of Siin. While authors have been careful to note that enslavement had limited currency in the Siin, they have also portrayed the polity as a strongly centralized administration, dominated by aristocratic elites and their armies. Farming communities, by contrast, have been placed on the receiving end of pillages, living under the threat of terror, at the mercy of authoritarian rule.[5]

The analytical investment in kingdoms has by all accounts been productive. By centering attention on questions of governance, it has highlighted the consolidation of power into the hands of aristocratic families and the development of increasingly abusive regimes in northern Senegal. At the same time, in reducing the political field essentially to the actions of the state, this "view from the kingdom" has also occluded other dimensions of the construction and negotiation of power. Three problems can be identified. First, commoners have been backgrounded. While this reflects their partial absence from many sources, one consequence is that the free peasantry is presented as a powerless bloc victimized by rulers blinded by greed and ambition. Farmers tend to be evacuated from the fields of political agency, only to be relocated on a more passive and conservative historical plane. A second issue is that the king-and-peasant couplet tends to reprise dubious disjunctions between politics and society where states stand for the former and commoners occupy the latter and whose articulation is portrayed as oppositional rather than co-constitutive. This happens at the expense of looking at how politics are fashioned in and through society. Or, in the instance of Senegal, how state projects and modes of rulership have acquired contingent shape in relation to resistance, consent, or composition on the part of nonelite actors.

A final difficulty lies in the way in which the state has been imagined in Senegal's Atlantic past. What the state is and does hovers around a configuration of features: pyramidal hierarchy; paramount rulers; centralized administration; control over people, resources, trade, and the means of destruction; territorial unity; and the capacity to make war, institute laws and distribute violence. These are not necessarily inaccurate, but positing the state as such—a centralized (raptorial, absolutist) entity—*presupposes* a particular functioning, instead of asking how power in different parts of Atlantic Africa might have been conceived, produced, and organized. In effect, the kingdoms evoked in Senegambian history bear a family resemblance to the models of the state born of the archives of European political thought. This can be problematic, since reading African political trajectories through categories hailing from other parts of the world may simply miss distinctive properties of political life on the continent.[6]

This chapter outlines a different vision of politics in Atlantic Senegambia, by putting the twinned images of potentate and peasantry to the test of Siin's material history. My premise is that, whereas these categories are consonant with the changing balance of power in Atlantic Senegambia, in their common scholarly usage they also cloud the specific qualities of governance in places like the Siin, which operated on the backstage of Atlantic commerce—and even possibly at its center. Instead of accepting the state as a concrete object with intrinsic characteristics, I prefer turning to the question of statecraft. This shift dissolves the concept of the state into an analytic of *processes*—*projects* of sovereignty, authority, and power—whose operation can only be understood in relation to specific historical and cultural environments. These milieus of power are not only restricted to state control but also structured by the work of customary institutions and grassroots energies. The resulting interplay between states and subjects has left numerous clues in the archaeological record, and I use data from the 2003 and 2011 settlement surveys as starting points for my analysis. Evidence of village distributions and arrangements between AD 1400 and 1900 invites new ways of reading archival records. Specifically, it stirs up some internal tensions that are seldom picked up in the historical literature, and these tensions expose trails of alternative interpretation about past political culture. Particularly interesting, I will argue, is the role of material worlds in *framing* and *limiting* political authority in precolonial Siin. I call special attention to how the political landscapes fashioned by village communities both constrained the operation of statecraft in the region and marked out certain material avenues for the performance of state authority—giving to the Siin kingdom an ambiguous and volatile character. Landscapes, here, emerge as contrarian terrains, their reluctant force in full sight. More than brute physicality, their materiality refracts *social* principles of power active in various provinces of Siin and echoed in oral traditions—moral sentiments of alienation and suspicion toward kingship—while offering a transcript of how this political unconscious acted on history.[7]

Altered States: Reimagining Political Life in African History

One cannot, therefore, write either the history of kings or the history of peoples; one can write the history of what constitutes those opposing terms, one of which is never infinity, and the other of which is never zero. M. FOUCAULT, *"SOCIETY MUST BE DEFENDED"*[8]

Before getting to the dynamics of power in Siin, let me make a brief excursus into the realm of theory, to examine how students of the African past have tackled the question of statehood. Since my analysis of Atlantic landscapes tacks between different source materials, the discussion moves freely between historical, anthropological, and archaeological literatures to highlight important debates and perspectives. I address two trends, specifically—first, how African state systems have been (and should be) conceptualized and, second, the relationship between states and the material world—with the optic of formulating suppler accounts of politics in Atlantic Africa.

The problem of state-like political forms in Africa's past can be approached in a number of ways. One response, favored by an earlier flavor of anthropology and still embraced today by certain segments of the archaeological establishment, might claim that most of the African polities referred to as states are actually not states at all but rather political types enjoying a lesser degree of organizational complexity than, say, the historical states and empires of Europe, Asia, and South America. In this perspective, then, the African state is closer to something like a complex chiefdom or an intermediate-level polity. There are difficulties with this line of argument, beginning with its developmentalist gospel.[9] Three incongruities come to mind:

The concept of chiefdom has been proved to be notoriously slippery, its bounds trespassing heartily into state territory.

A rigid category of state seems unable even to accommodate some of its exemplars; its contours have been constantly expanded, narrowed, or qualified to make room for inconsistencies and empirical evidence that challenge its typological premises.

Finally, because of these discrepancies, typological models underestimate the extent to which political orders in parts of precolonial Africa resemble the institutions of medieval Europe, which are viewed as instances of (archaic) states.[10]

Hidebound taxonomic units, in sum, seem mired in hopeless confusion; indeed, they are fated to founder on the bewildering variability of political arrangements that have proliferated throughout world history.

Other scholars have embraced a much different tack, underwritten by a drive to explain the idiosyncrasies of African forms of power. In effect, as Lonsdale reminds us, Africa's puzzle, its most distinctive "contribution to human history could be said to have been precisely the civilized art of living fairly peaceably together *not* in states."[11] More than seventy years ago, Fortes and Evans-Pritchard introduced the distinction between "stateless societies," where political structure consisted of a horizontal network of competing lineage segments, and "state societies," a loose agglomerate of variably centralized polities. Scholars on the continent have long recognized that *state* and *stateless* do not represent ideal types or essences per se but rather the poles of a graduated spectrum; indeed, they have been keenly attuned to the gamut of political expressions ranging between centralized and decentralized organizations.[12] Following Fortes and Evans-Pritchard, then, and eschewing any pretension of evolutionary thinking, Africanist historians and ethnographers have used the word *state* (or alternatively *kingdom*) more or less as a synonym for *centralized administration,* leaving the specification of its mechanics in various times and places to empirical scrutiny.[13]

Beneath this umbrella, accounts of the state have traveled a number of paths. Much ethnographic literature in the two decades preceding and following independence sought to dissect the cultural principles organizing political society in various parts of the continent. The outcome has been a flurry of classic analyses, often couched in the ethnographic present, that break down the rationalities driving inequality, stratification, and authority in local communities.[14] Collating society-specific observations into more general statements, these studies provide a series of caveats to universal models that locate power in centralized institutions, individual offices, vertical stratification, and economic accumulation. Rather, they show that "central authority, often of a ritual nature, [can be] paired with a power structure that is diffuse, segmentary, and heterarchical, as well as societies in which considerable complexity is achieved through horizontal differentiation and consensus-based decision making. The distribution of power among several corporate entities (e.g., lineages, secret societies, cults, age grades) can be regarded as a strategy that has successfully resisted in a variety of ways the consolidation of power by individuals."[15] Abstracting up from the turf of ethnography, other authors have sought to reflect more comparatively on the conditions informing African mechanisms of power and the singularity of African statehood. Herbst, for instance, drawing on earlier research by Goody and others, roots the specific physiology of African state building in demographic and geographic circumstances.[16] In precolonial Africa, low population densities mixed with the plentiful abundance of open land and widespread practice of rain-fed agriculture, which militated against the development of state systems grounded in territorial control, the exploitation of land and productive surplus, the management of specialized crafts, and the accumulation of wealth in staples, currency, or manufactured valuables.[17] Instead, central authority was constructed on the ability to mobilize human labor (wealth in people) and access long-distance trade, and power was located less in wealth or force (given the ease with which discontented subjects could move with their feet) than in the proliferation of political offices, ceremonial titles, and religious prestige.[18] Population and distance, moreover, acted as a break on the effective exercise—Herbst uses the term *broadcasting*—of power, which diffuses concentrically from the heartland in decreasing circles of efficacy, rather than unitarily across a bounded territory.

Another important strand of research has looked to the past and examined the formation and transformation of African political structures in the crucible of the Atlantic era. Many studies have observed the consolidation of power in the hands of individual rulers across West Africa between the seventeenth and nineteenth centuries. They document the growth of centralized administrations headed by absolute monarchs, their authority unrestricted by other decision-making bodies. While fueled by local dynamics, state expansion is largely attributed to the participation in long-distance commerce, which drew kingdoms into the updraft of enslavement, militarization, and regional conflict.[19] Studies of state building in Senegambia have very much focused on these processes. The stress on state predation and violence has also trickled into archaeological research, for instance by the late Brahim Diop in the kingdom of Bawol.[20] In the mirror of historical sentiment, Diop interpreted the village vestiges strewn across the region as indications of the desertions and displacement occasioned by the rise of absolutist regimes.

The great merit of these perspectives is to have clarified the bases of sovereignty in Atlantic Africa. Their downside is that, by foregrounding the political superstructure and instrumentality of power, they assume a sovereign gaze coextensive with state supremacy and do not go far enough into tackling the problem of consent and the relationship between central institutions and the societal tenets sustaining them.[21] This critique, in turn, has sparked the writing of more expansive accounts of precolonial states that have closely attended to the interpenetration of kingly power and social institutions nested in households, religious life, and gender structures. Other studies, in turn, have explored the establishment of intricate political organizations without centralized rulership, working horizontally through counterpoised corporate entities rather than vertically through stratified structures.[22]

In the end, the picture pieced together from this historical scholarship is consonant with David and Sterner's warning against the indiscriminate use of "statejackets" in the African past.[23] The root of the problem, as they see it, is that state categories tend to presume the forms, directions, and dynamics of political agency, that they force evidence into analytical blocks, and that ultimately they fail to account for political forms fuzzier than the "ideal types" of ethnological thinking. At their worse, state terminologies group under the same label political arrangements that may have not shared the same sources of power, logics of rule, and extent in authority. What David and Sterner recommend instead is a more productive strategy that requires unpacking the distinctive character and constitution of African political organizations. Their suggestion converges with an increasingly well-traveled body of literature in anthropology and the social sciences that critiques coherent visions of state (even in its modern garbs). A number of key points can be highlighted.

First, current scholarship cautions against glossing the state as a self-evident entity, a concentrated apparatus of rule and decision making casting its homogenizing shadow over a territory and population. Abrams, for instance, has shown that there is nothing obvious about the state, which he sees as an ideological fetish, a powerful illusion with concrete effects in the world.[24] The solution, then, is not to attempt to think through the state and smooth out its rough edges but to look past its mesmerizing aura. Indeed, we should reconfigure states (even highly authoritarian, highly centralized ones) as not-always-coherent ensembles of institutions, practices, and discourses organizing operations of power and political relations in given polities.[25]

In a second related vein, recent scholarship has sought to complicate heavy-handed ideas of sovereignty as accruing naturally to the state.[26] It shows how sovereignty does not represent a coherent domain of force contained in state forms but that stately claims to power are always in competition with other spheres of authority. These, in turn, have varying degrees of credibility for the different constituencies making up a polity; in other words, sovereignt*ies* are always plural, partial, overlapping, and gradated, which means that state-centralized power can never completely mold the spectrum of political choices and actions and the consciousness of actors navigating them.[27] State projects sometimes backfire; authority can be contested, law and order subverted; unintended effects abound, all of which work to (re)frame the horizon of state power.

A third element, which flows from the indeterminacy of state sovereignty, is that central power cannot just be asserted but that it has to be performed and reperformed ceaselessly, in order to shore up its legitimacy in the eyes of different social "audiences."[28] State injunctions always run the risk of being disrupted or discredited, and, to protect themselves from this risk, rulers must labor to cultivate receptive publics and seize the minds and imaginations of those they seek to rule. Some performances can be irruptive and violent, branded onto the flesh of bodies. What they consecrate there is the arbitrary right of the mightiest. Sovereignty is more gripping, however, when it seduces and infiltrates modes of thinking, its efficacy gauged in the extent to which it is picked up or recognized by imagined others. This restless oscillation between coercion and consent, between domination and hegemony, is precisely what was at stake in the theaters of power of Atlantic Africa.[29]

A last realization is that states are always *cultural productions—statements*, as Corrigan and Sayer intimate—that is, politics and culture twine up in the construction of statecraft.[30] Encounters between political regimes and their constituencies are inevitably mediated by cultural, moral, and religious sensibilities. The outcomes of power bids and their effectiveness—whether state mandates are viewed as fair or illegitimate and, thus, whether their prescriptions are accepted, resisted, or ignored, and by whom—are always partly dictated by local perceptions, positions, and calculations. Thus they are partly determined by the state's success in mobilizing culture and history as vehicles of power. In the end, the take-home message of these four points is that to decipher the riddle of statecraft in past African societies, we must first understand the institutions of power and their cultural bedrock and the ways in which they bound polities to their subjects. We must investigate, in other words, what Lefèbvre called "geometries of power," the evolving sets of *articulations*, from material encounters to symbolic contests, linking social classes and their political visions.[31]

Archaeologists are in a key position to capture these articulations—and their effects on all parties, including state formations themselves—in material-spatial terms. Indeed, recent archaeological conversations have taken stock of contemporary calls to replace the study of the state with a focus on sovereignty.[32] As outlined by Adam Smith, such "archaeologies of sovereignty" would explore the "practical regimes of authorization and subjection . . . that reproduce, and undo, sovereignty in interactions from the spectacular to the everyday."[33] Four important elements stand out from this formulation. First, politics is not just produced by the state, at the center, but in a constellation of places and contexts. Smith has clarified this relationship elsewhere, when he notes that "space is not prior to political relationships but rather created within them, [such that] not only must we examine spaces as political activities but we must also describe authority *in terms of the spaces it assembles*. Once space is understood as a set of relationships, conceptions of the political that rest on absolute foundations, such as the State, seem clunky and ill-fitting" (italics added).[34] Second, we need to consider the actions of rulers as well as subjects in the fashioning of political order and modes of power. Third, sovereign power is never a sure thing, a self-fulfilling prophecy. Centralized authority is often the ground of challenges, and state legitimacy must be constantly affirmed, negotiated, and effected. And, fourth, this perspective urges us to reframe analyses of political experience around an investigation of the fluid set of material practices, relations, and conditions imbuing political life in the past.[35]

Archaeologists in Africa have not been insensitive to these views, even if they have not addressed sovereignty sui generis.[36] Indeed, they have a successful track record of studying the construction of political authority and cultural rationalities informing historical expressions of power in Africa.[37] While the archaeology of African statecraft has produced compelling cartographies of political order, it has been more interested in their production from the standpoint of royal administrations than their intersection with popular institutions.[38] By focusing on the materialization of royal ideology in architecture and landscape, this work has sometimes been too Althusserian in its vision of state control, too generous in its portrayal of the state's ability to extend hegemony, too swift in assuming people's identification with the life created for them by political regimes.[39] On more material grounds, this perspective has also perhaps overplayed the instrumentality of space as a vector of royal domination and medium for the diffusion of royal power. One way to expand these portrayals of African political life entails paying closer attention to the roles of elites and commoners and center and periphery in the making of political milieus. It also demands closer inquiries into the multiple spheres of sovereignty cohabiting in landscapes. Finally, it requires an attunement to the ambiguous workings of power and the incompleteness of hegemony. Materially, this means acknowledging that spatial worlds may not always be a foolproof conduit for the manufacturing of obedience but may at times contravene projects of statecraft and embody implicit statements of critique for or against centralized power.[40] It means paying attention to a later aspect of Althusser's thinking, what he referred to as the "aleatory" nature of materialism: the chancy, unforeseen outcomes of material encounters.[41] In other words, it means investigating what in chapter 1

I called the reluctance of landscape and how it has historically configured the shape of state politics in Atlantic Africa.

Lest the concept of reluctant landscape be mistaken for its affinities with recent research, I should note that it does not represent an "art of not being governed" encrypted in geography and conditioned by it, as James Scott posited for the stateless societies of Zomia. Nor does it simply allude to the materialist determinism underwriting Herbst's study of the state.[42] I am uneasy with the former for the opposition it marks between people and state and with both for their naturalist views of landscape as a material determinant that precedes and constrains human possibility. Unlike these perspectives, reluctant landscapes do not locate power's limits in essential nature or culture but rather in a thoroughly *political* geography, fashioned in the meeting of state, society, and the material world. In this reading, centralization is a tentative *process* shaped in relation with peasant landscapes and gradated in time and space.[43] Much as monarchies contended with spheres of power organizing rural life, state sovereignty oscillated depending on its ability to coax and coopt grassroots politics as dependent provinces cycled between moments of greater centralization and self-determination.[44] The why and the how of these rhythms is what must be determined.

Histories of Statehood in Siin

The intelligence which Maissa Waly had demonstrated in this occasion permitted him to be recognized as worthy of kingship. The people of Mbissel elected Maissa Waly in a plebiscite, who accepted to be king provided he was seconded by the wealthy Wa Ngom who thus became the first *Diaraf* of Sine. N. DIOUF, "CHRONIQUE DU ROYAUME DU SINE"[45]

Histories of the state are deeply implanted in Siin and interlaced with trajectories of statehood elsewhere in Senegambia. On the one hand, the Siin kingdom is given foreign origins. The "gift" of sovereignty came from the southeast, carried by Gelwaar exiles fleeing war at home. In exchange for hospitality, their guide, Maisa Wali Joon, placed his qualities of leadership in the service of Siin, on the condition that rule be equitably shared with Seereer representatives. At the same time, Siin's monarchy is also portrayed as ambiguously local, its roots fusing with Wolof myths of originary statehood in Waalo and Jolof, at least according to some oral narratives. Traditions brim with tensions, of course, which make them difficult to read. For instance, some Seereer accounts vehemently deny that Siin was ever under the yoke of Jolof. More intriguing, however, are other narratives in Siin and Waalo that accord a seminal role to the Gelwaar ruler. In these traditions, it is Maisa Wali himself who gave Njajaan Jaay (the first Wolof king) his name and recognized his supernatural qualities. It is also Maisa Wali who willingly subjected himself to the authority of the Jolof monarch and, leading through example, convinced other regional leaders to follow suit.[46] Temporal lines are dissonant, in the sense that nearly two hundred years supposedly separate Njajaan Njaay and Maisa Wali. Yet the two moments meet nonetheless, an encounter that seems to mark a certain excess in the burden of sovereignty, which cannot be fully absorbed by the local. The king of Siin is seminal to the existence of Jolof, even as he relinquishes his own power and submits to the new empire, much like foreignness is supplementary to autochthony. Both buttressing and interrupting the identity of power, the foreign enchants and perturbs. This supplementary knot also signals a seeming aporia in ideologies of indigenous kingship: the initial sovereign owes his crown to an earlier king (whose office cannot yet exist!), and the latter inherits his rulership from historical precedence (that he somehow already created!). Sovereignty seems like a risky business resting on the shaky foundations of an endlessly deferred origin.[47]

At once inside and outside the space of Senegalese sovereignty and yet central to the genesis of Jolof, Siin ironically resurfaces on the historical stage at the moment of Jolof's dislocation—the king maker turns into king slayer. A critical chapter in Jolof's demise began when, around 1510, king of Siin Mbegaan Nduur invaded Saalum and defeated a number of Tukulor chiefs to found a new kingdom. This act of sedition reflects the new deal of Atlantic exchanges. From its commercial ties to the coast, the royal family of Siin acquired wealth and military power that an enfeebled Jolof could not contain. The creation of the Saalum kingdom sowed the seeds of secession, and other polities followed in its steps. The final and decisive strike was administered by the king of Kajoor, which had grown too big for Jolof.[48]

If oral traditions locate Siin's political institutions somewhere between corporate monarchy and heady rulership, written accounts add their own ambiguous strokes to portrayals of the Siin kingdom in the sixteenth and seventeenth centuries. Cadamosto inaugurates this narrative confusion as early as the mid-1400s when he describes the Seereer of Siin as living free from the yoke of "the King of Senega [Jolof] and any other seignior." This passage is obscure since it claims not only that monarchical institutions, supposedly created in the 1350s, were no longer in place one hundred years later but also that the province refused Jolof's sovereign reach. One possible explanation, suggested elsewhere by Cadamosto, is that his visit found Jolof in a state of vulnerability, headed by a puppet king propped up by lesser lords and always under the threat of deposition—observations supported by later observers like Gomes and Münzer. This period of regional fragility might have also spilled to Jolof's vassal kingdoms, and Cadamosto's description of Siin may refer to a period of momentary interruption of Gelwaar rule and ascendance of lamanal authority, perhaps corresponding to the reign of common man Panga Yaay Sarr recounted in oral traditions. In the last quarter of the sixteenth century, Cape Verdean explorer André Donelha offered a different assessment when he affirmed that all Senegambian kingdoms, including Siin, were vassals of the *farim Cabo* (king of Kantora) on the Gambia River and that all paid tribute to the *Mandimansa* (king of Mali), claims that fly in the face of commonly accepted scenarios. Less than two decades later, Rainolds describes the kingdom as ruled by *Jocoel Lamiockeric* a possible match for the *Jokel Laba* of dynastic lists. However, the name *Lamiockeric* does not figure in oral memory, though it has been hypothesized that the term could refer to *lam*, short for *lamaan*.[49]

Contrasting accounts, however, also exist. Contemporaries of Donelha, for instance, portray local monarchs as strong rulers. Dapper speaks of a certain Walla Silla, described as "a great fetisher" capable of fielding a large army from all over the country. While the numbers advanced—five thousand men and six hundred horses—are fanciful, they nevertheless convey the power and authority of the king. At the same time, Dapper is careful to mention the king's weak power of taxation or the fact that important decisions were made in concert with a council of advisors; he echoes here an earlier observation by Almada that while the king was "war-like . . . a good and brave general . . . [w]hen he decides to make war, he first takes council with those whom he calls together for this purpose." Should we see clues of a rising concentration of royal power in Dapper's indication that Walla Silla's influence rippled across the Siin, from Joal to the interior? The fact that those living in Diakhao were said to possess large numbers of horses also suggests the pooling of wealth and military power near the capital. Other observers provide related accounts of Siin's king as a powerful monarch able to enforce security throughout the kingdom. Speaking more generally of royal authority on the Petite Côte, Lemaire remarks that "no princes in the world [are] more respected, and more absolute than these negro kings. Such deference is an effect of their severity: indeed, for the smallest thing committed by one of their subjects, and that would be disagreeable to the Prince, ensues an order to cut his head, confiscate all his goods, and enslave all his family."[50]

What are we to make of these various descriptions of the *maad a Sinig* as alternatively weak, of lamanal extraction, and subservient to other polities, or reigning over the kingdom with an iron fist? One option is to blame the unevenness of written testimonies on Europeans' distant knowledge of coastal societies and mistaken reportage. In a more hopeful vein, evidential disparities can also hint at the historical dynamism of political traditions in Siin. They may indicate that political arrangements did not remain stable or move in a straight line from stateless to state but that the polity's internal organization fluctuated over time and space. They might also attest to the continued relevance of nonnobles to the affairs of the state, at least through the 1600s.

By the first two decades of the eighteenth century, the situation appears clearer. With some consistency, archival records represent the king as a tyrannical ruler and allude to repeated internal wars of succession, where the French variably sided with the king or his contenders depending on the perceived interests. Royal exactions targeted village resources through pillages, theft, and forceful retributions. Le Brasseur indeed observes that unlike the *damel* of Kajoor, who frequently enslaved the subjects of his realm, the king of Siin "does not have this right or . . . does not want to have it because his kingdom has fewer people" and only wants captives he can seize during wars. In fact, several authors remark that the bulk of the captives traded in Joal in the eighteenth century were not enslaved by the king of Siin but captured further north and into the interior by Moor traders or neighboring kings and brought to the *comptoir* via overland caravans.[51] As elsewhere in northern Senegal, European writers comment on the monarchs' increasing hold on power at the expense of free persons. Le Brasseur, for example, described one such successful ruler, who is sometimes identified as the Biram Pate of oral traditions. This king was apparently a consummate politician and negotiator, connoisseur of just prices and quality merchandise. When captives abounded, Biram Pate traveled to the coast and took charge of trading activities himself, fixing prices and demanding certain commodities. This king was also adept at political calculations, mobilizing and arming political exiles and dissenters in neighboring polities, with the objective of overthrowing leadership in Kajoor, Siin's sworn enemy.[52]

Written sources also document the growing role of crown captives in the expansion of the state; captives acted as security forces against the expansionist designs of other polities, a military police to ensure the payment of taxes, and the primary producers of slaves. Domestic slaves were also instrumental in supplying the royal court and provincial administrators with agricultural goods and craft products. Slave labor, in other words, provided the material foundations of the *maad*'s power, and it is unsurprising that the political influence and economic position of enslaved warriors (*ceddo*) benefited handsomely from the revenue of the coastal trade.[53] Conversely, the rise of the *ceddo* has been viewed as detrimental to free peasants, who were de facto hunting ground for warrior parties commissioned by neighboring polities and subject to random exactions by slave bands carrying out the wills of the Siin monarch and his noble titleholders. While it is possible that these depredations were sometimes tempered by the presence of royal village representatives, the monopolization of power at the state center was synonymous with royal encroachment upon the rights, privileges, and lives of peasant communities. This process took place gradually. On the basis of oral accounts of peasant-state relations, for example, Galvan has hypothesized a slow erosion of peasant prerogatives, which began with the progressive ousting of grassroots notables from decision-making circles and kingly councils, and accelerated with the extension of royal control over the political domain once managed by the *jaraaf*, culminating in some regions with the annexation of lamanal territories that were gifted to loyal followers. However, Galvan is also careful to note that this process of subjugation had limits, insisting, with Seereer oral memory, that the Gelwaar ultimately remained reliant on peasant elites for supernatural services, a delicate balancing act, since spiritual forces were the guardians of the polity's good fortunes.[54] Galvan's insights are important not just because he wisely cautions against exaggerating the power omnipotence of royal administrations but also because the idea of mutual paradoxical dependences between the domains of state, peasant, and spiritual power finds intriguing support in archaeological landscapes.

Archaeologies of Politics: Settlements in Siin during the Atlantic Era (1400s–1900)

What clues does the archaeological record hold about past political life, then? Before getting to this question, it is necessary first to delineate Siin's phenomenal landscape, as one might track it archaeologically after circa AD 1400. This reconstruction rests on two regional survey datasets collected in 2003 and 2011 (figure 4). This work located over 385 occupations, 313 of which were inhabited between the fifteenth and twentieth centuries (using changes in pottery styles and well-dated imported artifacts as chronological devices).[55] Many of these sites were settled, abandoned, and resettled over the years and thus contain more than one occupational context. They range, on average, from light material scatters to dense and extensive clusters of trash/habitation mounds (table 2). Settlements tend to leave thin material signatures, which indicate a pattern of residential mobility over time, a tale of sites inhabited for short periods of time and relocated elsewhere. Artifact collections consist chiefly of locally produced pottery, followed by smaller quantities of imported and local manufactures (glass bottles, beads, tobacco pipes, glazed ceramics, metal objects, spindle whorls). My discussion in this chapter will focus on the *spatial attributes* of residential vestiges—their structure and distribution in the broader milieu—spanning the 1400s–1870s period (phases Va and Vb). The object assemblages associated with these settlements will be discussed in chapter 6, and material evidence from later sites spanning the mid-nineteenth to the mid-twentieth century (phase Vc) will be examined in chapters 7 and 8.

It is important to stress, given the current state of archaeological knowledge in Siin, that my depiction of settlement dynamics is impressionistic in a number of ways. First, because the evidence discussed below derives primarily from survey research, the material landscapes it conjures unfold like a pointillist canvas. Sites coalesce into a cloud of dots, each node standing as a proxy for complex (and often intractable) bundles of historical and spatial relations. Surveys record archaeological sites whose traces are visible on land surface. While one gets a useful sense of horizontal exposure, these data tend to shortchange vertical layering. They generally underrepresent older, deeply buried sites, whose deposits have lower superficial presence. Moreover, for lack of chronological precision, they also often presume that all sites within one phase are cotemporal when these might have been occupied at different points in a time interval. Second, the landscapes examined here are largely residential. They focus sharply on settlement histories but provide a more limited assessment of other types of historical sites: sacred groves, cemeteries, religious places, and so forth. Finally, settlement space is difficult to "read" in Siin, due to the impermanence of sites and poor preservation of architecture. House remains are almost never encountered. Rather, the best signatures of past residence come in the shape of artifact aggregates of various sizes and extent. In some areas, centuries of farming activities have disrupted archaeological ruins and dispersed them beyond their original location. Site deposits in Siin unfold as a near-continuous artifact cover stretching unevenly across sandy fields. While breaks loosely mark where sites might begin and end, site boundaries and sizes are sometimes difficult to make out beyond loose estimates. However, while

Table 2 2003 and 2011 surveys: Site counts and ceramic phases

Phase	Chronology	2003 site counts	2011 site counts	Local ceramic assemblages	Historical context and benchmarks[a]
Phase III	ca. AD 700–1000	2[b]	5	Paste characteristics: sandy, gritty paste, wide variation in texture and firing. Characteristic vessel forms: (1) jar with everted lip; slip or twine impressions (interior rim and exterior); (2) collared oblique jars; fish-vertebrae roulette, multiple twine decoration, or twine-incision combination; (3) closed ovoid jar; slipped rim.	Construction of sand and shell tumuli; evidence of connection with Saharan political economy
Phase IV	ca. AD 1000–1400	11[b]	30	Paste characteristics: sandy, gritty paste; medium to medium-fine texture; occasional airy pasted fabric; sand-, shell-, organic-, or grog-tempered. Characteristic vessel forms: (1) beveled open bowl/platter; (2) open bowl; twine decoration; (3) short-collared oblique jar; slipped rim and twine below collar or multiple decoration (slipping, wavy comb-dragging, incisions, appliquéd dots or cordon; twine or fish-vertebrae roulettes); (4) long-collared oblique jars; slipped rim and twine below collar; (5) carinated jars; burnished; slip, twine, rib-and-groove; (6) ledged jars/pots; lipped rim, and twine below. Note: explosion in diversity of forms and decor and heterogeneity of vessel types.	Migrations of Seereer from Senegal River valley (11th century); Gelwaar migration and formation of the Siin kingdom (mid-1300s); continued contacts with Saharan political economy
Mixed phase III–IV	ca. AD 700–1400	25	—		
Phase Va	AD 1400s–1700s	33	27	Paste characteristics: sandy, gritty paste, well-consolidated; medium-fine with occasional medium texture; sand- and grog-tempered. Characteristic vessel forms: (1) closed oblique jar; slipped rim, groove, and twine; (2) closed oblique jar; twine field and overlapping incisions; (3) open bowl; slipping, twine or comb channeling. Note: homogenization of vessel types.	Early phase of Atlantic system; consolidation of Siin kingdom

(*continued*)

Table 2 *(continued)*

Phase	Chronology	2003 site counts	2011 site counts	Local ceramic assemblages	Historical context and benchmarks[a]
Phase Vb	18th century–ca. 1870s	70[c]	80	Paste characteristics: hard-pasted, homogeneous fabric; medium-fine to fine texture; sand-, grog-, or shell-tempered. Characteristic vessel forms: (1) closed ovoid jar; flat or beveled lip; slipped rim; twine (lip top, body), comb channeling, or incisions; occasional shell or millet cob impressions; (2) closed globular jar; same as closed ovoid jar; (3) open bowl or plate (flattened lip or T-rim); burnished and reduced surface; plain or occasionally slipped or twine decorated; occasional finger-grooving below rim giving the appearance of a faint carination; (3) globular jar with short everted neck; dusky red or purplish red slip/paint at rim; row of punctuations/stamping followed by twine or incisions; red/white paint on later vessels; (4) steamers; open bowl or pan with perforations across the body. Note: early phase marked by resurgence in ceramic diversity, followed by a reduction of variability over time.	Height of Atlantic slave trade (18th century); transition to "legitimate commerce" (post-1807); lead-up to formal colonial annexation (1861); movements of Islamic resistance (1860s)
Phase Vc	ca. 1870s–1950s	15[c]	78	Paste characteristics: hard-pasted, homogeneous fabric; generally medium-fine to fine with medium-coarse texture for certain vessel types; sand- or shell-tempered; smooth, waxy or dry, rough surfaces. Characteristic vessel forms: (1) globular jar with short or long everted neck; slapdash painting (red and white); geometric incisions; (2) closed ovoid jar (beveled or flat lip); *enduit* or paint; (3) deep open bowl or platter (beveled or flat lip); black vegetal *enduit*; twine; (4) globular jar with long everted neck and heavy shell-tempered fabric; twine with dusky red or pinkish orange slip; (5) steamers; paint, twine roulette. Note: phase marked by reduction in quality of decoration and manufacture.	French colonial occupation (1861–1960); dissolution of Siin kingdom (1898); independence of Senegal (1960)
Mixed phase Vb–Vc	18th–20th centuries	10	—		

Note: Because settlements often contain multiple chronological contexts, counts refer to identifiable occupations rather than sites per se. The table includes only residential contexts and does not list tumuli and iron scatter sites.

[a] These benchmarks and time lines are based on conventional oral and documentary history.

[b] These sites often contain mixed phase III and IV deposits, making it difficult to confidently assign a date range. Because of depositional conditions, counts tend to overestimate phase IV contexts and underestimate phase III ones.

[c] Phase Vb and Vc are often mixed on eighteenth- to twentieth-century sites, preventing definite chronological assignments. Phase Vb counts are probably inflated at the expense of phase Vc numbers.

this geographic gestalt is fuzzy, it is not inscrutable.[56] Archaeological landscapes are not disfigured beyond recognition. Settlement topologies are blurry, but they consistently pattern. Sheets of artifacts and heaps of debris across the countryside signal the presence of sites, like a smeared fingerprint of past settled life. Let us now review what picture of habitation and movement obtains for the Atlantic era.

We saw in chapter 3 that archaeological site distributions, in the centuries preceding European explorations, conform to a pattern of relative human mobility. Many communities in the Siin were small and transient, hugging the coast and tidal corridors. This moving geography, however, was anchored by a number of villages that larger populations occupied for several centuries. Deposits from the 2011 survey—which yielded three large village-sized sites close to the coast, in addition to the two villages previously documented in 2003—suggest that longer-lived, sedentary occupations might have been more numerous than previously expected. The exact nature of linkages between smaller and larger sites is unclear. One possibility, since bigger occupations appear to predate smaller settlements, is that the latter are the product of a gradual process of village dissolution over time, perhaps in relation to resource depletion, social conflict, or declining rainfalls. Another, given the fact that village locations are discrete and some areas contain only ephemeral residential remains, is that different parts of the Siin experienced different occupation histories, falling on a spectrum between centripetal and centrifugal habitat.[57]

Following the advent of Atlantic contacts in 1444, settlement densities sharply declined along Siin's littoral, although human communities persisted around Joal, the kingdom's principal port during the Atlantic era (figure 19; table 3; figure 20). Concurrently, interior areas witnessed a demographic explosion, as occupations sprouted up over the hinterland, perhaps in relation to the organization of the kingdom and growth of the Atlantic trade. Oral traditions credit this period with a wave of village formation, as the kingdom's political center inched its way toward the interior after the fifteenth century, from Mbissel and Ndiol to Ndiongolor and Sanghaie, before settling on Diakhao. Although political change appears to have rippled across the landscape, no major urban center or rigid settlement hierarchies stand out from the survey. European testimonies support this picture as they describe regional capitals as small villages that only departed from neighboring settlements in their labyrinthine and security-oriented internal organization. Archaeologically, settlements present no real sign of regional concentration, stratification, or centralized organization. In fact, the settled landscape

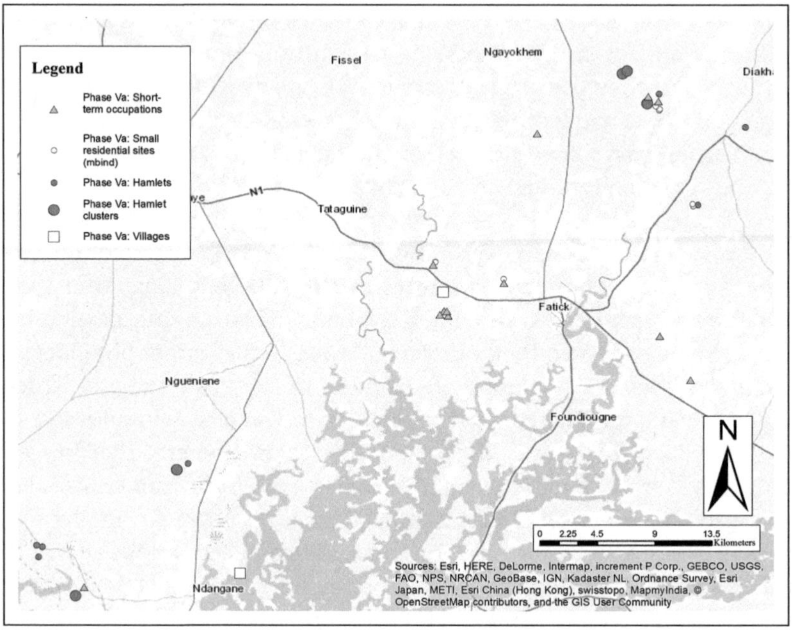

19 Siin settlement landscape, 2003 site inventory, Fatick, Diakhao, and Petite Côte regions, phase Va, ca. AD 1400–1700

Table 3 2003 site inventory: Transitions in settlement types by survey region, ca. 1400–1870s

	Phase Va			Phase Vb			
Site types	PCO	FAT	DIA	PCO	FAT	DIA	Total
Short-term occupation	1	8	3	4	17	12	45
Mbind		2	5	4	9	9	29
Hamlet	4		3	2	4	7	20
Hamlet cluster	2		3	3	2	6	16
Village	1	1			1	4	7
Total	8	11	14	13	33	38	117

of the fifteenth century appears to have given way to a more homogeneous residential geography. Sites are broadly comparable in structure, generally an assortment of small mounds, blanketed by a variably dense mantle of artifacts. While settlements show some areal variability, their sizes are surprisingly even across the surveyed areas. Sites tend to be modest (over 80 percent of the 2003 site assemblage falls below the 1.5-hectare

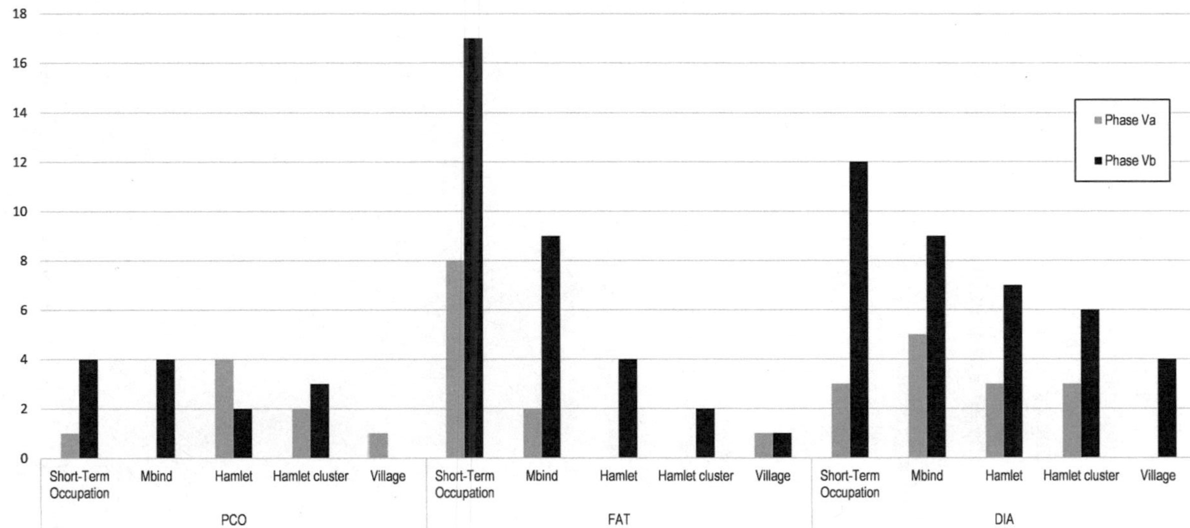

20 Phase Va and Vb settlements (2003 inventory): comparison by survey region

mark). They seem to correspond to clusters of hamlet-sized habitations. A few more substantial occupations also exist, including the coastal site of Mbissel, which regional traditions remember as Siin's first royal capital. Further in the interior, we also note a site complex near Ndiongolor, which corresponds to a former capital mentioned in historical and oral records. Problems of boundary determination make it difficult to assess whether the stretched out deposits formed a single residential ensemble or a constellation of one or more aristocratic residences surrounded by smaller satellite sites, possibly settled by slaves, retainers, or commoners. Diohine, deep in the Siin interior, is another larger village site of the early Atlantic era, though oral traditions collected from village elders insist on its resolutely nonaristocratic origins.[58]

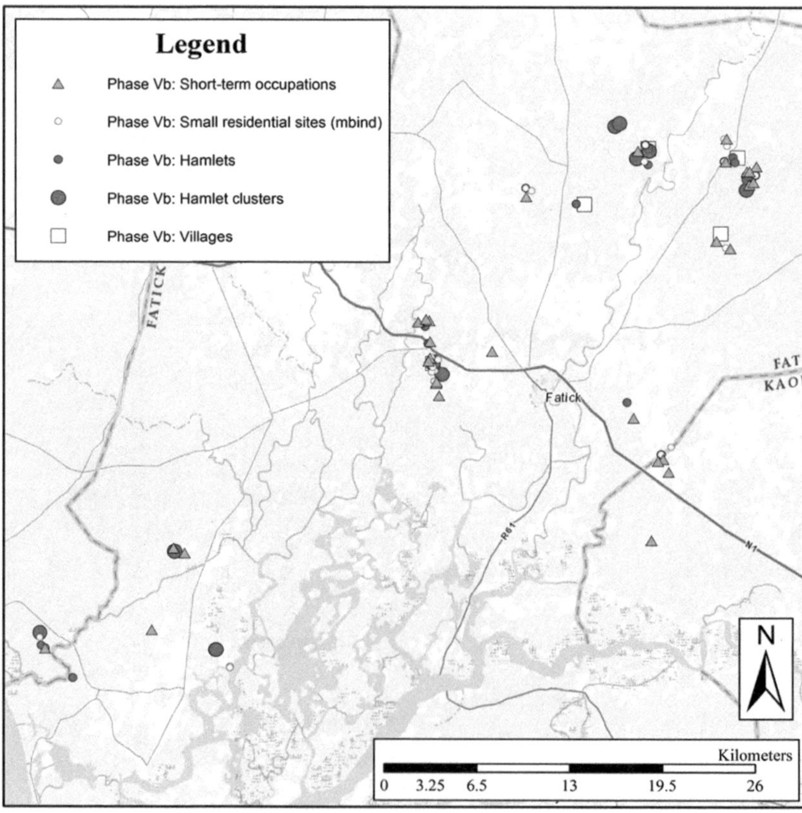

21 Siin settlement landscape, 2003 site inventory, Fatick, Diakhao, and Petite Côte regions, phase Vb, ca. AD 1700–1870

Table 4 2003 site inventory: Settlement frequencies by survey region, phases III–IV, Va, Vb, and Vc

	Phase III–IV	Phase Va	Phase Vb	Phase Vc	Total
FAT	15	11	33	15	74
DIA	19	14	38	9	80
PCO	27	8	13	1	49
Total	61	33	84	25	203

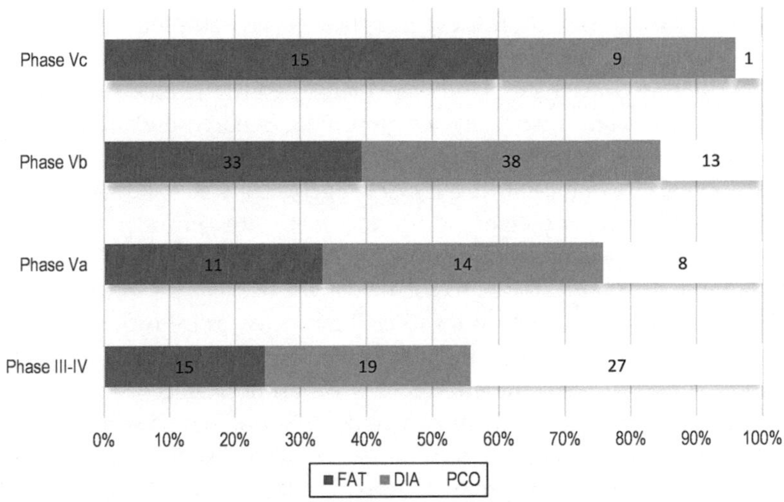

22 2003 settlements: frequencies by phase and survey region

Settlement organization in Siin experienced further mutations during the eighteenth century (figure 21; table 4; figure 22). First, this period marks an effective withdrawal of villages and their population away from coastal areas. Second, we note changes in the character of the spatial habitat, with a distinct increase in site counts, transiency, and mobility. There are more than twice as many archaeological settlements during the 1700–1850 period than in the previous phase. Compared to AD 1400–1700 habitations, sites of the eighteenth and early nineteenth centuries are generally much smaller and more ephemerally occupied, mostly short-term residences and single-concession habitations, resulting in a diffuse human landscape. Exceptions can be seen in the development of a few large bona fide villages, often in the most inland part of the province, that feature rosaries of mounds strung around one or more open areas, reminiscent of the central plazas associated with quarters in modern-day rural areas.

These spatial changes likely coincide with the intensification of Atlantic exchanges and political strategies of the Siin state, which created conditions ripe for human displacement. Archival correspondence suggests recurrent conflicts and skirmishes between Siin and Kajoor, its powerful northern neighbor, and alludes to frequent but low-intensity military activity along border villages during the seventeenth and eighteenth centuries. Written sources also mention that interkingdom conflicts spurred the desertion of political frontiers and, possibly, oscillations in territorial control between Siin and Bawol. Exactions and raids conducted by slave warriors on farming communities also appear to have amplified, especially in the course of the nineteenth century.[59]

The rise of a constellated landscape seems tied to the escalation of insecurity, in particular migrations away from exposed borderlands toward the more insulated center. Archaeological patterns, however, are not completely straightforward, and the dispersed geography that slowly crystallized in Siin during the eighteenth and nineteenth centuries compares oddly to contemporary peasant strategies recorded elsewhere in West Africa. A more familiar response to the onslaught of slavery sees the retreat of endangered rural communities to well-protected or inhospitable areas or the development of large, fortified settlements where residents could combine forces to repel the attacks of royal armies. Indeed, this is precisely what we observe in the hilly regions of Bawol, which served as refuge for decentralized Seereer communities, or among stateless societies in Casamance.[60] By contrast, the scattering of villages would have left rural residents more vulnerable to predation, though migrations to the hinterland, closer to the king's sphere of political influence, might have ensured greater protection from enemy kingdoms or royal warriors. Perhaps, then, it signals a trade-off, relinquishing autonomy and tolerating state racket for greater security from the dangers of captivity.

Sticking to a descriptive register, all we can say is that village dislocation was probably caused by the escalation of elite exactions on rural communities but that occupation patterns stand in sharp contrast to previous arguments that the Atlantic slave trade caused massive depopulation in coastal kingdoms. Oppositely, we observe a massive demographic *increase* expressed in an explosion of small, scattered concessions and hamlet-sized sites. Though by no means panregional, similar changes have been observed elsewhere—in the Falemme, for instance, where settlement patterns also contradict earlier scenarios of human abandonment. Further up the coast, European writers report the presence of large villages and high human densities. Also striking is the near absence of overt signs of militarization, such as gunflints or fortifications, which frequently turn up in other areas.[61] While the absence of material evidence offers weak ground for pronouncements on the consequences of violence, it lends tempting support to the thesis that political instability in Siin never approached the catastrophic proportions reached in neighboring polities; it might also buttress documentary claims that the Siin monarchy refrained from enslaving its subjects.

More provocatively, changes in settlement landscape suggest that the dispersed habitat that so fascinated colonial observers, who saw it as an ageless feature of Seereer cultural traditions may actually be a product of Atlantic conditions. By extension, it is quite possible that other Seereer social features long thought to be traditional and embedded in scattered spatial assemblages (see chapter 4)—such as the system of land tenure, agropastoral management, or residential mobility—also took shape during this period.

Lastly, settlement transformations also seem to externalize changes in social organization. Most new habitation sites literally sprout up in the political space stretching between Ndiongolor and Diakhao, in areas that were previously loosely inhabited. Many of these sites gravitated into the orbit of the two royal capitals. Some of them could represent small satellite settlements associated with retainers and craft specialists working for the monarchy, the traces of which linger today in the higher incidence of caste and slave patronyms in the Diakhao area.[62] However, artifact assemblages provide less definite evidence of specialized activities, except perhaps for the manufacture of pottery and smoking pipes at the small village of Sagn Folo.

Suspicions of Power: The Ambivalence of Foreignness

As we scan Siin's archaeological landscapes during the Atlantic era, it is striking that the region displays few if any of the correlates conventionally associated with state centralization. While written and oral archives record a modest administrative structure made up of governors and village overseers, survey evidence shows no marked spatial hierarchy with multiple levels of settlement and a paramount capital at the top. At best, one discerns a near-continuous spectrum ranging from ephemeral settlements to more permanent concession of clusters and hamlets. A handful of medium-sized villages, some compact and others more dispersed, stand out, though there is little indication that they acted as political magnets drawing in their orbit an archipelago of dependencies. In fact, oral traditions collected around these larger sites explicitly identify their past occupants as nonaristocratic. What is more, though these villages may have roots in the eighteenth century, their artifact inventories place them conclusively in the nineteenth century, if not the latter decades of the 1800s.

The lack of centralization and differentiation observed at the level of the built landscape is also mirrored at the scale of object worlds. Given the vagaries of surface disturbances, survey assemblages can be difficult to quantify accurately. Still, material assemblages recovered during survey and excavations are relatively homogeneous across the region. Surely, some of the more ephemeral sites have thin artifact collections and large villages sites boast more consequential material inventories. Barring these extremes, however, the same categories of objects invariably turn up across the Siin. Likewise, no major disparities or exponential differences in wealth exist among identified sites—or, at least, no differences that would speak to a royalty/nobility/commoner divide. For example, artifacts collected from trash heaps at the elite residence of the *lingeer* (king's wife or mother) showed no profound difference in quality and quantity from artifacts retrieved at large, nonelite villages (table 5). Surely, it would be an exaggeration to claim the complete absence of wealth differentials between elites and nonelites in Siin, as those would have been materialized in media leaving no durable archaeological presence (textiles and slaves, especially). For all that, however, it is clear that large stretches of material expressions *were* shared between commoners and nobles, which over time caused social anxiety (chapter 6).

It seems difficult to reconcile Siin's changing material worlds with a story of inescapable absolutism. Although the Atlantic economy undeniably reshaped demography, social strategies, and spatial practices in Senegambia, archaeological materialities question the image of an unflinching court brutalizing its subjects to keep itself afloat. Why, then, are the taken-for-granted expressions of state power not apparent in the Siin landscape or present in such subdued form? Or, to pose the question more usefully, what *were* the coordinates of state power in Siin? How was state political authority inscribed in rural environment? And under what conditions? As I have already intimated, Siin's archaeological ambiguity may simply bear the traces of different histories of power, moved by certain fundamental tensions rather than coolly integrated by force or hegemony. This might explain how, upon being confronted with social geographies inherited from earlier times, would-be statesmen may have been compelled to

Table 5 Diakhao region: Artifact inventories at aristocratic, peasant, and enslaved/casted artisan settlements

			Glass containers[a]						Other glass		Tobacco pipes fragments				
Occupation context	Closest village	Settlement type	Case bottles	Cylindrical alcohol bottles[b]	Mineral/ soda water bottles	Medical/ cosmetic containers[c]	Other bottles	Misc. bottle fragments	Tableware	Flat glass	Local	Imported	Imported ceramics sherds	Metal objects	Spindle whorl
S89	Cupaan	Hamlet													
S89—Mound A			43	9	1	7	1	2	1		3	1	4		
S89—Mound E			3	6	2	6							3		
S89—Mound G			10	4	2		2	4		1					
S33	Nguékokh	Hamlet													
S33—general surface			3	5	1			2			8			1 horse harness	
S37	Diadiel	Hamlet													
S37—Mound A			1	5		2					1				
S37—Mound C			23	5		3		13			2		1		
S37—Mound B			5	3		4									

(*continued*)

Table 5 (*continued*)

Occupation context	Closest village	Settlement type	Glass containers[a]						Other glass		Tobacco pipes fragments		Imported ceramics sherds	Metal objects	Spindle whorl
			Case bottles	Cylindrical alcohol bottles[b]	Mineral/ soda water bottles	Medical/ cosmetic containers[c]	Other bottles	Misc. bottle fragments	Tableware	Flat glass	Local	Imported			
S51	Ndofène	Hamlet cluster/ village													
S51—general surface			17	10	1	7[f]		14	1		1				
S51—Area A			6	2[d]	2	1		5	1		1				
S51—Area B			8	4[d]	3	6		4	1		1			1 bracelet	1
S57	Famb	Hamlet cluster/ village													
S57—general surface			20	2	1	3		39	2				1		
S57—Mound A			17	4[d]	1	3		16		1	5		1		
S57—Mound C			18	3	3	1		21			2				

S75	Sorokh	Hamlet									
S75—Area A			3	1		6	4	1			1
S75—Area C						1					
S75—Area D			3	1			2				1
S77	Sorokh	Village									
S77—Mound A			9	2		1	4		10	1	
S77—Mound L			16	1[d]	1	5	13		2		
S77—Mound N			23	9[d, e]	2	16	20				

Note: Sites listed in the table all orbit Diakhao, Siin's historic capital. Cupaan is the *lingeer*'s historic residence and associated with the nobility. Oral traditions identify Nguékokh, Diadiel, and Ndofène as tributary villages of Diakhao and thus potentially associated with casted artisans and enslaved dependents. Sorokh is a farming village. All selected contexts date to the late eighteenth and nineteenth centuries.

[a] Counts refer to minimum number of containers.

[b] Mostly wine bottles; small proportion of modern beer and whisky bottles.

[c] Variety of cylindrical medicine bottles (esp. embossed *alcool de menthe* containers) and small machine-made perfume bottles.

[d] Includes demijohn bottle fragments.

[e] Includes a whole Pernod bottle.

[f] Includes glass stoppers.

construct political legitimacy and authority *around* and *through*—rather than *over*—existing institutions of power.

Oral traditions provide a suggestive beginning here. Like other sources, collective memory does not transcribe past events transparently. It is a site of poetic and cultural production, where histories are debated, negotiated, and edited, and where the lessons of many historical moments are compressed into single texts. Yet, it is precisely the accretional quality of oral discourses (as opposed to a temporality of sequential description) that opens insights into the political past—and brings it closer to archaeology, with its collapsed nonlinear times, than history.[63] In lieu of granting exact access to what happened long ago, oral accounts often encode a record of collective *representations* about history and society—what McCaskie calls "fables of power."[64] In Siin, these fables take the form of a commentary about the ethics of power—about the political good and how power *should* be distributed among social constituencies—which embodies moral principles that informed past political actions.

Dyed in the fabric of Siin's dynastic traditions is a paradox: on the one hand, they celebrate noble lineages and their achievements, yet, on the other hand, they express quiet concern with royal power. This contradiction finds a positive outcome in scenarios that place the birth of the kingdom in the crucible of conciliation and cooperation between foreigners and autochthons. Galvan dubs this process a Norman-style "conquest," effected through marriage, cultural blending, and federalism rather than through coercion or force of arms. Dynastic chronicles portray state formation in Siin as a democratic process, the product of an exchange of services between aristocrat-outsiders and Seereer commoners, the former offering mystical wisdom, cohesion, and protection in return for a home; the latter trading culture and hospitality for governance.[65] One assumption is that the integration of village peer communities into a confederacy of sorts may have provided a desirable mode of organization in a general climate of political volatility associated with the ascendance of Jolof. Another is that early rulers may have been consensual and charismatic, possibly basing their authority on leadership and supernatural faculties. Power derived not from domination but reciprocity built into a system of checks and balances, a situation captured in the ideal political architecture described by colonial writers (see discussion in chapter 4), where major social stakeholders—nobles, commoners, and enslaved—were represented in the royal council and bore responsibility in decision making, at least in theory. Politically, the (federal) compromise involved working through local cultural institutions.

More abstractly, oral traditions also sketch out elements of a compelling philosophy of sovereignty. At one end, we find motifs reminiscent of the stranger-king figure in other parts of the world, where foreignness is the harbinger of order and power, the condition of their possibility—a broad sentiment that also underwrites the appropriation of foreign commodities. However, as Danilyn Rutherford remarks, the fetish of foreignness conveys not just the seductions of power but also its anxieties and thus becomes a site of deep uncertainty and conflicted feeling. The ambivalence that foreignness translates in Siin is that of sovereignty sui generis, as *both* an object of desire *and* a site of perilous excess.[66]

In his brilliant analysis of Seereer oral literature, Amade Faye details numerous instances of moral discomfort with state-derived authority, especially in the early days of cohabitation between Seereer and Gelwaar. As Faye demonstrates, oral narratives do not always praise the cordial marriage of political traditions, depicting instead the genesis of the state as a rocky and disputed process. In some instances, disagreements are remembered in episodes of violent resistance featuring lamanal opposition to Gelwaar projects, most famously expounded in the deeds of everyday man Panga Yaay Saar. Elsewhere, the seminal discord between strangers and hosts is translated symbolically. One such story invokes the image of an illicit liaison between king Maisa Wali's niece and a handsome wrestling champion, quintessential figure of the Seereer common man. Angered by the defilement of his lineage with impure blood, the mercurial Maisa vows to kill the offender. His councilors, however, warn that this action would be out of line, reminding him that "power is nothing but a title." They insist that it is the young wrestler, who in besting Siin's most valiant fighters, is the kingdom's true conqueror. More humiliation ensues when Maisa sends a delegation to consult with the wrestler's father, Biram o Ngoor. Forced off their horses by the thick layer of manure encircling Biram's village, the envoys must continue on foot to the peasant's house. The old man greets them with mockery. He questions Maisa's authority, referring to him as "the tolerated," and claims that he possesses more cows, horses, slaves, and wealth than the king himself, insinuating that the monarch would be foolish to oppose a marriage. In another version, Maisa's niece falls in love with Marga Caac, a powerful healer and hunter (another symbol of the Seereer terroir), and conceives an illegitimate child. Once again, the furious king seeks revenge. On the day of the child's baptism, Marga travels to the capital accompanied by followers, cattle, and other riches to celebrate the happy event. Maisa refuses to host the hunter, leaving him and his entourage stranded outside in the throes of a terrible thunderstorm. The next day, trusting that the torrential rain would have humbled Marga and spoiled his property, Maisa steps out of his house to find the unwanted guests and their baggage untouched by the rain. The dumbfounded king is forced to accept Marga's mystical prowess and consents to an alliance.[67]

Staged in these different stories is a confrontation between different regimes of truth about power, one grounded in locality and terroir, the other in alterity. Seereer and Gelwaar symbols size each other up (*lamaan*/wrestler/hunter vs. king, manure vs. horse, commoner magic vs. king's fetishes, wealth vs. title, humility vs. nobility), the opposition reaching momentary resolution when the former upstages the latter and when the Gelwaar half-heartedly concedes a truce (marriage). More importantly, narratives locate a crisis of legitimacy in the Gelwaar order, originating in the violation of the promise of unconditional hospitality on which the Siin state is founded. They expose the monarch's bad faith, the refusal of parity or complementarity, between host and guest, between local and foreign. Standing in for the Gelwaar, Maisa Wali may be a unifier and state maker, but he is also a poor host and a bad guest to those who welcomed him as stranger and tolerated him as ruler—here again, oral traditions gesture at a fundamental paradox haunting sovereign power.[68] This suspicion of sovereignty or, more precisely, of sovereignty centralized in the hands of the ruler is an enduring sentiment that mediates the history of power in Siin, and orients its reluctant geographies. It is also here that oral traditions recoup material history.

Reluctant Landscapes: Siin's Uneven Topographies of Power

The theory of politics distilled in oral accounts opens profound reflections on the kingdom's functioning and becoming, with consequences for the materiality of political worlds in Siin. Cultural memory posits a state grafted onto a bedrock of peasant political structures, balanced on tenuous compromise between centralized control and decentralized village authority. This dialectics of powers and counterpowers impulsed political fields at various moments in time and modulated the development of the kingdom. This volatile political environment was also eminently concrete, saturated by material relations and threaded through spatial worlds. While the state grew around material assemblages that developed their own logics, life, and potency, they also confronted a set of peasant institutions expressed in a spatial order of villages, agropastoral production, and collectively distributed land and natural resources. This vibrant material world could not be ignored, in part because politics, society, and religion remained strongly interbraided in Siin, a codependence woven into the landscape. State control may have hinged on military force and the management of external commerce, but coercion was not enough. As Doumet remarked of Kajoor, a king whose rule rests on force is master "only by the superiority of his strength, and ceases to be so when his strength goes lacking. Force is thus not regarded as a right."[69] In Siin, sovereignty also needed the endorsement, or collaboration, of spirits and ancestors residing in rural places. Effective rule, in other words, depended on domesticating a complex spiritual geography (religious shrines, landscape-dwelling ancestors, and sacred sites) that grounded social practices and formed a diffuse grid of power scattered across the landscape and managed by local actors. There, landscapes were as much a brake on royal power as a vehicle for its enforcement. Historically, land could not be owned or appropriated, partly because it was the repository of ancestral histories that buttressed collective identities and the home of local spirits with allegiances to peasant communities.[70] Given these grassroots solidarities and the state's limited means of political enforcement, it is likely that rulers were never in a position to fundamentally reform local political landscapes and subsume local spheres of sovereignty. Unlike other parts of the world, where leaders might have been at liberty to naturalize their regimes in space, in Siin, central power remained tethered to existing sociospatial assemblages—villages, landholdings, shrines, sacred groves—as structures of governance solidified. Reluctant materialities made implacable demands on social actors. The mixtures of power, culture, ancestors, and nature they contained pulled people in. They drove others away. They impressed their presence on human actions, and affected political projects. They materially resisted the pooling of power at the center, making state centralization unstable over time.[71]

The picture of power that seemed so confusing for the fifteenth and sixteenth centuries can now be reinterpreted in light of the historical tensions between royal and peasant structures. There, written sources seem to capture the contested construction of royal rule as it happened. What of the seventeenth and eighteenth centuries, however, when rulers gradually expanded their authority into a bona fide kingdom? Why was the concentration of political resources not inscribed in earth, wood, or stone? Principles of "wealth in people" and composition might provide one set of clues. Olfried Dapper suggested one possible explanation when he wrote that "the strength of [Senegalese] states consists more in a large number of men than in a few castles or fortresses." There, as in many other parts of West Africa, power derived as much, if not more, from the mobilization of human potential and social relations, from the composition of human skills and knowledges, than the accumulation of material goods—from wealth in people rather than in things. Because of their enmeshment with ancestors, peasant identities, and rural socialities, village landscapes in Siin remained inalienable terrains, which would have rendered the legitimate manipulation of material settings difficult. The inalienability of terrestrial space is manifest in the *lamanat* landholding system, which largely lay beyond the king's control.[72] On rare occasions, particularly during the troubled decades of the nineteenth century, royals may have taken over portions of lineage estates and appropriated management rights from land stewards (the *foxos* concessions described in chapter 4). These measures were probably highly exceptional. Land seizures were clear violations of the Seereer moral economy, where rightful control of land rested on genealogy and where land could not be divided by political fiat. As the old Seereer adage goes, land belongs to no one but *Roog Seen* (God). Moral outrage and condemnation were not sound principles of government.

If rulers had limited ability to remake their subjects through the landscape, royal power was nevertheless expressed in space—only it was channeled through people, social relations, and the agents of the crown. State power was *embodied* in the intrusion of notables and province governors; in the pillages and violence of roving royal war parties; in crown slaves and political entourages; in the person of the king himself, in his military actions and ritual prowess.[73] The transformations that we see archaeologically—demographic expansion, multiplication of villages in the vicinity of the capital, possible creation of specialized settlements and royal satellites—speak to a certain increase in the "density" of sociospatial relations, compatible with an effort to accrete power through the harnessing of wealth in people.[74] Note that these continue to be inscribed in a local logic of settlement: the new villages do not increase in size, segmentation, hierarchy, or complexity of arrangement; they rise in number and possibly functional diversity, if indeed some of the small sites created near aristocratic centers housed slave dependents and craft specialists (though archaeological evidence of this is tenuous)—reflecting both an accumulation of people and selective composition of their skills and labor. Nor does the capital fundamentally depart from other settlements. It moves, however, to the center of the web of social and political relations.

Other mechanisms of social control and political integration existed. Even as coercion and exactions played a pervasive role in state building leading into the colonial period, the ritual realm offered a less effusive arena for crafting authority in early Senegambian history.[75] An early passage by Cadamosto is edifying in this respect: "The king of this realm had nothing save villages of grass huts, and [he] was lord of only a part of this realm—a thing of little account. Such men are not lords by virtue of treasure or money, for they possess neither, nor do they expend any money; but on accounts of ceremonies and the following of people they may truly be called lords; indeed they receive beyond comparison more obedience than our lords."[76] While Cadamosto refers specifically to the Wolof kingdom of Kajoor, the political aesthetic of ceremonialism to which he alludes was part of a substratum of authority propping up kingdoms across northern Senegambia.

Ritual theater and politics appear to have intersected in a number of ways in Siin. First, sovereignty partly rested on spectacle, since, as elsewhere, the state was not just a political form but also a series of "statements," ways of affectively and aesthetically addressing subject audiences through public representations. One visual register lay in the performance of what MacEachern has called "stateliness."[77] Bereft of the means to fully subjugate rural dwellers, Senegambian statesmen partook in an aesthetics of sovereignty that drew the trappings, symbols, and practices of statehood from a regional grammar of rule: the building of slave armies, cavalry, and weapon arsenals; participation in enslavement and international commerce; diplomatic decorum; increasing use of recording technologies; redistributive largess; the assembly of clients and followers; acquisition of regalia; participation in conspicuous consumption; and the constitution of a loose administration of province chiefs—in other words, material signs that would be recognized by populations as statements of authority and would perform to other polities (even enemy ones) the transcript of common belonging. Sharing into this economy of appearances mattered just as much to the construction of state apparatuses as the capacity for brute force, war, or military protection.

Second, political elites built patronage networks through the strategic management and disbursement of foreign objects, exotic symbols, religious knowledge, labor, and marriage partners. Public ritual events—feasts, in particular—likely provided an important venue for the (re)production of political relations portrayed in the idiom of generosity, hospitality, and reciprocity. On one level, commensal rituals generally convey representations of the social and cosmic order that can rally groups with conflicting interests under a shared ideological umbrella. On another level, feasts and rituals of ostentation are public actualizations and manifestations of royal power. They reinforce the material foundations of the king's authority and fulfillment of his responsibilities toward the collectivity, kingdom, and ancestors. As Le Brasseur warned, great political misfortune awaited the king who neglected ancestors. Finally, ceremonies are important arenas of political investment, through the circulation of goods and gifts. Note here that elites acquired imports and exotics, without prodigious or long-standing personal accumulation: these were instead redistributed to followers to create political debt, providing one more instance of compositional strategies. They were also used to bolster regimes of taste that furthered the aesthetic of stateliness.[78]

Third, shared cosmology and ancestral worship provided technologies of regional cohesion. Ethnohistoric accounts tell us cultural and political unity in Siin was maintained through state performance: religious ceremonies, agricultural rituals, ritual hunts, burials, and the celebration of dynastic traditions that purported to speak both to local and statewide interests. Power flowed to the king from his role as spiritual leader, who interceded between natural, social, and mystical agencies. His authority rested in part on the ability to ensure the scheduling and proper functioning of religious ceremonies critical to the reproduction of the state. Public spectacles were staged in the terroir and anchored to Siin's sacred geography. They were often highly symbolic and spatialized affairs, involving journeys across the landscape that connected ritual places, spirit shrines (*pangool*), and ancestral sites into a narrative of continuity and harmony.[79] Boilat described one such annual ritual when the king visited a number of "genies" at the tomb of Maisa Wali at Mbissel, to whom he offered the soul of a parent in sacrifice, and the *pangool* of Fadiouth and Joal. In Joal, the *buur* "goes to sleep in front of the genie's hut until the sun sets; he consigns the kingdom's political affairs to the protection of infernal gods, and gives . . . to the priestess who purifies him all the clothes he was wearing and puts on new ones."[80]

Historic archives also make clear that funeral ceremonies punctuated the political calendar, ritually reinstating the office of the king and, through prestations and consumptions of food, symbolically enacting the participation of all social constituencies in the body politic.[81] Burials in the Seereer tradition are materializations of social relations. They embody in earth the labor of those—close family, lineage members, friends—who partake in their construction. The more respected the defunct, the larger the funeral crowd, and the more monumental the tomb. Funerary mounds were thus visible reminders of wealth in people in the landscape. In the same way, the burials of kings were rare occasions on which the idea of the polity came alive, when its body took on flesh even as that of the king passed away; they were moments when sovereignty's audiences could be constituted.[82]

To the extent that they succeeded, state rituals owed it to their reliance on antecedent ceremonial landscapes, which grounded and legitimized authority. Sovereigns employed the services of diviners (*saltigi*) and ritual functionaries originating from modest classes. They left offerings at provincial *pangool*, commemorating spirits that ensured the well-being of communities. Royal dignitaries officiated at village processions and festivities, writing themselves into the ritual calendars and social hierarchies of rural collectivities. Kings made pilgrimages to earlier capitals or regional sacred sites in an attempt to reinforce links between their reigns, places of memory, and historic rulers.[83] This ritual insertion has left loose traces in rural landscapes. For instance, while historic capitals did not stand out for their material grandeur (figure 23)—in fact, Diakhao's archaeological footprint suggests that it was probably smaller than a number of adjacent settlements—they were strategically located close to places of history and tradition, close to important *pangool*, and close to centers of religious power and spiritual-social reproduction. Because it relied on surrounding villages for food and thus did not suffer from soil exhaustion, Diakhao does not appear to have moved much if at all during the historic period—which may also reflect its central position in Siin's sacred geography.

During the Atlantic era, spiritual institutions contributed to keeping a system of working disequilibrium in place. Conversely, power's partial footing in cosmology and sacred sites also placed a check on the monarch's ability to fashion space in the image of power. To preserve and strengthen modes of authority, elites had to rely on a mixture of force and consent. Agricultural festivals had to be celebrated, local spirits propitiated, rituals of social reproduction honored, and ties to the sacred and natural landscapes reinstated. The need to gain access to the means of spiritual production, which were shared with local elites and ritual specialists, often provided rulers with incentives for not disrupting local social and spatial organization.[84] Angry spirits could easily turn political fates around, and, channeling Pierre Clastres, they periodically sided with society against the state.[85] In more structural terms, wagering sovereign fates in the ceremonial arena always entailed an element of risk. Ritual chains routinely break down and fail to deliver the desired effects, endangering the political projects they support. Even when successful, collective performances do not mechanically engineer unity. They are also stages for the negotiation of social dissent and often become catalysts of alternative projects and even change. While they affirmed the tenets of Gelwaar royalty, rituals of the state in Siin also paradoxically valorized the institutions (and political claims) of rural subjects.[86]

23 Postcards, early twentieth century. *Top*, "Diakhao, Residence of the King of Siin" (ANS, Iconographie, no. 0031). *Bottom*, *buur* Siin Kumba Ndofeen Juuf (r. 1898–1924) (ANS, Iconographie, no. 0701) (both reproduced with permission from Archives du Sénégal).

While material factors like military power, control of trade and slave labor, and extraction of small agricultural surpluses consolidated state rule in the eighteenth century, the documentary record hints, in hushed tones, that the process of centralization may have been more syncopated than once thought, and that grassroots political elites (lineage heads, land custodians, and caretakers of matrilineal wealth and patrimony) maintained structures of authority at the local level, the more efficiently the farther from the centers of royal power. Reading between the lines of historic archives, for instance, we discern variations in political power where central authority contracted or expanded depending on the individual monarch's ambitions, kin relations, and political alliances.

Although the kingdom's armies appear to have kept relatively firm control in the hinterland, especially around Diakhao, villagers along the coast seem to have enjoyed greater autonomy than interior populations and are periodically described as independent republics unto their own. In 1683, for instance, François de Paris argued that the community of Joal "cared little to obey the orders of the kings d'Hamel [*damel* of Kajoor] and Barbeçin [*buur* Siin], and conduct[ed] a great portion of the country's trade." A century later, a commercial memoir from Peyries de Jalvert mentioned that the king of Kajoor was trading in Joal, which is historically part of Siin's territory. Since there are no records of Kajoor taking over Siin's coastal strip at the time, a possible scenario is that Joal was a free port of trade, implying a period of independence from the king of Siin. In the 1780s, Senegal veteran Golberry depicted the Siin as subordinated to Saalum and noted that "all the expense that the country of Bur-Sin should foreseeably occasion, is reduced to [the payment of] customs for the king, for some of the village chiefs that abut the coast, *but above all for the master of Joal*" (italics added). Writing on the eve of French colonization, Father Gallais's ethnographic sketches are replete with references to the perfidy and free spirit of Joal's Christian community and their perpetual run-ins with the king's soldiers. So much so that *buur* Siin Hamat Diouf described them as "the most perverse of his subjects." Ironically, eighty years earlier, the king of Siin exulted to Demanet that Joal's Christians were his most faithful subjects. Likewise, the Mbayar, a frontier province along the kingdom's northern border appeared to retain considerable hold over its historical destiny over time, by virtue of its interstitial position between rival polities and its ability to side with one or the other depending on its interests.[87]

The existence of competing spheres of power built a fundamental instability in the structure of state power, translating into cycles up and down the scale of centralization during the precolonial era. Changing conjectures could tilt the kingdom toward central control or provincial autonomy, while reshaping the conditions of power in the process. These systems were clearly uneven. A strong king could strategically station administrators, deploy troops, mobilize social alliances, and marshal spiritual resources to manage distant provinces, monitor trade circuits, win followers, and consolidate his authority regionally and locally. However, under times of social strife or civil war, a weakened king, doubted by friends and foes, with overstretched resources, could easily see his authority challenged in one or more provinces and lose political ground to local elites or aristocratic contenders. These fluctuations could be temporary or durable, their effects discrete or cumulative. Whatever expressions the state did take rested on the specific articulation of local structures and broader forces at particular points in time. In turn, these oscillations and gradations in power reverberated against a backdrop of increasing state power and authority.

Because of the fine-textured scale at which it unfolded, the microhistory of these reconfigurations is somewhat beyond the reach of Siin's archaeological chronologies.[88] Moreover, because settlement patterns lend themselves to a number of possible readings, more research will be necessary to conclusively determine the cultural expressions of power in the region. That said, the maintenance of a relatively unstratified village landscape throughout the Atlantic era fits with the interpretation that royal rule interdigitated with local sociospatial forms, even as monarchies became more centralized. The endurance of this spatial arrangement perhaps also denotes the viability of a political system founded on a working imbalance. Though sketchy, this picture of contested and overlapping sovereignties exceeds the scenarios of linear state power that have featured so prominently in classic depictions of Atlantic Senegambia.

Conclusion: The Unease of Sovereignty

I fear the king
The king has no siblings
SEEREER EXPRESSIONS[89]

While unassuming in appearance, the state-peasant couplet holds certain keys to the Atlantic story in Senegal. For one, it condenses some of its problems, a kind of historical packaging, where kings and commoners move along to the beat of a plot not quite tuned to the historicity of local societies. Yet the tableaux of state-peasant interactions are also full of incongruous traces and choppy little strokes; individually, these can be dismissed as oddities marginal to Atlantic portraiture, yet, once inspected together, they conjoin into intriguing historical patterns. Tracking these puzzling threads is what I have tried to do in this chapter. Sifting through the rubble of archaeological, oral, and documentary archives, I have attempted to decompose the categories of state and peasant in order to better recompose the nature of their relationship. While archaeology carries its own burden of limitations and other sources are often tentative, they dare us to revisit accepted ideas about political history in Senegal and make room for obstinate materialities in historical imaginations of the Atlantic world.

Some of these provocations are keyed to historical and theoretical concerns, in Africa and elsewhere. In effect, a serious consideration of the social physics of milieu prompts a three-way deconstruction of state-centered visions of politics. First, it disintegrates the state *object* into a historical project of state*craft*. The kingdom has no essence. Its presence is schizophrenic, its institutions shifting, its order always under construction (which does not mean that they do not achieve moments of stability). Second, state sovereignty is never absolute. Rather, it coexists with other sovereign spaces that decenter the locus of power. And, third, centralization is a *process* not a fait accompli. It gradates in time and space, though in ways more complicated than commonly assumed or presented here. On one level, the Siin materials question the smooth model of concentric authority circles radiating across frictionless space presented by authors like Herbst. Political topographies *matter*. The social, spiritual, and historical intensities crystallized in landscape texture political geographies beyond simple inverse equations between distance and power. Political reluctance pools differentially across geography. The faraway villages of Joal or Fadiouth held on to their autonomy, but so did villages closer to Diakhao, like Diohine, that constantly butted heads with the king's officials.[90] The same goes for the temporal dynamics of statehood. Centralization is not a predictable pendulum swing between royal and rural power. It is disjointed. Sadly, the events of intensification, stabilization, decline, and reversal that punctuated monarchical rule get lost in the coarseness of archaeological imaging. Still, the resulting picture is a rather dynamic one, where the state seems much less encysted a notion than previously envisioned. Part of that uncertainty translates into the spatial realm to give shape to the reluctant landscapes evoked above. The idea of reticent geographies adds nuance to the hierarchy commonly structuring the relation between space and power. If states are often credited with the production of landscape, then aleatory materialities strike back by interfering with power. Space is unreliable, and power is not absolute. States are indebted to society, and neither one is external to the other. Peasants must be plugged back into Atlantic political life as partners, unequal to be sure, in the production of history and power. In turn, refining the history of state-peasant relationships by way of space-power clarification also provides a bridge into historiography. If Siin's (supposedly) highly centralized kingdom can be unmasked, then the same analysis in northern Senegal, home of the predatory absolutist state, might fundamentally reshape our understanding of state building in Atlantic Senegambia.

Finally, I have argued that the state-peasant dialectic harbors deeper currents of ambivalence toward sovereignty and its doubleness—a political unconscious materialized in space. Until recently, such discomfort was on full display in the ceremony of *tod't*, the annual crowning of the king of the sea (*maad no maah*) in Fadiouth. An ambiguous figure, drawn from the ranks of the village's founding matrilineages, the *maad no maah* is a priest king, whose role is to appease the caprices of land and sea and the collective anxieties to which they give rise. According to Bruzzone, he embodies a Seereer utopia of kingship: he is king but does not govern; he has no subjects; his authority is restricted to the family; he shares decision making with village elders; he acts on the world through sacrifice and prayer; he mediates between people and spirits for the good of the community.[91] Of course, the king of the sea is reflexively tied to the king of Siin, whose legitimacy he puts in question. If the former metaphorizes desirable power, the kind that is homespun, inclusive, and oriented to the commonwealth, then the later stands for a distorted species of sovereignty, one that is alien and alienating. While today largely symbolic and in decline, the *maad no maah* in earlier times possibly had more historical substance, delineating a sovereign space effectively counterposed against the *maad no Jaxaaw*, which held more local credibility and potency than the Diakhao monarchy ever did and which joined a brimming geography of power that comprised the rebellious residents of Joal, ambitious noble families whose eyes coveted the throne, and reluctant peasants elsewhere.

Even in death, Siin's monarchy illustrates the laboriousness of sovereignty and travails of giving a legitimate face to the state, and their transhistorical echo. Imaginations of power, encoded in memory, cross between past and present, and find receptive audiences today. Surely, the jury is still out on the precolonial state, as many parties find it an attractive foil to the inefficacy of government in the present. Yet, just as many rural residents denounce its excesses. Cue the oral narratives in the village of Diohine, which one moment politely recount the amity binding peasants and royalty but soon after rattle off a long list of grievances, from the king's unlawful encroachment upon lamanal lands to the dreaded taxation days when royal soldiers swooped in and stole anything in sight, leaving behind only cooking pots and their steaming contents.[92] Behind the powerful imagery is a reminder that violence is less an index of sovereign might than a symptom of its weakness, and that the flexing of state muscle in the eighteenth and nineteenth centuries perhaps signaled kings' recourse to domination as their legitimacy was being undercut by other modes of order, as raison d'état was tripped by its own raison d'être.

Past and present here speak to each other, and the unease of sovereignty, part fascination and part distrust, is not just a thing of Atlantic history but very much the stuff of power today.[93] In effect, this ambivalence has historically organized Seereer social activities and sentiments regarding political centralization. By extension, the reluctant landscapes in which it has found its form have mediated encounters with subsequent projects of rule—from French colonization to postcolonial governance. We will pick up this later story in chapters 7 and 8.

SIX

Object Trajectories: Atlantic Commerce and Genealogies of Material Practice

And because there were so many of those blacks on land that by no means could they disembark either by day or night, Gomez Pirez sought to show that he desired to go among them on peaceful terms, and so placed upon the shore a cake and a mirror and a sheet of paper on which he drew a cross. And the natives when they came there and found those things, broke up the cake and threw it far away, and with the assegais [spears] they cast at the mirror, till they had broken it in many pieces, and the paper they tore, showing that they cared not for any of these things. G. E. DE AZURARA, *THE CHRONICLE OF THE DISCOVERY AND CONQUEST OF GUINEA*[1]

Overture: Witnessing Things

If we believe Portuguese chronicler Gomez Eannes de Azurara, contacts between Senegambians and Europeans started off on rocky foundations. As Portugal's voyages of exploration added, one stroke at a time, new coastlines and continents to the *mapa mundi* of Iberian rulers, Africans' own worldviews stretched to make room for the crews of rugged adventurers that the tides of god, gold, and glory washed upon their shores. This tale of mutual discovery was marred by enmity and misunderstanding, driven more by chance than design. The first brick in this edifice of unthinking decisions, relates Azurara, was laid down in 1434 at Cape Bojador, in the western Sahara, where Portuguese sailors, choosing the heroics of human seizure over petty commerce, scoured the landscape for unsuspecting victims. By the time they sailed back to Portugal, the slave-raiding fleet had amassed a cargo of forty-six "Moors." These abductions were not just the fruits of whimsy but inspired by a marauding tradition perfected a century earlier during Portugal's expeditions to the Canary Islands, a tradition they transported southward as they leapfrogged from deserted beaches and inlets to river mouths around West Africa's coast. When they alighted in the bay of Dakar in 1445, the Christian mariners were repelled by coastal dwellers. Captain Dinis Diaz waited for nightfall to venture on shore and captured two prisoners, which sparked an armed tussle and forced the intruders to beat a hasty retreat aboard their ships. A year later, a new fleet of caravels reached the entrance of the Senegal River. There, one Estêvão Affonso led a small group of men along the banks, where they seized a young boy and his sister until they were driven away by the children's father. Defeated, the soldiers of fortune sailed onward to the Cap Vert peninsula, where their peace offerings of cake, mirror, and paper met only the approval of arrows.[2]

A hundred years later, the same beach scene south of Dakar would have looked quite different. No longer the sacrificial victims of a failed encounter, mirrors now entered a widening stream of foreign manufactures making their way into African societies. Once abandoned to the blowing wind, strips of paper enjoyed new life as prized occult artifacts; inked with Koranic versets and folded into leather pouches, they moved from the hands of clerics to those seeking the protection of magical charms. Long lost to the sand, cake crumbs gave way to sturdier foods—grain, livestock, fish—circulating in the opposite direction, from African men and women to European traders. Holding on to their spears and arrows, coastal rulers now also eyed imported iron and metal weapons, despite Portuguese efforts to cordon off access to the matériel of warfare. In paper, mirrors, cakes, and javelins (and many other *things*), we find humble allegories of Atlantic transfers, dwelling in cultural spaces largely invisible to the picaresque machismo of early Portuguese chronicles or the mercantilist concerns of later Europeans. Rather than a testament of negation, these objects were the vehicles for species of social contracts that activated new relationships between Africans and Europeans, women and men, rulers and commoners, warriors and clerics.[3] They bear witness to the failings of European persuasion, to the fact that their mere presence was insufficient to ensnare native peoples but that they could become instead concrete manifestos of refusal, partial adoption, or social invention. They translated new kinds of history.

This chapter aims to complicate the broad premises of Atlantic political economy in northern Senegal. I follow in the footsteps of recent scholarship, which locates the Atlantic trade not in an agonistic joust of supply and demand but in a history of articulations between production, consumption, and social actors. While this critical history performs its labor of analysis through a rereading of written archives, my examination catches the plane of economic history through the world of things that upheld Atlantic-era commercial transactions and social practices in their aftermath.[4] As Bill Brown reminds us, material things are instructive; they refrain from conforming to expectations. Contrasting "objects" and "things," he notes that

> As they circulate through our lives, we look *through* objects (to see what they disclose about history, society, nature, or culture—above all, what they disclose about *us*), but we only catch a glimpse of things. . . . We look through objects because there are codes by which our interpretive attention makes them meaningful, because there is a discourse of objectivity that allows us to use them as facts. A *thing*, in contrast, can hardly function as a window. We begin to confront the thingness of objects when they stop working for us: when the drill breaks, when the car stalls, when the windows get filthy, when their flow within the circuits of production and distribution, consumption and exhibition, has been arrested, however momentarily. The story of objects asserting themselves as things, then, is the story of a changed relation to the human subject and thus the story of how the thing really names less an object than a particular subject-object relation.[5]

Things' interruptive quality extends to archaeological artifacts; it is a trait of the epistemology of fragments they support, which provokes the following questions: How do things and artifacts undercut and expand our interpretive fetishes? How do they pose a rethinking of subject-object relations? What historical alternatives do they point to? In the context of Atlantic Senegal, shifting the focus to things seems to qualify the extent of global trade's deleterious impact on local economies. Pottery making's vitality to this day suggests that not all industries capitulated to the Atlantic trade, just as the fact that coastal Senegal likely imported its iron at the time of European contact tell us that some technological traditions may have been interrupted before its advent. While cursory, these examples illustrate the general point that the different activities making up Senegambian economies did not rise or fall in unison but often followed idiosyncratic paths.[6]

Unwrapping the Atlantic package in Siin, in short, requires more molecular visions of the economic flows and practices that buttressed the region's global past. To peek into the matter of African political economy—the once lively universe of material transactions welding nobles, traders, and commoners to coastal markets—I reexamine Siin's Atlantic history through the prism of past things whose imprints are retrievable archaeologically or legible in documentary archives. I draw on materials collected during the 2003 and 2011 survey seasons and track variations in artifact distribution, composition, and frequencies over the past five hundred years. Rather than lumping these object histories together into a single account of economic change, I parse them into discrete classes of material culture—bottle glass, imported and local ceramics, beads, tobacco pipes, and spindle whorls—and, with the assistance of textual and oral documentation (when available), attempt to extract the stories of social transformation embodied in each category of artifacts and the different ways in which Atlantic goods intersected with local people, ideas, and objects, and reframed the conditions of existence in Siin.

Brown tells us that "things" are both "baldly encountered" and "not quite apprehended." So it is, too, for artifactual remnants. They are intensely, sensuously present yet always partly elude intelligibility. In the objective "thereness" of artifacts, we find the residue of congealed gestures, mundane habits, and social dispositions. This material culture puzzle enables us to approach the questions of markets, labor, production, and society from the intimate angle of consumption practices and cultural premises underwriting commercial decisions. At the same time, archaeological objects never quite add up to more than a tattered testimony of the logics that drove actions one way or another, an incomplete conjuration of the "what really happened" of Atlantic history. While some material trajectories are easier to trace, others falter, vanish, or never become visible, casting wide shadows over our depictions of Atlantic experiences. This is particularly true of the artifacts considered here, which were largely retrieved from the surface of residential settlements and not in their primary context of use. This limits our ability to use archaeological things to reconstruct the histories of culture making that objects supported. This partiality aside, the patterns that emerge from Siin's archaeological record nuance assertions that the simple showing of a ship full of trade goods would stimulate African commerce. In effect, the circumspection with which Siin residents accepted imported goods and the long-standing refusal of certain types of commodities throw into relief whether the introduction of European merchandise in Senegambia was as "revolutionary" as Abdoulaye Ly once rhetorically surmised.[7]

Object Lessons

We have to follow the things themselves, for their meanings are inscribed in their forms, their uses, their trajectories. It is only through the analysis of these trajectories that we can interpret the human transactions and calculations that enliven things. Thus, even though from a *theoretical* point of view human actors encode things with significance, from a *methodological* point of view it is the things-in-motion that illuminate their human and social context.

A. APPADURAI, *THE SOCIAL LIFE OF THINGS*[8]

Methodological fetishism, then, is not an error so much as it is a condition for thought, new thoughts about how inanimate objects constitute human subjects, how they move them, how they threaten them, how they facilitate or threaten their relation to other subjects.

B. BROWN, "THING THEORY"[9]

To properly comprehend how worldwide economic forces influenced African societies, it is important to go beyond the pendulum swing of supply and demand; indeed, we must also consider the social principles that mediated between Africa and the world and shaped African desires, reception, and use of imported products.[10] Drawing inspiration from a thriving anthropological literature on exchange and consumption, recent Africanist scholarship has emphasized the need to uncover how African material practices and *regimes of value*, some of which predated the Atlantic trade, informed the *recontextualization* of trade materials—their appropriation in locally meaningful terms—and how contacts with global markets opened new horizons of social practice.[11] It is pivotal, in other words, to document the cultural translation of economic encounters before and during the Atlantic era and the different experiences forged in these interactions.

One effective way to gain insights into these entanglements is to examine the objects at their center, the things that literally were the stuff of economic transactions. In his seminal essay on "the social life of things," Appadurai celebrated the quiet wisdom of things, their uncanny capacity to expand human-centric analyses with their focus on actors, agency, and deliberate signification and to speak to the unspoken underside of exchange. Instead of beginning with people to get at the meaningful substance of exchanges, Appadurai advocated the virtues of "methodological fetishism," a stance that tracks the movements and paths of objects across terrains of social action to reveal more ineffable, if no less constitutive, dynamics of economic relations.[12] Mapping the circulation of objects in and out of spheres of production, exchange, and consumption, between different dramatis personae, and along and across social boundaries can illuminate the evaluations that regulated the trade, the ideologies determining what could be exchanged and what could not, the cultural preferences that guided the African demand for foreign goods, and how Atlantic commodities articulated with existing social practices and systems of objects. In turn, it can also better our comprehension of how the strange things and ideas introduced by oceanic commerce became familiar fixtures of Africa's daily worlds and how they could, in time, be converted into new forms of collective experiences, wealth, and social relations.

Object trajectories can also inform us about value, a keystone of discourse about Atlantic transactions. European merchants' paternalistic marvel at the fact that valuable materials could be obtained for cheap manufactures—in their perception, Africans' misapprehension of "real" value—is a staple of documentary archives. These preconceptions are largely dispelled by the tale of moving objects, which converges with the philosophies of Marx and Simmel to depict value not as something naturally inhering in things, but as a way of reckoning significance symbolically and materially *constructed* by multiple actors in different contexts and transactions.[13] In Atlantic Africa, value and values both drove economic encounters, just as the actuality of transactions (re)fashioned valuation in its wake. Borders of all sorts were key sites of value production, and the passage of things across thresholds of monetary, sociological, cultural, and political difference generated new meanings, imaginaries of worth, and spaces of agency.[14] These processes highlight that value is not just agreed upon collectively but contested and thus profoundly political. Trading parties come to the table of exchange with varying agendas. Economic partners or antagonists are not equal in their capacity to make effective demands, actualize their goals, and activate the movement of desired goods. Projects of value making and unmaking and the economic access they open or foreclose are intimately connected to an architecture of privilege and control. In this sense, the sociology of things is implicated in a politics of value, which plugs into a sociology of power.

This means that objects, people, and the representations and institutions organizing society are enmeshed in processes of mutual constitution. Things are actively involved in (re)creating the social orders that coordinate human interactions. As Bourdieu recognized long ago, the categorizations on which material value is predicated find equivalences in the domain of social rank and economic distinction between people.[15] Here, hierarchies of objects are linked to hierarchies of people, and the taste for certain things translates into judgments about social class. By extension, given the porous membrane between humans and the objects they use, things also enter the making of personhood and subjective understanding. Not infrequently, the personality of objects dissolves into the character of social actors or becomes irrevocably tied to who they are and the social image they project. Sometimes, people wager their identities on the acquisition of certain goods and the world of promise they contain. At other times, people and things are bound by estrangement, where exclusion from particular object spheres defines the parameters of identity. Finally, thanks to their ability to breach regulatory frameworks, things also work, deliberately or not, to transform social relations. Critically tied to dominant institutions of power, objects are nevertheless mobilized by competing political projects to transgress social classifications, contest traditional structures, and fashion new avenues of action. As elsewhere in West Africa, these aspects of things' social history find expression in the story of Atlantic exchanges in Siin. More precisely, what needs to be established is the nature of residents' investment in commercial goods, the contexts that shaped them, and how material items contributed to the construction, maintenance, and transformation of the kingdom's sociopolitical landscapes.

In recent years, archaeology has looked for answers to these questions in Kopytoff's famous essay on the "cultural biography of things," which has inspired a genre of narratives aimed at reconstructing object "histories" or "biographies."[16] This literature has monitored the various phases composing the long-term social life of singular objects and certain categories of material culture. More importantly, it has examined the processes of memory construction and social interpretation lining the passage of objects into different contexts as they operate in their original cultural setting, outlive owners and manufacturers, get recuperated by subsequent generations, and enter afterlives as archaeological artifacts. Though object biographies remain popular in archaeology, they have given way to a rising interest in genealogies of practice. The latter orientation has widened the biographic focus beyond unique or exceptional artifacts, to consider the embeddedness of object histor*ies* in broader webs of material practices. The goal has been to document how culture making emerges in fields of materiality forged between people, objects, and milieu. Studies have successfully mapped associations between object classes and different contexts of deposition to show how nonhuman materialities—habitual object uses, building gestures, earth strata—influence human action and the genesis of new practices.[17]

My approach shares affinities with these perspectives, beginning with their methodological fetishism and concern with the entwinement of objects and practice, but its ambitions are tempered by the constraints of Siin's archaeology. Because artifacts come chiefly from the surface of surveyed sites and not from well-stratified excavated contexts and primary deposits, it is difficult to follow how different sets of objects change or endure *in relation to* others, which is why my focus is on the trajectories of single classes of mundane objects, with limited attention, when context allows, to their *intersections* in time and space. My effort, then, is to capture salient moments in the course of things as they moved in and out of the spheres of production, exchange, and consumption.[18] One advantage is to highlight the heterogeneity of object worlds; rather than apprehending Atlantic assemblages as wholes, we can track different sets of objects, their distinctive pathways, spheres of circulation, and entanglements with local cultural practices.[19] As we do so, we must also cultivate an acute sensibility to the temporality and movements of things. This pursuit entails more than an appreciation of change and continuity in the material record; it requires that we scrutinize the *qualities*, *intensities*, and *durations* these processes acquire in given historical contexts.[20]

While they can never be completely recomposed, these fragmented histories do have a significant upside: connecting peoples, places, and processes across space and time, they enable us to travel the "awkward scales" on which social experiences of the Atlantic were fashioned.[21] As they cycle between contexts, consumable objects interpolate people into new geographies of experience: they link constituencies across locales into new communities of practice; they restrict social membership in consumption spheres; they introduce African collectives to foreign moods and desires; they participate in the local domestication of worldwide phenomena; and they stretch cultural senses of time, space, and identity.[22] The web of things, consequently, is intrinsic to the making and remaking of African political landscapes. It is also instrumental in linking these landscapes to an imperial geography of power shaped by a dynamic set of forces—centers of manufacture and production, commercial institutions, commodity flows, metropolitan consumer markets, projects of wealth creation and accumulation, and mechanisms of political control, all bearing on African economic history and its relationship to the world.[23] As a result, object trajectories privilege neither global sense nor local sensibilities, nor do they gloss the matrices of power in between. Standing at the meeting point of different societies and economies, things open vistas into the production of global trends in localities and the carving of local worlds by forces beyond them.[24] In so doing, they also capture something of the clumsiness of historical entanglements—the tensions and uneven integration that punctuated life in the Atlantic system and the frictions that fueled globalization and capital expansion.[25]

Things also convey something of their slipperiness in Africa, marred as they were by uncertainty, improvisation, and misunderstanding on the parts of all involved.[26]

Atlantic Immersions: A *Short* Economic History of Siin, 1500–1900

The opening of oceanic commerce reoriented economies from the Saharan edge to the coast, bringing in new products and demands and creating new modes of consumption. Yet, Senegambia's history of commercial engagements with long-distance trade long predates Europe's mercantile expansion, connecting coastal products (salt, fish, seafood) and Sahelian resources (iron, slaves) to Sudanic and Saharan markets. When the Portuguese made landfall on its shores, the Siin was teeming with circulating goods.[27]

The province participated in this dynamic commercial landscape at an early time, both as a supplier of leather, cotton cloth and agricultural goods, and as purchaser of horses and iron. As early as the mid-1400s, Diogo Gomes reports commercial activities in a coastal locality named Zaza, possibly the present-day village of Joal. He depicts a vibrant trade in slaves and horses along this portion of the coast. By the end of the fifteenth century, trading points had mushroomed along the Petite Côte, and European canoes navigated twenty leagues up the Siin-Saalum estuary to trade with interior villages, according to Pereira. Joal is mentioned for the first time by Valentim Fernandes. Commerce continued to thrive during the 1500s. In the late sixteenth century, for instance, English navigator Rainolds referred to Joal and Portudal as "the towns of the chiefest trade" on the Petite Côte, a sentiment echoed a few years later by Almada. This period of commercial intensification was also one of increased cultural and biological intermingling, materialized in the emergence of Luso-African communities along the littoral of Senegambia and Upper Guinea, which are frequently referenced in the sixteenth- and seventeenth-century documentary record and established themselves as a prosperous network of middlemen connecting the coast with interior supply areas.[28]

By the 1590s, English and French merchants had supplanted the Portuguese in Senegambia and were increasingly challenged by Dutch traders, who became involved in the hide trade. Around the same time, Lavanha depicts the coast as a floridly cosmopolitan place, marked by amicable economic and cultural exchanges between Africans and European nations. Contemporary authors place hides at the forefront of regional exports, estimating annual outputs at several tens of thousands. De Marees indicates that entire cargoes of salted hides were bartered for iron bars and assortments of other commodities (liquor, cloth, brass basins, beads) in coastal ports.[29] He adds that these hides did not come from the Petite Côte, where bovines were highly valued and a store of social wealth, but were obtained from the interior. Fuuta Tooro, where cattle abounded, was the main supplier of hides. They were acquired in return for finished iron products, which coastal smiths fashioned from traded bars into weapons, agricultural instruments, and fishing tools.[30]

Numerous authors also record that cotton was grown on the Petite Côte and supported a vibrant local cloth-making industry, likely integrated into regional circuits before the Atlantic trade. Late sixteenth-century authors like Almada and Andrade report that popular currency-cloths produced in the Rio São Domingos were made of Cape Verdean cotton and Rio Nunes dyes (putting into question what might as counted as local), while the Portuguese traded Sierra Leonean kola for cotton goods from the Petite Côte, and resold the latter for slaves in Cacheu. Blue-and-white striped cloth was the most prized article, which enjoyed great popularity on African coasts and was traded as far as Spain! Central to the regional economy until the seventeenth century, the cloth trade descended into oblivion after the French seized hold of Gorée. Marine resources provided another significant source of commerce in the Siin-Saalum. Salt making is documented by numerous European observers from the sixteenth to the eighteenth century and provided a solid foundation for the Saalum kingdom's influence in regional commerce. Jobson mentions that slaves were the "chiefest commoditie" traded for sun-evaporated salt by Juula merchants in the Saalum River and that the king profited handsomely from the proceeds of this trade, which made up the bulk of his revenue. Saalum's salt, in turn, was resold further inland in exchange for gold, kola, and ivory. Captain John Leach's *Map of the River Gambra* (1732) features saltpans on both banks of the estuary belonging respectively to Siin and Saalum and refers to an abundant commerce in salt and grain departing from the Saalum Islands. This area is also associated with the gathering and processing of mollusks, which, once cured and sun-dried, were traded into interior markets. Again, these various regional exchanges boasted considerably greater antiquity than Atlantic circuits.[31]

Written documents paint a vivid portrait of local kings' involvement in the external trade (figure 24). Foreign traders were required to pay

24 King of Kajoor negotiating anchorage fees with the captain of a European vessel (O. Dapper, *Description de l'Afrique*, Amsterdam, 1686, p. 237; http://gallica.bnf.fr/ark:/12148/bpt6k104385v/f21.image)

taxes and customs to port officials and often describe their dealings with royal agents trading on behalf of the king.[32] In some situations, kings themselves conducted negotiations with European merchants. In Siin, oral traditions indicate that the *maad* exerted a royal monopoly on salt, slaves, and horses, items that might have given an economic edge to political rivals. What also transpires from European accounts is that Africans were not gullible puppets in the hands of wily foreigners, as is sometimes portrayed in historical writings, but knowledgeable merchants, tough negotiators, and savvy businessmen. The architecture of captains, *alcatis* (king's representatives at trading factories), royal officers, and customs collectors certainly denotes a measure of African control over the terms of the trade, and, notwithstanding frequent complaints, Europeans accepted with resignation the burden of payments and Africans' meticulous inspection of their goods. The perceived benefits of African riches demanded these concessions.[33] While mutual adjustment, assessment, and hard bargaining continued to frame exchanges until the nineteenth century, the economic parity between Africans and Europeans appeared to last through the Dutch period before beginning to fracture toward the late seventeenth century with the French occupation of Gorée.

With the turn of the eighteenth century, Siin became caught in an intricate web of processes with varied effects on its political economy. Commercially, Siin seems to have distanced itself from Atlantic exchanges after the hide trade period, at least in relation to neighboring areas. The kingdom was still active in oceanic commerce but retreated considerably with the rise of Kajoor, Bawol, and Saalum, and the growing importance of the ports of Rufisque and Portudal. The ascending Franco-British commercial hegemony and rivalry in Senegal triggered a shift from a hide- and textile-centered trade to one focused on slaves, which may explain Siin's demotion to the rank of secondary player in regional politics and economy, insofar as the kingdom was never a major supplier of captives.[34] Commercial activity did not remain uniform throughout the eighteenth century, and vast annual variations characterized the trade in captives and other supplies, depending on political fluctuations, wars, and incidences of famines or locust infestations. Regional conflicts occasionally produced surges in captives that fed the export trade at Joal. Yet, Le Brasseur points out that unlike other coastal kingdoms, Siin only traded slaves in times of war; while at peace, the polity supplied grain (millet, rice), cattle, and other basic necessities to Gorée and Saint-Louis, thus suggesting a more distant involvement with the Atlantic slave commerce.[35]

Against this backdrop of relative disengagement, however, the Siin was gradually drawn into relations of mutual dependence with the European *comptoirs*. The pangs of reliance on Atlantic supplies and their impact on the state were already visible by the 1730s and 1740s. This period was marked by frequent trade cessations in Joal due to political disruptions, wars, and the souring of European-African commercial relations. The king of Siin, who was caught in regional wars at the time, made repeated pleas with Europeans for the reopening of coastal exchanges.[36] When a war with Bawol interrupted Siin's commerce during several months in 1744, the superior council of direction in Gorée observed that "Barbessin king of Joal is every day courting to reestablish our *comptoir* in his country but it is apposite that we punish the people of this *canton* for the number of vexations it did to us, as we do not [presently] need their services." Later, in the 1770s, de Rocheblave noted that while the *maad* was greedy and exigent, "his needs continually place [him] back in our dependence, forc[ing] [him] to ask a composition; liquor, judiciously distributed, straightens the worst affairs."[37]

Commercial dependence, however, was not unilateral, and the French administration often was equally tied to the vagaries of supplies coming from Joal. As famines, millet shortages, and warfare escalated throughout the eighteenth century, Siin's produce repeatedly bailed the French out of delicate situations. As early as the 1720s, Dubellay recognized that "fortunately, Joal has been and will always be of great rescue to Gorée and here [Saint-Louis], for millet in case of shortage or trading dispute, even though we have been obliged to increase the price because of the scarcity of it in Baöl or Cayör." Thirty years later, Estoupan worried that "the kings of Cayor, Baol and Sin [would] take advantage of the need that we have for them, and either through trade interdictions, or frequent and unreasonable demands, place us in the situation, either to yield and consent to all of their whims, or to expose ourselves to the confiscation of our cattle."[38] While some observers readily admitted that Joal's trade was of moderate consequence, most emphasized the *comptoir*'s centrality for the provisioning of the French colony.[39] More generally, the commercial situation on the coast often made it necessary for the French to accommodate local monarchs. In the early trade, for instance, concerns with protection, boycott, and European competition obliged French *résidents* to advance goods on credit, despite existing debts. Conversely, throughout the 1700s, the deepening cycle of debt and credit pushed the kingdom closer to the interests of the French colony.[40]

The passage into the nineteenth century ushered profound reconfigurations in Senegambian economies, inspired by the British abolition of the slave trade in 1807 and gradual transition to "legitimate commerce." Existing merchant networks quickly compensated for the abandonment of human commodities, offering new economic options (gum arabic, incipient cash crops) that consolidated local kingdoms' dependence on trade goods.[41] Due to the lack of documents, little is known about the Siin during the first part of the nineteenth century, and we can conjecture that the region probably had limited interactions with French agents and authorities during that period. After 1850, however, the region was slowly absorbed into France's nascent colonial economy as a producer of cash crops. Siin's involvement in Atlantic grain and produce markets created a precedent for the transition to colonial commodity farming.

Assorted Entanglements: Cultured Trade, Consumptive Paths, and the Logic of Composition

He begs you, Gentlemen, to send him a striped garment, six pairs of red stockings, and as many black ones, with a golden sword, with a fairly large blade, made of Damascened steel, with a few ornaments and gilded on the top: he can put up to the value of ten captives at the Senegal rate of

50# per *pièce d'Inde* [slave]. Because this king is six feet and four inches in height, what we send to him must be proportionate to his size.

N. D. DE SAINT-ROBERT, "LETTRE À LA COMPAGNIE," 1720[42]

Two sets of clues stand out regarding the culture of trade in Atlantic Senegambia. First, sources underline the importance of consumptive practices, as they depict a world of African economy peopled by sophisticated negotiators and demanding clients. Senegambians did not just buy anything.[43] Rather, they were careful about the quality, amount, and content of merchandise. Secondly, written documents contain promising insights into the calculi and ideologies of value underwriting Senegambian dealings with Atlantic markets.

Extending Jane Guyer's argument regarding "wealth in people" (and her analysis of the combinatory principles whereby people are turned into valuable assets), I suggest that Atlantic exchanges, early on and continuing into the nineteenth century, were locally mediated by what Guyer has called a "logic of composition." The term describes social economies where social power is created not only by *accumulating* rare or precious commodities but also by selectively *combining* and *arranging* different classes of goods and the substances, knowledges, and use-values they embodied. Value thus inhered not solely in particular goods but in the *assortment* of varied commodities.[44]

Throughout the Atlantic era, commercial memoirs and merchants' journals list extensive compilations of objects, which, in shifting arrangements, permitted traders to secure certain categories of local goods or others. Thus, in the early seventeenth century, Ruiters documented equivalences between imported and local goods—what could be obtained in return for what—making it all too clear that local consumption tastes regulated the direction of exchanges. In 1610, Lancaster, while briefly stopping on the Petite Côte, complained that "although the natives catch much fish, they [the crew] did not buy any, the expedition being devoid of crystal beads, white and blue *counter* [glass beads], bloodstones [carnelian beads], knifes with yellow handles, iron bars, liquor bottles, without which one can procure neither cattle, nor goats, nor chickens, nor wood, nor water, etc." In 1720, Brüe indicated that beads had to be strung by color and in particular arrangements to be sellable on the coast. In the mid-1760s, Demanet remarked that baubles were absolutely necessary to obtain captives and foodstuffs, in conjunction with iron, liquor, beads, weapons, ammunitions, and gunpowder. Ten years later, Le Brasseur lamented the indispensability of assortments to obtaining certain local products in return.[45]

These various accounts underscore the importance of compositional practices in coastal trading and the distinct modes of valuation on which they rested. Just as wealth flowed from the strategic mobilization of people and relations, "things" could be selectively combined to meet local demand and tastes. While "real values" slid up and down against absolute price scales depending on the combination of goods being exchanged, imported commodities became imbued with economic meaning as parts of trade *assemblages*, whose content varied on the basis of what was being transacted. These dynamics pulsed through the operation of Senegambian money, whose elasticity has been demonstrated by economic historians.[46] For instance, although grain was traded directly for livestock—or hides for iron, or horses for slaves—in various parts of Senegal at different points in time, a variety of currencies emerged as fictional benchmarks for exchange. Historically, these included textiles, cowries, silver, and liquor, though starting in the late seventeenth century, the "iron bar" was institutionalized as a standard of price-reckoning. Iron bars, however, served as ideal yardsticks. On the ground, transactions gave way to a fluid system of payments expressed in a variety of assorted commodities. These goods each had a different relationship of convertibility to the iron bar, and their exchange rates were at variance with each other, such that an iron bar of beads might not be worth an iron bar of rum or long cloth. What is more, while the iron bar remained relatively stable until the late eighteenth century, its value fluctuated considerably over shorter periods, as did the bar prices of different trade goods.[47] In consequence, trade typically entailed a frenetic ballet of bargaining calculations, where each trading party sought to take advantage of the cacophony of equivalences: African merchants tried to obtain goods fetching the highest prices in interior markets, while European traders sought to maximize the amount of cheap goods included in an assortment.

The widespread nature of composition in African commerce at the time of contact suggests the probable antiquity of these modes of valuation. Its persistence throughout the Atlantic era attests to its continued relevance as a compass for acquisition and a general framework in which objects near and far could be slotted, equivalences between them consistently determined, and exchangeability guaranteed.

Liquid Trajectories: Glimpses of the Social Lives of Bottle Glass

As elsewhere along the coast, historic documents stress the early popularity of trade alcohol in Siin. Liquid intoxicants frequently recur on lists of traded items in the sixteenth and seventeenth centuries, and official correspondence between local administrators and French charter companies documents increasing local demand for alcohol and iron throughout the 1700s, with *alcool de traite* (trade liquor) moving to the strategic center of commercial exchanges in northern Senegambia.[48] Hard economic information is anecdotal for the Atlantic era, which makes quantification somewhat unreliable. Keeping this in mind, estimates computed by Curtin from commercial records between 1718 and 1838 nevertheless show a steep increase in the volume of alcohol (surpassed only by imported textiles) matched by a comparable decline in prices. In the context of regional economy, many authors mention that liquor was more heavily prized on the Petite Côte than further to the south where populations were more heavily Islamized. These assessments find some documentary substantiation, at least for the early eighteenth century. For instance, a commercial memoir for the French Compagnie des Indes, which serviced northern Senegambia, estimates that in 1718, "brandy" or "spirits" represented 25.4 percent of all imports (in value) into the Siin, easily outpacing Bawol and southern Kajoor, the second-greatest importer of alcohol at 11 percent.[49]

How the inflow of liquor affected alcohol consumption in local settings during the eighteenth century is difficult to evaluate. One of the persistent difficulties we face is the virtual absence of evidence on alcohol drinking in coastal Senegal before the onset of Atlantic exchanges. Archaeological research has been too limited to suggest much of anything before the sixteenth century. On the documentary side, while it is known that populations on the Petite Côte made wine out of grain (millet) and the fruit of the palm tree in the early days of contact, coastal observers say little about the sociology of alcohol use and offer thin comparative ground for evaluating later archaeological trajectories.[50] More intriguing still, considering its well-documented antiquity, is that the liquor trade has left few material traces on regional sites before the late eighteenth century. Preservation factors may account for this phenomenon. It is also possible that *alcool de traite* was traded in perishable, nonglass containers that would have no archaeological visibility.

This changes with the turn of the nineteenth century. In effect, the ubiquitous presence of alcohol bottles on archaeological sites of this period in the Siin offers a material reminder of the central importance of liquor in international exchanges in Senegal. While liquor was one element in a complex assortment of barter items during the seventeenth and eighteenth centuries, it rapidly eclipsed other goods during the nineteenth century and came to dominate the sphere of trade imports on the

25 Gin bottles, Diakhao region, late nineteenth-century archaeological contexts

coast. Archaeologically, case bottle assemblages illustrate the reign of gin after the 1850s (figure 25). Writing in the last decade of the nineteenth century, Noirot, who administered the Siin province, admitted that "genever liquor" was the main item traded on the coast and indispensable to obtain local products. The sheer magnitude of gin bottles also speaks to the dynamics of colonial capitalism and supply circuits in Senegambia at the time. The liquor trade reflects the economic success of the Dutch distilling industry, whose products inundated Africa through the marketing channels of other European nations. Embossed lettering on case bottles retrieved from settlements in the vicinity of Diakhao point to the products of Dutch manufacturers: J. H. Henkes, Handels, and E. Kiderlen feature as recurrent brand marks. Before that, as archival references appear to hint, alcohol imports were maybe more diverse in provenance and included French liquor and rum from the Caribbean and possibly wine.[51]

The liquor trade had a considerable impact on local consumption in nineteenth-century Siin. This much is refracted in what European sources portrayed as the generalized practice of drunkenness on the coast. Colonial observers perceived the abusive local alcohol consumption as a sign of degrading mores and social anarchy. The extent to which we can trust these depictions is debatable.[52] On one level, colonial documents are ideological artifacts that consciously highlight the vitiated morals of the local aristocracy and exploit the rhetoric of oppressiveness to justify European intervention. In this light, colonial reports of systemic alcoholism seem built as much on cultural stereotypy and strategic instrumentalism as the perils of liquor consumption. On another level, the consistence with which writers of all backgrounds discuss local liquor consumption and inebriation over time suggests that alcohol use in Siin was no simple political fiction but a social fact that intensified to the beat of global flows. This is expressed all-too-concretely in the hundreds of liquor bottles collected on regional sites, from aristocratic residences to peasant villages.[53] Survey evidence thus confirms that alcohol consumption was not limited to social elites but encompassed the full breadth of Seereer society in the nineteenth century. Lack of reliable measurable evidence makes it impossible to know if people drank more *sangara* (moonshine) in the Siin or if neighboring regions were similarly affected—on this point, colonial writers seem equally determined to lament the rampage of alcoholism among the nobility of Kajoor or Bawol—but there is little doubt that the liquor trade wore a disruptive face, as the landscape of commotion that hardened in the second half of the nineteenth century would seem to suggest.[54] In this, Siin joins a long list of examples stressing the part of alcohol in colonial world building as a vehicle of deleterious social and economic relations and a component of imperial technologies of domination.[55]

As with all material histories, however, there is a flip side to scripts of colonial imposition. In this regard, if alcohol had adverse effects on precolonial and colonial public health and served as a tool of empire, it also clearly became inscribed in local fields and rituals of social power; that is, drinking was a political act.[56] This much was visible, for instance, in the way in which drinking was attached to the *habitus* of *ceddo* warriors, for whom *sangara* drinking translated to bravery in battle and invulnerability to enemy blows, in addition to cementing martial subjectivities and solidarities. Nuances of cultural politics are also traceable in the material record of nineteenth-century consumption. In effect, variations in artifact assemblages seem to illuminate the social dimensions of drinking and its role in the fashioning of social distance. Regional archaeological transcripts indicate that while alcohol containers remain abundant on all nineteenth-century sites, a disparity emerges in the content of bottle assemblages between royal and aristocratic residencies and settlements inhabited by nonelites. Specifically, the former not only revealed denser and more diverse bottle assemblages but also featured higher proportions of wine bottles in relation to gin case bottles. Wine containers, for example, were very common in the nineteenth-century trash mound assemblages at Thioupane, the domicile of Siin's *lingeer* (the kingdom's first lady), and Pecc Waagaan, a secondary royal residence near Ndiongolor, and most recently the refuge of renegade king Sanumoon Faay in the 1870s. Inventories at these sites contrasted with those of neighboring settlements, whose collections contained high frequencies of case bottles (table 6; figure 26).[57]

While this trend may partly index preferential participation in commodity circuits, excavated material suggests a subtler set of cultural dynamics at play, denoting the enmeshment of wine in local practices of taste and boundary making. During the excavation of an open plaza at Pecc Waagaan, a strange feature emerged: a deep pit (more than two meters below the surface) made up of stacked layers of greasy organic soil containing dense amounts of charcoal and ash and crammed with solid cultural materials—burnt ovicaprine, bovine and fish debris, ceramic cooking and serving wares, and an enormous amount of bottle fragments. The deposits broke down into thinner and thicker layers, which were chronologically contemporary (clustering around 1870–1890) and were apparently laid down in short succession. If culinary trash and food remains are normally discarded into garbage mounds in Siin, this feature seemed better interpreted as the outcome of successive feasting episodes accumulated at roughly the same time. More curious still, in stark contrast with artifact inventories elsewhere, 70 percent of the feasting pit's bottles were wine containers (figure 27). While this is slim evidence, the repeated association of wine with aristocratic contexts and its presence in prestational ceremonies in Siin makes it tempting to wonder whether wine may have carried different symbolic weight from other types of alcohol. As a highly public and collective ritual experience, feasting frequently forms an arena for the elaboration, reproduction, or consolidation of strategies of power. The feasting ground of Pecc Waagaan could represent an instance of what Michael Dietler has called "diacritical feasts," where the display and selective consumption of precious or prestige items serves to mark and remake social boundaries. Perhaps, then, at a time when gin seemed to diffuse widely to all echelons of society, wine evolved into an icon of social distinction, publicly distinguishing elite consumption practices from those of commoners.[58]

Contemporary documents provide discrete allusions to such an elite aesthetic in the Siin. In one of his letters to governor of Senegal Pinet-Laprade, after requesting a war horse, a double tent, a rifle, and a pair of shoulder pads, *Maad a Sinig* Buukaar Jiilaas went on to express his great urge to have "some of that red beverage which is called *bique* (wine)."[59]

Table 6 Fatick region: Glass bottle inventories at Pecc Waagaan (S6) and neighboring sites

		Glass containers[a]									Other glass			
Site name	Context	Case bottles	Wine bottles	Medical/ cosmetic[b]	Mineral water bottles	Soda	Other bottles[c]	Liquor bottle fragments	Other bottle fragments	Jars	Tableware[d]	Lighting glass	Flat glass	Comments
S6C	Unit 1 (all levels)	2	46				6	93			3		1	
S6C	Unit 2 (all levels)	3	2				3	24	4					
S6C	Surface collections	1	18	1	2		2	63	6		1			
S6 complex	STPs	3	7[e]				1	12	2			1		
S6 complex	Surface collections	24	122[e]	16	10		16	60	30		2		1	
S7	Surface collections	18	18	14	2		1	1	1					
S10	Surface collections	3	2	2										Site featured uncharacteristically small amounts of imported artifacts
S11	Unit 1 (all levels)	47	28	34	8	5	11	14	78	6	17	2	22	
S11	Unit 2 (all levels)	56	32[e]	45	10	2	4	120	172	2	8		6	

(continued)

Table 6 (*continued*)

Site name	Context	Glass containers[a]									Other glass			Comments
		Case bottles	Wine bottles	Medical/ cosmetic[b]	Mineral water bottles	Soda	Other bottles[c]	Liquor bottle fragments	Other bottle fragments	Jars	Tableware[d]	Lighting glass	Flat glass	
S11	Surface collections	31	13	8	11	1	3	4	3					
S13	Surface collections	2	1				1	5	1					Site featured uncharacteristically small amounts of imported artifacts
S17	Surface collections	3	11	6	1[f]	2	1	1						Presence of late 18th-/early 19th-century bottles skews the case-to-wine-bottle ratio
S23	Surface collections	27	15	33	5		1	100	9	2			1	

Note: All sites dated to 1850–1950, with late nineteenth-century/early twentieth-century occupations. All are located within a three-kilometer radius of the contemporary village of Ndiongolor. S10, S7, and S23 are single-family residences (*mbind*); S11 is a large hamlet; S13 and S17 are small hamlets; and S6 was a village, the precursor of Ndiongolor. Deposits at S10, S11, and S23 are typical of regional hinterland sites.

[a] Counts refer to minimum number of containers.

[b] Variety of cylindrical medicine bottles (esp. embossed *alcool de menthe* containers), apothecary containers, and small machine-made perfume bottles.

[c] Made up largely of beer bottles, blue-green/aqua-green flacon fragments, wide-mouthed containers, and small cylindrical amber containers.

[d] Tableware consists largely of tea glasses and tumblers.

[e] Includes a small number of demijohn bottle fragments.

[f] Includes an early twentieth-century Perrier bottle.

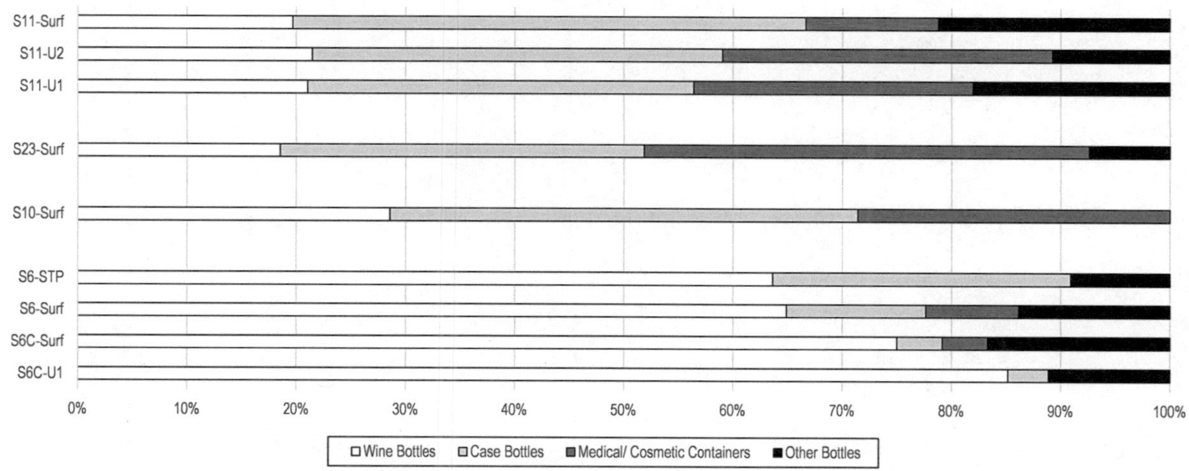

26 Comparing bottle type frequencies near village of Ndiongolor (S6 complex, S10, S11, and S23)

27 Village of Ndiongolor, Pecc Waagaan site (S6C), unit 1: feasting pit feature; pit deposits consist of layers of greasy, silty soil with ash lenses and high charcoal content packed with material culture

In admitting his unfamiliarity with wine, the *buur* seems to hint that this beverage may have enjoyed limited circulation on the coast and maybe in Senegambia in the 1860s. By the end of the nineteenth century, however, oral memory recalls that wine (rather than any alcohol) was an essential element in the *lingeer*'s initiation ceremony. The fact that an *imported* commodity held central ground in local ritual practices and in the induction of high functionaries of the state speaks volumes about the enrollment of foreign objects into local social practices and logics of power.[60] While different variants of liquor may have shared a common path across the various domains of consumption in Siin, wine may have become invested with social value, translated as ritual potency, and replaced local and imported liquor as an embodied substance associated with political power. Differentiating between imported products enabled aristocratic elites to alter regimes of taste and demarcate different classes of people; it assisted them in holding onto a social order showing signs of erosion by creating new hierarchies of consumption.[61] Because it was readily available to the average villager and thus less manipulable as a material symbol gin was kept out of the calculus of invented traditions. At the same time, based on colonial and ethnographic sources, there is much evidence that, among commoners, trade liquor operated in the same ceremonial capacity as wine in aristocratic circles. While milk and millet porridge once served as primary ritual substances, by the end of the nineteenth century, liquor was commonly used for commensal rites, the propitiation of ancestral spirits, annual festivals, public ceremonies, funerals, and work parties. Mirroring observations in the previous chapter about the potency of the foreign, the passage of trade imports into the habitual world of social production and reproduction seems to exemplify the eagerness with which Siin residents sought to cajole the social efficacy of certain outside things.

While *alcool de traite* was a permanent fixture of the nineteenth-century political-economic landscape in Siin, we would be remiss to look at glass assemblages through the single lens of hard liquor. Pharmaceutical and cosmetic bottles made up the second largest component of glass artifacts, showing that consumptions markets were not restricted to gin and wine. "Medicine" bottles consist of molded or machine-made cylindrical containers sporting classic "prescription" lips, whose date ranges cluster toward the last decades of the nineteenth century. The most common types of pharmaceutical containers are *alcool de menthe* (peppermint water) bottles, which turn up in abundance on recent historic sites.[62] These artifacts sometimes showcase embossed labels—Alcool de Menthe de Daver and Alcool de Menthe de Ravol being the most frequent brands—located on the body of the bottle or stamped on the base inside a starburst pattern. Greater variety is found in perfume and toilet water bottles. Early types comprise tiny bottles with molded, paneled bodies and free-blown necks. These are sometimes accompanied with finials and stoppers. Most cosmetic vials, however, are machine made and date at the earliest to the last decade of the nineteenth century. They boast threaded lips and cylindrical necks, as well as a variety of adventitious body shapes involving paneling, ribbing, and geometric forms. These are generally embossed on the base with numbers or brand labels, the most common of which are Crizma Paris, Kelkar, Islamia, and Dagron et Cie. These names dovetail with labels listed in colonial trading inventories.[63]

If alcohol and imported beverages appear to have constituted a *qualitative* index of social difference, pharmaceutical and cosmetic glass assemblages perhaps provide a more *quantitative* expression of social disparities (table 6). As with other classes of material culture, medicine and elixir bottles, vials, perfume and toilet water flacons, and other cosmetic containers are found indiscriminately on nearly all post-1850 habitation sites, speaking to the active radiation of colonial market forces in the late nineteenth century. More than their presence or absence then, it is the size and composition of these assemblages that seem to yield a few clues to local consumption. Specifically, the diversity and sheer number of medicine and toiletry bottle fragments on residences of aristocratic families and district chiefs may denote regional imbalances in purchasing power and access to commercial spheres. Unfortunately, surface material patterns say little about how these artifacts were used or incorporated into local practices, how they were combined with Seereer pharmacopoeia, medical and magical knowledge, or ideas of hygiene, cleanliness, and aesthetics.[64]

Of Other (Small) Things: Sketching the Cultural Economy of Beads, Pipes, Ceramics, and Textiles

Beads: Strings of Trade

Against the growing popularity of textile and liquor in Atlantic exchanges, beads continued to be imported at a steady rate. In European correspondence, beads are often depicted as essential items of trade, modes of payment, gifts, or components of customs assortments along the coast and were incorporated into local aesthetic and adornment practices.[65] Coastal writers make frequent references to African men and women clad in bead paraphernalia and the fervent demand that existed for them. This trend was vividly captured by Demanet who observed that "it is inconceivable for the Europeans who have not witnessed it, how many trinkets are consumed along the coasts of Africa. Negros, negresses, mulattoes and mulattresses wear them in prodigious belts that are sometimes a foot in length and three or four rows thick. . . . Thus all the kinds of baubles are absolutely necessary for the trade in slaves, as well as to procure the necessities of life."[66]

Documentary sources seem to echo anthropological and archaeological analyses in other parts of the continent, which have underscored beads' centrality to cultural and power transactions as barter, token of currency, money, luxury goods, and ritual, religious, or decorative objects.[67] The partiality of archaeological information makes it difficult to understand the role that beads played in processes of social and ritual reproduction in Siin and how their introduction transformed local practical embodiment. Clearly, beads were not exactly a novelty at the time of early oceanic encounters but had already been a part of local and regional exchange networks—another reminder that the Atlantic trade often did not bring items that to which Africans lacked access but simply redirected economic gravities away from hinterland areas and grafted itself onto existing commercial circuits. While bead assemblages have been recovered from funerary contexts in the Senegal River valley, megalithic and tumulus belts, and Saalum Island delta after AD 500, beads in Siin match other imported materials by their invisibility in pre-Atlantic settings. The earliest recorded beads are chevron beads retrieved from early Atlantic-period deposits at the sites of Mbissel, which is thought to have been Siin's first royal capital, and Diohine in Siin's interior. While the chronology of chevron beads is somewhat delicate, these artifacts were included in European overseas trading inventories between the sixteenth and eighteenth centuries, and the strata in which the Mbissel and Diohine finds originated fit well with a seventeenth-century attribution.[68] While this discrepancy probably stems from problems of archaeological sampling and distortions associated with bead curation and heirlooming, it might also point to Siin's distant connection to Saharan economic spheres prior to the Atlantic era.

While comparisons between pre-fifteenth-century contexts and Atlantic-period ones are difficult, it is possible to pick up the trail of beads across later social settings by juxtaposing material archives against the textual records. As with other trade materials, one notes a discrepancy between sixteenth- and seventeenth-century European sources that shows the economic significance and cultural appropriation of imported beads and their near absence from archaeological sites dating to that period. Although we surely owe this incongruity to conditions of deposition and preservation and to the difficulty of identifying early bead specimens with accuracy, the absence of beads may simply indicate that the Siin was not as active in local exchanges as portrayed in European sources.

Alternatively, it is possible that, in the early decades of the Atlantic trade, the circulation of overseas commodities like beads (and access to them) may not have been as widespread as documentary evidence suggests but subject to tight control on the part of political dignitaries. Archaeological evidence to date is too limited to suggest differences in the geography of bead distribution that would support preferential consumption or their use as badges of prestige and social valuation, but it is quite possible that relevant contexts have yet to be investigated. In effect, some seventeenth-century sources comment upon the local use of beads to delimit social difference, a form of "practical logic" that has been documented in other parts of Africa.[69]

By contrast, the omnipresence of Venetian and Czech beads in historic settlements in Siin offers unambiguous evidence of the widespread demand for imported beads. This is all the more informative because this period appears to have experienced a precipitous decline in bead imports as they were supplanted by liquor and weapons.[70] The ubiquitous presence of beads at eighteenth- and nineteenth-century sites in various parts of Senegal leaves little doubt that they remained important elements of regional cultural landscapes, as many colonial authors observed.[71] Despite the relative modesty of its size and composition, the Siin assemblage shows greater diversity than material collected in some neighboring regions. To compare, the Falemme assemblage recovered along the Upper Senegal yielded 474 beads and 108 types, compared to 728 beads and 171 types in Siin's 2003 collection. This could reflect chronological disparities. In the 2011 survey assemblage, which was dominated by post-1850 occupations, beads were fewer (numbering 450) and less diverse, with 23 percent of plastic and 43 percent of Prosser-molded specimens. Yet it also could lend some credence to Curtin's contention that beads were a more popular import in southern Senegambia than in more northerly areas or hinterland regions, where textiles appear to have predominated.[72] Also interesting is the chromatic dominance of blue in Siin's assemblages (both 2003 and 2011) in contrast with the Falemme beads that boast a more diverse color palette, which brings apparent support to the textual hints of distinct regional tastes in commodities and African intransigence in enforcing principles of cultural preference.

A more nuanced expression of the continued economic, cultural, and aesthetic significance of beads in Siin can be seen in the growth of a local ceramic bead tradition during the 1700s, which probably has roots in the seventeenth century. These hand-rolled clay beads were primarily associated with excavations at the two small hinterland settlements of Sagn

Folo and Dioral, whose main occupations date to the eighteenth and nineteenth century, respectively. While perhaps fortuitous, the archaeological emergence of a clay bead manufacturing industry might also signal a connection to the expansion of Atlantic commerce and shifts in commercial fluxes, although the meaning of these entanglements is uncertain.[73] Were local clay beads used to emulate imported beads, and, if so, by whom, and in what social situations? Did they acquire different values, functions, and social messages? Perhaps clay bead production developed to substitute for episodic shortages or the possible decrease in bead circulation documented by historians. Perhaps artisans tried to harness the local taste for beads by producing items that could replace their imported counterparts? The small nature of the assemblage (thirty-five ceramic beads retrieved in 2003, two in 2011) and limited information on the contexts of clay bead use and production afford only hypotheses.

Tobacco Pipes and Ceramics: Resisting Global Commodity Flows

While beads inflected local regimes of preference, smoking pipes and ceramics demonstrate different internal dynamics. It is likely that pipe production followed the introduction of American fumigants, but the conservatism of local assemblages over time and the near absence of imported specimens in archaeological contexts until the late nineteenth century suggest that pipe smoking may have been a relatively democratic activity practiced by all regardless of status.[74] Seventeenth-century depictions of Siin people as consummate smokers would support this view, attesting to the widespread quality of tobacco-smoking, which was practiced indiscriminately by aristocrats and commoners. Lemaire, for instance, described peasants as "scrap[ing] the earth, . . . holding their pipes in their mouths all the time," while mentioning that kings and women also liberally enjoyed pipe smoking. Later accounts indicate that smoking and drinking went hand in hand, and that men and women, young and old, equally indulged in such recreational activities. Following these descriptions, the homogeneity of local pipe assemblages may derive from confinement to the recreational sphere, unlike other parts of West Africa, where the role of fumigants in ritual, divinatory, medical, or political activities encouraged the production of a more complex range of styles and social uses.[75]

Uniformity also extends to imported assemblages, which are comprised nearly exclusively of deep red clay, lustered and molded imitations of African pipes mass-produced by the French for African colonial markets in the terminal decades of the nineteenth century (table 7). In a nod to the dynamics of colonial supply, these pipes appear to have originated from a limited number of manufacturers, since nearly all the identifiable stamp marks point to the Bonnaud workshop in Marseilles. Only four tiny fragments of white ball clay pipe have been recovered so far. In this, the Siin can be contrasted with excavated French military posts and multicultural settlements in other parts of Senegal, where white ball clay pipes were far more popular.[76] What is more, imported models are scarce in the Siin, and survey and excavated collections are dominated by local forms. This disproportion seems to show that, unlike the Gulf of Guinea Coast, where local pipes are replaced wholesale by imports or parts of Senegal more widely exposed to French influence, villagers in Siin did not abandon traditional pipes in favor of European-produced ones.[77] Consistency in pipe usage could in turn reflect the strength of local industry or a cultural choice, as well as unsuccessful marketing, lack of availability, or restricted patterns of circulation for imported pipes on this part of the coast.

In similar fashion, European ceramics never appeared to gain much traction on local pottery consumption. So far, regional sites have yielded a small eclectic assemblage of European-manufactured pottery, amounting to a little under two hundred sherds between 2003 and 2011. These numbers pale in comparison with local ceramic manufacture, which thrived long before the 1400s and continued unabated until the twentieth century after undergoing repeated changes in vessel forms and decorations. Beyond their negligibility, another striking feature of imported ceramics is their lateness. While some eighteenth-century inventories list gifts of faience chargers and other ceramics as customs payments to the Siin monarch and possibly local retainers as well, excavated and survey assemblages have produced absolutely no material antedating the 1800s.[78] The imported pottery we do find in the Siin—plates, platters, and bowls of pearlware, faience, or whiteware with painted or transfer-printed decorations, annularware and spongeware dishes, porcelain jars and teacups, as well as more utilitarian earthenware, slipware, and stoneware vessels—mirrors other trade goods and largely clusters toward the second half of the nineteenth and the twentieth century.[79] A final element involves the skewedness of ceramic imports, which center on a small number of sites (table 8). In the 2003 sample, a total of nineteen sherds came from nine of the forty-six sites of the Diakhao region with an identifiable historic component, mostly from the royal settlement of Pecc Waagaan and Thioupane, while only fifty-one sherds came from eleven of the forty sites in the Fatick region datable to the eighteenth

Table 7 2003 and 2011 site inventories: Tobacco pipes

	2003 site inventory: Tobacco pipes				2011 site inventory: Tobacco pipes		
Site name	Locally produced	Imported molded red clay	Imported white ball clay	Notes	Site names	Locally produced	Imported molded red clay
S1, S7, S12, S13, S14, S17, S23	15	15			S243	38	
S6C—Units 1 + 2	51		1*		S249	21	
S6 complex	22						
S11—Units 1 + 2	46	1			S184A, S218, S231	17	
S61—surface	7						
S61—Unit 1	126			Possible 17th century dates on early pipe contexts			
S61—Units 2 + 3	27						
S89—STPs	5	2			S154A, S154B, S154C, S158, S180, S181, S184, S195, S204, S207, S212, S213, S215, S225, S230, S254, S259	24	1
S57, S37, S51, S56, S62, S69, S81, S87	30	3					
S33, S77, S82	28						
S93, S97, S101, S102, S104, S106, S107, S108, S111	20	1					
Total	377	22	1		Total	100	1

* Two additional imported ball clay pipe fragments were collected during test excavations in the village of Diohine (S260).

Table 8 2003 site inventory: Imported ceramic assemblages

Site names	Lead-glazed earthenware	Slipware	Faience	Pearlware (1820–1840)	
				Plain	Painted
S2—surface					
S4—surface			1		
S5A—surface					
S6C—surface	3	1	1		
S6C—Unit 1 (all levels)		1			
S7—surface	2				
S11—surface					
S11—Unit 1 (all levels)					
S11—Unit 2 (all levels)					
S18—surface					
S21—surface	3			1	
S23—surface	1	2			4
S24—surface				1	
S37—surface					
S41—surface					
S50—surface					
S51—surface					
S56—surface					
S57—surface					
S71—surface				1	
S75—surface	2				
S89—surface					
S93—surface			1		
S95—surface				1	
S106—surface		2		1	
S108—surface					
S111—surface					
S115—surface					
S121—surface					
Total	11	6	3	5	4

through twentieth centuries. In the 2011, two sites made up of four residential contexts (including the residence of an indigenous colonial chief) accounted for nearly 44 percent of the ceramic collection.

What these trends suggest is that, unlike areas such as the Gold or Slaves Coasts and possibly other parts of Senegambia, European commodities did not quite permeate Siin's consumption spheres until well into the colonial period.[80] From the paucity of imported material in Siin, we can adduce that European ceramics never quite found their way into everyday activities. On one level, limited supply probably contributed to the estrangement of European ceramics from local cooking practices. More centrally, this trend reemphasizes that some European

Whiteware (1820s+)				Porcelain		
Plain/molded	Painted	Transfer-printed/decal	Spongeware (1845–1930)	Plain/molded	Decorated	Utilitarian stoneware
1					1	
	1					
2		2	1			1
						1
1	1					
1	1					
1	2			6	1	1
	1					
1						1
				1		
						1
						1
	1					1
						1
						2
						1
1						
		1		1		4
						1
						4
						5
			1			
						1
8	7	3	2	8	2	26

commodities simply filled no demand that was not already satisfied by local industries. There was little incentive for imported ceramics when indigenous pottery industries thrived during the Atlantic period. The abundance of local ceramic inventories suggests that Siin potters met local domestic needs until cheap, mass-produced cookware began to flood African markets in the twentieth century. Before that, European ceramics were simply too costly to penetrate local foodways and were ill adapted to local food preparation, serving, and consumption. Ethnographic data for the Siin and ethnohistoric sources for northern Senegal indicate that meals were one-pot affairs cooked in clay dishes and consumed in communal vessels made of wood, a practice that continues to this today, even if the kitchen paraphernalia has been replaced by gas burners, cast iron cooking pots, and enameled metalware.[81]

Like other regions of Senegal, in Siin ceramics were largely utilitarian objects associated with cooking and domestic activities, not metrics of prestige or social difference. Atlantic-period pottery assemblages fit this scenario well, consisting of few representative vessel types: restricted jars and pots of various sizes (many with traces of soot on them), steamers, and open bowls or platters, highly generic over the region and modestly (and expediently) decorated with twine roulettes and incisions.[82] Considering the peripheral position of pottery in local grids of value, European ceramics were literally screened out due to their lack of social translatability. In Seereer material symbolism, food and the items associated with its collection, production, and preparation, though heavily gendered, evoke an ethos of sharing, commensality, and social belonging rooted in matrilineal identities. European ceramic sets or vessels, by contrast, with their focus on individual consumption and partition, may have exuded a halo of asociality clashing with local conceptions of moral gastronomy, where the communal ingestion of millet grown on the fields and kept in the granaries of the maternal hut (*ngak*) cemented social bonds among family members. It should perhaps not be a surprise that the most diverse and largest imported sherd inventories were found on aristocratic settlements, contexts in which they might well have trumped utilitarian considerations and functioned as symbols of status and conspicuous consumption. Interestingly, ongoing research on Gorée Island has also documented the enduring importance of African food preparation and consumption practices but in a resolutely Creole and cosmopolitan setting.[83]

Cloth: Economic and Social Fabrics

Although less studied because of its limited archaeological visibility, the fate of cloth seems to tell yet another story in Siin. As mentioned earlier, the Siin is described in Portuguese and Dutch sources as a textile-producing area whose products were valuable items of trade in various parts of the African coast. Because local cotton cloth also served a domestic market, it is possible that textile production kept the demand for imported fabric much lower in Siin than in other parts of Africa until the eighteenth century and maybe later. Other documents, however, show that by the 1630s, Petite Côte traders purchased on the Gambia River cotton cloth from which they fashioned their valued garments.[84] Observers also note that local cloth probably embodied forms of social differentiation during the seventeenth century; certain garments seem to have distinguished nobles and elites from commoners. As in many societies, by virtue of its pliability, tactility, and gradability—its intimate linkages to bodies and selves—clothing constitutes a veritable social skin, deployed and redeployed as political artifact in daily negotiations of social geometries.[85]

After playing a central role in exchanges with Portugal and Holland, the trade in local textiles declined with the rise of Franco-British commerce in the late 1600s. These changes probably heavily impacted Siin's economy and position in exchange circuits, since the region lost an important source of revenue and medium of exchange.[86] The gradual peripheralization of Siin in the Atlantic economy may date back to these reconfigurations, after what appeared to be an enterprising start.

What is less clear, however, is how the collapse of a coastal market for indigenous textiles affected Siin's cloth-making industries. It is unclear whether artisanal production experienced a decrease, though European accounts report that imported cloth was increasingly popular throughout the eighteenth century.[87] We can legitimately wonder how foreign cloth influenced the meaning and uses of textiles in Siin and mechanisms of distinction reported a century earlier. How were imported textiles incorporated and reframed into local social aesthetics and body politics? What kind of value did they acquire, and was the meaning of local cloth redefined in the process? Transformations surely occurred, but their cultural significance unfortunately lies beyond archaeological interpretation at this point. A very small collection of highly variable spindle whorls scattered across the region and spanning at least three centuries bespeaks considerable heterogeneity in manufacture. This demonstrates some historical continuity in the practice of cotton spinning into the nineteenth century, although the concurrent scarcity of spindle whorls in recent archaeological contexts may reflect the fierce competition that imported textiles posed to local cloth-making industries.[88]

Because of small sample sizes, no real geographic or temporal patterning emerges from the artifact assemblage. Following oral and historical accounts, one might have expected to see some spatial clustering of spindle whorls in the vicinity of royal settlements and attached satellites, where servants and craft specialists appear to have resided. At the same time, ethnohistoric accounts also remind us that spinning probably was a domestic activity practiced by all women, while loom weaving may have been confined to enslaved artisans or casted weavers. While we should be cautious about assuming continuity in craft traditions and technologies, the heterogeneity of the spindle whorl assemblage is congruent with scenarios of part-time or unspecialized cotton spinning and suggests the decentralized production of cotton threads.[89]

Democratizing Rural Consumption?

While the Atlantic era bred disruption and turbulence, there is another side to the story that must not be overlooked. Atlantic entanglements entailed a certain democratization of the trade economy by bringing commoners into contact with new goods and possibilities. While kings and court retainers may have held special control over the movements of precious commodities (slaves, horses, iron), particularly early on, textual references about rural women's bead assortments from the sixteenth century onward hint that Atlantic commodities slowly came to elude royal monopolies to fall within the reach of Seereer peasants—something also attested to by the unrestricted presence of European imports at all levels of Siin's settlement system.

By the late eighteenth century, most villagers would have been able to trade cereal surpluses for imported merchandise as a way to fulfill the French trading posts' need for grain and provisioning. Witness Le Brasseur, who wrote in 1776 that "almost all the women on the continent have obtained [the right] to sell millet so they could request that the [trading] assortment contain all the baubles that they need. Have we ever traded such large quantities of millet without being obliged to give in exchange all the necessary merchandise?" The congruence of documentary and material patterns lends credence to Searing's suggestion that Senegambia's engagement with the Atlantic economy was structured by a "dual seller's market, one dominated by consumption goods valued by the peasants, the other by aristocratic prestige goods."[90] Simple farmers may not have been able to buy horses, weaponry, or other vanity objects that moved along networks of elite consumption, but through parallel exchange spheres they acquired beads, metal goods, liquor, and many other things. While political violence surely worsened during the eighteenth and nineteenth centuries, the convertibility of peasant foodstuffs into Atlantic commodities ensured the wide circulation of trade imports in local economies and the participation of peasants in external exchange on an unprecedented scale. These new transfers and trade relations bypassed the restrictions that traditional circulation spheres and sumptuary laws imposed on peasant consumption and accumulation.[91] By opening commodity circuits to nonelites, the Atlantic trade challenged local power relations and the practices of distinction that reproduced them. This reached a uniquely concrete expression in the nineteenth century when peasants were able to trade agricultural products for weapons and ammunitions, which they could employ to protect themselves against state violence.[92] In return, the entry of peasants into a wider world of trade and consumption demanded adjustment on the part of elites, as the example of wine discussed earlier perhaps illustrates.

That a broader swath of Siin society was drawn into global political economy thus does not entail its subjection to interests fashioned in Western capitalist centers. The recent dates on trade import assemblages indicate that European goods do not make a visible material impact on the regional landscape until the second part of the nineteenth century. Early colonial documents corroborate the relative autonomy of economic choices in Siin at a time when the French went out of their way to encourage rural participation in commerce as a conduit for the dissemination of colonial authority.[93] Thus, in 1892, Noirot lamented that the Seereer were largely indifferent to European goods. Four years later, he reported that colonial attempts to substitute imported textiles for alcohol as the chief means of barter proved largely unsuccessful, since the Seereer were unwilling to let go of liquor and preferred African cloth.[94] The advent of the twentieth century, however, turned a new page in the history of material practices in Siin. While, as a whole, Senegal's dependence on the world market had remained minimal until the late 1800s, the explosion of colonial commerce and export agriculture progressively tethered local lives to French products, generally at the expense of local modes of subsistence, production, and sociality.[95] Framed by the peanut trade and consolidation of colonial authority, this period was one of dramatic socioeconomic transformations, yet, true to nearly five hundred years of global enmeshments, one permeated by local negotiations and cultural syncretism. We will recoup part of this story in chapters 7 and 8.

Lights and Shadows in Portraits of the Atlantic Past

Glissant . . . urges us to acknowledge that "history has its dimension of the unexplorable." There exist pasts the reality of which we cannot deny but that we may never find ourselves able to evidence unless "we reevalu[ate our] conventions of analytical thought." For the recognition of such systematically obliterated past realities—as well as the recovery of the historical subjectivities of those who lived through them—"has as much to do with the problematics of investigation as with a historical organization of things." S. PALMIÉ, *WIZARDS AND SCIENTISTS*[96]

The Atlantic era was a period of momentous change, which reconfigured a wide range of local social fields. Some transformations have left tangible traces, while others are bound to remain indistinct. One particularly understudied phenomenon, for instance, is the impact of violence and

responses to global political economy, challenging conventional writings on Senegambia.

Rather than shifting wholesale or not at all—an impression sometimes left by historical treatments, particularly as regards matters of culture—material practices, via their agents, locked unevenly with global market forces and thus acquired their own social histories filtered by different conceptions of what is good or acceptable, different senses of what is possible, different imaginations and representations of a changing world. It is in this context that we should understand why such avid smokers as Siin villagers never quite adopted imported pipes, or ceramics for that matter, but quested after liquor and beads; why local and imported cloth became caught in a frantic dance of gains and losses; or why the social trajectories of wine and gin may have bifurcated, as liquid commodities became embroiled in the politics of consumption. In this sense, I have also tried to show that any moment of consumption is also a form of cultural production or that production processes always already envision corresponding spheres of consumption animated by needs and desires. The same can be said of change and continuity, which are not either/or absolutes but whose expressions are tied to the production of scale, moral economies, and cultural sensibilities.[100]

Charting out these dynamics requires particular attention to configurations of time, space, and experience visible at different scales and in different sources. In navigating between feasting pits and settlement networks, between aristocratic residences and peasant villages, between Siin and other parts of Senegal, with an eye on commercial flows radiating from Europe, I sought to craft a narrative sensitive to worldwide political economy and the eventual stranglehold of geocapitalism and to their imbrication in local places—the way rural communities in Senegal made and unmade their worlds in the face of tidal changes they tried to domesticate but could not fully control.

Clearly, these initial steps leave much unturned. In part, this is because the effects of loss and turbulence are doubly compounded by what we could call the "pathos" of objects, to stretch Simmel's phrase, in that artifacts embody not only the limits of social relations but also the limits of their own ability to fully represent what these relations entailed.[101] Remember Bill Brown's "things": nakedly encountered but never quite mapped out. Objects work in fields of social relations, and when the latter are no longer present or have transformed into something else, things only afford skeletal reconstructions of the broader sociology in which they were inscribed. Another difficulty, specific to archaeology, is that we are often left to gaze at the processes of *production* (of things, values, peoples) and *exchange* through the recovery of artifacts in their contexts of *use, consumption,* or *discard,* which introduces shortcuts in our portrayals of material histories.

Within these constraints, this chapter said too little about power, or gender, or state regulations, which were undoubtedly pivotal constituents of life. Also, much of the interpretation stays within object classes and fails to examine transactions *between* different categories of goods and the regimes of value sustaining them; in this sense, it falls short of the demands of a true "compositional" analysis.[102] For lack of historical and archaeological resolution, the analysis reads the process of value production and the kinds of people it created through a rather coarse sociology, separating elites from nonelites but struggling to refine, historicize, or problematize these categories. A more nuanced exploration of value must involve more systematic analysis of the *properties* of objects: qualities (color, tactility, sensuousness, material, shape, size, interior-exterior), quantities (numbers, ratios, densities), scales of use and circulation, and relationality (asymmetries, ranking, grading, equivalences, compositionality). Given the centrality of compositional politics in Senegambian trade, it is critical to look at artifacts in relation to the broader *assemblages* of which they are a part.[103]

At the same time, parts of the analysis show flashes of what a thicker historical description might look like. For example, the sinuous object trajectories traversing Siin's Atlantic past rub against notions of history directed, irreversibly, by the arrow of progressive global time or regressive capitalism; rather, they motion toward a more laminated sense of historicity, made up of different times and processes of engagement with European imperialism. Relations of force are immanent to this story, and here again the tale of artifacts is a cautionary one. Instead of simple formulae of imposition-coercion, archaeological objects show that global forces variably shrunk or expanded Senegambian fields of action. While the compass of African agency may have grown narrower over time, which lessened indigenous abilities to dictate the terms of trade or tweak them in their favor, exchanges continued to be negotiated within a portfolio of options. African actors did not just passively accept trade goods. Guided by cultural tastes, they appropriated some commodities and rejected others. Some trade goods interfered with existing industries and fueled destructive passions while others sparked new craft productions and valuations. Atlantic objects plugged themselves into existing spheres of consumption and opened new ones, keeping old and new connected through mechanisms of conversion, redistribution, and invention. By linking different categories of actors to Atlantic markets, they wove new social solidarities within social classes and redefined relations between them. Albeit schematic, these archaeological mappings provoke new reflections about value and modes of action, the formation of subjects and persons, and the making of social power. Indeed, as they navigate political topographies, objects also help to reorganize political landscapes. They rearrange subjects' relationships to social order and sovereign institutions and thus recompose political identities. In doing so, they also instantiate forms of culture making that structure future actions and possibilities.

When arguing that the Atlantic system in Senegambia had unpredictable effects, which created new economic opportunities, opened coastal commerce to the wider populace, spurred social strategies outside of traditional ways, and redrew the power balance between elites and commoners, I do not suggest we succumb to a gauzy celebration of consumption and exchange as salvation. The Atlantic trade is filled with ghosts and violence, historical dead-ends, and aborted pathways, some of which carried forward into the colonial era. Furthermore, consumption choices are never untrammeled but partially shaped by inequities in productive forces and economic power. Consumption also has unintended consequences, and some of the long-term dependencies forged by global commerce were decidedly not beneficial to political and economic development on the African continent. What the tale of material things allows, however, is a remapping of the problem-space of Senegambian history. Rather than dwelling on the Atlantic past as a long episode of loss, suffering, and devastation—a big part of the story, admittedly, yet one that plugs Africa into a prefigured historical script—an object-centered perspective acknowledges the forms of agency, relationality, and possibility imbricated into the violence of Atlantic exchanges. Through the refuse of global transactions, it recuperates of the Atlantic moment as a historical space—indeed, a space of historicities—that was not just a process of negation and alienation but absolutely fundamental to the shaping of African memories, identities, and subjectivities into the present.[104] These accounts force us to confront Africans not as passively subjected to the time of Atlantic modernity but as subjects of it, as genuine producers of history and culture.

PART FOUR

Colonial Indeterminacies: Entangled Landscapes, Overlapping Sovereignties

The peanut thus begins to weave, bit by bit and insidiously, a whole system of commercial, monetary, and psychological customs, whose establishment we can clearly follow in Sedhiou and its surroundings, and to which migrant seasonal cultivators are tightly subjugated right away, even if they attempt, at least early on, to ward off its most constraining aspects. P. DAVID, *LES NAVÉTANES*[1]

In *Les navétanes* Pierre David recounts the historical experiences of "strange farmers," the itinerant foot soldiers of the agricultural economy that sprouted in Senegal and the Gambia after 1820.[2] On the face of it, David's story is one of economic transformations in the aftermath of the slave trade, a transition that promoted the commercialization of cash crops and created a demand for new sources of labor in the absence of ready reservoirs of captives. David's account is also a profoundly human tale of resilience and creativity, as seasonal migrants flocked to central Senegal in search of quick money and new opportunities and adapted to the rigors of an economic system rigged against them. Yet, the book is also an it-narrative of sorts, a quiet story of the peanut, which emerges as an unsung actor possessed of uncannily determining character.

While David's intuitions are more poetic than sociological, his portrayal has a certain Latourian charm, one in which Sudanic peasants entered an unholy alliance with networks of animate and inanimate things in which peanuts were a foremost actant. Better yet, his insights ex ante actor-network theory advance a subtle, understated theory of colonial materiality that is full of analytic potential. The subtext is that peanuts enmired people in a web of entanglements that rewired their relationship to soils, cereal crops, agrarian programs and calendars, social wealth, kin and communities, among others. This set off a chain reaction of dependencies and entrapments, which in turn helped to sustain the economic and social ecology of colonialism. Peanuts at different moments of their lives with humans—plucked from the ground, dried and stored, sold to itinerant merchants or at colonial *escales*, exchanged for cash, eaten as raw snacks or processed in sauces—exerted independent material force in the field of colonial life itself, which in some ways eclipsed the realpolitik of administrators, blueprints of imperial thinkers, and wills of African farmers.

What I want to do over the next two chapters is to use David's discussion of "peanut imperialism" as a loose heuristic to gaze at the experience of colonialism in Siin. As *Les navétanes* intimates, peanuts offer a valuable prism into the colonial order that congealed in coastal Senegal during the second half of the nineteenth century. First, they provide a hyphen between the Atlantic system and colonial economy, which evinces some of the structural continuities and inheritances linking these two historical moments. Second, they place in relief the material networks of colonialism: its vessels, conduits, and scaffolds. Lastly, and consequently, peanuts hold important insights into the work of statecraft that underpinned the French colonial presence. Taking seriously the role of peanuts as an appendage of power complicates our conceptions of the colonial state and operations of colonial rule in rural Africa. It tempers perceptions of colonial power as intentional, instrumental, and agentive with a humbler focus on the unintended effects and obscure vehicles of colonialism. And it fosters reflection on how the putting-in-place of colonial worlds was not just a tale of forceful imposition but a story that unfolded through mundane, tactile, and often banal channels—a story in which Africans, buoyed by their own modes of doing and living, created themselves anew while they took part in the forging of colonial power. In other words, much as I argued in the preceding chapters that statesmen and farmers (and all social groups in between) contributed uneven strokes to the making of political worlds, I now want to examine the mutual participation of French administrators and rural Seereer communities in the making of colonialism in Siin.

My narrative has two parts: chapter 7 explores the conditions of colonial governance in rural Senegal. It sets the stage for the second part, in the following chapter, which analyzes how the Seereer navigated colonial rule between 1850 and 1950. Both are connected by a concern with what Trouillot called the "geography of imagination" and the "geography of management."[3] The first domain applied scientific and political discourse to facilitate the operations of rule and produce knowledge about conquered territories and colonized others. These representations, in turn, informed the second domain, which entailed the reorganization of indigenous political and economic spaces for purposes of control. These geographies of power, however, did not go unchallenged. Both met the resistance of a tangible social world. Colonial images, for instance, were confronted by pesky forms of cultural life, which they generally failed to elucidate, let alone domesticate; concurrently, techniques of colonial management often foundered on the shoals of implementation, as they were translated to rural habitats. In the Siin, then, colonial strategies, the physical milieu of Seereer villages, and ethnographic images converged in restless ways and became locked in a process of mutual adjustment, improvisation, and constitution.

SEVEN

Hesitant Sovereignties: Logics, Logistics, and Aesthetics of French Rule

How did a notoriously small handful of white men rule gigantic territories?

K. FIELDS, *REVIVAL AND REBELLION IN COLONIAL CENTRAL AFRICA*[1]

This chapter lays out the coordinates of colonial governance in Senegal. Extending the remarks in chapter 5, I begin with a theoretical look at the literature on colonial statecraft. Using Michel Foucault's later writings, I propose an approach to colonial rule that eschews binary visions of colonialism as omnipotent or impotent in favor of integrating materiality, government, and the productivity of power—that is, placing colonizers and colonized in a shared field of power, treating neither as external to the other. I then shift from theory to history to examine the transitions in the first half of the 1800s that moved Senegal from the slave trade to "legitimate commerce" and from there to the onset of formal colonization. The following section outlines the conditions of colonialism in Senegal: its logics, logistics, and aesthetic dimensions. Echoing the epigraph from Karen Fields, I reflect on the material constraints facing French bureaucrats and administrators and how they shaped the philosophy and practice of colonial sovereignty in rural areas. Because of limited resources, the "long arms but weak fingers" of imperial France clung onto the paradoxical projects of preserving/exploiting and reforming/improving indigenous societies, which drove the colonial administration toward peanuts as an offhand agent of rule and human management.[2]

I end the chapter with an "archaeological" (indebted to both Foucault and the trowel) look at one aspect of colonial rule—namely, the production of representations of otherness (the geography of imagination, to reprise Trouillot's terminology). There, I go back to the images of Seereer peasant archetypes encountered in chapters 3 and 4 and reexamine them in the light of archaeological materials. In archaeology, the tangible forms expressed in sheets of earth and text combine to expose the fictions of colonial ideology and evoke more credible accounts of indigenous social existence. My argument, however, is that these mixtures can *also* reveal facets of past epistemologies. Expanding the critique begun in earlier chapters, I match ruins and representations to reinterpret ethnographic images not simply as the byproduct of colonial fantasy, invention, or make-believe but as a symptom of what Michael Taussig sees as the "epistemic murk" oozing out of the colonial project itself. In doing so, I attempt to lay the initial foundations of an archaeology of colonial knowledge in Siin, where materialities disclose aspects of ethnographic common sense and the anxieties, disquiets, and disregards of empire coursing through it.[3]

Topologies of Colonial States: History, Anthropology, Archaeology

Scholarship on the nature of colonial governance in Africa has been somewhat bifurcated. In the broadest of brushstrokes, one strand of literature has portrayed colonial rule as despotic and oppressive, emphasizing its vocation for domination, despotism, and sovereign violence. Other studies have adopted a more skeptical tone, pointing out the limitations and internal contradictions of colonial regimes (most notably their reliance on precolonial institutions) and their inability to monitor African labor and agricultural economy and downplaying their transformational effect on African societies. Herbst corroborates these propositions when he notes that colonialism did not mark a fundamental break with the way in which power was exercised in Africa.[4] While these different views capture salient aspects of colonial rule, there is a danger of slippage into an all-or-nothing understanding of power and its capacity to alter the social relations of colonized peoples. This split has not escaped recent research, which has adopted a more temperate perspective: one recognizing that colonial governments varied considerably in time, space, and over the course of their existence; that some administrations were strong and intrusive (and meted out power instrumentally) while others were weak and indifferent (allowing power to dissipate along many channels); and that others still were sometimes *both* at once. In the face of these textured political worlds, the venerable category of the colonial state as an integrated entity and definitive political type appears somewhat chimerical. Collapsing under its own unwieldy weight, the state has given way to more pliant definitions: a variably coordinated ensemble of institutions, loci, programs, and discourses held together by legal frameworks and broadly working (through cadres, agents, bureaucrats) to define a political community, administer rights and resources, legitimize a regime of order, institute cultural conventions fostering acquiescence to rule, and regulate the behavior of different political actors.[5]

Part of the instability of colonial rule stemmed from the fact that these different projects did not always converge toward a coherent vision. The cracks between them nurtured sizable dysfunctions, contradictions, and shortcomings. Nor were colonial designs always synchronized with the cultural terrains they attempted to police and reform. While colonial authorities at times managed to align their representations with reality, political initiatives were often out of joint with an Africa that European bureaucrats failed to comprehend in full. Another source of imbalance flowed from the cohabitation of colonial administrations with other assemblages of power (which frequently enjoyed more legitimacy in the eyes of Africans): the worlds of village chiefs, lineage heads, land custodians, rain priests, and diviners. At various points in time, colonial administrators may have combated these other spheres of power (such as precolonial aristocracies, Islamic brotherhoods, or labor unions), actively cultivated them (for instance, traditional ruling elites repurposed as chiefs or colonial functionaries), or actually manufactured them (such as African clerks and interpreters, who were pivotal cogs in the machinery of colonial affairs). More ambivalence accrued from the fact that colonial policies did not always elicit anticipated responses from subject populations or meet their consent. Africans openly resisted, subverted, and appropriated colonial idioms, rituals, and other trappings of power for their own devices. Additionally, the goal of subjecting Africans to colonial law sometimes backfired and opened new avenues of native agency. In rural Senegal, for instance, after the 1900s, indigenous tribunals rapidly worked their way into peasants' daily life, and villagers increasingly used legal recourse to adjudicate matters of land rights, inheritance, marriage, family dispute, and theft, turning a modern institution into the arbiter of social tradition and transforming both in the same breath. Likewise, in urban areas, educated mixed-race and black Africans frequently used the law to magnify contradictions in colonial ideology, contest state power, and carve out a space for the expression of the rights of the colonized.[6]

The take-home message is that colonies were not absolute systems of order but "twilight zone[s] of multiple indeterminate configurations of power and authority." To properly grasp the nature of colonial sovereignty requires an understanding of the different registers of power at play in given territories, how they articulated with each other, the uncertainties permeating the government of subject populations, and the ambiguous responses to which they gave rise. In other words, the key to unpacking the metaphysics of colonial rule lies in the microphysics of its functioning.[7]

A relative newcomer in cross-disciplinary conversations about colonialism, archaeology stands to make pointed contributions to our comprehension of colonial statecraft. In the past two decades, historical archaeology has been active in writing counterhistories of colonialism that eschew totalizing portrayals to focus on the microdynamics of colonial world making. Where earlier annals once centered analyses on European achievements or on colonial structures and discourses, archaeologists have drawn on the material debris generated in routine interfaces between colonizers and colonized to advance a ground-level view of colonialism highlighting the daily ordeals and shifting lives of colonized peoples.[8] This work has been keenly attuned to the asymmetries and fluidity of power permeating colonial situations and has thoughtfully examined the capacity of indigenous actors to negotiate or subvert the diktat of colonial prescriptions and engage in meaningful social action.

If archaeological analyses have not engaged nearly as readily with colonial states and their material forms, recent studies suggest that archaeological evidence can be a prime source of insights into imperial governance, its working contradictions, and its manifestations in the material world.[9] To make a finer point, given that many archaeologists labor at the contact zones between people and the state—where people lived, worked, and felt—it can be argued that the discipline has much to say not only about the tangle of relations binding regimes and subjects but also about the shadowy horizon of power that stands past coercion and confrontation and strives to configure comportment through the mundane ether of social practice. In other words, I would suggest that archaeologists are ideally positioned to examine the mechanics of colonial government.[10]

I take *government* here in its Foucauldian inflection to refer to a mode of power concerned with the "conduct of conduct," in which people are the bearers of their subjection to a political order. The work of government (or governmentality), according to Foucault, entails the construction of a "population"—through various instruments of knowledge (censuses, statistics, surveys, social-science research, bureaucratic institutions, public health, urban planning)—as the object of state intervention, whose life can be managed and optimized through rationalizing programs. These interventions, in turn, necessitate the existence of a milieu, a domain of "life, existence, and work" with predictable and accidental dimensions that tangibly organizes the bodies and relations of those living in it. If milieus preexist populations, they can nevertheless be acted upon, adjusted, and harnessed to define and monitor collectivities—which makes them the notional terrain of government.[11] Government's fundamental embeddedness in materiality makes it appealing as an archaeological field of study. Much like Jacques Rancière stresses that politics is about struggles over the configuration of the sensible world and the signs through which it is made intelligible—to whom, for whom and, more importantly, by whom—Foucault reminds us that government is about the "right disposition of things," about the proper arrangement of milieus in pursuit of the effective management of people. In light of this observation, we can argue that the archaeological vestiges of colonial settings provide ready-made windows into the logics and techniques of colonial government. While distorted by formation processes, material assemblages compose a piecemeal portrait of human activities shaped in colonial power fields, in contexts that were often deliberately targeted by colonial programs. Colonial state operations, in other words, can be read aslant, through the effects they left on the concrete indigenous worlds archaeologists so frequently study.[12]

In addition to capitalizing on materiality and the types of information encoded in archaeological data, the study of governance underscores the dense linkages connecting states and subjects and invites us to examine their co-constitution. Foucault remarked that, in becoming subjected to regimes of authority, individuals internalize certain predicates of order and dispositions that orient their deeds and decisions. These sensibilities are thus folded into the subjectivities of social actors and partake in the construction of who they are.[13] Thus, rather than cleaving power and people, we need to view state power as a diverse spectrum of designs whose effects scatter widely between the poles of negation and possibility. In addition to condemning the repressive dimensions of power and revealing ways in which colonized people sought to avert them, we also need to heed power's *productive* side and how it (purposely or not) helped configure native actions.[14] My intent here is not to paint a roseate picture of colonialism and deny its infrastructure of domination, exploitation, alienation, and violence. Surely, force and discipline centrally featured into the colonial equation of power, but so did government. My point, rather, is that power and agency are intertwined: institutions of power create conditions in which people can act in certain ways but not in others, in which they recognize certain choices as feasible, delicate, or impossible, in which they perceive certain regulations as desirable or illegitimate. Matrices of power *both* constrain *and* authorize social projects. But note the flip side of that dialectic: as colonized people blazed new territories of practice around, through, or against colonial policies, they also (again, not always consciously) reframed the terms of power and the conditions of its applicability. Taking account of government, along with other aspects of colonial state making, enables us to interrogate the various reasons, processes, and institutions of rule at play in colonies and to determine precisely how they intersected with native lifeworlds and political experiences. In Senegal, and I suspect other colonial settings, administrations variably ignored, restrained, or coerced colonized subjects, but in doing so they also offered a certain freedom to act, which became part of Africans' evolving social traditions.

Peanut Transitions: Senegambia from Legitimate Commerce to Colonization

The British cessation of the slave trade in 1807, though frequently violated in the French portions of the Senegambian coast, left France looking for economic options when it reoccupied Saint-Louis in 1817–1818, after fifteen years of English rule. Suddenly deprived of its chief linkage to the world economy and lacking resources, the colony embarked at first on a scheme of agricultural colonization, which revolved around the development of tobacco, sugar, and cotton plantations in the Lower Senegal and the use of existing pools of servile labor to cultivate the crops. In 1819, hopeful that the Saint-Louis hinterland would replace the Caribbean island of Saint-Domingue, the French signed a treaty that effectively turned the devastated kingdom of Waalo into a commercial protectorate. This policy of resource maximization (*mise en valeur*) was halted in its tracks by a resurgence of regional political violence in the region, repeated incursions by the Trarza Moors, acts of popular resistance and sabotage by local people, and rancor from the merchant community, all of which culminated in the abandonment of agricultural colonization in 1831.[15]

Despite these hiccups, the phase of adjustment to legitimate commerce was swift and relatively seamless, mostly because the same networks of merchants and labor that had supplied the Atlantic slave trade continued to supply the new exports. Moreover, the new trade built on preexisting commodity circuits, such as gum arabic and peanuts, which had operated alongside the slave export economy and proved quite lucrative. The economic ascendance of cash crops also preserved the one-export pattern that characterized Atlantic Senegambia, while leaving regional systems of production mostly untouched.[16]

The period of structural adjustment unfolded over the first half of the nineteenth century in two loose phases: a gum cycle that spanned from 1800 to 1840 and, after 1840, a long period dominated by peanuts and cash cropping, which lasted into the twentieth century. The first phase is marked by the dominance of the Senegal River Valley, which formed a dynamic river empire centered on Saint-Louis and its surroundings that extended along waterways to link the markets and production areas of the Upper Senegal and Middle Niger regions and engulfed the ecologies of the savanna and western Saharan desert within its orb.[17] Because of its riverine geography and commercial orientations, this economic system operated effectively without territorial conquest.

Gum had been a key export at the mouth of the Senegal River since the late seventeenth century, and its prices had been steadily on the rise since the mid-1750s, which facilitated economic reconversion. Gum production stayed consistent after 1780, and export volumes dramatically picked up by the 1820s, steered by the prospect of profitable returns and demand from fabric manufacturers in Europe. During the first half of the nineteenth century, gum made up about two-thirds of the total value of Senegalese exports, and by 1830 virtually all commercial activity in the colony centered on gum.[18]

The economic boom did not last very long, however, and production began to retract in the 1840s as divisions erupted between colonial administrators, French merchant houses, Saint-Louis traders, and Moor suppliers.[19] These conflicts ushered in a period of commercial speculation, saturated markets, and currency inflation that brought into salience structural constraints internal to the gum trade. Disagreements within the merchant community hinged on contradictory interests between river traders and big, heavily capitalized import-export houses. These were compounded by a phase of environmental degradation that inaugurated the nineteenth century. Extended droughts and overexploitation of gum groves' fragile ecology edged the geography of gum extraction away from the desert and into the savanna-Sahel zone, which shrank outputs. Another long-standing problem was the dependence of gum exchanges on the erratic supply of *guinées* (blue-dyed cloth from India). Oversupplies, as observed in the commercial crises of the 1830s and 1840s, flooded the market with cheap cloth and caused gum prices to drop. Finally, gum's twilight was accelerated by the succession of civil wars, Trarza expansion, and French scorched-earth policy that laid waste to the Lower Senegal in the 1830s and resulted in massive population displacements. Despite the production slumps, gum remained a chief export of the Lower Senegal in the second half of the nineteenth century along with millet, though the river trade was now dominated by rapidly expanding peanut production.[20]

Gum's commercial exhaustion and the demand for oleaginous products in Europe opened an outlet for the peanut trade after the 1840s. As soon as the 1830s, traders in the Gambia began experimenting with peanuts, shipping small quantities to England to test their suitability for home markets. Senegalese merchants soon followed. With the developing soap industry and need for industrial lubricants in the metropole, peanut production soared from a measly one metric ton in 1840 to five thousand tons in 1850; in 1898, export had reached ninety-five thousand metric tons. For those regions that had depended on the sale of captives during the era of commercial slavery but lay outside of gum trading circuits peanuts offered a way out of the transition crisis caused by the ending of the slave trade. These areas made the switch while building on the rural networks that had delivered millet, cattle, and foodstuffs to Gorée and the French colony in the eighteenth century. As they diffused the Gambia northward, peanuts' growing weight in the balance of trade recentered the Atlantic economy after the 1850s from the Senegal River toward the peanut basin in west-central Senegal. The provinces of Kajoor and Bawol established themselves as principal producers in the early decades and were replaced by the Siin-Saalum on the eve of the twentieth century.[21]

Because of its direct reliance on peasant producers, peanut agriculture drove a wedge between France's interests and those of local aristocracies, who could no longer act as intermediaries and reap benefits from the international trade. Whereas the gum trade had favored the income of traders and those who oversaw gum plantations, peanuts were true instruments of social promotion for African peasantries.[22] From being dependent to the nobility and occasionally commodities themselves, peasants rose to the ranks of bona fide economic partners—as producers and vendors but also consumers of goods once restricted to the aristocracy or limited in circulation (weapons, especially). Peasants also reclaimed control over the fruits of their labor, which had been subject to aristocratic appropriation.

While the grain trade afforded access to Atlantic commodities prior to the 1850s, peasant consumption remained limited in scale, focusing mostly on local markets and basic subsistence needs. With peanut cultivation came linkages to a broader sphere of exchanges, which enabled peasants to gradually replace *buur* and *ceddo* as beneficiaries of the external commerce by becoming instrumental, if unequal, agents of that economy.

These internal conflicts and the threat of peasant economic independence triggered a period of unbridled military reprisals. Facing declining incomes, local aristocracies attempted to tap the newfound peanut wealth by pillaging peasant villages and imposing tribute and customs on the trade.[23] This period of instability offered a convenient pretext for intervention by the colonial administration insofar as French peanut traders found themselves frequently threatened by *ceddo* exactions in demand for protection. The merchant community found a zealous advocate in the person of Louis Léon Faidherbe, whose appointment to the post of governor in 1854 marked an aggressive turn in French foreign policy that placed Senegal on the path to formal colonization. Military action was also justified as a way to curb the threat of Islam, targeting the jihad begun in the 1850s by al-hajj Umar Tal in Fuuta Toro and Upper Senegal.[24]

Faidherbe used France's technological edge and African troops immune to tropical diseases to surmount logistical difficulties, budgetary concerns, and limited military personnel. Waalo, which had by then become a dependency of Saint-Louis, was annexed in 1855. Faidherbe launched a series of punitive expeditions against the Moors, which was followed by military campaigns in Fuuta Toro and in the kingdoms of Kajoor, Siin, and Saalum between 1859 and 1861. As Klein points out, "his goals tended to be similar in all areas: suppression of all subsidies to African rulers, establishment of a 3 percent export tax, and construction of a fortified post." This first wave of territorial conquest gave the French a toehold on the coast and mainland and a stepping-stone toward the establishment of *pax gallica*.[25] However, after the defeat of Umar Tal, the 1860s were swept by widespread Islamic revolutions mounted by his successors. These religious movements disrupted commerce, devastated the countryside, and aggravated political rivalries within the various monarchies. For instance, the jihad led by Ma Ba Jaaxu, which briefly united a broad swath of the regional Muslim community, and subsequent spin-off movements left the Saalum and Gambia torn by insecurity, depopulation, and production crises. The failure of the holy warriors coincided with the traditional aristocracies' swan song, which was delivered as a series of last-ditch resistance efforts against the French penetration in the 1870s and 1880s.[26] For a time, the game of alliances binding Muslim revolutionaries and secular leaders proved threatening to French interests, but these ententes were unstable, and could not muster the kind of supraregional challenge that broad-scale jihads had achieved. As alliances unraveled, and as the French were courted for support, rulers were one by one defeated on the battlefield, leaving France in charge of Senegal north of the Gambia by the late 1880s. The pacification of southern Senegambia, from Casamance south, came much later and much more painstakingly, practically on a village-by-village basis.[27]

What were the repercussions for Senegambian societies? For one, while the transition rode the crest of antecedent trade patterns and did not significantly reform economic institutions, it stimulated a gradual reorganization of commerce and acted as a catalyst for the replacement of networks controlled by Saint-Louis métis and African traders by colonial economic structures paced by the agendas of metropolitan investment, merchant capital, and industrial interests. Second, the loss of royal monopolies and the democratization of exchanges accentuated the antagonism between the old regime and cultivators. The economic crises of the 1830s and 1840s ignited a crescendo of state violence, as *ceddo* warriors sought to harvest slaves and resources by raiding villages on the periphery of neighboring polities or, at times, within their own kingdoms. Because peasants outside of the Siin were often Muslims, these attacks deepened the rifts between Islam and the unruly *ceddo*. Aristocratic depredations continued with the civil wars that swept northern Senegambia between the 1850s and 1880s, and Islamic revolutions appear to have intensified internal enslavement.[28] Against this background of social tensions, famines, and political chaos, French pacification campaigns introduced further instability by torching fields and villages. In this troubled climate, peasant communities were left with precious few options. They often sought to resist the rapacious *ceddo* regimes either by taking up arms, which were increasingly accessible through peanut sales, or by joining Muslim resisters. They also fought aristocratic predation and colonial penetration with their feet and became part of the massive population movements that deserted Fuuta Tooro, escaped Saalum and the Gambia to seek asylum in Siin, or relocated from war-torn Waalo into Kajoor. The monarchies were shaken by the political-economic turmoil. The colonial administration largely eliminated traditional regimes and prerogatives and strove to enroll the members of former ruling families as agents of the colonial state. The demise of monarchies, however, was a gain for Islamic political leadership, not only because *marabouts* led much of the resistance against kings and colonizers but also because some brotherhoods, the Muridiyya especially, emerged as powerful political partners and mobilizers of agricultural labor during the colonial era.[29]

The changes implemented by legitimate commerce also carried forward historical currents incubated by Atlantic transactions. First, the Wolof, Muslim, and urban regions of northern Senegal consolidated as centers of political and economic activity—a formative stage of the "Islamo-Wolof model" born of the geography of early trading partnerships and the economics of grain, gum, and peanuts.[30] Second, while the gum boom and peanut revolution built on old food circuits (grain, fish, cattle, salt), they also quietly conspired with politics to draw local peasantries into the commercial machinery of colonialism, gradually yoking them to the cycle of debt and credit, and fostering dependencies that precipitated the loss of economic autonomy, especially in the Wolof parts of the peanut basin, where many early groundnut cultivators were emancipated slaves.[31] Finally, while slavery was officially abolished in 1848 in the French empire, the colonial administration was slow to regulate internal captivity, owing mostly to the logistics of enforcing prohibition, a concern with maintaining social and political status quo, and the centrality of bonded labor to the economy. The French conquest, however, forced the breakdown of slave production, leaving a labor vacuum that was filled by migrant workers—the *navétanes* of David's book. Circuits of labor migrations already crisscrossed the countrysides, stretching as far back as the 1840s in the Gambia, as both free and enslaved workers were lured by economic growth in peanut-growing areas. The completion of the Kajoor railway in 1889, which began to integrate production zones across the peanut basin, created additional demand for field hands and brought flows of seasonal migrants from as far as Mali and Guinée to the Gambia, Siin, Saalum, and Kajoor-Bawol (figure 28).[32] In addition to shoring up the success of colonial export crops, the new labor system also had considerable impact on the demography and social organization of peanut-farming regions.

Anatomizing Colonial Statecraft: Logics and Aesthetics of Rule in Siin

By the late 1870s, stability was restored over most of northern Senegal, and local polities were by and large operating in the orbit of France's dominion. Military surrender, however, did not mean total subjection or formal incorporation into the colony. In effect, many of the provinces under France's mandate were administered as protectorates, where

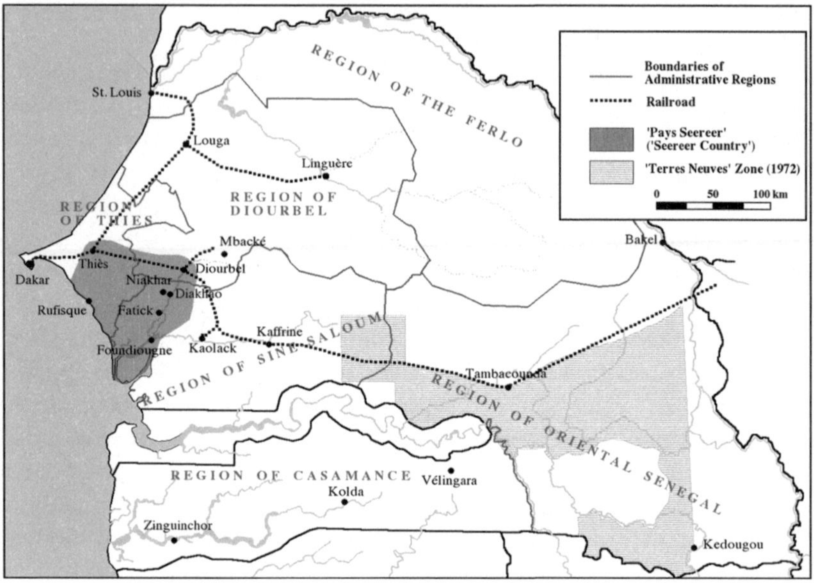

28 Circle of Sine-Saloum: Dakar-Niger railroad and Terres Neuves (1972)

traditional elites often retained considerable power and influence. For example, after being invaded twice in 1859 and 1861, the Siin became a protectorate in 1887. It took eleven more years for its monarchy to dissolve (1898), and twenty more for the region to be officially absorbed into the colony (1920). One outcome of this political bricolage was the nurturance of registers of power that could not be fully assimilated into colonial law. During the troubled years of colonial expansion (1850–1880), for instance, state authority met many challenges as it competed with other political actors for control over territories and populations. Thus, secular ordinances regarding the destiny of African bodies and souls were often disputed by Catholic missionaries spreading the gospel in the region, just as large trading houses (*maisons de commerce*) did not always see eye to eye with colonial and metropolitan politicians regarding matters of commerce. Similarly, French administrators consistently clashed with the remnants of African aristocracies and grassroots leaders (village authorities, lineage heads, ritual specialists) over questions of labor, taxation, trade, and security.[33] Under colonialism, sovereignty remained a gradated affair.

French rule also had to contend with opposing forces internally, which muddled policy orientations, expenditure programs, and ideas about how to best secure French political presence and commercial interests on the continent—in other words, France's capacity to govern effectively its African empire. Between 1854 and 1895, successive administrations and ministries vacillated between programs of territorial conquest and consolidation through trade; they oscillated between fiscal conservatism and shouldering the inflationary costs of expansion; even the general commitment to trade liberalization was halted by bouts of protectionism. Assertive military governors like Faidherbe, Pinet-Laprade, and Brière de l'Isle, with the backing of expansionist ministers like Peycinet and Jauréguiberry, often defied the directives of their metropolitan superiors and launched vast programs of territorial conquest that left their successors with the challenges of an enlarged empire that had to be paid for and managed. The coexistence of separate imperial visions between civil, military, and commercial leaders bred incongruities between local, municipal, regional, and metropolitan levels of government and discontinuities in rule. It fostered conflicts over jurisdiction, taxation, and trade integration between different territorial districts. The establishment of the Government General of French West Africa in 1895 aimed to remedy these discrepancies by setting up a federation pooling revenues, fiscal and financial institutions, and policy making in a centralized administration headquartered in Senegal and tasked with integrating authority across colonial districts. These efforts at hierarchy notwithstanding, structural tensions persisted. Practically and financially, governor-generals were limited in their ability to control subordinates and enforce policy, such that central decrees rarely went unchanged as they traveled to administered territories.[34]

The fractured, shifting nature of sovereignty in Senegal and other French colonies flowed in large part from the partial grafting of state institutions onto older political fields, which itself was a function of the financial austerity buttressing France's imperial edifice in Africa. From the very beginning, France had been unwilling to open national coffers to support imperialist expansion south of the Sahara. Relatively cash poor, the French government was a miserly sovereign, reluctant (and often unable) to disburse the colossal sums required for development and modernization in the colonies and thus reliant on political and economic institutions already present in subjected territories. In effect, the primary tenet of French colonialism was that its African empire was to be realized on the cheap, built on local labor and raw materials rather than investments in technology, infrastructure, or production. A correlate to this principle was that colonies were largely expected to pay for themselves. Unsurprisingly, this policy of budgetary parsimony added fuel to the disagreements splitting the interests of colonial and metropolitan governments, but, more importantly, it fundamentally structured the political economy of rule in colonial Senegal by rooting it in agriculture.[35]

In effect, while Senegal had few natural riches, it had no shortage of agricultural savoir faire, a human resource that could be put to use in the pursuit of colonial interest. The deceptive peanut fitted ideally into this schema. Peanuts had been known to local agricultural economies since the seventeenth century and were well adapted to Senegal's sandy soils and tenuous rainfall. Growing them also required no specialized training. Using local knowledge and cultivation methods, peanut yields could be improved by extending acreages planted in cash crops. Because commercial farming had historical antecedents in Senegal, peanuts could be seamlessly plugged into existing infrastructures of exchange and social relations at minimal costs of development. In turn, the revenues generated by peanut sales and taxes would help to support the costs of administration. Finally, the demand for soap and industrial lubricants in France created a niche for oleaginous plants at home, such that peanut oil literally greased the wheels of industrialization.[36]

Given the colony's economic orientations, the Siin became uniquely attractive to French imperial designs. While the province had long been known to European merchants and served as a key supplier of foodstuffs to Gorée in the eighteenth century, French administrators rediscovered its agricultural potential in the 1850s. After all, the Siin was home to one of Senegal's most accomplished peasantries, and thanks to its unique system of rain-fed farming, which combined animal and vegetal fertilization, regular field rotations, and ecological management, the region had achieved human densities and cereal yields that surpassed those of surrounding regions.[37] Its suitability for cash-crop production was not lost on French observers.

Siin's integration into the colony's economic machinery took time, however. In effect, France's frugal moods notwithstanding, the realities of export agriculture *did* demand a modicum of material investment to assist the operations of commerce. Colonial development programs thus involved the construction of roads, bridges, port facilities, and towns that functioned primarily as centers for the administration of trade and headquarters for commercial houses and, secondarily, hosted basic institutions of colonial governance (forts, judicial courts, administrative buildings, post offices, markets). As a consequence, the histories of peanut exports, transport routes, and economic growth strongly interweave in Senegal. The Dakar–Saint Louis railroad, built between 1883 and 1885, was a primary conduit of French commercial penetration and information diffusion. The kingdoms of Kajoor and Bawol, which were the first regions to be traversed by the railroad, dominated peanut exports until the end of the nineteenth century. As commercial infrastructure extended east and south, however, and port facilities were put in place in Kaolack in 1896 to accommodate oceangoing vessels, peanut tonnage in Siin took off: from a mere eight thousand tons shipped out of the Saalum River in 1884, exports (out of Kaolack) increased to 25,480 tons in 1909, 183,444 in 1929, and peaked in 1936–1937 at 310,419 tons. At its zenith, the Siin accounted for over 50 percent of Senegalese peanut exports and was one of the premiere agricultural producers in French West Africa.[38]

Siin's slow transition to peanut cash cropping also reflects the constraints of budgetary restrictions. Part of the difficulty encountered by colonial policy makers was a chronic shortage of funds and personnel, which resulted in yawning asymmetries in the reach of the colonial state.[39] This unevenness was first and foremost geographical, splitting largely along urban and rural lines (though many linkages connected town and country). France's effective political control was restricted to the *quatre communes*, the four towns of Saint-Louis, Gorée, Dakar, and Rufisque, and their immediate periphery. These coastal centers boasted larger European populations; they were developed around the orderly dictates of urban planning, and their white and mixed-race residents were accorded the same rights as French citizens.[40] These conditions facilitated the creation of a political community around colonial legislation, government, and ideologies. By contrast, in the rural hinterland stretching beyond these littoral enclaves, things looked more ambiguous, due to France's attenuated presence. For example, for much of the 1890s, the Siin-Saalum region, by no means a small area, was under the supervision of *one* French administrator assisted by a handful of African clerks. Although personnel grew steadily—from one clerk and one interpreter in 1892 to fourteen employees in 1897 and twenty-nine in 1902—the French administrative presence remained dwarfed by the vast and diverse lands under its supervision.[41]

Colonial governments attempted to patch over geographic hurdles through the realm of law, which played an important role in carving out what Africans could and could not do. Colonial law, however, could not escape the human and physical challenges it to sought to transcend. The political, material, and cultural disparities between town and country were reinscribed legally in the form of two spheres of jurisdiction.[42] Through the creation of protectorates, colonial countrysides were constructed as distinctive legal spaces defined by their own special system of laws, rights, and obligations. One of such impositions was, after 1891, the payment of a head tax for all rural dwellers, which would finance the projects of the colonial state. Another peculiarity was the legal status of its residents, who, unlike the citizens of the *quatre communes*, were considered to be French subjects (*sujets*). The *sujets* occupied a complex legal terrain organized by different regimes of law. On the one hand, under the observances of indigenous justice, and depending on the confessions of plaintiffs and defendants, Muslim or customary law would inform the settlement of civil matters of marriage, land dispute, or property inheritance. Criminal offenses were prosecuted by different courts. On the other hand, native justice was generally subordinated to the *indigénat* regime. This framework was an ensemble of provisions derived from the French criminal code that authorized the summary use of force and penalty without recourse to judicial courts to ensure abidance to the letter of the law. Under the system of the Native Code, imprisonment, deportation, random fines, and forced labor were legitimate tools of rule, which were frequently mobilized by European administrators to suppress resistance, discipline the masses, and coerce African participation in colonial projects. In the late nineteenth century, for instance, African chiefs were encouraged to resort to force when villagers did not pay their taxes.[43] In the *indigénat*, we find one particular expression of colonial sovereignty—namely, the instrumental application of power in all of its repressive and arbitrary quality. Yet inconsistency was also symptomatic of colonial law as a whole and was allowed to flourish under the scissors-and-paste conditions of authority in the countryside. As it sought to reconcile principle, necessity, and contingency, colonial governance was an intricate juggling act that promoted both order and its subversion, to the point that they became mutually constitutive.[44]

These dynamics were particularly acute in the day-to-day of the state's operations, where thin staffs imposed an amount of rule by proxy, alongside the official bureaucratic apparatus manned by French personnel. Much of the business of colonial power was administered through *precolonial* African institutions and offices and exercised through a network of former ruling elites—kings and nobilities—recycled as state employees. Their main activities were tightly integrated into the cash-crop economy and revolved principally around collecting taxes, recruiting labor, overseeing peanut cultivation, conducting military conscription, levying fines, and adjudicating simple matters of justice.[45]

This system of indirect administration engendered furious headaches. If African intermediaries were sometimes reliable executors of the law, more often than not they also used their prerogatives for political gain and the maintenance of social privileges. Provincial and local chiefs commonly wielded their influence to extort gifts and favors and ensure their fields were cultivated. They often supplemented their small salaries with fines and penalties, which they channeled toward maintaining entourages, itself an outward sign of authority. Thus, the machinery of rule in the countryside tended to veer toward a sort of entropy, characterized by chronic diversions of power as self-serving abuses, excesses, and exactions were committed at every link in the chain of authority.[46] French administrators were not unaware of the dysfunctions of a system of native chiefs connected to former ruling families and dreamt of a cadre of loyal French-speaking bureaucrats free from the attachments of locality and family. They were, however, pragmatists and understood that outsiders seldom made effective leaders since they lacked hereditary claims to legitimate command.[47] For this reason, some of the most efficient province chiefs turned out to hail from the ranks of former noble elites—people like Kumba Ndofeen Juuf (r. 1897–1924), a man whom Administrator Lefilliâtre described as "loved by his subjects and very devoted to the French cause" and whose success he attributed the fact that the Siin commoner "does not like to see his country divided. . . . He will accept another chief only with a great deal of difficulty; I believe . . . that without force, we cannot obtain such results in any other way." By contrast, in 1898, when the French tried to split Siin into two equal-sized administrative territories, villagers rejected the authority of Kumba Ndofeen's rival, Kumba Njimbi, appointed chief of the western province; they refused to pay taxes and even chased out a French *résident,* until the cavalry intervened. Similarly, efforts to directly influence and monitor the actions of indigenous chiefs were often in vain.[48]

In more structural terms, the reliance on local institutions of power, which had their own goals and logics, compelled colonial authorities to walk a tightrope between enforcing the values of French Republicanism and making concessions to African leaders that contradicted these very principles. The state's attitude toward slavery prior to World War I, for example, saw officials walking a treacherous course between rhetorical condemnations of the practice but the toleration of its existence in various regions. Even the French took captives in their wars on the Upper Senegal, which they promptly resold to local leaders.[49]

These ambivalences were fundamental features of what Wilder calls imperial France's "colonial humanism." The term captures the contradictions of a political rationality at once predicated on institutional racism and difference making yet also preaching the values of metropolitan productivism, statism, and welfarism, at once rooted in self-interest, profit seeking, and exploitation while committed (at least notionally) to native improvement: "a political order that was unconditionally colonial (illiberal, authoritarian) yet incontestably modern (rationalizing, modernizing)." This constitutive paradox was glaringly exposed in policy makers' quest for "hegemony on a shoestring": while the success of colonial governance was in part predicated on the development of new forms of African civility, clothed in the moral discourse of *mission civilisatrice* (civilizing mission), the colony's economy largely rested on the maintenance of traditional social relations, thus implying minimal direct political involvement in reforming local lifeworlds. These limitations did not, however, mean an abdication of the idea of "native improvement" but that this project should take place through less interventionist channels.[50]

There, again, as the cornerstone of the colonial economy, peanuts would also be the instrument of its politics. Working in concert with economic philosophy and techniques of government (such as community-run credit and cooperative associations [*sociétés de prévoyances*]), cash crops would penetrate the social worlds of peasants and engineer transformations from within. This harkens back to the belief, held by the architects of colonialism in Senegal, that economic liberalism and the interests of capital were critical mechanisms for the work of governmentality and the cultivation of good subjects.[51] To French bureaucrats, Commerce was a de facto civilizing force, which would eventually bring natives within the fold of colonial modernity. The goal was to combine law, taxation, and monetization to create a structure of incentive for the production of agricultural commodities and participation in colonial markets: peasants would adopt cash cropping so they could obtain enough money to cover the dreaded head tax; cash cropping would force peasants to abandon subsistence agriculture and become consumers of French goods; consumption would interpolate African peasants in circuits of debt and credit, while deepening their dependence on cash and imported commodities for the requirements of social reproduction; exposure to French goods and commerce would teach natives the blessings of civility, property, and entrepreneurialism; due to their connections to the domestic realm, women held a key role in these schemas as primary agents of commercial development. More generally, the work of government would partly be outsourced to the agencies of peanuts, commodities, and money, which were to regulate the collective conduct of African rural masses and, in time, gradually sensitize habits and hearts to the virtues of industry, private ownership, and individual responsibility.[52] And, when policies designed to regulate the actions of colonized people fell short, or when African farmers refused to acquiesce, the provisions of the Native Code would step in and compel obedience in more sinister ways.

The Geography of Imagination: Tradition as Biopolitics

Unsurprisingly, as we saw in chapter 3, formal French colonization went hand in hand with the birth of colonial ethnography. This complicity was partly necessitated by the gap between the logics and logistics of rule, between political and economic aspirations and the capacity to enforce them. Yet, the fashioning of ethnographic images was also intrinsic to the biopolitical rationality that emerged in rural Senegal—a regime that governed best because it governed least (in part because it had no choice), that sought to regulate colonized populations with the prospect of peaceful economic extraction, yet partly outsourced the work of human improvement to other agencies (in this instance, market forces working through the channel of peanuts). The somewhat schizoid process of defining, managing, and transforming African populations all at once would find resolution in the harmonizing of imagination and rule.

Ethnography joined a wider panoply of practices of enumeration, designation, and description designed to assist the fiat of colonial governance in two ways. First, along with the "putting to use" of African natural resources, it fueled another sort of *mise en valeur* focused on managing human resources. Ethnographers sought to identify existing racial assets and weave them into programs of economic development. In doing so, they fixed indigenous populations into an ethno-racial-linguistic order of things, which served the promotion of social order (a cornerstone of Governor General Ponty's *politique des races*).[53] Second, French West Africa's territorial immensity and the bewildering diversity of its peoples demanded the construction of forms of biopolitical knowledge—through ethnography, census data, and statistical compilations—to render African cultural milieus intelligible to colonial authorities and thus rulable and to capture the internal functioning of their normative culture. Extensive information was thus compiled about indigenous systems of kinship, marriage, law, property, and inheritance. The eventual goal was to distill these customs into a set of consistent principles that could guide the development of appropriate policies, ensure native compliance with colonial authority and economic requirements, and aid the proper administration of justice while assisting Africans on their paths to Civilization. In this regard, archetypal peasants were part and parcel of France's *politique indigène* and colonial humanism. Historically, peasants have often been constituted as objects of state management to be improved by state policy. Similarly, under French rule, as for other ethnographic or taxonomic states, the definitions of *custom* and *tradition* became instruments of administration, which reframed the social parameters of colonized populations.[54]

The image of the traditional peasant so yearned for by colonial administrators and the agricultural sensibilities of Siin residents mutually hailed and inhabited each other to the point that history and ideology became tied into an inextricable knot. So much so, in fact, given the metonymic propensity of colonial discourse that the Seereer came to stand for the region and its agricultural potential. As explained in chapter 4, the consolidation of a peasant archetype in Siin rested on a certain representation of milieu that fused rural people into a naturalized landscape of residential anarchy, cultural immobility, and deep attachment to agricultural traditions. In light of the economic goals of the administration, this image also had pragmatic resonance for French officials. Many indeed underscored that the Seereer provided exactly the kind of small-scale production and agricultural diligence required by the project of *mise en valeur*. Thus, Bérenger-Féraud saw early the promise of the Seereer as both valuable producers and consumers for the colonial economy, who would supply "our commerce with products of serious value in very satisfying quantities," while becoming "very desirable tributaries for our commerce if we manage, through a series of long-term measures, to diminish their inclination for drunkenness and protect them against incursions from their neighbors, who under the pretext of converting them to Islam, devastate their country from time to time."[55] At play here is the very kind of hands-off logic of government examined above. Yet, not all observers agreed with Bérenger-Féraud. Indeed, while they were ideal subjects *in potentia*, the Seereer also seemed to stand at the limits of French colonial rule and pose the problem of its effective implementation. Many lamented their hostility to technology, modernization, and commerce and wondered about their capacity for assimilation into the colonial economy, in stark contrast to the Wolof, for instance, who were lauded for their innate sense of enterprise and "progress."[56] Frustratingly, the Seereer both shone and flickered in the ethnoracial maps of colonial government. The more they became fixed to the imaginary geography of colonial Senegal, the more they seemed to resist the projects that colonial representations were supposed to bring about.

An Archaeology of Ethnography: Re-excavating the Archetypal Peasant in Siin

One could find comfort in writing off colonial depictions of the Seereer as mere inventions of tradition and identity, thus making their incapacity to match cultural reality a nonproblem. As recent historians have cautioned, however, the "traditions" of colonial ethnologists were never entirely made up but complexly indebted to African cultural practices.[57] In effect, as our review of colonial writings on Seereer farming showed, the ethnographic optic applied to the Siin was not entirely baseless. There is good evidence throughout the colonial period that the Seereer *were* adept cultivators, living in dispersed settlements, with an acute sense of terroir and strong connections to their land and lineage. However, since colonial writings here are both judge and jury of their own empirical integrity, they can only inform us so much about the making of ethnographic images. By contrast, because colonial representations so readily equated physical milieu with Seereer modes of being, a turn to archaeology might help us to perceive the tangible landscapes that rooted these depictions and help to shed light on both the historical and ethnographic Seereer and the processes of construction binding both.

Let us briefly review the evidence, drawing on the 2003 survey. More than 80 percent of the sites dated to the nineteenth and twentieth centuries found in this corpus were smaller than two hectares in size. A majority (62 percent) consisted of sparse remains probably corresponding to single family concessions (*mbind*), while others (30 percent) contained a handful of mounds likely representing the vestiges of small hamlets (table 9; figure 29). These sites were inhabited for fewer than two hundred years. They also tend to spread across the landscape, rather than converge into concentrated settlements, forming constellations of single residences and loose clusters of habitations. A handful of exceptions stand out in the form of small and large villages (figure 30). These sites are found exclusively in the central and northern portions of Siin. They were occupied chiefly in the 1800s, with possible roots in the previous century. Survey evidence suggests considerable dynamism and movement in Siin's archaeological settlements with interesting patterns emerging. After their foundation and being inhabited for several generations, sites follow a number of trajectories: (1) they move elsewhere, though rarely more than a few hundred meters from the originary settlement; (2) they hive off, and parts of the settlement relocate a short distance away; or (3) some occupations merge with nearby sites to form

Table 9 2003 site inventory: Settlement types by survey regions, eighteenth through twentieth centuries

	Phase Vb			Phase Vc			
Site types	PCO	FAT	DIA	PCO	FAT	DIA	Total
Short-term occupation	4	17	12	1	8	6	48
Mbind	4	9	9		6	1	29
Hamlet	2	4	7			1	14
Hamlet cluster	3	2	6		1	1	13
Village		1	4				5
Total	13	33	38	1	15	9	109

Note: Sites from the 2003 inventory tend to contain remains from both phase Vb and Vc, making it difficult to attribute them to one or the other. The numbers in this table reflect this overlap, and some occupations were counted both as phase Vb and Vc. However, phase Vc settlements remain undercounted and thus underrepresented in the 2003 inventory.

larger residential units. Contemporary settlements are often found in the vicinity of archaeological sites or partially overlap with them and seem to represent the most recent episodes in this history of village mobility. It is also worth noting that, by and large, the geography of eighteenth- through twentieth-century deposits maps quite well with the present-day distribution of spirit shrines (*pangool*); in fact, many deposits contain such shrines or have become sacred places themselves.

Archaeological portraits here partially dovetail with colonial visions, showing that in the middle of the nineteenth century Siin's human habitat *was* ostensibly quite scattered and would have been so perceived by colonial observers. Like ethnographic sources, archaeological documents depict village communities, for the most part, as dispersed clouds of habitations variably integrated into larger ensembles. Likewise, the pattern of village (re)settlement in the vicinity of founding sites, contemporary villages, and *pangool* suggests a certain attachment to place and lineage-managed land. Scribbled between the lines of these very broad trends, however, one also encounters evidence of the bubbling underside of the "typical peasant" trope, which points to the limits of ethnographic representation. As they resist the conformity of images, archaeological landscapes reveal that colonial science's chief errancy lay in its quest for the age-old coordinates of an essential Seereer character. By generalizing ethnographic snapshots that held empirical validity in Siin's heartland out to Seereer communities across the region and through time, colonial representations severely flattened the history and heterogeneity of the Seereer country.

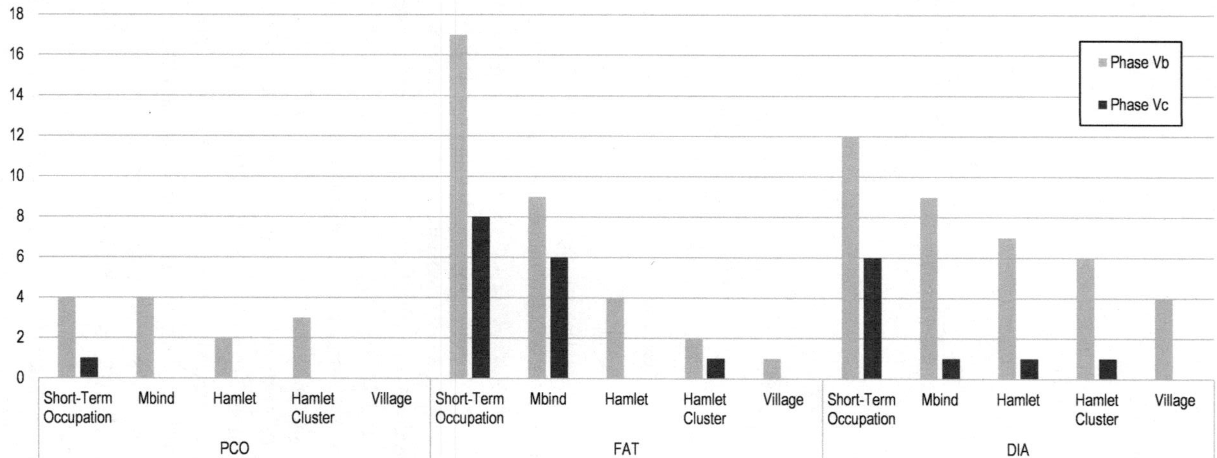

29 2003 settlements: site types by survey region, phases Vb and Vc

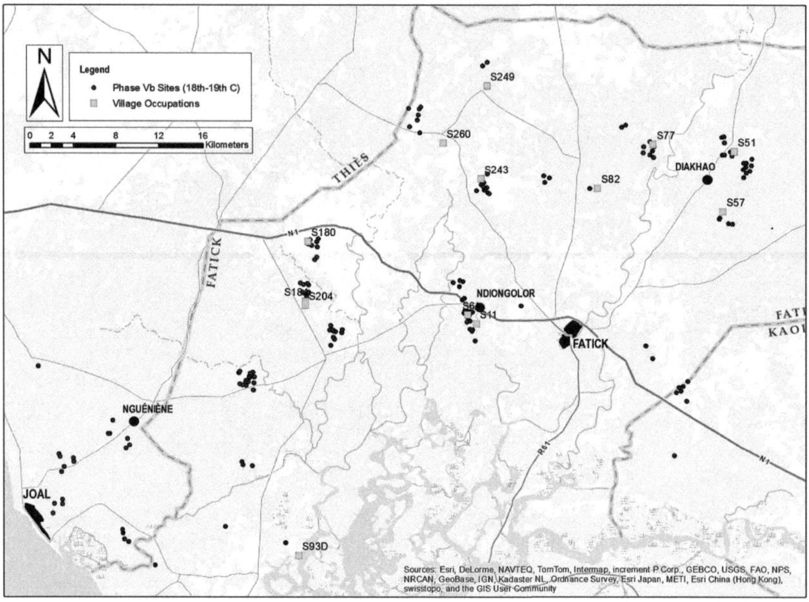

30 Large village occupations, 2003 and 2011 site inventories, phase Vb, eighteenth and nineteenth centuries

Earlier, we saw that Seereer modes of spatial occupations at the time of colonial expansion were fairly recent phenomena indebted to reconfigurations associated with Atlantic exchanges.[58] While occupations in Siin had been relatively stable and concentrated before the 1700s, the constellated landscape that so fascinated colonial observers actually took shape in the eighteenth and nineteenth centuries in response to political turbulences generated by the oceanic commerce and postabolition era. Not only was the Seereer countryside not the placid landscape of customs portrayed in the colonial imagination, it also exhibited a great deal of internal diversity, which dispels the notion of a cultural core condensing the character of Seereer ethnicity—a diversity anxiously acknowledged in the margins of ethnographic canons, you will recall from chapter 4. Mirroring these accounts, the structure of archaeological settlements points to broad differences in the built environment between coast and hinterland. While villages in the interior tend to conform to the model of dispersion recorded above, their counterparts on the littoral tend to be compact and nucleated.[59] Traces of such spatial templates endure today in the congested urban fabric of coastal towns like Joal and Fadiouth, and their labyrinths of narrow streets snaking around densely packed houses and compounds (figure 31). Likewise, material assemblages retrieved along

31 Postcards, early twentieth century. *Top*, "Inside a Cérère village" (ANS, Iconographie, no. 0357). This image is representative of the aesthetics of colonial photography in the Siin, whose depictions folded culture into nature by merging Seereer lifestyles into their geographic surroundings. Photographs here were mobilized to create visual proofs of Seereer primitiveness. *Bottom*, "Village of Fadiouth," (ANS, Iconographie, no. 0996). Fadiouth's densely packed housing is representative of compact village arrangements along the coast. (Both reproduced with permission from Archives du Sénégal.)

ethnic borders also caution against equating materiality and ethnicity too rigidly in northern Senegal, given the strong similarities in the object inventories of colonial-era sites on both sides of the historical boundary separating Siin from the Wolof kingdom of Bawol.[60] Finally, the tunnel vision animating colonial representations, intent as it was on writing the Seereer out of modernity, also edited out overt signs of local involvement with external market forces and the myriad imported objects that had come to reshape the calculi of daily existence since the eighteenth century.

The problem of colonial images, then, is that, in consigning Seereer communities to the immutability of the ethnographic present, they missed the stories of mutation and permanence woven into Siin's rural landscapes. The kind of dynamism observed in the archaeological record anticipates the quandaries faced by colonial administrators—namely, the fact that French portrayals of the Seereer offered more frustrations than solutions. First, they failed to account for the variability of Seereer social practices, again something that field administrators conceded with some uneasiness.[61] As images of the Seereer became standardized into a peasant archetype, such disjunctures became accepted as necessary evils and were increasingly overlooked. Second, in their insistence to view sedentariness as intrinsic to the Seereer "race," observers overlooked the complex logics of mobility—the histories of movements, fissions, and fusions—that structured the social life of the Siin countryside during the colonial era, including reconfigurations unfolding before their very eyes in response to peanut agriculture (which we will explore in the next chapter).[62] Lastly, ethnographic knowledge could not explain why the Seereer did not respond to colonial incentives and modernize their rural habitat in the image of their Wolof neighbors—beyond the circular recourse to the rhetoric of stubborn Seereer backwardness and innate Wolof initiative.[63]

These dissonances underscore some founding paradoxes in the colonial power/knowledge nexus. First, its representations of rural Africans were both *descriptive* and *prescriptive*, both intended to *depict* and *construct* colonized subjects. They were shaped by the tense relationship between cultural worlds and the demands of governance. While the engineering of a certain type of Seereer subject—the docile peasant—required some grounding in ethnographic realities, it also necessitated the streamlining of ethnographic information into preconceived notions of native capacities for development. The ethnographic Seereer were thus constructed around this gap, which said as much about what they were as what they were not (e.g., *not* modern, *not* civil, *not* Wolof) and recalled earlier constructions of Seereer ethnicity through the lens of alterity, as seen in chapter 3. Second, the application of ethnographic inventories to the terrain of rule also revealed profound weaknesses in the links between colonial knowledge of African farmers and the state's capacity to produce peasant subjects. Colonial programs did not encounter an empty human terrain to be freely molded in the desired image but a culturally carved milieu already embedded in its own configurations of power, perception, and materiality. The resource- and personnel-thin French administration did not so much challenge these spheres of authority as it half-heartedly conceded their influence and created so many discordant territories under a single colony.

One irony of the fixity of colonial codifications is that they allowed cultural life to effervesce below the orderly façade of ethnic customs, as new hybrid practices bubbled up to creatively usurp customs in the service of personal or collective ends. For example, while the Seereer were often officially depicted as a matrilineal society, they reckoned kinship both through paternal and maternal lines. Thus, strategically claiming rights of descent, inheritance, and debt devolution through one or the other line often enabled those whose deceased relatives had defaulted on their debt to escape the demands made by commercial companies seeking reimbursement on unpaid purchases or loans. Likewise, Muslim converts often invoked Islam's mode of patrilateral succession to avoid taking on the arrears of maternal relatives. Of course, instances of conversion to Islam or Catholicism also generated tensions within families, as inheritance came to be disputed among relatives of different confessions, each citing allegiance to a different system of rights.[64] What rendered these social acrobatics possible, indeed what became their guarantors, was precisely the ethnographic imagination of tradition. As a technology of imperial control, the compilation of customs came to bear more heavily on Seereer social practices over time. And how could it not? What had been fluid sets of relations before were increasingly crystallized in their tussles with the word-processed cultures of ethnographic notebooks. At the same time, recorded customs did eventually take on a life of their own. They never floated completely unmoored from cultural practice, but, in slowing colonial perceptions of natives to a standstill, they paradoxically preserved a degree of cultural autonomy for rural people.

More than just expressions of disingenuousness or error, more than figures of instrumentality or false consciousness, the imaginary geographies of ethnicity in Siin might be more usefully approached as illustrations of what Taussig calls the "epistemic murk" of colonial encounters. This space of confusion glosses a condition of knowledge in which fantasy and reality do not stand as separate but as conditions of each other's possibility. Born of colonial condensation, the mists of murky truths enshroud situations of translation across culture, difference, and otherness. These cloudy knowledges were both byproducts of colonial government and constitutive aspects of its regimes of truth. Under the mantle of rational administration and objective implementation, they allowed the proliferation of sincere fictions and honest myopias, the kinds of representations of African culture that served the purposes of colonial exploitation while undercutting its efficacy.[65] They are also a reminder of the disquiets and disregards inhabiting colonial common sense. As Stoler recently noted, colonial agents were not the charmed audience of ideology but at times were nervously aware of the cracks in colonial systems of knowledge, which often prompted them to shift their gaze away from inconvenient contradictions standing on the edge of perception.[66]

Conclusion: Entangled Sovereignties

In his pathbreaking *French Colonialism in Tropical Africa*, Jean Suret-Canale offered a mixed assessment of the effects of French rule in rural Africa, quipping on the one hand that "the despotism of lower officials was limited only by the despotism of their superiors," yet concluding on the other hand that before 1945 "the significant changes affected only the main towns and the big commercial ports. In the bush, nothing changed."[67] These two passages echo the two families of motifs that have bookended visions of the colonial state in Africa. One pole depicts the colonial moment as a radical break with precolonial life, mired in irrationalism, excesses, and brutality. It is an account where the peanut marks a chronological caesura between a pre-peanut world of untrammeled culture and a post-peanut universe of colonial alteration.[68] At the other pole, the reality of colonialism seems to have translated into very little change at all. Peanuts don't quite feature into this story. Charting a path between chromatic conceptions, I prefer to conceive of colonial rule as a more heterogeneous terrain whose effects both transformed and preserved different aspects of African rural life at different paces, at different times, through different media, and never quite in the manner anticipated by French administrators. This is a perspective interested in conduits and technologies, a story featuring peanuts as picaresque agents of imperialism, doing the bidding of colonial government.

To do due diligence to the complexities of colonial world making, we need to attend to the middle ground of colonialism, that shadowy horizon of power that engulfed French colonists and colonized Africans. Practices of government are important here because they targeted explicitly the material existence of indigenous villagers, leaving concrete imprints of their passage in rural landscapes. Landscapes, in turn, provide useful mementos of both the mechanisms of colonial rule and how the colonial order was translated into village life. As previously argued, we cannot analyze the construction of politics under colonialism without accounting for the entanglement between colonial sovereignty and preexisting structures of power in the Senegalese countryside. Nor can we look only at the coercive, planned dimensions of colonial statecraft, given that colonial proscriptions lost much of their intransigence when they touched ground. Rather, the gap between the logics of rule and its logistics added a measure of unpredictability to colonial governance. Surely, colonial policies reconfigured the coordinates of life in village communities; yet, these reconfigurations also became the grounds on which Africans fashioned new identities, aspirations, and modes of action. The fields of power woven by the colonial state were sometimes repressive, but they could also be productive. They were also interrupted, subverted, and altered.

I began my analysis of colonial statecraft in Siin by looking at the political rationalities underwriting colonial government and the modes of knowledge it produced. The imperatives of the cash-crop economy introduced a curious gambit. It entailed valorizing the agricultural dispositions of African peasantries while aspiring to reform their modes of life—an impossible project that demanded at once the cultivation of "the native within" and its opposite.[69] The representations of Seereer agriculturalists that developed in the first seventy years of colonial rule are saturated with these contradictions, as they alternately celebrate the Seereer's traditionalism or condemn their conservatism, without ever quite harnessing the first or reforming the second for the benefit of economic *mise en valeur*. Of course, we can also see here the paradox of colonial humanism in its full effect and interpret the uncanny African peasants that people the colonial imagination as symptoms of the hazy truth of colonial knowledge, which alloyed fantasy and objectivity, which needed a savage archetype to better imagine the prototype of tomorrow's African *sujet*, the right mix of obedience and civility.

Archaeological vistas shed light on the construction of ethnographic visions where colonial representations met Seereer lived worlds. Under the canopy of science, depictions of Seereerness often captured facets of peasant realities at the time of observation, but they did so selectively and with little regard for history. Ethnographic portraits melded facts and fictions into ethnic categories. These strange amalgams imparted a great deal of instability to ethnographic images and the subjects they aimed to define. Such uncertainty translated to the terrain of colonial government, as representations of African identity, tradition, and custom (and the silences they contained) came to organize the management of colonized populations. To be sure, ethnographic categories steered policy, yet they never quite accounted for the material milieus they purported to reshape—an inevitable consequence of the process of "simplification" of colonial modernity.[70]

The gap around which ideas of Seereerness were structured—a lack of civility and its orderly expressions—was also a potentiality, which afforded opportunities to work around colonial control, as illustrated indeed by the messiness and resistances of rural materialities. It also formed a slippery foundation for the process of rule and management of geography. It is little wonder, then, that colonial sovereignty remained a tentative project, frequently recomposed by the circumstances of interests, places, and events, in dialogue with other fields of power. And no small irony, correlatively, that colonial policies inadvertently fashioned different kinds of African *sujets* from the frugal, reliable, small-holding farmers they had hoped to craft out the Seereer. How the latter apprehended the changing conditions of colonialism—their lived experiences of French rule—is what we will examine in the next chapter.

EIGHT

The Politics of Absence: Peasant Lifeworlds and Colonial Government

The peasant could never see the white man.

B. THIAM, INTERVIEWED IN 1975[1]

Postcolonial Preamble: The Benevolent Neglect of the State

In a recent study of community-based development in West Africa, Dennis Galvan examined the conditions that favored effective grassroots mobilization in rural Senegal. His study focused on the Association des Paysans de Toukar, a farmer's collective from the village of Toukar, deep in the Siin heartland. Charting the rise and fall of the association, Galvan explains that the success of its initiatives depended in some measure on its founders' capacities. They were an enterprising group of young men with university educations who were able to use their village background, technocratic skills, and urban contacts to attract funding for local development projects. Some of these initiatives included the establishment of a cholera-prevention program, a water-retention basin for garden irrigation, a revolving credit fund for cattle husbandry, and a general goods store. Yet, if visionary leadership and money connections gave continued lift to the association, Galvan also underscores the central importance of two other factors: the Senegalese state's "benevolent neglect" of the region, which shielded the association from the potential siphoning off of resources and knowledge into political patronage networks, and a willingness to recycle elements of traditional social relations (especially solidarities based in kinship and age-group cohorts) in the name of community development.[2]

As Galvan aptly notes, the recombinant use of "tradition" and ambivalent relations between society and state structures are not new phenomena in Siin's peasant world. Their specific expressions today may be original, but they rest on a deeper historical stratum, stretching back to the colonial era, where the roots of Siin's marginalization from state-assisted development can be found. It is also during that period that hybrid repertoires of practices, combining past and present, became legitimate forms of mediation between state and community. Two elements are interesting here. First, contemporary modes of being and acting in Siin are infused with social orientations that were shaped in relation to colonial authority. Second, Siin's relationships to state power (both past and present) have been paradoxical: on the one hand, they have turned the countryside into a political backwater insulated from the sphere of clout, influence, and favor in a country where national politics revolve increasingly around large cities. On the other hand, this peripheralization has also proved productive, affording certain political possibilities for community empowerment in the present. To be sure, state and society have been imbricated differently at different moments of the past, but the point is that the history of their interplay binds political trajectories between colony and postcolony and that the social worlds that African peasants have built over time are outcomes of that history.

My concern in this chapter is with the colonial phase of this long story of interactions. While the previous chapter unfolded the logics of colonial rule, here I am interested in its practical side and application, what I called colonial *government*, between 1850 and 1960, the hundred years or so of French occupation in Senegal. Drawing on historical evidence gleaned from colonial archives and archaeological sites dating to the past 150 years, I extend the analysis begun in chapter 7 to unpack Trouillot's geography of management. This entails, on the one hand, dissecting the colonial state's encounter with rural people in Senegal, mapping the efficacy and derailments of its technologies of power, accounting for the hurdles French administrators stumbled into as they sought to institute order in the countryside, and keeping a close eye on the tensions internal to empire as a form of political practice.[3] On the other hand, one cannot develop a sense of colonial management without examining what was being managed—namely, Seereer peasants and their cultural universe. Consequently, the bulk of this chapter follows the experiences of Seereer residents as they grew entangled with the sticky webs of peanut imperialism and learned to navigate and reframe, with various degrees of success, the new worlds of power unloosed by colonialism.

What particularly moves my analysis is a simple puzzle: how do we reconcile perceptions of colonial power (both lay and learned) as invasive and transformative with the recollections of Saalum farmers like Biram Thiam, at the beginning of this chapter, who remember the *inconspicuousness* of the late colonial state—a sentiment widely echoed in my conversations with Seereer elders who were children in the fading days of colonialism. Forging a dialogue between Galvan's idea of "benevolent state neglect" and peasant commentaries about the invisibility of colonial rulers on the ground, and extending the tale of peanut as agent of power begun earlier, I propose that a key modality of colonial governance in the Siin was a politics of absence. Absence here does not mean vacuum or nothingness; rather it evokes a material register of power that did not require direct physical intervention but, rather, worked obliquely through an assemblage of nonstate, market-based, or parastatal actors, media, and institutions held together by peanut agriculture. This politics of absence braided with more frontal state strategies to organize the quotidian of peasant populations, though its results did not always play out as predicted.

My analysis takes up these ambiguities of government—where efficacy met incertitude and where the two could not always be differentiated—and explores how they reverberated across the Seereer milieu. There the hesitations of French rule met the Seereer's own hesitancies, those they harbored toward central command and which they inherited from earlier times—hesitancies that, in turn, achieved physical form in things, places, and landscapes. The quivering geographies that once hampered statecraft during the Atlantic era endured, in a transformed (and transforming) state, to continue overseeing the Seereer's tussles with French colonialism. And reluctant they remained, as we will see below.

Materialities of Government in Rural Senegal: Toward a Politics of Absence?

Buoyed by decades of research, historical scholarship has given us an increasingly substantive picture of imperial and colonial governance in Senegal, attentive to its organization, administration, institutions, programs, and structural impacts, as well as African responses to colonial order.[4] These portrayals, however, remain incomplete, especially in a colony like Senegal where the topography of rule was uneven and where the colonial state wore different faces between town and country. Portraits of colonialism have sharper resolution in urban settings, where abundant and detailed archives offer fertile ground for the analysis of life, politics, and culture under French rule. The range of research has been more modest in rural Senegal, where archival densities do not always permit reconstruction of the full texture of colonial entanglements, though the Siin fares better than most farming regions. Our understanding of colonial rule's structural properties and their impact on African economic life is indebted to Klein's canonical work, which, nearly fifty years later, remains the most authoritative treatment of political history in the region, in no small part because of its deft integration of oral sources and written documents. The other landmark is Mohamed Mbodj's study of Siin's colonial economy, which unpacks the complexity of peanut agriculture and commerce, both qualitatively and quantitatively.[5]

This work has created insightful maps of colonial rule in Siin, and the broad mutations it occasioned in rural political institutions and economy. As such, it provides a valuable stepping-stone for more in-depth analyses of the phenomenology of colonial rule and its reverberation on African cultural worlds and a more explicit theorization of its material expressions.[6] Here, I believe that combining an analytic of government (keyed to the tactility, multiplicity, unpredictability and productivity of power) with an analytic of materiality (attuned to the tangibility of colonial processes) has the potential to highlight dimensions of colonial experiences that often fall out of oral and written texts. As the loci of power transactions, material settings sharpen our focus on the vehicles of colonial governance and how the latter was received in village life, thus opening insights into (1) power's microphysics and how it meshed with African actors and (2) how colonialism was lived and the cultural productions to which it gave life. As the infrastructure of colonial government and the reluctant landscapes of Seereer politics locked horns, they fashioned a hesitant geography of power that brought rural residents into the fold of colonial markets while preserving a certain measure of cultural and political autonomy. More importantly, village entanglements with colonial rule became part of the experiential raw material out of which African peasants (re)fashioned their identities and subjectivities.

Reviewing the question of modernity and power in French and British West Africa, Frederick Cooper has critiqued the urge to indiscriminately associate colonial regimes with the all-out implementation of "modern governmentality," as is sometimes seen in postcolonial scholarship. As Cooper points out, a major difference separating European governments from colonial states was that the latter did not so much focus their efforts on systematically transforming Africans and creating individual subjects as on governing through collectivities and developing institutions designed to keep them in check. And, even there, colonial regimes in Africa proved notoriously "unable to routinize and normalize their exercise of power, and they were equally incoherent in their efforts to harness 'tradition' and 'traditional rulers' to a stable pattern of governance."[7] Instead, he discerns periods of mutual adjustment between colonial policy and the initiatives of colonized peoples: an early and euphoric imperial agenda of reform, improvement, and rationalization (1850–1914); a more sobering period of rule through indigenous institutions until the late 1930s, followed by a decade of social and economic tensions that colonial ideologies could no longer rein in; and, by the late 1940s, the implementation of programs of modernization and development targeting African workers, which African political organizations recuperated as a claims-making device.[8]

Cooper's warning against tumorous and ahistorical visions of governmentality is pointed, though I am less certain about his separation between the collectivizing and individualizing tendencies of government. Foucault insisted, for instance, that homogenization and differentiation—that is, the construction of populations and individuals—were two sides of the same governmental logic. Likewise with the conflicted logic of "productivism . . . and welfarism," the will to "transform and preserve indigenous societies simultaneously," which Wilder sees as intrinsic to France's colonial humanism.[9]

Cooper's injunction to historicize governmental logics and practices is welcome and important. In this light, his periodization is heuristically useful and matches quite well the terrain of colonial Senegal, which Cooper has studied for many years. That said, its broad lines do not completely account for the idiosyncrasies of colonial governance as it was translated to different regions. In the Siin, for instance, direct intervention and indirect rule cohabited on the ground very early on.[10] More generally, Cooper's periods are also crosscut by certain rationalities of rule, such as the paradoxical project of native exploitation/improvement or the idea that subject populations can be managed both through and in conformity with the progressive laws of commerce and the economy.[11] In Siin, then, state institutions, market forces, and social forms combined and recombined to shape each other and how rural people understood their circumstances, constructed their choices, and imagined the broader world. This, in turn, imparted particular shape to colonial state projects in the province and the tensions generated by their implementation. It also generated materialities of rule and colonial power that straddle some of Cooper's periods.

In his thought-provoking study of Catholic evangelization in Waluguru (Tanzania), Pels argues that colonial missionizing—and the colonial enterprise, more generally—did not just consist in forging a new representational order but also involved a "politics of presence." By this, he means that colonial transactions were mediated through matter and physicality, that colonial contact was a profoundly tactile, embodied, and sensuous tale of encounters. While colonial world building often evokes metaphors of language and vision, the "long conversation" between colonizers and colonized, the yearning to sway native consciousness, and the rearrangement of signifiers triggered by imperial ventures also implicated arguments of gestures, practices, customs, and things.[12]

Pels's point about the materiality of empire making is very well taken. However, in advancing the idea of physical *presence*, he seems to consider only one aspect of the materialness of colonial power plays at the expense of a more diverse palette of media for exercising rule. Materiality, surely, works through propinquity and sustained contact, but it also operates through absence, invisibility, deferral, infrequency, ephemera, and sidelong mediations.[13] What happens, then, when political projects leave few material residues of their passage or when they may not have rested on the production of new social geographies per se—say, when they rode the chain reaction of effects welling up in the tracks of peanut farming? By extension, how do we study processes that have limited archaeological visibility? When it comes to the state, as we saw previously, archaeologists have often underscored the bold, in-your-face character of power, materialized in its capacity to reconstruct landscapes in its own image. By contrast, when viewed through an archaeological lens, one of the most curious aspects of Siin's countryside is the relative mutedness of colonialism, the faintness of its material traces, the seeming absence of overt state signatures. Surely, old colonial buildings survive, though those are overwhelmingly confined to urban settings. In the countryside, other than the occasional ruined fort, bridge, dispensary, or school, few built structures appear to have been erected, and the ones that exist stand few and far between. Likewise, other than the contemporary road grid, railway system, and a handful of towns, which follow the footprints of colonial penetration, Siin's rural milieu contains limited evidence of colonial infrastructure building. Concurrently, there is little hint of systematic attempts to synthesize a new order into the landscape or reform local practices by realigning their material referents. Instead, the panorama of rural life over the past two hundred years, outwardly at least, remains crisscrossed by material continuities: village arrangements owe more to local cultural histories than modernist planning, building technologies are firmly rooted in local savoir faire, the bocage is underwritten by local kinship solidarities, ancestral shrines stand as testimonies to a vibrant sacred geography, local ceramic traditions dominate local assemblages. And, yet, colonial influences stain, with variable intensity, the fabric of local livelihoods. Historically, they surface in the ubiquity of peanut crops, in the growing incursion of mass-produced commodities, or in the establishment of settlements of seasonal workers.

How must we account for these hybrid political landscapes that weld old and new elements without overhanded attempts by colonial authorities to dominate social space? Playing on Pels, I would suggest that, in Siin, weaknesses inherent in the structure of colonial rule imposed the deployment of a politics of absence: Because French authorities never had the resources to infiltrate and remake the livelihoods of African peasants, they often settled for more offhand modes of governance—that is, delegating the business of government to institutions that were *not* under direct control of the state, such as the wirework of cash cropping. Absence, defined in this broad sense, was an important register of colonial statecraft and joined more vigorous forms of power and interventionist technologies as primary avenues through which colonial rule was meted out. The inability to consistently engage in a politics of presence—one mobilizing permanent personnel and markers of sovereignty on the ground—laced the management of peasant populations with contradictions. By extension, the gap between colonial intentions and the actual effects of policies on rural communities introduced systemic unpredictability into the exercise of rule.

As we began to appraise at the end of last chapter, these histories of power find partial expressions in Siin's rural landscape, which I seek to unlock further here through the combined lenses of archaeology, ethnohistory, and ethnography. I continue to mobilize archaeological evidence derived from the 2003 survey near the villages of Mbissel, Fatick, and Diakhao, focusing specifically on sites dating to the past two hundred years. As previously noted, the chronology of these settlements is rather indefinite. They tend to contain remains attributable to both ceramic phase Vb (which is a bit unwieldy for our purposes since it falls in the 1700–1870 range, a period that spans the era of Atlantic trade, legitimate commerce, and early colonization) and phase Vc (which ranges from the late nineteenth century to the mid-twentieth century). Chronic issues of surface admixture often blur chronological assignments to one or the other period. To remedy these problems, I also draw on materials from the 2011 survey, which targeted areas around the villages of Nguéniène, Loul Sessène, and Diohine. While these data are still being processed, they provide greater resolution in the chronology of recent settlements. Of the 215 occupational contexts retrieved during the survey, seventy-eight were conclusively ascribed to phase Vb, and seventy-seven fell squarely into phase Vc. These archaeological pictures are important historical transcripts in that they get at changing trends and departures in human mobility, residential logics, community making, and object use tying together the before, during, and after of colonialism—the kinds of stories faintly impressed, if at all, in the forgotten margins of official annals. To remedy the problems of interpretive resolution posed by surface archaeology, I try to introduce some attention to such microhistorical details—the realm of rationales, intentions, and ideologies that underlays the actions of colonizer and colonized alike—by picking up narrative threads present in archival and oral evidence gathered between 2002 and 2013. I also attend to contemporary features of the Seereer milieu, which, in some sense, is a cumulative product of long-term cultural histories and contains important clues about the transformations spurred by the colonial conquest.

In this sense, more than ever, my view of archaeological landscapes in this chapter is expansive and recognizes that rural milieus are palimpsests made up of complexly intertwined temporalities. While they coexist in the present, not all elements of a landscape have the same history, longevity, or pull on social action. Some were fashioned earlier or later, others were altered, and still others destroyed or replaced. In this light, contemporary social topographies can be just as archaeological as buried ones and just as revelatory of deeper histories (even as they sometimes entail a measure of historical flattening). For instance, material infrastructures like roads are colonial inheritances that have become integral parts of present-day geographies. Likewise with Siin's system of agricultural fields, which preserves a concrete, multigenerational record of landed patrimony, lineage ownership, and occupational history. In some sense, the juxtaposition of different sources, each calibrated to certain scales of social change and speaking to different histories, offers critical vistas into the slow-moving and faster-clipped processes that shaped political landscapes over time. If similarities among different sources bring a level of assurance to our recounting of the past, disjunctures between them are equally valuable as they invite new questions about our rendering of historical process.

Competing (for) Sovereignties: Peasant Life in Early Colonial Rule in Siin

The early decades of French colonial rule in Siin were marked by considerable instability. This volatility had roots in the political soil of the Atlantic era, though it appeared to increase exponentially after the passage to legitimate commerce.[14] Between the shift to legitimate trade and the creation of the Siin protectorate in 1887, the kingdom witnessed an expansion of internal tensions and political repression. While missionary sources in the late 1840s and 1850s portray the *buur* Siin as a likable monarch loved by his subjects, they have no kind words for his violent and undisciplined soldiers, who made an art of harassing traders and peasant populations.[15] In fact, *ceddo* exactions likely worsened after the abolition of slavery and adoption of peanut agriculture.

France's annexations campaigns did not improve the climate of violence. In 1859, the Siin was traversed by expeditionary forces, which resulted in the torching of Fatick. Backed by technological and military arguments, the French exploited growing divisions between noble lineages and the interkingdom conflicts spawned by Muslim revolutions to extend their authority over the Siin. In the 1863–1870 period, the Siin-Saalum was swept by Ma Ba Jaaxu's Islamic warriors, who caused significant devastation, food crises, and human dislocation. Ma Ba's attacks caused a massive migration and relocation of Saalum villages to the Petite Côte, which provided an attractive refuge for defenseless peasant populations. King of Siin Kumba Ndofeen Juuf and his army were instrumental in defeating Ma Ba's troops at the battle of Somb in 1867, preserving their autonomy from Islam yet ironically paving the way for a subsequent colonial takeover.[16]

This highly charged atmosphere gave considerable freedom to slave warriors, who seem to have acted increasingly independently of their masters and continued to terrorize peasant populations well into the 1870s. In an early report to the Minister written in 1863, Pinet-Laprade lamented that the *ceddo* reigned supreme in Siin. Later French correspondence indicates that émigrés from inland villages moved en masse to Joal to escape raiding and seek the protection of colonial authorities. Coastal villages, as a result, became prey to the pillages of slave warriors, forcing French soldiers to send the refugees back to their villages and the law of the *ceddo*. Not only did France's loose mandate fall short of imposing order in the Siin, it could not even ensure the protection of its citizens. Traders, for instance, were warned that their security could not be guaranteed beyond the cannons of the military post in Joal. With regard to internal affairs, the word was to avoid getting involved in local politics, while urging the *maad* to control his minions. This policy also applied to slaves owned by notables, who, once escaped or hired in town, had to be returned to the king.[17]

Colonial sources also signal profound tensions between the monarchy and its coastal periphery, which extended fractures grown during the Atlantic era. An early gubernatorial report mentions the secessionist intentions of the "Joal Republic," whose "velleities of independence" are underscored in subsequent correspondence, thus throwing doubt on the monarch's centralizing hold over its coastal provinces.[18] These relations grew tenser as the French immersed themselves in local political affairs. With the presence of the military post in Joal, the French were at liberty to incorporate the entire village into the colony with the help of coastal residents eager to dissociate from the kingdom. The 1860s and 1870s were the stage of intense conflicts between the king of Siin and the colony, as the latter gradually encroached upon the Seereer kingdom by annexing coastal villages in the vicinity of Joal. This process of limited expansion triggered frequent clashes between Seereer villagers and *ceddo*. The villages of Fadial, Ndiodior or Dionewar, which were placed under the French protectorate, saw their autonomy repeatedly challenged by the *maad a Sinig*, who attempted to reestablish his authority over them. The king's rule met more contestation as Seereer villagers residing inland began to take their herds to French-controlled regions to escape warrior exactions.[19]

If voting with one's feet afforded resistance to the arbitrary imposition of royal rule, peasants had other grassroots strategies at their disposal to defuse aristocratic predations. In a rare allusion to Seereer cultural worldviews, Noirot notes the existence of a spiritual check on *ceddo* anarchy. The mighty warriors were fearful of Seereer mysticism, suspicious of the spells of *baadoole* (commoners). Writing in the 1890s, Noirot admitted that French colonial policies had curbed the peasants' ability to defend themselves against the king's envoys, but that, prior to colonial rule, "at the slightest alert, the Sereres belched rallying ululations, and in the blink of an eye the women and children retired to the granaries while the men, armed with guns or bows, outnumbered the thiedos [*ceddo*], who often had no recourse but to retreat." Sacred geography was also a powerful ally of the peasants, and there were numerous places and parts of the landscape where "a thiedo would not dare to fire a gun or ride a horse without fearing the worst calamities. The Bour himself cannot enter certain villages without running the risk of dying within the year."[20] Ancestral spirits, however, also had dangerous and exigent appetites. It is said that in the old days, for instance, villagers of Diohine killed bulls and young people to appease their *pangool*'s anger. Likewise for King Sanumoon Fay (r. 1871–1878), whose legendary cruelty was matched only by that of his protective genie, who fed on human sacrifices.[21]

What we are seeing in the first thirty years of colonial occupation is a confused and changing landscape of power, which Seereer peasants sought to negotiate to the best of their ability, if not always by choice. The picture that emerges is a dynamic one. Already weary of state authority, village communities were likely heavily affected by the intensification of *ceddo* exactions. Some were forced to resettle to escape political violence, yet doing so also meant abandoning their fields, means of subsistence, and the land that housed their ancestors. The archaeological record seems to support this picture. While the fragmentation of the village landscape has roots in the previous century, and problems of chronology notwithstanding, there is a good chance that a number of phase Vb–Vc sites encountered near Joal, Mbissel, and Fadial are associated with the commotion of the 1850s–1870s and founded during this period. The French presence further tested villagers' unease with state projects, though it also opened possibilities. Stuck between a derelict monarchy desperate to hold on to power and France's ambivalent, cash-strapped sovereignty, Seereer villagers tried to make the best of adverse conditions and went with whoever seemed to offer the most attractive options. Some villages willingly placed themselves under French protection to extend the lease on their independence or protect their wealth in cattle from theft and depredation. In other cases, the refusal of central rule spoke through sacred landscapes. To borrow from Nancy Munn, spiritual "law's visible signs [were] topographic markings," which placed ancestral land off-limits.[22] These unstable and contested terrains of power endured until the 1880s, when they were altered once more by the takeoff of peanut farming and the establishment of the Siin protectorate.

As mentioned previously, the expansion of commercial agriculture drove a decisive nail into the coffin of ancien régime economic order. With the liberalization of trade, peasants were allowed to meet the market as producers and bypass customary authorities and sumptuary channels. Peanut farming also eroded the economy of *ceddo* predation and privilege as it enabled farmers to channel the proceeds of agricultural sales toward the acquisition of weapons for protection against pillages. Mbodj analyzes these relations with great clarity:

> peanuts are a product which completely escapes the traditional economico-social circuits. It is a product that the peasant does not need to transform like cotton. He produces it directly. Its culture does not have specific locations that the Buur can control. It is the object of no possible regulation because custom has not predicted its existence. Thus, considering the precarious situation imposed by the ceddo, peasants will exchange their peanuts for weapons. Numerically important, constantly threatened, armed, there needed only a trigger so that these peasants once terrorists would become warriors.

At the same time, commercial agriculture was effortlessly inserted into the triadic logic of colonial capitalism underwritten by "the initiator State, the indigenous producer, and the European buyer."[23]

The era of the protectorate (1887–1924) witnessed major transitions in political power, bringing about transformations in chiefly authority as well as a gradual decrease of the *ceddo* entourage and its eventual dilution into the growing mass of the peasantry by the end of the 1890s.[24] French administrators chose to work within Seereer sociopolitical structures and collaborate with local chiefs and monarchs to anchor the armature of the colonial system to local rural settings. Unlike Kajoor, where the monarchy was obliterated in the aftermath of Lat Joor's resistance, the Gelwaar aristocracy was left in place and operated until World War II under a regime of indirect administration. Colonial authorities worked through traditional rulership and the Gelwaar aristocracy, who were delegated institutional functions, tax-collection duties, and cash-crop supervision.[25] By the late nineteenth century, considerable changes in the form and distribution of power had happened at the expense of traditional grassroots institutions, mostly *lamaan* and village authorities, though, as we will see, they maintained traction at the local level. Further, the influx of seasonal laborers and the installation of Wolof colonizers that accompanied the expansion of peanut agriculture altered the social geography and occupation of space. New villages were created, which did not answer to the Seereer system of land partition, taxes, and dues.[26]

The protectorate introduced two interrelated policy changes in Siin: first, the head tax and, second, a commitment to expanding peanut cultivation and the agricultural trade. Prior to the 1880s, Siin's peasants had been relatively modest peanut producers and were only distantly integrated into the circuits of colonial economy.[27] Taxation, as mentioned in the previous chapter, created incentives for the expansion of both. However, in the process of implementing these plans, the French administration confronted commercial houses, international markets, and Seereer communities whose respective interests were not necessarily isomorphic with those of the colonial officers. The 1891 head tax seems to have jolted peanut production overnight. Despite a downturn in the world economy and low global prices, exports from Siin-Saalum grew from five thousand tons in 1890 to eleven thousand in 1893. Prices dropped further, however, and local commercial houses insisted on driving them down, which caused a reduction of peanut exports in the two years that followed.[28]

Responding to these commercial policies, Noirot wrote the governor with the following plea:

> I beg of you, please make our merchants understand that in wanting to obtain industrial products at too low a price, they expose themselves to the possible desertion of their shops. . . . Our influence over these peoples is not yet sufficiently established to enable them to do without our commercial activity. The needs that we are trying to encourage in the natives are not yet so imperious as to force them to produce in spite of everything. We have in the east of Saloum 40,000 people who have little or no contact with our commerce, and who are capable of living and of clothing themselves. . . . If he [the peasant] were not obliged to get money in order to pay his tax, he would make no effort to seek out European commerce.

Noirot here clairvoyantly assesses the hurdles to French political sovereignty and its solutions. He also embodies the precepts of colonial liberalism examined in chapter 7, a belief that commerce would bring about social change and that good prices and French commodities would irresistibly drive African farmers to European traders and thus to peanut cultivation. Noirot's tug-of-war with the merchant community continued as he perpetually encouraged the replacement of barter with monetized exchange, the establishment of a minimum price, and unrestricted access to French goods.[29]

Trading houses' commercial policy also dragged the colonial administration into a series of confrontations with the rulers of Siin and Saalum. Since the advent of formal colonizations, these kings had occasionally resorted to the interruption of the trade (called *laff*) when they felt that the terms were no longer favorable. This was implemented in the 1860s by Kumba Ndofeen Juuf as a strategy of resistance against colonialism in the hope that the trade prohibition would drive the French away. In 1889, both monarchs imposed the *laff,* which lasted for a month until the kings received generous presents. Afterward, the rulers continued to extend the *laff* episodically. Correspondence between Noirot and the two kings reveals their disenchantment with mercenary peanut prices and their adverse effects. In 1892, for instance, Buur Saalum Geedel complained that low prices were not advantageous to him because "I have debts that I can only pay when the peanut trade goes well; I have nothing but the *coubeul* [tax on peanut sales imposed on French traders] for my expenses." The following year, *buur* Siin Mbake Ndeep Njaay wrote to the director of political affairs that "the Sine-Sine [farmer], after having cultivated peanuts in order to pay his tax, is forced, because the price is so low, to go look for work in the Gambia in order to provide what the peanuts cannot get for him." While the *laff* rapidly lost its power after 1893, these letters reveal the grievances generated by the expansion of the peanut trade and contests over the legitimacy of French law and sovereignty.[30]

Disapproval also extended to the peasant population, who expressed its resistance in arguments of gestures (since we have no correspondence from farmers). Indeed, Noirot's hopes and elated predictions notwithstanding, Seereer peasants did not take to the seductions of commercial crops, cash, and commodities as readily as expected. As Roitman reminds us, colonial truth regimes could not just be forced on colonial subjects; rather, colonial visions of social order and "appropriate comportment" generated both acquiescence and disputes over the legitimacy, intelligibility, and signs of regulatory authority.[31] Thus, in the early days of the protectorate, sections of the peasant body in Siin and neighboring Saalum responded to French taxation through defiance rather than compliance. Colonial archives document episodes of tax evasion, the exploitation of loopholes in the tax system (mostly by migrating from high-tax to low-tax areas), and refusal to pay, as residents from the village of Diohine reportedly did in 1891 and 1892.[32] In subsequent decades, villagers gradually surrendered to the inescapability of the *impôt* (head tax), though not without questioning the legitimacy of colonial fiscality. Thus, Siin farmers chronically underreported household members and heads of cattle in their herds, which were the bases on which personal wealth was determined. They also quietly opposed the diktat of peanut cultivation and the social transformations that came in its wake through acts of passive resistance that entailed both harnessing and responding to signs in the landscape. The conflation of religion, political resistance, and peanuts in the Seereer cultural imagination is clearly captured in a letter by Noirot addressed to the governor. The administrator describes an incident in the Foundiougne area where Seereer farmers refused to take part in a collective effort to eliminate locusts. When queried about their decision, the Seereer answered that "they did not want to destroy the locusts, hoping that they would eat all the pistachios [peanuts] and that the Mandingoes, Wolof, and Tukulor [who were practically all Muslims, as Noirot carefully notes] seeing their cultures destroyed would become disheartened and leave. The locusts were sent by Rook Sène, the local god to help the Seereer chase the strangers away from their country."[33]

These attitudes also translated to French goods, as reported by one of Noirot's Saalum informants: "Why would we go a long way to buy objects we can do without . . . [already having] excellent indigo-dyed cotton cloth, millet, peanuts, tobacco. . . . Ah! If traders came here perhaps women would want beads, coral, *tubab* [white people] textiles. But the traders stay home, and our wives don't travel; they are content with what we have."[34] Even when trade started pressing inland and the Seereer gradually accepted the realities of cash cropping after the 1900s, they often produced just enough peanuts to meet tax requirements and acquire consumption goods. As explained by Administrator Genèbre, "today the cultivator possesses sufficient reserves of millet for his own food and would like to sell his peanuts at a higher price than the commercial houses want to pay. In these circumstances, he is largely supported by his king, whose *coubeul* [export tax] will be that much higher if the products of his country are sold at a higher price." Indeed, until the early 1930s, not only were most Seereer villages economically self-sufficient but families continued to produce enough millet to feed themselves, while deferring the choke of debt.[35] We also continue to see the contingency of political alignments as peasants variably sided with or against ruling authorities, with or against colonial agents, to suit their own projects.

When the political technologies designed to regulate the actions of colonized farmers proved ineffective, colonial power generally showed a more repressive side, sanctioned under the auspices of the *indigénat* regime. No longer delivered through desirable goods and the appeal of trade, persuasion came in the summary form of imprisonment, deportation, fines, and forced labor.[36] In these instances, colonial authority was less grounded in the African adoption of self-policing or participation in their own rule than in the public enactment of violence, punishment, and exploitation on the bodies of rural dwellers. These performances of sovereignty complemented France's politics of absence. They were predicated on a muscular kind of presence, a politics of concrete and visceral visibility, which camouflaged under displays of brutal force the failures of subjectivization, government, and rule by consent. As with the previous monarchical regimes, force here did not reveal authority as much as the lack of it. Nor did it breed consent, as Noirot wrote in 1896; for the fines and penalties levied on behalf of Europeans not only ruined peasants but also turned Europeans into objects of indigenous fear, dislike, and suspicion.[37]

Governing Space and the Challenges of Milieu

Until the late 1920s, lack of personnel and resources confined the colony's dealings with indigenous spheres of power to a dual strategy of conciliation and outsourcing. It also effectively located colonial authority in a restricted number of places and bodies (those of administrators, soldiers, merchants, doctors, and indigenous clerks), thus limiting its intrusion into the daily life of Seereer villagers. While colonial forms of control could be more successfully deployed in urban settings, the state often had a patchy physical presence in rural areas. Until the late nineteenth century, for example, complaints from missionaries and merchants about bands of thieves roving the countryside echoed those made twenty years before, often eliciting the same contrite admission that colonial protection did not radiate far beyond the perimeter of military posts.[38]

Although its power of police increased over time, prior to the 1930s, the colonial state achieved concrete expression in largely episodic spectacles and punctual acts of presence, its trappings glimpsed in military forts and expeditions, administrative delegations, medical campaigns, school creation, the building and inauguration of infrastructure, or annual celebrations of Bastille Day. Despite their limited visibility, state institutions were palpable through the effects they left in the landscape. For instance, public construction projects (roads, wells, bridges) showcased the arbitrary face of colonial power, built as they were on brutal *corvée* labor requirements. And, indeed, by 1898, the Siin-Saalum boasted 555 kilometers of dirt roads.[39]

While much has been made, drawing on the early Foucault, of the capillary extension of power, Cooper argues that the colonial state asserted its presence in more "arterial" fashion, that it was *channeled* through a system of disciplinary techniques—tax collection, fining, policing, labor recruitment, imprisonment, and native courts—mediated by a network of native administrators and collaborators often handpicked from precolonial elites.[40] The reliance on African employees created intermediaries nodes of personal and charismatic power, which unlocked new opportunities for illicit personal accumulation. Colonial correspondence is littered with the testimonies of simple villagers condemning the brutality of village and district chiefs and the rapacity of aristocratic elites, over whom colonial authorities had the most nominal of influence. France tolerated these necessary evils, as evidenced in classified assessments of African intermediaries from the late 1800s, which reported evidence of petty crimes and power abuses committed by district chiefs but proposed few corrective measures.[41]

By and large, however, most Seereer villagers stayed estranged from sites of colonial spatiality: administrative towns, commercial centers, or port facilities (figure 32). Prior to the 1930s, the scattering of these sites and the porousness of colonial sovereignty opened vast spaces of autonomy, where the Seereer continued to practice old and new spatial forms away from the watchful eyes of colonial law, even as the latter increasingly redefined the conditions of local subjectivities. Galvan provides a powerful illustration of these dynamics in his discussion of the institution of pawnship (*taile*).[42] *Taile* emerged in response to colonial attempts to reform rural landholding and institute new regimes of individual land ownership. Instead of selling land considered inalienable under Seereer principles of collective custodianship, a farmer could pawn his use rights to a land plot to another peasant as collateral for a cash loan. The money would enable the first peasant to pay off his taxes or debts (as often was the case), while the land parcel would enable the second peasant to extend his cultivated acreage or pasture for cattle herds. This system, in other words, allowed the temporary conversion of unsellable resources into cash without compromising their inalienability; it performed an illusion of commodification that actually upheld traditional conceptions of landholding.

The aftermath of the world economic crisis of 1929 saw a consolidation of colonial governance marked by a shift in state materiality and its politics of absence. The modes of sporadic presence and arterial intervention that had prevailed until the late 1800s were supplemented by a regime of present absence working primarily through the channels of political economy to refashion the field of local possibilities. Gradually planting its roots in rural Senegal after 1900, this regime intensified

32 Two views of Foundiougne. *Top*, "Port of Foundiougne" (ANS, Iconographie, no. 0696; reproduced with permission from Archives du Sénégal). *Bottom*, old colonial cooperative built in the 1920s (photo by author, 2013).

during the first fifty years of the twentieth century with the indirect assistance of state programs like farming cooperatives, and after the economic crash, with more direct involvement of the state in driving agricultural policy and development.[43] Archaeological landscapes offer useful (if not completely concordant) clues of these transitions and how they were internalized into Seereer livelihoods. I will briefly examine their manifestations in artifact inventories and settlement logics.

Consuming Colonialism

One unquestionable archaeological trend in Siin involves the explosive increase in imported artifacts over the past two hundred years. While trade goods are negligible in pre-1700 surface and excavated contexts and while foreign manufactures (glass objects, especially) become essential components of site assemblages (even as local ceramics continue to dominate), one sees a marked expansion in the quantity and diversity of imported objects in post-1850s occupations. Although village communities in the region had long engaged with Atlantic commerce and had a long history of making foreign objects and ideas their own, the colonial moment ushered in new worlds of peasant consumption and, over time, cemented farmers' dependence on commodity circuits and cash exchanges. However, Seereer relations with the global "empire of things" were by no means unilateral, and different classes of artifacts reveal different histories of appropriation.[44]

Glass assemblages, for instance, contain an overwhelming proportion of gin and schnapps bottles, a preference that appears to have been driven by consumer choice. It was also fueled by the commercial availability of *alcool de traite* (trade liquor), which was an essential component of economic transactions and often served as currency in the early decades of colonial exchange. As we saw in chapter 6, while many colonial administrators lamented the socially destructive effects of alcohol and its hand in propagating violence in Senegalese provinces, liquor also became an intrinsic part of Seereer practices of social reproduction—as a commensal gift to reward workers in labor parties, as a libation to honor spirits and ancestors, and as a ritual substance to assist rites of passage and agricultural ceremonies. The increasing democratization of trade liquor (gin, especially) also appears to have motivated aristocrats at the end of the nineteenth century to devise new ways of controlling alcohol and construct new markers of status, as perhaps revealed by the central role of wine in the elite feasting deposits discussed earlier. What is interesting, though not easily quantified, in the 2011 collections is the appearance of new kinds of liquor (such as Pernod) on twentieth-century settlements, as well as the increasing quantities of wine fragments on these sites. Perhaps this reflects the observation of economic historians that, in looking to find niches for their products, French trading houses and manufacturers created demands and markets that fanned the flames of colonial mercantilism.[45] At the same time, more in line with the sociology of alcohol consumption delineated in this book, these new consumer goods might also illustrate that former elites were losing control over markers of economic privilege and distinction. Perhaps the market ensured that nonaristocrats would also covet wine or develop a taste for other alcohols. If so, what did these shifts indicate about changing identities in Siin?

If archaeological assemblages inform us about broad categories of elite and commoner practices, they also chronicle the development of finer-grained social stories. For instance, a number of French documents from the late nineteenth and early twentieth centuries note, with amused condescension, the emergence of a Muslim taste for *alcool de menthe* (peppermint water) or *Menthe Ricqlès*.[46] While technically an all-purpose medicinal drug, peppermint water contained moderate amounts of ethanol and would have enabled Muslim enthusiasts partially to reconcile religious restrictions on alcohol with the satisfaction of recreational drinking. The recovery of *alcool de menthe* bottle fragments on phase Vc residential sites might index the presence of such consumptive syntheses tied to the expansion of Muslim modernities in the Seereer countryside.

In another example, the recovery of Perrier and Evian bottle fragments after 1890 in the proximity of colonial *escales* (trading posts) speaks to variability in beverage consumption. In his correspondence with the director of indigenous affairs, Noirot provides rare insights into the social life of mineral water in late nineteenth-century Senegal: "Vichy water can be considered as a luxury drink or as medicine [to cure liver problems]. . . . Allow me to bring to your attention that we do not always find Vichy water here, and that, when we do find it, we must pay 1.25 F per bottle, and this is a discount rate."[47] These remarks convey the possibility that mineral water, at least early on, was associated with village chiefs, local authorities, and petty colonial elites. In fact, the discovery of Vichy water bottles in the village of Ndianda on an early twentieth-century site identified as the residence of a certain Pierre Ndiaye, an indigenous district chief (*chef de canton*), seems to signal the development of yet other registers of distinction, no longer predicated on inherited status but on social occupation. Other than its cost, Vichy water might not mean much by itself. What seems to support the idea of mineral water as a statement of taste, however, is the fact that the bottle fragments were paired with glazed pottery sherds and buttons that index commodities (European ceramic wares and manufactured clothes) rarely encountered on rural sites of the colonial period. As an assemblage, these items perhaps deliver an unassuming testament to the new forms of wealth, disposable income, and purchasing power accrued by certain colonial employees and to the rise of Seereer subjectivities merging the desire for material icons of taste with aspirations toward ideas of colonial civility.

33 Postcard, early twentieth century, "Céréres—Preparation of an alcoholic beverage with fermented millet" (ANS, Iconographie no. 0348; reproduced with permission from Archives du Sénégal). Note the metal cooking pot in the foreground.

Glass containers in Siin embody something of the successful side of colonial commerce and its program of subjection through consumption. Other artifacts, however, document the failure of colonial commodities to capture the practical imaginations of Seereer peasants. We mentioned in chapter 6 the absence of popular demand for mass-produced ceramic vessels in the eighteenth and nineteenth centuries, and these apparently remained largely estranged from Seereer households for the first fifty years of the twentieth century (table 10). Glazed plates and bowls were poorly adapted to local foodways, which demanded large containers capable of accommodating communal eating. The bulk of imported ceramics on colonial-period sites consists of utilitarian stonewares, which were probably acquired for what they contained rather than the function fulfilled by the containers themselves. Note that culinary traditions did not remain stagnant during the colonial era; in fact, they changed fairly dramatically, most notably through the incorporation of vegetables (peanuts, tomatoes) and condiments and the Indochinese rice that increasingly flooded Senegalese markets.[48] Likewise, we also note the increase of metal cauldron parts in the archaeological record, which points to the adoption of new cooking technologies over time (figure 33). Finally, while whitewares and porcelaneous ceramics never quite fully made it into colonial assemblages, they do increase after the 1930s in

Table 10 2011 site inventory: Imported ceramic assemblages

Sites	Lead-glazed earthenware	Tin-glazed earthenware	Pearlware (1820–1840) Plain	Pearlware (1820–1840) Decorated	Whiteware (1820s+) Plain/ molded	Whiteware (1820s+) Painted	Whiteware (1820s+) Transfer-printed/ decal	Spongeware (1845–1930)	Annularware (1820–1900)	Porcelain Plain/ molded	Porcelain Decorated	Stoneware Utilitarian	Stoneware Tableware	Other
S151					3					1	1			
S154—general collection	1				1	1	1							
S154A			1		5	2		2	3			2		
S154B			1	2	3	2	1	1	2	3	2			
S154C	3				9	1	3			1	1	2		
S157			1		2								1	
S163					1		2							
S164	4													
S177	1	1					1						9	
S183							1			1			1	
S195		2			1									
S204					1				2					
S235					3				1					
S246					2				1					
S249					1						2			

S257											3			
S155, S159, S161, S162, S180, S182, S215, S228, S230, S241, S243, S254*					6	2	2	1	4	2	3		2	2
S133C, S137, S144, S147, S148, S156, S158, S160, S166, S176, S178, S179, S196, S199, S202, S206, S211, S218, S220, S222, S225, S229, S237, S253, S259**	3	2	2		7	3	2			1	4		2	
Total	12	5	5	2	45	11	13	4	13	9	16	4	15	2

Note: Most of the ceramics listed here point to late nineteenth- and twentieth-century occupations, with the exception of sites containing later pearlware (ca. 1820–1840), S157 and S154, which have components dating to 1800–1850. Nearly all the lead-glazed earthenware is of the Vallauris variety. All the tin-glazed earthenware is recent. The majority of pearlware, whiteware, sponge-ware, and annularware fragments come from plates, platters, and saucers. With the exception of an Imari revival teacup sherd dating to the nineteenth century, the porcelain fragments are all from the twentieth century, especially post-1960. They include a majority of cups and mugs. The same goes for the stoneware tableware, which is uniformly recent and consists largely of mugs/cups with a small number of sugar pots and teapots. The "other" category consists of slipware and yellowware.

* Sites containing two imported ceramic sherds.

** Sites containing one imported ceramic sherd.

34 Diohine region, 2011 site inventory, coin assemblage. The British half sovereign coin is on the far right.

archaeological inventories. For example, in the 2011 inventory, which contained a large proportion of twentieth-century sites, modest quantities of China-made mass-produced porcelain teacups and stoneware coffee mugs entered the garbage of post-1960 villages, alongside ubiquitous fragments of glass cups used to drink mint tea. A related transition since independence has seen the replacement of locally made ceramics by cheap plasticware or enameled tinware (although there remains a market for ceramic braziers and large water jars, often reinforced with cement because of their fragility).

A final set of objects raises a caveat about overestimating the power of French commerce. In effect, trade artifacts suggest an unsuspected knack for navigating commercial networks manifested, for instance, by the presence of British coinage in contexts far away from the British colony in Gambia. Particularly notable is a 1908 British half sovereign gold coin found on a site near Diohine (figure 34). The date is interesting because the area had long been under French influence at that time. We cannot be sure of how the coin wound up in Siin. It could have been traded or gifted or exchanged for produce across the porous political and commercial boundary between French and British colonies. Perhaps, then, it is a predecessor to the informal, illicit economic networks vibrating along the Senegal-Gambia border, taking advantage of opportunities for "marginal gains" at currency frontiers. At the same time, the fact that some of these and other coins are perforated indicate that they had been taken out of circulation. More generally, along with French colonial currency, they act as a reminder that money followed in the footsteps of cash cropping, penetrated into the Seereer countryside, and grew increasingly relevant to social life.[49]

What these objects' trajectories indicate is that, as the Seereer struggled to accommodate change while remaining the same, the new things they used joined old ones to reconfigure the sensible world in which rural folks acquired a sense of personal and collective identities. In short time spans, as peanuts threaded into the countryside a new suite of productive and consuming habits, goods that had little currency a few decades earlier became the stuff of familiar sights, sounds, tastes, and smells. Along with the cash they commanded for sale or purchase, imported goods became dyed into the fabric of everyday interactions and social reproduction (marriage payments, inheritances, loans, barter exchanges, debt repayments). That said, while the spell of commodities was quite successful in binding the Seereer to market conditions they could not control, it fell short of conjuring a population of submissive farmers adapted to the demands of colonial accumulation.

Mapping Spatial Transformations

The remodeling of Seereer modes of consumption also parallels broader reorganizations in Siin's social space. These are manifested archaeologically in the form of changes in settlement structure and regionally through changes in village location. One of the most palpable trends coming out of the 2011 survey is the fragmentation of the village landscape after the late 1800s (figure 35; table 11; figure 36). While the eighteenth century inaugurated an increase in settlement numbers but a decrease in average settlement size and occupation, phase Vc sites are generally smaller, more ephemeral, materially poor, and dispersed than their predecessors. Many of these sites, moreover, are located in previously empty areas between well-established villages. This atomization of the social environment points right back to colonial political economy and processes unleashed by the normalization of cash crops, commodities, and currency in the countryside.

First, the fragmentation of Siin's habitat is connected to the massive conversion to peanut farming after the 1920s, which triggered a growing individualization of property relations and dissolution of matrilineal

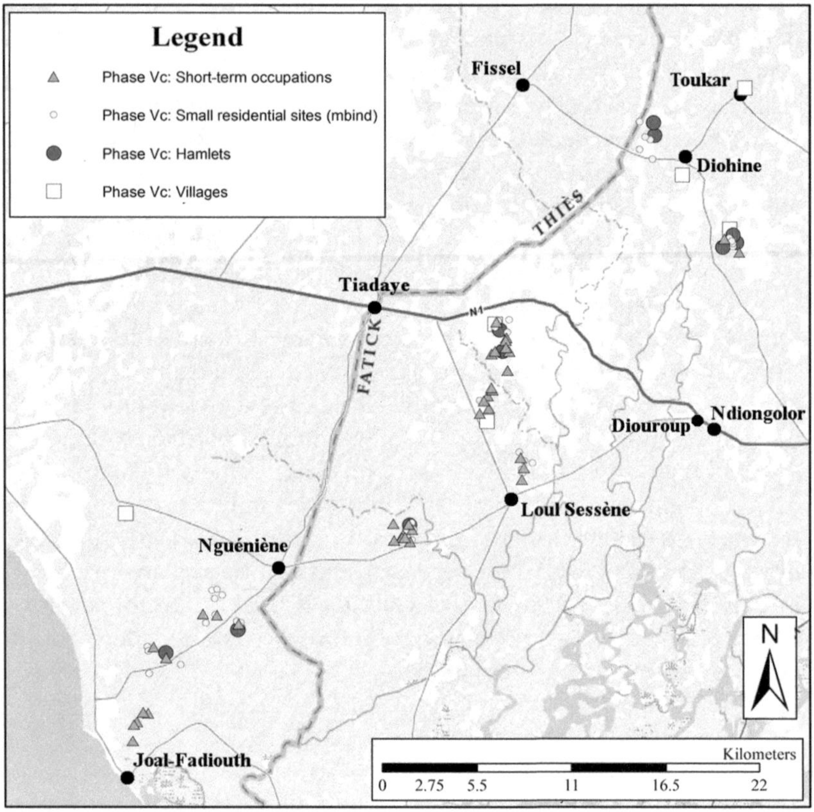

35 Siin settlement landscape, 2011 site inventory, Toukar, Nguénièné, and Loul Sessène regions, phase Vc, 1870–1950

Table 11 2011 site inventory: Settlement types by survey regions in nineteenth and twentieth centuries

	Phase Vb			Phase Vc		
Site types	NGE	LOUL	TUK	NGE	LOUL	TUK
Short-term occupation	6	22	5	6	18	6
Mbind	5	17	7	10	16	6
Hamlet	2	4	5	2	4	4
Village	1	3	3	1	2	3
Total	14	46	20	19	40	19

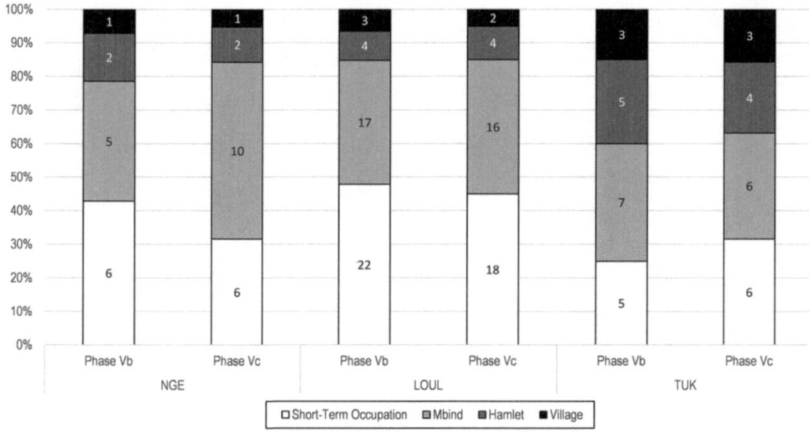

36 2011 settlements: site types by phase and by survey region

holdings. Part of the loose network of phase Vc habitations orbiting in the periphery of large villages reflects the multiplication of interstitial agricultural concessions as peanut farmers broke off from familial units, claimed their own fields to cultivate, and moved to the fringes of existing settlements. This trend also intensified the fuzziness of settlement boundaries that so startled colonial observers and their successors.

Second, the mobile geographies outlined by archaeology were a product of the new organization of labor accompanying the shift from subsistence farming to commercial cultivation. Peanut cultivation in high-yield areas like the Siin required much manual labor and attracted migrant workers who came to assist with agricultural tasks.[50] While labor movements were often seasonal, some non-Seereer migrants established hamlets in the vicinity of existing villages; indeed, some of the archaeological occupations surveyed in 2003 were identified by nearby residents as having been founded by migrants coming from Wolof regions to the north, and The Gambia and Guinea to the south. Faced with the pressures of land, labor, and drought, Seereer residents themselves were also prone to population movements as they left crowded terroirs and increasingly small parcels of land to look for better opportunities. A number of sites documented in 2011 in the region of Nguéniène traced original settlers to inland areas near the villages of Fissel, Toukar, Diohine, and Diouroup, according to residents we interviewed (figure 37).[51] The residents confirmed the shallowness of historical settlement in this region. Most were descendants from people who had come from the

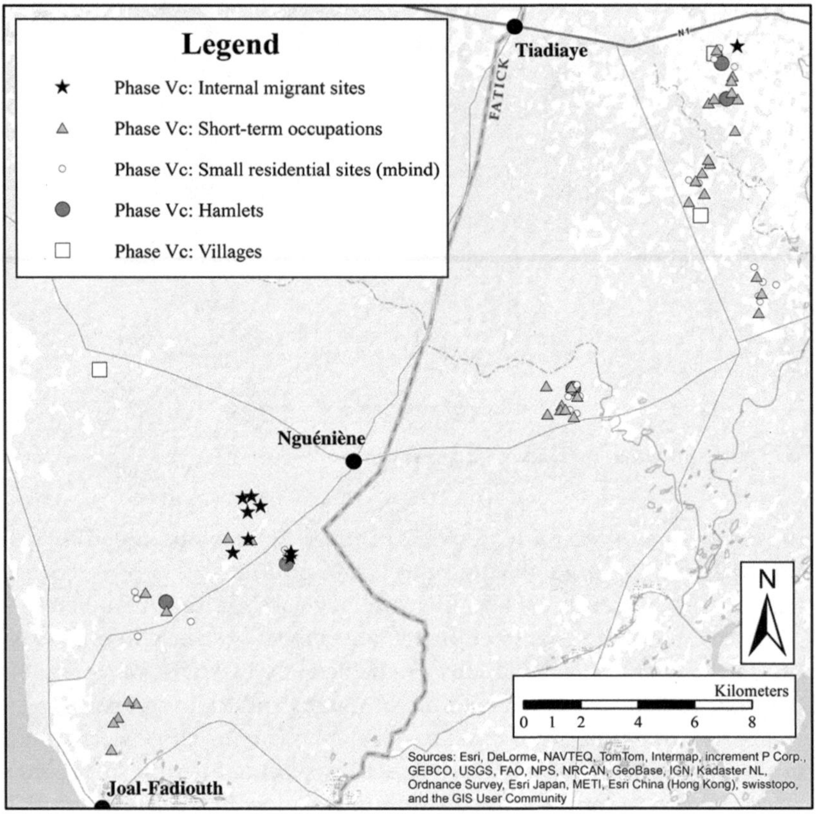

37 Internal migration: recent site movements from Toukar area to Nguéniène

interior and settled uninhabited areas between the 1930s and 1950s. In our conversations, residents consistently struck the same note about the conditions of migration: land-poor sons from Siin's hinterland near the peanut-growing centers, forced out of saturated matrilineal estates, looking to the south for pasture for their herds and water and land for their crops. Their stories recoup the testimonies of peasants interviewed by Guigou: "Some men, who resided in villages of the Ndiafadj country and lacked land, left to settle in villages of Hiréna, in the Diakhao zone or that of the Gandiaye arrondissement, so they could benefit from more abundant and fertile lands. Some went to rejoin a maternal relative, others who left were attracted by land tenure opportunities. These movements took diverse shapes, ranging from the seasonal agricultural migrations of young men to the temporary or definitive migrations of adult men accompanied by their families."[52] In some instances, these displacements afforded new economic opportunities, avenues of accumulation, and forms of social advancement that had been proscribed under customary arrangements. They also engendered less felicitous effects. Most frequently, the arrival of newcomers sparked off disputes over land, resources, and identity, which are prominently recounted in village traditions.[53] Relocation also sometimes failed to deliver on the promises of economic betterment. In effect, the lands on which the new settlers established their homes were often marginal, and their fragile, ferruginous, and often poorly watered soils were not always able to support a comfortable living. Many migrants, in other words, faced a future of poverty, one that was accelerated over time by overcultivation and drought cycles, a situation visible today in many parts of the Siin. Lastly, on a more experiential plane, regional movements may have unsettled the horizon of Seereer migrants, whose identities were solidly anchored to soil, place, and spiritual forces rooted in lineage estates. To palliate the effects of dislocation, peasant migrants may have improvised strategies like those of Seereer seasonal workers in the eastern Saalum during the 1960s and 1970s, who incorporated soil from their homeland into their spiritual altars.[54]

Archaeology suggests other—structural—reorientations in Siin's residential landscape, apparently set off by the French bureaucratic and commercial presence.[55] Beyond documenting a dispersal of the Seereer habitat during the colonial era, settlement maps also signal the parallel emergence of unprecedentedly large villages. Some of the largest residential sites recorded in Siin emerged in the nineteenth century, with six of the nine villages larger than seven hectares dating to that period. These sites frequently contain well over fifty mounds, with distinct quartiers clearly identifiable in surface remains. Why this size increase happened is not entirely clear, though it can probably be related to the relative political stability created by colonialism and the demographic increases spurred by export agriculture.

Residential sites of the colonial period also appear to converge toward administrative and economic centers as well as commercial axes and major roads. Closer proximity to colonial infrastructure would have been desirable for logistical and economic reasons. In towns, peasants found weighing stations and points of collection for peanut harvests, where selling prices were better than those offered by merchants servicing the countryside. Towns also hosted regional markets where surplus food and crafts could be exchanged for valued commodities: moonshine, kola nuts, metalware, or cloth.[56] Being near roads and bridges would have considerably eased the transportation of peanut harvests and reduced travel times, which could be lengthy.[57] Over time, the development of commercial axes appears to have influenced settlement layouts. Today, many villages are wound about major roads as residential quarters agglutinate in ribbons along each side of the thoroughfare. This clearly is a departure from the dispersed modes of occupation reported in the hinterland in the early decades of colonial rule. In this process of community reconfiguration, settlements have gradually dislocated from matrilineal landholdings, and today original lineage estates and the boundaries of contemporary villages no longer really overlap.[58] As noticed earlier, these alterations of the Seereer milieu should be read as spatial symptoms of a broader process of transformation toward individual ownership, freeholding, and the loosening of matrilineal allegiances. These features, in turn, have intensified to an even greater degree since Senegal gained its independence in 1960, and national political directions in the past fifty years have followed a path of land reforms, economic austerity, liberal governance, and the promotion of Islamic modernity. Particularly injurious to Seereer peasants was the nationalization of agricultural lands in the 1960s, which completely upset the subtle architecture of traditional land management and gravely affected many communities. Later, in the 1980s, programs of structural adjustment initiated a gradual withdrawal of the state from rural life, which continues to fuel local animus toward sovereign authority and suspicion toward state centralization.[59]

Conclusion: Colonial Postscript

This chapter began with a story of absence, a contemporary vignette evoking the relative disengagement of the Senegalese state from the dealings of Siin's peasant communities. I have suggested that this state of affairs and the political experiences flowing from it are indebted to a much longer history of interactions between peasants and centralized authority. The elusiveness of the postcolonial state and the productive gaps it has engendered for Seereer farmers are connected to earlier narratives of absence. Working back from the present and forward from past settings, I have attempted to expose some of the historical threads bridging the today and yesterday of power in the Siin countryside. While these political genealogies are messy and tangled, harkening back to the reluctant landscapes of the Atlantic era, much of my attention has been focused on the *colonial prehistory* of present-day formations of power and the modes of action, political possibilities, and subjective understandings they have configured. Landscape here works as a hyphen between history and ethnography: a dialectical image juxtaposing different political times and temporalities of power, an archive of the ruptures and continuities that have made and redefined Seereer modernities over the past two hundred years.

Throughout this chapter, my goals have been multiple. First, I have sought to show that archaeological materials can be used to study practices of colonial statecraft and permit reflections about the materiality of the state and its mediations of power. Archaeology is therefore positioned to contribute to historical and anthropological conversations about the problematization of colonialism and theorization of its operations in Africa and beyond. Second, archaeological landscapes offer prime evidence of how colonial programs were translated to rural Africa and the traces they left on peasant lifeworlds. In this way, engaging with colonial government helps us to elucidate the milieus of power in which African agencies, identities, and social practices were molded. It also lends insights into the material conditions and dispositions that oriented native modes of subjective understanding. Lastly, by adding material and temporal strokes to current thinking on the tensions between (post)colonial state rationalities and possibilities, archaeological archives provide support to Africanist recastings of notions of governmentality and sovereignty hatched in the Euro-American library.[60]

In addition to these general considerations, this chapter has also tried to think through the possibilities introduced by the problem of absence in past settings. Epistemologically, I have tried to show that archaeological reasoning can be sparked as much by what is there as by what isn't—absence of evidence here does not necessarily connote evidence of absence. Failing to find expected signatures of colonial power might imply limitations in one's data, but it can also trigger new ways of approaching historical questions. In this instance, material resistances provoked fresh questions about the nature of state power and its mediations (rather than endorsing certain a priori notions about how states become substantiated in the world). Conceptually, I have tried to examine how absence might feature as a technology of rule, and thus this work joins a growing body of writings on emptiness, invisibility, and immateriality as they relate to matters of power.[61]

Landscapes complement the story of L'Association des Paysans de Toukar in useful and surprising ways. They root the social fact of state neglect in a political rationality that sought to reconcile the costs of governance with anemic budgets. This style of rule lay partly in the institution of a kind of power by proxy, a power exercised through the African chiefs, peanuts, and commodities that did the unsung business of government. In this way, the distance of the colonial state gave a certain autonomy to peasant communities, observable in a number of broad continuities that orchestrated the countryside, village space, and consumption practices over time. Some of these linger today. For instance, old villages like Toukar or Diakhao retain a polynucleated organization that defies the rectilinear axes of Cartesian grid maps, which tend to be reflected in more recent villages like Diouroup that were built and structured around the road. Other onetime continuities are disappearing: millet, for example, has for a few decades slowly given way to rice as a Seereer staple, except among the poorest families who can't afford this expensive commodity.[62] Yet, these zones of autonomy were also indebted to the chancy, reluctant geographies that precolonial states could not tame and that colonial administration tolerated with resignation. Continuity does not mean immobility. These geographies were recombinant and shifted shape and organization with the introduction of new commodities, the construction of roads, the emergence of trading points, or the building of towns. However, they continued to translate collective feelings of unease about foreign power—whether the sovereignty of Gelwaar aristocrats or that of the French—across a landscape rapidly reoriented by peanuts, which admitted first a trickle of money and later a flow of commodities that altered the coordinates of social life away from collective institutions.

While the optic of landscape affords broad vistas, linking disparate histories across territorial space, it also glosses over the microhistory of single communities.[63] As materialities coterminous with the peasantry at large come into focus, smaller sociological details fade out of sight. The modest rebellions and vexations of everyday life cannot be grasped. The many fates, faces, and feuds *within* villages cannot be glimpsed. And yet, the story of French rule is very much about how the lives of individuals and families were unevenly tethered to the programs of colonialism. After all, some farmers consolidated their holdings and grew wealthy, while others lost their land to poor decisions, desiccation, or the decomposition of lineages, and many more saw their economic prospects decline steadily. Some rose to influence in village politics and others faded into oblivion. Some migrated to towns, others moved to the Terres Neuves in eastern Saalum to cultivate peanuts, and others relocated, permanently or temporarily, to other villages or provinces, each displacement rearticulating their position in the web of colony and society.[64] We catch the occasional glint of these smaller histories in the upstart aspirations conveyed in the trash of a *chef de canton* or, more poetically, in the discovery of a perforated coin once held around the neck of its owner and humbly curated by him or her. At the same time, landscape materialities speak to the aggregated force of collective experience, and, in doing so, they sometimes provoke us by exposing the lively histories, good or bad, that stretch across (post)colonial biopolitics. One such story—the other face of state neglect—is one of impoverishment, the palpable poverty littering the Siin countryside. This marginality stood with particular force in the landscape of small makeshift concessions, the tattered homes of farmers eking a living out of inhospitable soil that we encountered in areas near the prosperous village of Nguénième. These areas, it appears, are among the regions that over the past seventy years welcomed internal migrants forced by circumstance to relocate on the outskirts of settled landscapes. In this sense, the vestiges of abandoned homes and today's extant houses stand as allegories of the ruin and decay linking colonial agriculture to the conditions of marginalization experienced by Seereer peasantries in the postindependence era. And so we return, fittingly, to the peasant malaise with which this book opened, though we perhaps understand it a little better this time, or at least now know it differently.

Conclusion: Archaeological Pasts, Postcolonial Presents, Traditional Futures

To lay the past to rest thus means not that we should forget it but that we have no choice but to relate it, no choice but to live on within the full knowledge and unending of it. Time does not pass but accumulates. Why? Because what has been begun does not end but endures. Because this fatal Atlantic "beginning" of the modern is more properly understood as an ending without end. Because history comes to us not only as flash or revelation but piling up. Because this is, not was. Because this is the Atlantic, now. Because all of it is now, it is always now, even for you who never was there. I. BAUCOM, *SPECTERS OF THE ATLANTIC*[1]

Places of Re-memberings

Before they consolidated as arguments of history and theory, the ideas of this book took shape in the present through years of archaeological encounters with Siin's rural past. I was perhaps first introduced to the politics of Seereer memory when I traveled to Diakhao, Siin's former capital, in 2001 (figure 38). A small enclaved village, Diakhao is a reference point of Seereer culture, a *lieu de mémoire* saturated with myths, stories, and traditions. This omnipresent past is also a cumbersome heritage "weigh[ing] like a nightmare on the brains of the living."[2] Having long outlived its former grandeur and fallen off the map of colonial and postcolonial favor, the village has clung to a bygone past and seeks consolation in the Sisyphean task of arbitrating a Tradition increasingly slippery, contested, and perhaps even irrelevant.

38 Diakhao, royal residence, interior courtyard (photos by author, May 2001)

In Diakhao, the past is continually workshopped. This much was made manifest at our arrival as a village elder greeted us defiantly, an old issue of the *Bulletin de l'IFAN* in hand. Brandishing the yellowed journal, the man launched into a fiery condemnation of historians studying Siin's past from the comfort of their air-conditioned offices in Dakar. The province's *real* past, he insisted, did not flow from the pens of urban academics; it was "rooted in the soil" and declaimed by the heirs of tradition. We defused the tensions by mentioning that we were interested in the more remote past, before the Gelwaar royals, and walked away from the confrontation.[3]

During a three-month stay two years later, our team was routinely exposed to the politics of authenticity in Diakhao. Our excavations at Thioupane, the historic residence of Siin's *lingeer*, hosted a constant stream of local elders who traveled the narrow trail to the site and "set us straight" on the true history of place. Conversations around the village revealed a more fractious topography of memory, some (often the descendants of royal dependencies) speaking in support of the aristocracy's past glory, others contesting the ideologies of history expounded by the royal family. Many interlocutors regarded the nobility as controversial figures then and now, expressing skepticism about idealized accounts of Gelwaar exploits and monopolistic claims on the past. They countered such romanticizations with their own recountings of popular political wisdom and oppressive precolonial regimes. We often found ourselves in the crossfire of contests of legitimacy. One time, the royal family used our excavations to discredit village political functionaries who had green-lit our work and reestablish authority over important sites of memory.[4] This is reminiscent of the uneasy poetics of authority and autonomy that have shaped Siin's landscape history (chapter 5), only this time conflicts between *baadoole* (commoners) and nobles, between Gelwaar and the state, were symbolically waged on the terrain of memory.

The politics of memory have taken on different expression in Mbissel, another locus classicus of Siin's *cosaan* (deep history). A quiet village lost in a blur of mango orchards, Mbissel is remembered as Siin's first capital, home to Maisa Wali Joon, the founder of Siin's royal dynasty; it is also his resting place, as the mythical king is said to be buried in the village and serves as the locality's main *fangool* (figure 39). Less concerned with claims and counterclaims over history's entitlements, remembering has centered on Maisa's tomb, soldering past and present into a chronotope of sacred continuity and ancestral consecration. The first time I visited the tomb in 2001, Mr. Faye, its caretaker, handed our group a set of printed instructions. The document was a faded photocopy of President Senghor's preface to Father Gravrand's first volume of *La civilisation sereer*, an influential treatment of Seereer historical traditions. The preface recounts Senghor's mystical journey back to his homeland during a difficult political campaign. In the vicinity of Mbissel, he encountered a group of women who performed purification rituals and sacrifices designed to secure his first seat on the National Assembly. We were invited to relive Senghor's experiences as we walked to the tomb, including paying the five thousand CFA francs that he gave to the women to guarantee his political victory. Unlike Senghor, we received no mystical bath, though we were told that sacrifices would be made in our honor. We were forbidden to speak French or Wolof. Only Seereer was authorized. At one point, the caretaker motioned toward the outside of the tomb and inquired whether we had seen the women of Senghor's narrative: they had come to give us their blessing.

When I returned to Mbissel nearly fifteen years later, a greying Mr. Faye still tended to the tomb. The *fangool* was encircled by a palisade, its access blocked by a rusty iron gate. The ritual had changed, too. Gone were the written instructions. No more background story, the king's mythical fame perhaps speaking for itself. No suggested fee. Of course, we compensated the caretaker for his trouble, but the gesture—now a banal cash transaction—had lost its enchanted veneer. The *fangool* still imposed the Seereer language, but it no longer permitted photographs. Muslim women were also required to remove their headscarves in its presence.

Maisa's shrine is another instance of the myriad recompositions that have enveloped history and storytelling in the Seereer countryside since

39 Mbissel, *fangool* of Maisa Wali Joon (photo by author, May 2001)

the Atlantic era. If ritual has often labored for the preservation of sacred institutions and traditions, it has also nested spaces of innovation in the name of keeping things the same. As it creatively folds together the foundational moments of Siin's creation and Senegal's genesis and folds them back upon Mbissel, Faye's story also stakes out tradition as the bridge connecting the province's past and the postcolony. Maisa Wali, the king maker, is also a nation maker (a point revisited below). It is also a crushing rebuttal to Sarkozy's reveries about African nature, showing that, at one of Siin's most traditional sites, tradition is, well, irreverently modern—mediated by the money sign, mechanical reproduction, a French missionary-turned-expert-on-tradition, and ideas of the nation. Tradition has never been Sarkozy's eternal return to the same. Its repetition always entails difference, new events and signs, and cultural entrepreneurialism.[5] Its political claims extend beyond locality.

More recombinations await as the *fangool* is dragged into conversations about modernization, stretching its taciturn agencies in new ways. In 2012, Maliam Sagne, Mbissel's chief, took to the newspapers to deplore the absence of electrification in his village. Construction had begun a decade earlier but had been suspended without explanation, though he had heard that the cancellation came from executives at Senelec (Senegal's energy company), who believed that his village was haunted and that the irascible Maisa would harm outsiders bringing change. Deploring these stereotypes, Sagne wondered why the *fangool* would stand in the way of development when Maisa's presence, and the significance it gives to Mbissel as Siin's oldest village (*saax maak*), is precisely why the village deserved better.[6] Why indeed would Maisa want to keep villagers in the dark, literally and metaphorically? Keenly attuned to the ironies of superstitious modernizers and electrical *pangool*, Mr. Sagne knew that spirit shrines and state projects have always combined into a proliferation of mixtures collapsing the boundaries of tradition and modernity. Or maybe even that Maisa has all along been made and remade in his embrace with global flows and expectations. He also knew that progress is the graveyard of many dreams, and modernity's promises do not alleviate the burdens of poverty. While the newspaper campaign has since successfully brought electrical infrastructures to the village, as of 2016 the latter stood idle, a future-perfect beyond the reach of most Mbissel residents, who cannot afford to pay the subscription for electrical service.[7]

Collectively, these anecdotes problematize central concerns of this book about the shifting relationship between landscape, history, and tradition. Attending to the representation side of history, they also reverberate with the premises that opened the prologue. They show that places are conflicted terrains of memory oozing with political affect. They convey Seereer preoccupations about their positions within history, the nation, and the world. And they demonstrate that what appears most intrinsic to culture is structured in relation with other places, peoples, and ideas.

They also remind us that politics is never an abstract thing. Born of concerns anchored in concrete cultural milieus, political feeling actualizes itself in the world; it needs materialities to "take place." Today, as in the past, Seereer worlds exude a certain uneasiness about projects of sovereignty radiating from the Elysian fields of the state, the market, or the West. This moral sentiment is, however, plastic in time, space, and society, and, depending on the outcome of situated encounters, it achieves different forms: the Gelwaar maneuvering for influence between citizens and the state, Maisa Wali's caretaker's sophisticated cultural tinkering, which endorses certain forms of outsideness and rejects others, or when anxieties surge up about modernity's broken hopes as in Mbissel. Provoked by encounters, these political materialities exact demands on students of the past, leaving us no choice but to engage.

Reluctant Engagements and Landscape Politics in Atlantic Siin

What I have attempted in this book is an examination of the material conditions that have shaped life, politics, history, and representation in Siin's peasant worlds over the past five hundred years. In the broadest of sense, this study has taken the shape of an oblique meditation on tradition. Tradition has served as a complex historical force that has mediated Siin's modern political experiences; it has been mobilized as both an argument for exclusion and subjection and a mode of inclusion and connection to the world. At one level, traditions of landscape and object use have been composed and recomposed over time to respond to the realities of markets, globality, and colony. On the other hand, as shown by the chapters on the construction of ethnographic knowledge and colonial government in Siin, tradition has been mobilized as a technology of political imposition and marginalization—the opposite of a desired condition of modernity; in its discursive form, it has painted the province as an island of timeless culture and camouflaged the distinctive properties of its history. Looking at various archives, however, I have sought to show the flaws in images of Seereer conservatism; it is clear that social lives and identities in Siin and popular orientations to past, present, and future have been indelibly fashioned by material and imagined links to elsewheres. In historiography, this engagement with the world has often been perceived as driven by the stifling forces of global commerce and colonialism. My suggestion, however, is that these presumptions and the references points guiding their visions of African history do not adequately account for the minor-key histories of peasantry saturating the African countryside, those *longue durée* temporalities of power roping the experiences of farmers in the past to the discontents that farmers feel today.

To get at these histories, I have proposed to rearticulate the problem-space of Siin's past around the material world. This has led me to examine how Siin history has been fashioned by a political unconscious that has achieved material substance in the terroir. Materiality's trails have led me to speculate on the historical force of Siin's reluctant landscapes (chapter 1). Like the suspicions of sovereignty animating political discourse in Siin today, geographic reluctance does not refer to a spatial ethos of resistance. Rather, it is a broad orientation to the political, built around tensions between the virtues of decentralization, federalism, and local government and the dangerous attractions of power rooted in hierarchy, centralization, and the outside (chapter 5). Further, reluctant spatialities have been a *mode of historical engagement* that has mediated Siin's relationship to the world and been transformed by it. Reluctance has been as much about bringing in as keeping out. It has also creatively pivoted around the question of foreignness as something to be feared, embraced, or even harnessed.

At the genesis of the kingdom, Siin's rural communities accepted the promises of foreign power. Over time, they tiptoed around the gap between rule and autonomy, sometimes reticently siding with state authority (say, in the early days of colonialism, to protect themselves against indigenous rulers) or tolerating it in times of strong kings while seeking to preserve control over local affairs as states threatened to encroach on cultural terroirs. Throughout the colonial period, the grassroots spatiality of village landscapes interrupted French projects of government, while rural spaces were redrawn by the passage of roads and railroads, the emergence of colonial towns, and the new material relations spun out by cash cropping (chapter 8). These dynamics extend to object worlds. The objects of trade were judged through local grids of value, where not all differences were the same, where some foreign elements might be more foreign than others (glazed pottery), where new things (alcohol, beads, textiles) were compatible with a sense of the old, where new practices could be experimented with (smoking), and where new avenues of collective possibility and self-making could be explored (say, the democratization of Atlantic-era peasant consumption or the new kinds of elite personhoods that arose in colonial Siin)—at the same time that debt, capital, and global obligations pressed on local economies (chapter 6). Cultural identities created out of difference, such as Seereer ethnicity, have even over time been inhabited as authentic (chapter 3).

Perhaps most interesting (given my penchant for disagreements between sources) is how different historical registers broadly align on this account. Archaeology's corporate materialities echo written mentions of the fragile edges of kingly power or the toils of managing African farmers for French colonists. Likewise, archaeological repertoires accord in surprising ways with the stories of power conserved in various places of memory. They resonate in deep ways with Amade Faye's demonstration that Seereer oral literature celebrates the common man—the peasant and his works—in contraposition with the dubious legitimacy of other sovereigns. Faye paints a terroir vibrating with a practical sort of poetry, where songs, legends, and tales are called up by material activities like cultivating a field or journeying across the landscape.[8]

In like fashion, materialities provoke different mappings of the past—not only different interpretations of history but different forms of it, more attentive to incompleteness, uncertainty, and open-endedness. Mobilizing the epistemology of fragments nested in Siin's archives (chapter 2), Siin's reluctant landscapes restore some of the incoherence and messiness of global encounters in the region, with implications for other parts of Senegal and the continent at large. Likewise, looking at history from the standpoint of material fragments can help to crack some conceptual idols and expose their limits. I hope to have shown, for instance, that the idea of ethnicity might not adequately capture salient forms of identity in Siin's precolonial past (chapter 3), that colonial ethnography might tell us more about colonial knowledge making than about the Seereer (chapters 4 and 7), that the state does not quite occupy the whole field of politics (chapters 5 and 7), or that the histories of dispossession sparked by the Atlantic trade were crosscut by histories of indigenous choice and initiative (chapters 6 and 8). In passing, I have also advocated humility in historical portraits, as the resistance of material things and spaces or the agencies of peanuts and *pangool* invite pause about human-focused accounts of Atlantic Africa.

In the end, my use of materiality to address questions of history and epistemology in Africa stems from the conviction that the kind of "archaeology" I have proposed here not only approaches the past in fresh ways but also can help craft more critical arguments about the present. With James Holston, I believe that "the mappings of fieldwork have always suggested . . . that a particular social problem encountered in the field takes on a specific articulation because its historical formulation continues to structure its present possibilities."[9] Siin's current responses to modernity's predicaments only make sense in relation to earlier histories binding the province to the political fields of the Atlantic trade and colonialism. And archaeologies of the latter, concurrently, can open certain reflections on the present (and even the future). I will spend the rest of this conclusion on two such problems by briefly examining, first, tradition in relation to national modernity and, second, rural politics in relation to the state.

Ambiguous Modernity and the Future of Tradition

Despite its tortuous career as a tool for savage-slotting Seereer people, tradition is also a powerful vehicle of cultural pride in many parts of the Siin. Cultural conservatism and the respect of ancestral ways are often trumpeted as avenues of collective dignity, especially (but not exclusively) by older men and women, and the loss of tradition is lamented as a corrupting effect of modernity and urban life—tradition being mobilized here as a counterdiscourse against the vitiating influence of *Wolofization*. More surprisingly, the discourse of tradition has also brought together local ideas of self-definition and state projects of nation building since independence. In effect, tradition has been a ground for the positive valuation of ethnic difference in Senegal and received new investments from the state and capital.[10]

Witness, for instance, the conflicted public fascination with aspects of Seereer tradition like *xoy*, divination ceremonies where renowned *saltigi* (earth priests, soothsayers) meet every year to announce the first rains and forecast the fates of the agricultural season. The contemporary persistence of such ritual events, although their forms and contents have evolved over the years and although the Siin is now overwhelmingly Muslim and Christian, contributes to the view of the region as a backwater stubbornly clinging to its ancestral ways, but it has also been envisioned as a sign of cultural richness under the canopy of the nation. Agencies such as Senegal's Ministry of Culture have increasingly endorsed the sunny side of this discourse on the primitive other by portraying Siin's distinctiveness as an integral part of Senegal's diverse national patrimony. Promoting their own brand of salvage anthropology, cultural officials often paint romanticized pictures of rural landscapes as precious exotics whose dying customs must be recorded for posterity before they go extinct. In 2004, for instance, the Direction du Patrimoine (the heritage division of the Ministry of Culture) took great pain to film the full ceremony of Diakhao's *xoy* in its most authentic regalia—with one exception: the traditional event generally demands the sacrifice of a black bull, which could not be purchased in time for the recording.[11] While these efforts are undoubtedly well-meaning, their outcome is tangled up with more derogatory perceptions: despite the appreciative undertones, difference is still objectified as otherness. By scooping history and change out of cultural forms, the ministry's cultural discourse effectively resuscitates the old cabinet-of-curiosity perspective: Seereer traditions and culture are glossed as *objets sauvages* made of detachable parts to be preserved or abandoned based on an index of authenticity, artifacts that belong to a natural order of things rather than part of a changing cultural process.[12] In this perspective, Siin's countryside and its cultural landscape are made to inhabit a different temporality—the ethnographic past—which can be substituted for history and remains dislocated from the world of the present. It also provides an entry for selective incorporation into the nation, the terms of which are decided by institutions of the state. By the same token, the grounds on which Senegalese modernity has been defined—Wolof and Islam—are themselves traditions, political projects with storied histories of navigation between inclusion and difference, belonging and otherness, action and detraction. Again, here, controlling the terms of discourse makes a big difference.[13]

Yet, despite the diverse palette of political uses, it seems that tradition is somehow always already there and ambiguously central to the project of Senegal's modernity. The national obsession during presidential elections with Seereer *saltigi* and their capacity to divine—and maybe even *make*—the next president is a case in point. During the 2012 electoral campaign, news outlets and public conversations in Dakar were fixated on what the Seereer *saltigi* of the famous Malango Center in Fatick might reveal during their annual *xoy*. *Saltigi* commonly make predictions about economic and political life, which receive considerable coverage in the media, and debating them is something of a national sport. But in 2009 and 2010, their political prognoses often received the lion's share of national attention, as in this instance reported on Nettali.net: "One of the best-known *saltigués* in Senegal, dame Khane Diouf, did not hold back on her predictions. Without going into details, this soothsayer maintains that the next president of Senegal will be someone who says 'mbimi'—meaning that it will be someone who speaks Pulaar. And all the minds now turn to Macky Sall, the mayor of Fatick. Which is what seems to put in question the credibility of the xooy, as many believe that the *saltigués* would seek to please the mayor of Fatick."[14]

As it turns out, the *saltigi*'s omens proved right, and Macky Sall *was* elected—though, as the last sentence intimates, many skeptics believe that the Fatick mayor had generously compensated the diviners to make statements in his favor. Yet, beyond the intrigue surrounding the lucky candidate or the result of the elections, what is important here is how Siin's tradition is located at the center of the nation's future—once again. Recall, as I have argued in chapter 5, that some oral traditions already underscore Siin's ambiguous centrality to the making of state and ethnicity in Senegal. In Yoro Dyao's compilation, Maisa Wali crowns the first Wolof king, who proceeds to unify Senegal under the aegis of Great Jolof. The homology in discourses a century apart (since Dyao's account was recorded in the 1910s) is instructive and perhaps revealing of bigger things about the relationship between Senegal, nation, and modernity. In effect, just as oral traditions associate Siin with the birth of modern identity and state formation in Senegal, Senegal's politics today continues to make plenty of room for Siin's traditions, heeding them even as it decries them. The future of Senegal's politics, then, is perhaps never quite apart from the future of grassroots traditions.

Looking at the nation from the perspective of the Siin and, I suspect, its other cultural peripheries sheds light on its hidden history in ways that expand and complicate the Islamo-Wolof imaginary. On the one hand, references to ethnic traditions in Senegal expose a loose political project of othering, where Wolof slips out of the realm of ethnicity to become the unmarked ground against which ethnicity is publicly reckoned. Perhaps *this* is the true public secret of Senegal's political life (see chapter 3).[15] On the other hand, ethnicity and tradition are not just brushed off to the side and sublimated into the universal character of the nation. They are actively consumed at the center, and they actively contest Islamo-Wolof imaginations, seeking to reappropriate the terms of political discourse. They are constitutive of the nation and reveal the fragility of its hegemonies. Perhaps, by reemerging as tensions at the heart of Senegal's modernity, not just as rumbles on its margins, they might signal the kinds of formative contradictions that Latour locates in modernity as a condition of political thinking: that it is a quixotic project always unachieved, always interrupted by its others, and thus always hybrid. In fact, it nurtures the proliferation of hybridity.[16] Histories and archaeologies written from Senegal's fringes have long recognized this hybridity and offer the important reminder that peripheries have always been and continue to be of the nation, that their tradition is part of Senegal's modernity and that their past is always implicated in its future. They recognize that Senegal's modernity is always another tradition (or composition of traditions) and that Siin's peasants, by virtue of their tumultuous inclusion in the Atlantic world, have long been modern, if not postmodern.[17]

Longue Durées of Power: Archaeological Futures?

> In seeing the consequences of alternatives taken and alternatives lost, we raise important issues of responsibility and accountability. In contrast, searching for legacies or looking for a determining moment in the past risks misunderstanding not only the past, but the extent and limitations of alternatives for the future. Africans have imagined different sorts of political communities; they have worked creatively with the tension between citizenship in a state and personal loyalty, between their rootedness in place and particularity and their connections to a wider world. They will continue to do so in the future—in ways we cannot yet perceive and whose implications we do not yet know. F. COOPER, "POSSIBILITY AND CONSTRAINT: AFRICAN INDEPENDENCE IN HISTORICAL PERSPECTIVE"[18]

If the alternative pasts generated by archaeology can help us to revisit national myths, they also give us a chance to situate African rural experiences in longer histories of the state and longer *durées* of power that lasso together Atlantic, colonial, and postcolonial regimes of rule. Struggles over land and space initiated by precolonial and colonial rulers have been taken up by the postindependence state and structured Seereer life over the past 150 years. The intrusive tactics of postcolonial law, however, have cohabited with other modes of (non)intervention that preserve uncanny continuities with colonial-style governance. In Siin, the contemporary state has kept moving through a dialectics of presence and absence, alternating heavy-handed regulation (focusing on the management of peanut crop yields, sales, and commercialization) with a relatively hands-off investment in local affairs, development, and politics.[19] Against this background of stately aloofness, Seereer villagers have continued to enjoy a quiet autonomy in their everyday matters. More generally, if in the 1800s cultivating millet and working the fields to meet the subsistence needs of the household were central elements of Seereer self-identification, during the next century these principles were complemented or supplanted by export cropping and modern forms of consumption as key constituents of what it meant to be a Seereer peasant; today these activities continue to form part of the ground on which rural subjectivities are built and from which villagers meaningfully (if unevenly) articulate with state, market, and society in Senegal and beyond.

Archaeological examination of the production of power over time enables us not only to reincorporate the Siin as an active participant in the making of national history but also to reframe today's politics of difference in Senegal in a deeper arc of relations between states and subjects. Understanding the Seereer engagement with multiple registers of authority in the past four hundred years can unearth local narratives of experience that have been lost to posterity (as suggested by Cooper in the epigraph). Correlatively, analyses of the (im)materialities of government also clarify the conditions of power that have informed political actions and imaginations at different points in time, dynamics that are often obscured by the analytical breaks we make between colonialism and its aftereffects, between state and society, or between domination and resistance. In this sense, such explorations are not just historical exercises. Rather, their contemporary relevance lies in the capacity to sketch more robust maps of the present by illuminating the solidarities and subjectivities that local entwinements with modern power have made possible and, perhaps, the kinds of futures that may arise from them.

Lastly, and to return to contemporary times, I find hope in the fact that archaeology, broadly defined, can help to write more effective histories of the present. The layers of time permeating the archaeological record indicate that historical processes set in motion during colonialism (and quite clearly before) have deep resonances in the Siin today. Past, present, and future are not discrete horizons. Instead, they bleed profusely into each other and are traversed by processes of different durations, effectiveness, and predictability, which combine to alter the field of historical possibility.[20] This does not mean that the past is the mirror of the present (as colonial writers imagined about the Seereer) or that traditions have gone unchanged for centuries. Quite differently, it means that adjusting to new situations is intrinsic to the making of tradition and that slow and fast changes are continually absorbed into configurations of identity deemed stable.[21] It implies that the ways in which today's peasants go about crafting sustainable futures in uncertain times have antecedents and that the ways they face problems forged by centralized authority have been anticipated historically. It indicates, finally, that the past-, present-, and future-oriented histories embedded in archaeological landscapes have relevance for how time and memory are mobilized to negotiate the future and, thus, that archaeology may have something to say about social and political experiences sometimes held to be the exclusive province of postcolonial modernity.

At a time on the African continent when many people imagine futures elsewhere,[22] perhaps the past is an elsewhere that can give inspiration for the future at home, pointing to alternatives that were once present in people's minds, and have quietly endured since, their traces scattered across reluctant landscapes.

Abbreviations

ACSE	Archives de la Congrégation du Saint-Esprit
ANS	Archives Nationales du Sénégal
ANSOM	Archives Nationales de France, Section Outre-Mer
BNF	Bibliothèque Nationale de France
FC	Dépôts des Fortifications et Colonies

Notes

PROLOGUE

1. L. S. Senghor, "Le message," in *Hosties noires* (Paris: Éditions du Seuil, 1948).
2. Gallais, "Notes sur la mission de Joal" (1851), ACSE 3I1.5a5. On the mission's turbulent history, see M. Klein, *Islam and Imperialism in Senegal: The Sine-Saloum, 1847–1914* (Stanford, CA: Stanford University Press, 1968), 43–62.
3. Gallais, "Notes," 36, 38. One of the village's women greeted the building of the chapel with a terse: *Tubab ba nangu na suñu dekk bi* (The white man is taking over our village).
4. *Aperçu historique sur la Mission de S. Joseph de Ngasobil* (1875), 27–30, ACSE 3I1.12a4.
5. P. J. Faye, "Les Sérères sont-ils encore des Sénégalais à part entière?" *Walfadjri*, Sept. 16, 2003.
6. M.-C. Diop (ed.), *Gouverner le Sénégal: Entre ajustement structurel et développement durable* (Paris: Karthala, 2004); M.-C. Diop, *Sénégal (2000–2012): Les institutions et politiques publiques à l'épreuve d'une gouvernance libérale* (Paris: Karthala, 2013); M.-C. Diop, *Le Sénégal sous Abdoulaye Wade* (Paris: Karthala, 2013); S. Gellar, *Democracy in Senegal: Tocquevillian Analytics in Africa* (New York: Palgrave Macmillan, 2005).
7. M. Mbodj, "La crise trentenaire de l'économie arachidière," in M.-C. Diop (ed.), *Sénégal: Trajectoires d'un état*, 95–135 (Paris: Karthala, 1992); M. Niang (ed.), *Participation paysanne et développement rural au Sénégal* (Dakar: CODESRIA, 2004).
8. The full speech can be read here: "Le discours de Dakar de Nicolas Sarkozy," *Le Monde*, Apr. 7, 2009, http://www.lemonde.fr/afrique/article/2007/11/09/le-discours-de-dakar_976786_3212.html.

9. See A. Mbembe, "L'Afrique de Nicolas Sarkozy," Grioo.com, Aug. 2, 2007, on ethnophilosophy. For newspaper condemnations, see P. Bernard and C. Jakubyszyn, "À Dakar, Nicolas Sarkozy appelle l'Afrique à 'renaître' et à 's'élancer vers l'avenir,'" *Le Monde*, Jul. 27, 2007; B. B. Diop, "Le discours inacceptable de Nicolas Sarkozy," *Le Quotidien*, Jul. 27, 2007; and T. Hofnung, "Sarkozy l'Africain fait grincer des dents," *Libération*, Jul. 28, 2007. For academic dissections of the speech and critique of its Hegelian echoes, see El Hadj G. W. Ndoye, "Entretien avec le Professeur Mamadou Diouf," *Sud Quotidien*, Aug. 17, 2007; I. Thioub, "Ibrahima Thioub répond à Nicolas Sarkozy," LDH Toulon, Aug. 8, 2007, https://ldh-toulon.net/Ibrahima-Thioub-repond-a-Nicolas.html; M. Gassama (ed.), *L'Afrique répond à Sarkozy—contre le discours de Dakar* (Paris: Philippe Rey, 2008); and A. B. Konaré (ed.), *Petit traité d'histoire africaine à l'usage de Nicolas Sarkozy* (Paris: La Découverte, 2008).
10. Africa's entanglement with globality is evidenced by a long history of labor migrations: M.-C. Diop (ed.), *Le Sénégal des migrations: Mobilités, identités et sociétés* (Paris: Karthala, 2008); A.-M. Makhulu, B. Buggenhagen, and S. Jackson (eds.), *Hard Work, Hard Times: Global Volatility and African Subjectivities* (Berkeley: University of California Press, 2012). In Senegal, this entrepreneurialism is iconically captured in the success of the Murid trade diaspora: B. Buggenhagen, *Muslim Families in Global Africa: Money Takes Care of Shame* (Bloomington: Indiana University Press, 2012); M. Diouf, "The Murids and the making of a vernacular cosmopolitanism," *Public Culture* 12(3): 679–702 (2000). In the early 2000s, a popular urban Wolof phrase captured the grim realities of laboring abroad and economic despair at home: "Barça walla barsàq," which can be cynically translated as "to emigrate or to die" (*Barça* is short for Barcelona, then imagined to be an El Dorado of opportunities, while *barsàq*, in Muslim theology, refers to the resting place of defunct souls before the advent of Judgment Day—that is, a transitory purgatory). Dakar, like many African cities, has been shaped by aspirations of global culture since the 1970s; M. Diouf, "Re-imagining an African city," in G. Prakash and K. Kruse (eds.), *The Spaces of the Modern City: Imaginaries, Politics, and Everyday Life*, 346–372 (Princeton, NJ: Princeton University Press, 2008); and M. Diouf and R. Fredericks (eds.), *The Arts of Citizenship in African Cities* (New York: Palgrave Macmillan, 2014). Senegal's vernacular cosmopolitanisms have roots in the Atlantic era: F. G. Richard, "Thinking through 'vernacular cosmopolitanisms': Historical archaeology in Senegal and the material contours of the African Atlantic," *International Journal of Historical Archaeology* 17(1): 40–71 (2013).
11. In *Unclaimed Experience: Trauma, Narrative, and History* (Baltimore: Johns Hopkins University Press, 1996), C. Caruth observes that historical traumas are both events inflicted on the fabric of consciousness at the moment of wounding and the deferred effects of such wounds on the structure of experience. Mbembe has suggested that the Atlantic slave trade, colonialism, and

apartheid have been foundational wounds that have fundamentally stamped African modes of being; A. Mbembe, "African modes of self-writing," *Public Culture* 13(1): 239–273 (2002). For accounts of the ways in which the wounds of slavery and colonialism are enacted and silenced in Africa's political present, see N. Argenti, *The Intestines of the State: Youth, Violence, and Belated Histories in the Cameroon Grassfields* (Chicago: University of Chicago Press, 2007); R. Shaw, *Memories of the Slave Trade: Ritual and the Historical Imagination in Sierra Leone* (Chicago: University of Chicago Press, 2002); J. Cole, *Forget Colonialism? Sacrifice and the Art of Memory in Madagascar* (Berkeley: University of California Press, 2001); P. Stoller, *Embodying Colonial Memories: Spirit Possession, Power, and the Hauka in West Africa* (New York: Routledge, 1995); and R. Werbner (ed.), *Memory and the Postcolony: African Anthropology and the Critique of Power* (London: Zed Books, 1998). For analyses of how heritage tourism is reshaping narratives of the triangular trade and politics of memory on the continent: P. Ebron, *Performing Africa* (Princeton, NJ: Princeton University Press, 1999); B. Holsey, *Routes of Remembrance: Refashioning the Slave Trade in Ghana* (Chicago: University of Chicago Press, 2008). See J. Comaroff, "The end of history, again: Pursuing the past in the postcolony," in A. Loomba, S. Kaul M. Bunzl, A, Burton, and J. Esty (eds.), *Postcolonial Studies and Beyond*, 125–144 (Durham, NC: Duke University Press, 2005) on truth commissions in post-apartheid South Africa.

12. F. Fanon, *The Wretched of the Earth* (New York: Grove Press, 2004), 182.
13. The materiality of building proved particularly contentious in the history of encounters between Europeans and Senegambians. The conflict over the right to build *en dur* (stonemasonry) versus the use of mud-and-straw structures came into full view on Gorée in the 1780s, when Governor de Boufflers sought to reorder the habitat along geometric lines and stone architecture. These urban reforms were prompted by his belief that residence in African-style huts would tarnish French civility; M. Hinchman, "African rococo: House and portrait in 18th-century senegal" (PhD diss., University of Chicago, 2000). The politics of *en dur* architecture endured in the following decade, periodically cropping up in archival mentions. In the mid-nineteenth century, for instance, the chief of the Cap-Vert peninsula forbade the erection of stone-and-brick constructions in the fledging village of Dakar.
14. For analyses of the Wade regime, see Diop, *Le Sénégal sous Abdoulaye Wade*; and M. Ralph, *Forensics of Capital* (Chicago: University of Chicago Press, 2015). See D. Galvan, *The State Must Be Our Master of Fire: How Peasants Craft Culturally Sustainable Development in Senegal* (Berkeley: University of California Press, 2004) on Siin farmers' engagement with forces of historical change.
15. On "Afro-pessimism" and Africa's excision from global futures, see J. Ferguson, *Global Shadows: Africa in the Neoliberal World Order* (Durham, NC: Duke University Press, 2006), ch. 1; J. and J. L. Comaroff, *Theory from the South;*

or, How Euro-America Is Evolving toward Africa (Boulder, CO: Paradigm, 2013), 1–49.

16. A. T. Smith, *The Political Landscape: Constellations of Authority in Early Complex Polities* (Berkeley: University of California Press, 2003).
17. On Africa-Mediterranean networks, see P. Mitchell, *African Connections: Archaeological Perspectives on Africa and the Wider World* (Walnut Creek, CA: Altamira, 2005); R. Austen, *Trans-Saharan Africa in World History* (New York: Oxford University Press, 2010). On transatlantic connections, see S. Palmié (ed.), *Africa of the Americas: Beyond the Search for Origins in the Study of Afro-Atlantic Religions* (Leiden: Brill, 2008); and M.-R. Trouillot, *Global Transformations: Anthropology and the Modern World* (New York: Palgrave Macmillan, 2003).
18. M.-R. Trouillot, *Silencing the Past: Power and the Production of History* (Boston: Beacon Press, 1995).
19. M. Klein (ed.), *Peasants in Africa: Historical and Contemporary Perspectives* (Beverly Hills, CA: Sage, 1980); F. Cooper, "Peasants, capitalists, and historians: A review article," *Journal of Southern African Studies* 7(2): 284–314 (1981); A. Isaacman, "Rural social protest in Africa," in F. Cooper, A. Isaacman, F. E. Mallon, W. Roseberry, and S. J. Stern (eds.), *Confronting Historical Paradigms*, 205–317 (Madison: University of Wisconsin Press, 1993); also M.-R. Trouillot, *Peasants and Capital: Dominica in the World Economy* (Baltimore: Johns Hopkins University Press, 1988); M. Watts, "Marx and recombinant capitalism: The agrarian question redux," *African Rural and Urban Studies* 4(2/3): 127–160 (1997); M. Watts, "Antinomies of community: Some thoughts on geography, resources, and empire," *Transactions of the Institute of British Geographers* 29(2): 195–216 (2004).
20. Researchers have long written about Siin-Saalum's rich record of pre-Atlantic earthen tumuli, shell mounds, and megalithic formations and have attempted to fit these vestiges into the storylines of regional history; see F. G. Richard, "Historical and dialectical perspectives on the archaeology of complexity in the Siin-Saalum (Senegal): Back to the future?" *African Archaeological Review* 26(2): 75–135 (2009). Monumental remains, however, are largely funerary in nature and provide tenuous insights into the world of the living. Until fifteen years ago, no residential sites of any period had been analyzed in Siin, and there was practically no information on archaeological settlements. I carried out dissertation research between 2002 and 2004 with the explicit purpose of addressing these gaps. This work brought together survey and excavations to construct an initial information baseline about chronology, settlement patterns, and residential sites; F. G. Richard, "From cosaan to colony: Exploring archaeological landscape formations and socio-political complexity in the Siin (Senegal), AD 500–1900" (PhD diss., Syracuse University, 2007).
21. For exemplary historical-archaeological treatments of Africa, see C. R. DeCorse, *An Archaeology of Elmina: Africans and Europeans on the Gold Coast,*

1400–1900 (Washington, DC: Smithsonian Institution Press, 2001), and A. B. Stahl, *Making History in Banda: Anthropological Visions of Africa* (New York: Cambridge University Press, 2001). For studies outside Africa, see M. Dietler, *Archaeologies of Colonialism: Consumption, Entanglement, and Violence in Ancient Mediterranean France* (Berkeley: University of California Press, 2010); S. Fowles, *An Archaeology of Doings: Secularism and the Study of Pueblo Religion* (Santa Fe, NM: School for Advanced Research Press, 2013); B. Voss, *The Archaeology of Ethnogenesis: Race and Sexuality in Colonial San Francisco* (Berkeley: University of California Press, 2008); and S. Wernke, *Negotiated Settlements: Andean Communities and Landscapes under Inka and Spanish Colonialism* (Gainesville: University Press of Florida, 2013).

22. On the dangers of methodological anachronism and virtues of using sources in a manner sensitive to the context of their creation and use: Stahl, *Making History*; and F. Cooper, *Colonialism in Question: Theory, Knowledge, History* (Berkeley: University of California Press, 2005).
23. It is impossible to do justice to the enormous historical-anthropological literature. For a short sample of influential volumes, see B. Axel (ed.), *From the Margins: Historical Anthropology and Its Futures* (Durham, NC: Duke University Press, 2002); B. Cohn, *Colonialism and Its Forms of Knowledge* (Princeton, NJ: Princeton University Press, 1996); J. L. and J. Comaroff, *Ethnography and the Historical Imagination* (Boulder, CO: Westview Press, 1992); F. Cooper and A. Stoler (eds.), *Tensions of Empire: Colonial Cultures in a Bourgeois World* (Berkeley: University of California Press, 1997); A. Stoler, *Along the Archival Grain: Epistemic Anxieties and Colonial Common Sense* (Princeton, NJ: Princeton University Press, 2010).
24. For pioneering examples of this interdisciplinary perspective: V. Buchli, *An Archaeology of Socialism* (New York: Berg, 1999); V. Buchli and G. Lucas (eds.), *Archaeologies of the Contemporary Past* (New York: Routledge, 2001); S. Dawdy, "Clockpunk anthropology and the ruins of modernity," *Current Anthropology* 51(6): 761–793 (2010); A. González-Ruibal, "Time to destroy: An archaeology of supermodernity," *Current Anthropology* 49(2): 247–279 (2008); A. González-Ruibal, *An Archaeology of Resistance: Materiality and Time in an African Borderland* (Plymouth, UK: Rowman & Littlefield, 2014); M. Hall, *Archaeology and the Modern World: Colonial Transcripts in South Africa and the Chesapeake* (New York: Routledge, 2000); and Stahl, *Making History*.

PART ONE INTRODUCTION

1. A. Faye, "Senghor en perspective dans le champ littéraire seereer," *Éthiopiques* 80: 53–72 (2008), 55.
2. Like other forms of modern representation, maps tend to enframe the world as tableaus lifted out of history, which asserts both the objectiveness of a scene and the observer's control over its truth; M. Heidegger, "The age of the world picture," in *The Question Concerning Technology and Other Essays* (New York:

Harper Torchbooks, 1977), 82; T. Mitchell, *Colonizing Egypt* (Chicago: University of Chicago Press, 1988). More generally, on techniques of modern representation, see D. Cosgrove, *Social Formations and Symbolic Landscape* (Madison: University of Wisconsin Press, 1998); and J. Crary, *Techniques of the Observer: On Vision and Modernity in the Nineteenth Century* (Cambridge, MA: MIT Press, 1990). For a critical analysis of the "absolutist ontology" of Cartesian-Newtonian space, see Smith, *Political Landscape*, 33–54; and D. Haraway, *Simians, Cyborgs, and Women: The Reinvention of Nature* (New York: Routledge, 1991), 188–189, on the capitalist-masculinist politics of objectivist vision.

3. D. Gregory, *Geographical Imaginations* (Cambridge: Blackwell, 1994), 72–73, 75. On maps' complicity with power and metanarratives of Western modernity and their inability to contain inconvenient geographies, see D. Cosgrove (ed.), *Mappings* (London: Reaktion Books, 1999); J. Crampton, "Maps as social constructions: Power, communication and visualization," *Progress in Human Geography* 25(2): 235–252 (2001); P. Carter, *Dark Writing: Geography, Performance, Design* (Honolulu: University of Hawai'i Press, 2008).
4. W. Thongchai, *Siam Mapped: A History of the Geo-Body of a Nation* (Honolulu: University of Hawaii Press, 1994), 16–17, defines the *geo-body* as the spatial operations, technologies, and discourses involved in the production of territoriality and national sentiment.
5. O. Thiam, "L'occultation du Sine Atlantique du département de Fatick: Impertinences des politiques et malaises des populations," *Sud Quotidien*, Oct. 23, 2007; F. Offner and P. Diasse, "Foundiougne: Des opportunités économiques peu exploitées," *L'Observateur*, Nov. 10, 2007. Following the nomination of Macky Sall, then mayor of Fatick (the capital of the Siin region), to the Prime Ministry in 2004 and the hosting of the 2005 Fête de l'Indépendance (Independence Day) in Fatick, the regional road system showed promises of improvement. Despite initial enthusiasm, public and private money were chronically mismanaged, and, when funds did not dry up, infrastructure building exclusively benefited Fatick and its surroundings—a pattern of uneven development common in the countryside.
6. C. T. Mbengue, "Les humanitaires déplorent le déficit de moyens," *Sud Quotidien*, Sept. 14, 2007; M. Sarr, "Ouverture de l'hôpital de Fatick: Les populations interpellent le Président Wade," *Walfadjri*, Dec. 2, 2007.
7. On political imaginations of the postcolony, see A. Mbembe, *On the Postcolony* (Berkeley: University of California Press, 2001); J. Roitman, *Fiscal Disobedience: An Anthropology of Economic Regulation in Central Africa* (Princeton, NJ: Princeton University Press, 2004); J. L. and J. Comaroff, *Civil Society and the Political Imagination in Africa* (Chicago: University of Chicago Press, 1999). See S. Feierman, *Peasant Intellectuals: Anthropology and History in Tanzania* (Madison: University of Wisconsin Press, 2000) for a rich account of organic intellectuals in rural Africa.
8. M.-C. Diop (ed.), "La crise de l'agriculture africaine," special issue, *Sociétés-Espaces-Temps* 1(1) (1992); T. Dahou (ed.), *Libéralisation et politique agricole*

au Sénégal (Paris: Karthala, 2009); and G. Duteurtre, M. Dieye Faye, and P. Nouhine Dieye (eds.), *L'agriculture sénégalaise à l'épreuve du marché* (Paris: Karthala, 2010).

9. Launched in 2008, GOANA (Great Agricultural Offensive for Food and Abundance) aimed to make the country food self-sufficient by 2015. The first two years saw dramatic increases in food crops. However, the unprecedented rainfall during this period and the absence of region-specific statistics make it hard to assess the initiative's success. The program has been positively evaluated in government-friendly newspapers; e.g., special issues of *Le Soleil* titled "Goana" (Oct. 2008) and "Agriculture et ressources naturelles" (Dec. 30, 2010); S. F. Lô, "Sénégal: Goana an II—Tous les records de production battus," *Le Soleil*, Jan. 8, 2010. More independent assessments have been less optimistic: M. Diop, "Goana: Entre pari non maitrisé et fausse bonne idée," Afrique Développement Local, Aug. 6, 2011, http://www.sendeveloppementlocal.com/Contributions-GOANA-Entre-pari-non-maitrise-et-fausse-bonne-idee_a1044.html; "Le PIT évalue la politique agricole de Wade," *Le Blog du PIT-Sénégal*, Jun. 10, 2011, http://cinquieme-congres-du-pit-senegal.over-blog.com/article-bilan-de-la-politique-agricole-sous-le-regime-de-wade-76348585.html.

10. I have frequently encountered strong opposition among my Siin interlocutors to Abdoulaye Wade's right-leaning PDS (Parti Démocratique Sénégalais), the party in power between 2000 and 2012. Dominant political orientation in Siin, however, does not fall along neat partisan divides but tends to follow charismatic networks. If the province was a stronghold for the socialist regimes of Léopold Sédar Senghor and Abdou Diouf, who governed Senegal from 1960 to 2000, in part out of a sense of loyalty to Siin-born Senghor, it has also overwhelmingly supported Fatick native and liberal-party affiliate Macky Sall at parliamentary and presidential elections since 2007. More generally, cynicism is a primary mode of relating with state politics in rural and urban Senegal. As a structure of political feeling, it also upholds the work of fantasy through which citizens *both* deconstruct state power in public discourse *and* regenerate the state's aura and existence at the level of the collective unconscious; Y. Navarro-Yashin, *Faces of the State: Secularism and Public Life in Turkey* (Princeton, NJ: Princeton University Press, 2002), 4–5; A. Mbembe and J. Roitman, "The figure of the subject in times of crisis," *Public Culture* 7(2): 323–352 (1995).

11. Galvan, *The State*, ch. 3.

12. For analyses of governance in Senegal with extensive sidebars on the rural world, see D. Cruise O'Brien, M.-C. Diop, and M. Diouf, *La construction de l'état au Sénégal* (Paris: Karthala, 2002); Diop, *Gouverner le Sénégal*; Diop, *Le Sénégal sous Abdoulaye Wade*; Diop, *Sénégal (2000–2012)*; M.-C. Diop and M. Diouf, *Le Sénégal sous Abdou Diouf. État et société* (Paris: Karthala, 1990); Gellar, *Democracy in Senegal*; and D. Cruise O'Brien, *Symbolic Confrontations: Muslims Imagining the State in Africa* (London: C. Hurst, 2003).

13. On historical workshopping, see D. Cohen and A. Odhiambo, *Siaya: The Historical Anthropology of an African Landscape* (Athens: Ohio University Press, 1989), 30.
14. Diop and Diouf, *Sénégal sous Abdou Diouf*; M. Diouf, *Histoire du Sénégal: Le modèle Islamo-Wolof et ses périphéries* (Paris: Maisonneuve et Larose, 2001). On state fashioning of history and memory, see R. Roberts, "History and memory: The power of statist narratives," *International Journal of African Historical Studies* 33(3): 513–522 (2000); A. Apter, *The Pan-African Nation: Oil and the Spectacle of Culture in Nigeria* (Chicago: University of Chicago Press, 2005).
15. Diouf, *Histoire du Sénégal*, 9–10.
16. See J. Derrida, *Writing and Difference* (Chicago: University of Chicago Press, 1978), 292, 339, on margins' power to displace.
17. The expression "scandal of the nation" is from S. Dube, *Stitches on Time: Colonial Textures and Postcolonial Tangles* (Durham, NC: Duke University Press, 2004), 6, 20.
18. Gregory, *Geographical Imaginations*, 76.

CHAPTER ONE

1. E. Glissant, *Tout-monde* (Paris: Gallimard, 1993), 513.
2. A. Lericollais, "La dégradation de l'aménagement agraire," in A. Lericollais (ed.), *Paysans sereer: Dynamiques agraires et mobilités au Sénégal*, 117–138 (Paris: Éditions de l'IRD, 1999). Also C. Blanc-Pamard and L. Cambrézy (eds.), *Terre, terroir, territoire. Les tensions foncières* (Paris: ORSTOM, 1995).
3. Young women in the Siin have been disproportionately affected by the agricultural crisis and are the region's main urban migrants. The Fatick region is Senegal's primary reservoir of urban maids; see B. Guigou and A. Lericollais, "Crise de l'agriculture et marginalisation économique des femmes sereer siin (Sénégal)," *Sociétés-Espaces-Temps* 1(1): 45–64 (1992); and G. Pontié and A. Lericollais, "Migrations et relations à distance," in Lericollais, *Paysans sereer*, 555–591. For a broader view on urban Africa, see A. Simone, "On the worlding of African cities," *African Studies Review* 44(2): 15–41 (2001).
4. See L. Aujas, "La région du Sine-Saloum: Le port de Kaolack," *Bulletin du Comité d'Études Historiques et Scientifiques de l'A.O.F.* 12: 92–132 (1933); and L. Villalón, *Islamic Society and State Power in Senegal: Disciples and Citizens in Fatick* (New York: Cambridge University Press, 1993), on the development of Kaolack and Fatick. Beside Dakar, Touba (the spiritual capital of the Murid Brotherhood) has emerged as a focal point in contemporary urban migration; E. Ross, *Sufi City: Urban Designs and Archetypes in Touba* (Rochester, MN: University of Rochester Press, 2006).
5. On the notion of dwelling, see T. Ingold, *Perception of the Environment: Essays on Livelihood, Dwelling, and Skill* (New York: Routledge, 2000).
6. Although referred to as rivers, the two waterways are actually *rias*—that is,

incursions of marine water that penetrate deep into the continent, whose shallow valleys are fed by tidal fluxes and seasonal rainfall; F. Brigaud, *Études sénégalaises No. 9: Hydrographie* (Saint-Louis: CRDS, 1961), 57–59.

7. Colonial observers document that the Siin River once flowed far beyond its current limits, as far as Diakhao, Ndiob, or Kael; E. Mage, "Les rivières du Sine-Saloum," *Revue Maritime et Coloniale* 7: 673–679 (1863); E. Pinet-Laprade, "Notice sur les Sérères," *Annuaire du Sénégal et Dépendances* 1865: 121–179 (1865); and H. Hubert, "Le dessèchement progressif en Afrique Occidentale," *Bulletin du Comité d'Études Historiques et Scientifiques de l'A.O.F.* 3: 401–467 (1920), 419.
8. E.g., N. Munn, *The Fame of Gawa: A Symbolic Study of Value Transformation in a Massim Society* (Durham, NC: Duke University Press, 2002); B. Weiss, *The Making and Unmaking of the Haya Lived World* (Durham, NC: Duke University Press, 1996); also P. Bourdieu, *Outline of a Theory of Practice* (New York: Cambridge University Press, 1997).
9. P. Pélissier, "Les paysans sérères: Essai sur la formation d'un terroir du Sénégal," *Cahiers d'Outre-Mer* 22: 105–127 (1953).
10. M. Dupire, A. Lericollais, B. Delpech, and J.-M. Gastellu, "Résidence, tenure foncière, alliance dans une société bilinéaire (Serer du Sine et du Baol, Sénégal)," *Cahiers d'Études Africaines* 14(3): 417–452 (1974); J.-M. Gastellu, *L'égalitarisme économique des Serer du Sénégal* (Paris: ORSTOM, 1981); B. Guigou, A. Lericollais, and G. Pontié, "La gestion de la terre en pays sereer Siin (Sénégal)," in Blanc-Pamard and Cambrézy, *Terre, terroir, territoire,* 183–225; A. Lericollais, *Sob: Étude géographique d'un terroir sérèr (Sénégal)* (Paris: Mouton, 1972); Lericollais, *Paysans sereer*; J. Lombard, *Riz des villes, mil des champs en pays serer, Sénégal* (Pessac: Presses Universitaires de Bordeaux, 1993); and P. Pélissier, *Paysans du Sénégal: Les civilisations agraires du Cayor à la Casamance* (Saint-Irieix: Imprimerie Fabrègue, 1966).
11. For valuable readings of African moral economy at the interface of nature, culture, and history, see Cohen and Odhiambo, *Siaya*; D. Moore, *Suffering for Territory: Race, Place, and Power in Zimbabwe* (Durham, NC: Duke University Press, 2005); T. Ranger, *Voices from the Rocks: Nature, Culture, and History in the Matopos Hills of Zimbabwe* (Bloomington: Indiana University Press, 1999); T. Spear, *Mountain Farmers: Moral Economies of Land and Agricultural Development in Arusha and Meru* (Oxford: James Currey, 1997); and Weiss, *Making and Unmaking.*
12. For classic accounts of the relationship between place, identity, and memory, see E. Casey, *Getting Back into Place: Toward a Renewed Understanding of the Place-World* (Bloomington: Indiana University Press, 1993); E. Casey, *The Fate of Place* (Berkeley: University of California Press, 1997); and S. Feld and K. Basso (eds.), *Senses of Place* (Santa Fe, NM: School of American Research Press, 1997). While attentive to phenomenology, this literature skirts the political dimensions of place, which take center stage in K. Stewart's *A Space on the Side of the Road: Cultural Poetics in an "Other" America* (Princeton, NJ: Princeton University Press, 1996); G. Gordillo, *Landscapes of Devils:*

Tensions of Place and Memory in the Argentinian Chaco (Durham, NC: Duke University Press, 2006); and H. Raffles, *In Amazonia: A Natural History* (Princeton, NJ: Princeton University Press, 2002).

13. H. Gravrand, "Aux sources de la vie humaine d'après les traditions serer du Sine," *Psychopathologie Africaine* 1(2): 286–303 (1965); H. Gravrand, "Le symbolisme serer," *Psychopathologie Africaine* 9(2): 237–265 (1973); H. Gravrand, "Rites et symbols sereer face au sacré," *Cahiers des Religions Africaines* 20–21: 125–143 (1986); and H. Gravrand, *La civilisation sereer. "Pangool," le génie religieux* (Dakar: Nouvelles Éditions Africaines, 1990). As examined in chapter 4, Seereer religion has long been in contact with Islam and, after the fifteenth century, with Christianity and has often sought to appropriate their material elements and ritual efficacy into its own spiritual repertoires.
14. C. Becker, V. Martin, and A. Ndène, "Traditions villageoises du Sine. Arrondissements de Diakhao, Fimela, Niakhar, et Tatagin" (unpublished manuscript, Dakar, 2014); N. Diouf, "Chronique du royaume du Sine," *Bulletin de l'IFAN*, B, 34(4): 702–732 (1972); H. Gravrand, *La civilisation sereer. "Cosaan," les origines* (Dakar: Nouvelles Éditions Africaines, 1983); and A. Sarr, "Histoire du Sine-Saloum," *Bulletin de l'IFAN*, B, 46(3/4): 211–283 (1986–1987). The phrase "places of memory" (*lieux de mémoire*) refers to sites invested with affective energy and thus ripe terrain for the fashioning of collective identity; P. Nora and L. Kritzman (eds.), *Realms of Memory: The Construction of the French Past*, 3 vols. (New York: Columbia University Press, 1996). However, I wish to loosen the term from the moorings of Nora's original formulation, which tended to demarcate history from memory and mobilized the concept for a project of French national consolidation in times of anxiety about globalization; see critique in P. Hutton, *History as an Art of Memory* (Hanover, NH: University Press of New England, 1993).
15. H. Gravrand, "'Naq' et sorcellerie dans les conceptions sereer," *Psychopathologie Africaine* 11(2): 179–216 (1975); and Gravrand, *"Pangool."* On negative spaces, see N. Munn, "Excluded spaces: The figure in the Australian Aboriginal landscape," *Critical Inquiry* 22(3): 446–465 (1996).
16. A. Faye, *Le thème de la mort dans la littérature seereer* (Dakar: Nouvelles Éditions Africaines du Sénégal, 1997); and A. Faye, "La littérature orale seereer: Typologie des genres et problématiques d'analyse," 2 vols. (Thèse d'état, Dakar, 2011–2012).
17. Moore, *Suffering*, 22 (italics in the original).
18. W. J. T. Mitchell, "Introduction," in W. J. T. Mitchell (ed.), *Landscape and Power*, 1–4 (Chicago: University of Chicago Press, 2002), 1. The concept of spatial work is also prevalent in Henri Lefèbvre's seminal *The Production of Space* (Malden, MA: Blackwell, 1991). The literature on landscape is prodigiously generative and won't be summarized it here. An excellent discussion of its use in geography can be found in D. Mitchell, *Cultural Geography: A Critical Introduction* (Malden, MA: Blackwell, 1996). In anthro

pology, see B. Bender and M. Winer (eds.), *Contested Landscapes: Movement, Exile, and Place* (New York: Berg, 2001); E. Hirsch and M. O'Hanlon (eds.), *The Anthropology of Landscape: Perspectives on Place and Space* (Oxford: Clarendon, 1995); and P. Steward and A. Strathern (eds.), *Landscape, Memory and History: Anthropological Perspectives* (London: Pluto, 2003). For archaeological treatments, see W. Ashmore and A. B. Knapp (eds.), *Archaeologies of Landscapes: Contemporary Perspectives* (Cambridge: Blackwell, 1999); C. Crumley and W. Marquardt (eds.), *Regional Dynamics: Burgundian Landscapes in Historical Perspective* (San Diego, CA: Academic Press, 1987); C. Tilley, *A Phenomenology of Landscape: Places, Paths, and Monuments* (Oxford: Berg, 1994); and P. Ucko and R. Layton (eds.), *The Archaeology and Anthropology of Landscape: Shaping Your Landscape* (New York: Routledge, 1999).

19. Lefèbvre, *Production of Space*, 26.
20. Moore, *Suffering*, 22, defines landscapes as "historically sedimented practices that mix with environmental milieu." See also T. Ingold, "The temporality of the landscape," *World Archaeology* 25(2): 152–174 (1993), who makes a distinction between *taskscape*, the ensemble of practical acts through which humans meaningfully inhabit their world, and *landscape*, the milieu resulting from these activities as it is known by people who live in it. For different relational perspectives on space, see Gordillo, *Landscapes of Devils*; D. Harvey, *Justice, Nature and the Geography of Difference* (London: Blackwell, 1996); D. Massey, *For Space* (London: Sage, 2005); Smith, *Political Landscape*; and E. Soja, *Postmodern Geographies: The Reassertion of Space in Critical Social Theory* (London: Verso, 1989), ch. 3.
21. H. Lefèbvre, *Writings on Cities* (Malden, MA: Blackwell, 1996), 118.
22. Many authors have adopted Lefèbvre's contention that space is simultaneously lived, perceived, and conceived, or what he terms spatial practice, spatial representations, and representations of space (*Production of Space*, 33, 38–46); e.g., Smith, *Political Landscape*, 10, 73; and E. Soja, *Thirdspace: Journeys to Los Angeles and Other Real-and-Imagined Places* (Malden, MA: Blackwell, 1996), ch. 2, for useful interpretations. I refrain from using Lefèbvre's formulation here in part because I feel that even the best exegeses cannot quite purge his spatial triad of a certain inconsistency. At its most analytically robust, Lefèbvre's spatial trinity remains firmly grounded in the historical conditions of capitalist (late) modernity, which might limit its generalization to antecedent histories. This seems particularly true of the notion of lived space, which I read as strongly wedded to the historically charged Lefèbvrian category of the everyday; see A. Merrifield, *Henri Lefèbvre: A Critical Introduction* (New York: Routledge, 2006), ch. 6; and S. Elden, *Understanding Henri Lefèbvre: Theory and the Possible* (New York: Continuum, 2004), ch. 5. Rather, my account draws on explorations of space, time, and politics in Moore, *Suffering*; Massey, *For Space*; Gordillo, *Landscapes of Devils*; and W. Benjamin, *Arcades Project*, R. Tiedemann (ed.) (Cambridge, MA: Harvard University Press, 1999).

23. Smith, *Political Landscape*, 11. Space and place are cornerstones of spatial analysis. Conventionally, space refers to the forms framing material experience, while place represents locations charged with subjective identity. In most writings, space has connotations of geometry and abstraction, while place resonates with locality, feeling, and cultural density. Moore, *Suffering*, 19–20, has critiqued this opposition, and I too am wary of what gets lost in the separation. Moore notes that common definitions tend to essentialize ideas of space and place, and he underscores the need to think about them more dynamically and historically. After all, place is a deeply political process, which can be the basis of tension and alienation; in the same way, space may be devoid of affective attachment yet still be meaningful, just as it can be invested with cultural significance and appropriated as a resource in identity construction: D. Massey, *Space, Place and Gender* (Minneapolis: University of Minnesota Press, 1994); J. Brown, *Dropping Anchor, Setting Sail: Geographies of Race in Black Liverpool* (Princeton, NJ: Princeton University Press, 2005); Gordillo, *Landscapes of Devils*; Raffles, *In Amazonia*. Landscape bypasses these bifurcations in that it forms a bridge between space and place from which the nature of their articulation can be queried.
24. Massey, *For Space*, 24, defines space as "a simultaneity of stories-so-far"; also Raffles, *In Amazonia*, 34–35; and J. Shetler, *Imagining the Serengeti: A History of Landscape Memory in Tanzania from Earliest Times to the Present* (Athens: Ohio University Press, 2007). Dialectical thinkers have long recognized the spatial braiding of old and new, that social formations always contain the remnants of earlier worlds; e.g., Lefèbvre, *Production of Space*, 164; Benjamin, *Arcades Project*, 4–5.
25. Lefèbvre, *Production of Space*, 102, 191. While it dovetails with the sociological space of the terroir, the idea of landscape is at once more capacious and analytically precise. By virtue of its sensitivity to the mutual fashioning of people and place, it also bypasses the Durkheimian accents lingering in the concept of terroir, where space often figures as the precipitate of a priori social classification, such that milieu ultimately reflects society. On the intersection of Durkheimian sociology and French geography in the late nineteenth century and the essentialism/formalism fueling ideas of *territoire* (and terroir), see Gregory, *Geographical Imaginations*, 39–52.
26. This can be read as a spatial formulation of Marx's dictum that people "make their own history, but they do not make it just as they please; they do not make it under circumstances chosen by themselves, but under circumstances directly encountered, given, and transmitted from the past"; K. Marx, *The 18th Brumaire of Louis Bonaparte* (New York: International Publishers, 1963), 15. On the porous relationship between objects and subjects, see Weiss, *Making and Unmaking*; D. Miller, *Material Culture and Mass Consumption* (New York: Blackwell, 1987); and D. Miller (ed.), *Materiality* (Durham, NC: Duke University Press, 2005); also W. Keane, *Christian Moderns: Freedom and Fetish in the Mission Encounter* (Berkeley: University of California Press, 2007);

E. Kohn, *How Forests Think: Toward an Anthropology beyond the Human* (Berkeley: University of California Press, 2013); and Z. Crossland, *Ancestral Encounters in Highland Madagascar: Material Signs and Traces of the Dead* (New York: Cambridge University Press, 2014), from the perspective of Peircean semiotics.

27. Moore, *Suffering*, 22; also Gordillo, *Landscapes of Devils*; T. Mitchell, *Rule of Experts: Egypt, Techno-Politics, Modernity* (Berkeley: University of California Press, 2002); Raffles, *In Amazonia*. The idea that nonhuman entities have some sort of agency is a staple of actor-network theory; e.g., B. Latour, *Reassembling the Social: An Introduction to Actor-Network-Theory* (New York: Oxford University Press, 2005). While sensitive to Latour's call to unseat humans as self-proclaimed reality makers, I am concerned that his approach compresses the (social) world into a flat landscape of associations that sidelines the frictions, hierarchies, and differences that structure these associations and condition life and nonlife in them. History suffers a similar fate under the Latourian scalpel and gives way to a somewhat deflated temporality that does not do full justice to time's multiplicities. Like Moore, *Suffering*, 22–26, I think that an analytic of power and politics remains useful, and that the concepts of assemblage and mixture (rather than a generalized vocabulary of network and actants) provide valuable escapes from the fetishes of sociology and anthropology (e.g., society, culture, object-subject divide). Whether or not agency can be located in the nonhuman world, I prefer to think of how nonhuman entities have effects and efficacy that elude humans and participate in the construction of collectivities and self-understanding; cf. A. Gell, *Art and Agency: An Anthropological Theory* (Oxford: Clarendon, 1998), ch. 9. In Siin's oral legends, subjectivity stretches beyond the body to encompass the spiritual world. Spirits manifest themselves to people through animals and inanimate features of the landscape and influence human actions in seminal ways. In fact, they are depicted as central to the making of political community.

28. Lefèbvre, *Production of Space*. See also J. Allen, "Spatial assemblages of power: From domination to empowerment," in D. Massey, J. Allen, and P. Sarre (eds.), *Human Geography Today*, 194–218 (Cambridge: Polity, 1999); J. Crampton and S. Elden (eds.), *Space, Knowledge, and Power: Foucault and Geography* (Burlington, VT: Ashgate, 2007); and M. Foucault, *Power: Essential Works of Foucault, 1954–1984*, vol. 3, J. D. Faubion (ed.) (New York: New Press, 2000), 349–364.

29. J. Rancière, "Comment and response," *Theory and Event* 6(4) (2003); J. Rancière, "Ten theses on politics," *Theory and Event* 5(3) (2001); also J. Bennett, *Vibrant Matter: A Political Ecology of Things* (Durham, NC: Duke University Press, 2010), vii, 123. Note that Rancière's theory of politics prioritizes a fairly narrow register of the sensorium (voice and visibility) and privileges human subjects. As a theoretical formulation, his model also approaches politics in fairly abstract ways through the classical texts of Greek philosophy; see J. Rancière, *The Politics of Aesthetics: The Distribution of the*

Sensible (London: Continuum, 2004); and J. Rancière, *Disagreement: Politics and Philosophy* (Minneapolis: University of Minnesota Press, 2005). Rather than confining politics to arguments over speech and audibility, I adopt an expanded definition of the "configuration of the sensible," one that takes seriously Rancière's own appeals to bodies, practices, and materiality and considers the catalytic role of nonhuman elements. On this latter point, see Raffles, *In Amazonia*; Mitchell, *Rule of Experts*, ch. 2; Bennett, *Vibrant Matter*; Kohn, *How Forests Think*.

30. Smith, *Political Landscape*, 77; Mitchell, "Introduction," 2; and "Imperial landscape," in Mitchell, *Landscape and Power*, 5–34; D. Moore, J. Kosek, and A. Pandian (eds.), *Race, Nature, and the Politics of Difference* (Durham, NC: Duke University Press, 2003); and Shetler, *Imagining the Serengeti*.
31. Foucault, *Power*, 361.
32. Massey, *For Space*, 112.
33. Lefèbvre, *Production of Space*, 109; Moore, *Suffering*, 22.
34. Bennett, *Vibrant Matter*, ch. 1; see also B. Brown (ed.), *Things* (Chicago: University of Chicago Press, 2004); Keane, *Christian Moderns*; and W. J. T. Mitchell, *What Do Pictures Want? The Lives and Loves of Images* (Chicago: University of Chicago Press, 2005).
35. Massey, *For Space*, 111–117. The idea of space as a force and animated entity is evoked in A. Feldman, *Formations of Violence: The Narrative of Body and Terror in Northern Ireland* (Chicago: University of Chicago Press, 1991), 29. On the defiance of space, see Lefèbvre, *Production of Space*, 413; Moore, *Suffering*; also J. Holston, *Insurgent Citizenships: Disjunctions of Democracy and Modernity in Brazil* (Princeton, NJ: Princeton University Press, 2008), on autoconstructed spaces.
36. A. Mbembe's *Afriques indociles* (Paris: Karthala, 1988) uses "indocility" to refer to the forms of indiscipline deployed by populations in Cameroon as they (re)worked the Christian message to make it theirs. I am extending this idea to the *reluctant* materialities generated in the encounter between political projects and subjects in Siin.
37. Lefèbvre, *Production of Space*, 413.
38. F. Jameson, *The Political Unconscious: Narrative as a Socially Symbolic Act* (Ithaca, NY: Cornell University Press, 1982).

CHAPTER TWO

1. A. Mbembe, "African modes of self-writing," *Public Culture* 13(1): 239–273 (2002), 242.
2. Mbembe, "African modes of self-writing"; also Trouillot, *Global Transformations*. On useful alternatives to global/local determinisms, see B. Meyer and P. Geschiere (eds.), *Globalization and Identity: Dialectics of Flow and Closure* (Malden, MA: Blackwell, 1999); Cooper, *Colonialism*, ch. 4; and J. Prestholdt, *Domesticating the World: African Consumerism and the Genealo-*

gies of Globalization (Berkeley: University of California Press, 2008). See also J.-F. Bayart, "Africa in the world: A history of extraversion," *African Affairs* 99: 217–267 (2000); and A. Mbembe, "At the edge of the world: Boundaries, territoriality, and sovereignty in Africa," *Public Culture* 12(1): 259–284 (2000).

3. J.-F. Bayart, *The State in Africa: The Politics of the Belly* (New York: Longman, 1993). See also M. Diouf, "Des historiens et des histoires, pour quoi faire? L'histoire africaine entre l'état et les communautés," *Revue Canadienne d'Études Africaines* 34(2): 337–374 (2000), which anticipates some of my reflections.
4. A. Mbembe, "On the power of the false," *Public Culture* 14(3): 629–641 (2002).
5. G. Agamben, *Remnants of Auschwitz: The Witness and the Archive* (London: Zone Books, 1999), 12.
6. Much of the historical discourse on the Atlantic commerce over the past forty years has unfolded as a conversation with Philip Curtin's pathbreaking *The Atlantic Slave Trade: A Census* (Madison: University of Wisconsin Press, 1969). Intended as a point of departure rather than a definitive analysis, Curtin's thesis inspired broad reflections on the statistics and economics of the slave trade, setting the terms of analysis in resolutely quantitative colors. Subsequent research has questioned Curtin's projections for various portions of the trade and fostered critical reexamination of methods, computations, and sources. Scholarship concurs that Curtin's original export figures need to be revised upward. See B. Barry, *Senegambia and the Atlantic Slave Trade* (New York: Cambridge University Press, 1998), 61–69; C. Becker, "La Sénégambie à l'époque de la traite des esclaves. À propos d'un ouvrage recent de Philip D. Curtin," *Revue Française d'Histoire d'Outre-Mer* 64: 203–224 (1977); D. Eltis, "The volume and structure of the transatlantic slave trade: A reassessment," *William and Mary Quarterly* 58(1): 17–46 (2001); J. E. Inikori (ed.), *Forced Migration: The Impact of the Export Slave Trade on African Societies* (New York: Africana, 1982); P. Lovejoy, "The volume of the Atlantic slave trade: A synthesis," *Journal of African History* 23(4): 473–501 (1982); and D. Richardson, "Slave exports from West and West-Central Africa, 1700–1810: New estimates of volume and distribution," *Journal of African History* 30(1): 1–22 (1989).
7. See, however, J. Thornton, *Africa and Africans in the Making of the Atlantic World, 1400–1800* (New York: Cambridge University Press, 1998).
8. P. D. Curtin, *Economic Change in Precolonial Africa: Senegambia in the Era of the Slave Trade* (Madison: University of Wisconsin Press, 1975), 309. P. Lovejoy, "The impact of the Atlantic slave trade on Africa: A review of the literature," *Journal of African History* 30(3): 365–394, summarizes this debate. A "dress rehearsal" of these conversations initially opposed Rodney and Fage over whether the slave trade ripped apart African economies or could have been a factor of development. Eltis and Lovejoy have taken up a more nuanced version of the argument: the former using economic and demographic data to demonstrate that the slave trade and its aftermaths negligibly impacted

African histories; the latter suggesting that the economic and human costs of slave sales far outstripped whatever "advantages" they may have fostered; W. Rodney, "African slavery and other forms of social oppression on the Upper Guinea coast in the context of the Atlantic slave-trade," *Journal of African History* 6(3): 307–322 (1966); J. D. Fage, "Slavery and the slave trade in the context of West African history," *Journal of African History* 10(3): 393–404 (1969); D. Eltis, "Trade between Western Africa and the Atlantic world before 1870: Estimates of trends in value, composition, and direction," *Research in Economic History* 12: 197–239 (1989); P. Lovejoy, *Transformations in Slavery* (Cambridge: Cambridge University Press, 2000).

9. Thioub, "École." Curtin's critics reproach him for downplaying the human costs of the Atlantic slavery by inflating the importance of trans-Saharan slave markets. A similar charge has also been imputed to Webb's work on desert-side economies in northern Senegambia; B. Barry, *Senegambia: Advocating a Regional Historical Perspective* (Amsterdam: SEPHIS, 2001), 52, for a critique; also J. Webb, *Desert Frontier: Ecological and Economic Change along the Western Sahel, 1600–1850* (Madison: University of Wisconsin Press, 1995).
10. B. Barry, "Economic anthropology of precolonial Senegambia from XV–XIX century," in L. Gallistel-Colvin (ed.), *The Uprooted of the Western Sahel: Migrants' Quest for Cash in the Senegambia*, 20–49 (Baltimore: University of Maryland/US Agency for International Development, 1979), 41. See also Barry, *Senegambia*; A. Bathily, *Les portes de l'or. Le royaume de Galam (Sénégal) de l'ère musulmane au temps des négriers (VIIIe–XVIIIe siècle)* (Paris: Éditions l'Harmattan, 1989).
11. W. Rodney, *How Europe Underdeveloped Africa* (Washington, DC: Howard University Press, 1982); I. Wallerstein, *The Modern World System II. Mercantilism and the Consolidation of the European World-Economy, 1600–1750* (New York: Academic Press, 1980). On state centralization, see Barry, *Senegambia*; J. Boulègue, *Le Grand Jolof (XIIIe–XVIe siècle)* (Blois: Éditions Façades, 1987), and *Les royaumes wolof dans l'espace sénégambien (XIIIe–XVIIIe siècle)* (Paris: Karthala, 2013); and M. A. Klein, "The impact of the Atlantic slave trade on the societies of the western Sudan," in J. Inikori and S. Engerman (eds.), *The Atlantic Slave Trade: Effects on Economies, Societies, and Peoples in Africa, the Americas, and Europe*, 25–47 (Durham, NC: Duke University Press, 1992).
12. Barry, *Advocating*; also B. Barry, *Le royaume du Waalo: Le Sénégal avant la conquête* (Paris: Maspéro, 1972); J. F. Searing, *West African Slavery and Atlantic Commerce: The Senegal River Valley, 1700–1860* (New York: Cambridge University Press, 1993); J. F. Searing, *"God Alone Is King": Islam and Emancipation in Senegal. The Wolof Kingdoms of Kajoor and Bawol, 1859–1914* (Portsmouth, NH: Heinemann, 2002); and D. R. Wright, *The World and a Very Small Place in Africa* (Armonk, NY: M. E. Sharpe, 1997).
13. Because oral traditions make rare reference to the Atlantic commerce, most studies of early Atlantic contacts employ a combination of oral evidence and travel accounts to picture local pasts *before* the advent of European contact

and draw more heavily on textual documents (which grow exponentially after the 1700s) to chronicle the course of regional history *during* the Atlantic era; e.g., G. Brooks, *Landlords and Strangers: Ecology, Society, and Trade in Western Africa, 1000–1630* (Boulder, CO: Westview Press, 1993). For notable exceptions built on extensive oral corpuses, see R. Baum, *Shrines of the Slave Trade: Diola Religion and Society in Precolonial Senegambia* (New York: Oxford University Press, 1999); and W. Hawthorne, *Planting Rice and Harvesting Slaves: Transformations along the Guinea-Bissau Coast, 1400–1900* (Portsmouth, NH: Heinemann, 2003). Boulègue, *Royaumes wolof* and *Grand Jolof,* synthesize various sources on the Jolof empire before and after the Atlantic era. Oral sources grow increasingly rich in the nineteenth and twentieth centuries and are integral to analyses of colonial French Africa; e.g., C. Babou, *Fighting the Greater Jihad: Amadu Bamba and the Founding of the Muridiyya of Senegal, 1853–1913* (Athens: Ohio University Press, 2007); M. Klein, *Slavery and Colonial Rule in French West Africa* (New York: Cambridge University Press, 1998); R. Roberts, *Two Worlds of Cotton: Colonialism and the Regional Economy in the French Soudan, 1800–1946* (Stanford, CA: Stanford University Press, 1996); D. Robinson, *The Holy War of Umar Tal: The Western Sudan in the Mid-Nineteenth Century* (Oxford: Clarendon, 1985); and Searing, *"God Alone Is King."*

14. Searing, *West African Slavery*, 29.
15. The predatory model has been influential in other parts of Western Africa; e.g., R. Kea, *Settlements, Trade, and Polities in the Seventeenth Century Gold Coast* (Baltimore: Johns Hopkins University Press, 1982); J. Bazin and E. Terray (eds.), *Guerres de lignages et guerres d'états en Afrique* (Paris: Éditions des Archives Contemporaines, 1982); R. Law, *The Slave Coast of West Africa, 1550–1750: The Impact of the Atlantic Slave Trade on an African Society* (Oxford: Clarendon, 1991); and R. Roberts, *Warriors, Slaves, and Merchants: The State and the Economy in the Middle Niger Valley, 1700–1914* (Stanford, CA: Stanford University Press, 1987).
16. For recent perspectives on decentralized societies, see Baum, *Shrines*; A. Hubbell, "A view of the slave trade from the margin: Souroudougou in the late nineteenth-century slave trade of the Niger bend," *Journal of African History* 42: 25–47 (2001); Hawthorne, *Planting Rice*; M. Klein, "The slave trade and decentralized societies," *Journal of African History* 42: 49–65 (2001); cf. O. F. Linares, "Deferring to trade in slaves: The Jola of Casamance, Senegal, in historical perspective," *History in Africa* 14: 113–139 (1987), for an earlier study. On the social logics of African participation in enslavement, see C. Piot, "Of slaves and the gift: Kabre sale of kin during the era of the slave trade," *Journal of African History* 37: 31–49 (1996); S. MacEachern, "Selling the iron for their shackles: Wandala-Montagnard interactions in northern Cameroon," *Journal of African History* 34(2): 247–270 (1993).
17. See J. Inikori and S. Engerman (eds.), *The Atlantic Slave Trade: Effects in Economies, Societies, and Peoples in Africa, the Americas, and Europe* (Durham, NC: Duke University Press, 1992), for an example of this kind of framing.

On emplotment, see P. Ricoeur, *Time and Narrative*, vol. 3 (Chicago: University of Chicago Press, 1988); and H. White, *The Content of the Form: Narrative Discourse and Historical Representation* (Baltimore: Johns Hopkins University Press, 1987), ch. 2.

18. See accounts of precolonial culture in Barry, *Senegambia*, 26–35; Curtin, *Economic Change*, ch. 1; Diagne, *Pouvoir politique traditionnel en Afrique Occidentale* (Paris: Présence Africaine, 1967); and Klein, *Islam*, ch. 1. Early European descriptions of the Senegambian coast—Almada, Cadamosto, Donelha, Lemos Coelho come to mind—provide rich, almost ethnographic observations on local societies. Some later compilations rest on generic, frequently recycled knowledge about the customs of different kingdoms; O. Dapper, "Description de l'Afrique [1686]," in *Objets interdits* (Paris: Fondation Dapper, 1989); J.-B. Demanet, *Nouvelle histoire de l'Afrique françoise*, 4 vols. (Paris: Lacombe, 1767); J.-B. Labat, *Nouvelle relation de l'Afrique Occidentale*, 4 vols. (Paris: Guillaume Cavelier, 1728). Accounts tend to be more detailed for Wolof areas around *comptoirs* (trading points) and less informative for interior areas with which European nations had more diffuse relations. But see M. Adanson, *Histoire naturelle du Sénégal* (Paris: C. J. B. Bauche, 1757); P. Cultru (ed.), *Premier voyage du Sieur de la Courbe fait à la coste d'Afrique en 1685* (Paris: Émile Larose, 1913); and A. Lemaire, *Les voyages du Sieur Lemaire aux Îles Canaries, Cap-Verd, Sénégal, et Gambie* (Paris: Jacques Collombat, 1695).

19. For historical treatments of Wolof polities, see Barry, *Royaume*; M. Diouf, *Le Kajoor au XIXe siècle: Pouvoir ceddo et conquête coloniale* (Paris: Karthala, 1990); R. Fall, "Le Royaume du Bawol du XVIe au XIXe siècle: Pouvoir wolof et rapports avec les populations Sereer" (PhD diss., Université de Paris I, 1984); Searing, *West African Slavery* and *"God Alone Is King."* For economic histories in Senegal, see S. Gellar, *Structural Changes and Colonial Dependency: Senegal 1885–1945* (London: Sage, 1976); M. Klein, "Colonial rule and structural change," in R. Cruise O'Brien (ed.), *The Political Economy of Underdevelopment: Dependence in Senegal*, 65–99 (Beverly Hills, CA: Sage, 1979); M. Mbodj, "Un exemple d'économie coloniale: Le Sine-Saloum et l'arachide, 1887–1940," 2 vols. (PhD diss., Université de Paris VII, 1978). For analyses of labor migrations, see P. David, *Les navétanes: Histoire des migrants saisonniers de l'arachide en Sénégambie des origines à nos jours* (Paris: Nouvelles Éditions Africaines, 1980); and Klein, *Slavery and Colonial Rule.* For an authoritative compendium on colonial dynamics in French West Africa, see C. Becker, S. Mbaye, and I. Thioub (eds.), *AOF: Réalités et héritages. Sociétés ouest-africaines et ordre colonial, 1895–1960*, 2 vols. (Dakar: Direction des Archives du Sénégal, 1997). For geographic and sociological studies on Senegal's countryside, see J. Copans, P. Couty, I. Roch, and G. Rocheteau, *Maintenance sociale et changement économique au Sénégal. I. Doctrine économique et pratique du travail chez les Mourides* (Paris: ORSTOM, 1972); D. Cruise O'Brien, *The Mourides of Senegal: The Political and Economic Organization of an Islamic Brotherhood* (Oxford: Clarendon, 1971), and *Saints*

and Politicians: Essays in the Organization of a Senegalese Peasant Society (New York: Cambridge University Press, 1975); A. B. Diop, *La société wolof: Tradition et changement. Les systèmes d'inégalité et de domination* (Paris: Karthala, 1981); Gastellu, *Égalitarisme*; J.-M. Gastellu and B. Delpech (eds.), *Maintenance sociale et changement économique au Sénégal. II. Pratique du travail et rééquilibres sociaux en milieu serer* (Paris: ORSTOM, 1974); Pélissier, *Paysans*.

20. See critiques of Wolofo-centrism, in Diouf, *Histoire du Sénégal*, ch. 1; and Thioub, "École." Exceptions to the dehistoricizing of culture can be found in analyses of Atlantic-era social and moral economies: Baum, *Shrines*; J. Miller, *Way of Death: Merchant Capitalism and the Angolan Slave Trade, 1730–1830* (Madison: University of Wisconsin Press, 1997); S. Palmié, "A taste for human commodities: Experiencing the Atlantic system," in S. Palmié (ed.), *Slave Cultures and the Cultures of Slavery*, 40–54 (Knoxville: University of Tennessee Press, 1995); and Shaw, *Memories*. This critique also does not apply historical studies of urban popular cultural forms; cf. work by Ndiouga Adrien Benga, Ousseynou Faye, and Ibrahima Thioub.
21. C. Neale, *Writing "Independent" History: African Historiography* (Westport, CT: Greenwood, 1985).
22. On the silencing performed by world history narratives, S. Feierman, "African histories and the dissolution of world history," in R. H. Bates, V. Y. Mudimbe, and J. O'Barr (eds.) *Africa and the Disciplines: Contributions of Research in Africa to the Social Sciences and Humanities*, 167–212 (Chicago: University of Chicago Press, 1993); and S. Feierman, "Colonizers, scholars and the creation of invisible histories," in V. E. Bonnell and L. Hunt (eds.), *Beyond the Cultural Turn: New Directions in the Study of Society and Culture*, 182–216 (Berkeley: University of California Press, 1999); and J. Guyer, "Wealth in people, wealth in things," *Journal of African History* 36: 83–90 (1995). Cooper, *Colonialism*, 18, offers a compelling analysis of the tunnel vision sometimes produced by narratives of failure/success culled from the present, a mode of "doing history backward" that disguises "the paths not taken, the dead ends of historical processes, the alternatives that appeared to people in their time." These predicaments are not specific to Africa but features of postcolonies. Concerns over the possibilities/limits of Western archives and imaginations for retrieving the distinct quality of non-Western political experience have been central to the Subaltern Studies scholarship in South Asia; e.g., D. Chakrabarty, *Provincializing Europe* (Princeton, NJ: Princeton University Press, 2008); and F. Cooper, "Conflict and connection: Rethinking colonial African history," *American Historical Review* 99(5): 1516–1545 (1994), for a smart dialogue between postcolonial theory and Africanist perspectives. See also I. Thioub, "L'histoire vue d'Afrique. Enjeux et perspectives," in J.-P. Chrétien (ed.), *L'Afrique de Sarkozy. Un déni d'histoire*, 155–180 (Paris: Karthala, 2008), for a critical perspective from Senegal.
23. Quoted in Ingold, "Temporality," 162.
24. Benjamin, *Arcades Project*, 476.

25. Chakrabarty, *Provincializing Europe*, 6.
26. D. Scott, *Refashioning Futures* (Chicago: University of Chicago Press, 2001), 8; and D. Scott, *Conscripts of Modernity: The Tragedy of Colonial Enlightenment* (Durham, NC: Duke University Press, 2004), 23–57. Scott envisions "problem-spaces" as discursive configurations that frame historical inquiry and shape the mode of thinking, the kinds of questions and answers one pursues, and the imaginations and political projects enabled by these inquiries. Problem-spaces are situated in particular political and historical fields, to whose conditions they respond. In fact, problem-spaces often become the very stakes over which different modalities of power compete and can become instruments of power in their own right—or symptoms of particular configurations of power/knowledge. One correlate is that new modes of historical investigation are never posited abstractly but derive their pertinence from and must take stock of the political circumstances enveloping them; cf. J. Scott, "After history," in J. Scott and D. Keates (eds.), *Schools of Thought: Twenty-Five Years of Interpretive Social Science*, 85–103 (Princeton, NJ: Princeton University Press, 2001).
27. Following Trouillot, *Silencing*, 27, each history presents a particular bundle of silences, which demands a unique process of deconstruction.
28. See A. Appadurai, *Modernity at Large* (Minneapolis: University of Minnesota Press, 1996), who shows that global flows are actualized in the fashioning of localities.
29. Mbembe, *On the Postcolony*, 14–15; Chakrabarty, *Provincializing Europe*, 111–112. See also Bayart, "Africa in the world"; and Dube, *Stitches*.
30. Materiality is a contested concept in anthropological thinking. I use to the term to refer to the material engagements that line the social—how people interact with the (animate and inanimate) nonhuman world and how these transactions condition their social lives. For an overview of recent debates about materiality, see T. Ingold, "Materials against materiality," *Archaeological Dialogues* 14(1): 1–16 (2007) and responses to Ingold in the same journal issue. See also D. Miller, "Materiality: An introduction," in D. Miller (ed.), *Materiality*, 1–50 (Durham, NC: Duke University Press, 2005); C. Tilley et al. (eds.), *Handbook of Material Culture* (Thousand Oaks, CA: Sage, 2006); and D. Hicks and M. Beaudry (eds.), *The Oxford Handbook of Material Culture Studies* (New York: Oxford University Press, 2006).
31. D. Chakrabarty, *Habitations of Modernity: Essays in the Wake of Subaltern Studies* (Chicago: University of Chicago Press, 2002), 45.
32. M. Bakhtin, *The Dialogic Imagination: Four Essays*, M. Holquist (ed.) (Austin: University of Texas Press, 1981), 84. His analysis focuses on literary chronotopes but alludes to their presence in "other areas of culture" (ibid.). Ethnographers have extended the concept to account for the narrative constitution of place; e.g., Feld and Basso, *Senses of Place*; Stewart, *Space on the Side of the Road*; N. Munn, "The cultural anthropology of time: A critical essay," *Annual Review of Anthropology* 21: 93–123 (1992).

33. Benjamin's work attends to the disruptive potential of obsolescence rummaged through the wreckage of progress; see his "Theses on the philosophy of history," in H. Arendt (ed.), *Illuminations*, 253–264 (New York: Schocken Books, 1968). The most extensive treatment of dialectical images (which he called "dialectics at a standstill") can be found in *Arcades Project*, 456–488, though the discussion, like the book itself, is fragmentary and widely dispersed; but see S. Buck-Morss, *The Dialectics of Seeing: Walter Benjamin and the Arcades Project* (Cambridge, MA: MIT Press, 1989), 56, 67, 73, 219–222; and R. Tiedemann, "Dialectics at a standstill: Approaches to the Passagen-Werk," in *Arcades Project*, 929–945. Several geographers have extended the concept to landscapes and underscored Benjamin's relevance to readings of the material world; e.g., Gregory, *Geographical Imaginations*; and M. Watts and A. Pred, *Reworking Modernity: Capitalisms and Symbolic Discontent* (New Brunswick, NJ: Rutgers University Press, 1992). Similarly, thinking with Benjamin's archaeological imagination, archaeologists have argued for the revelatory optics of material ruins and rubbish, their ability to disclose unnerving stories throbbing beneath the surface of things; e.g., M. Pearson and M. Shanks, *Theater/Archaeology* (New York: Routledge, 2001); González-Ruibal, "Time to destroy"; L. Olivier, *The Dark Abyss of Time: Archaeology and Memory* (Walnut Creek, CA: Altamira, 2011); Dawdy, "Clockpunk anthropology"; and S. Dawdy, *Patina: A Profane Archaeology* (Chicago: University of Chicago Press, 2016). Note the convergence with J. Derrida's *Specters of Marx: The State of the Debt, the Work of Mourning, and the New International* (New York: Routledge, 1994), which reflects on the troubling pasts and uncertain futures that constantly invade the present (what he calls spectrality) and the open-endedness of history (though outside of a framework of materiality).
34. See Derrida, *Writing and Difference*; and J. Derrida, *Margins of Philosophy* (Chicago: University of Chicago Press, 1982).
35. Chakrabarty, *Provincializing Europe*, 47–71. Drawing on Bill Brown, I suggest that landscapes' epistemological promise flows from the distinct "historical ontologies" that they congeal. Borrowing the term from Ian Hacking, Brown understands these object ontologies as the residues of muted (and often inconvenient) pasts encoded *in* materiality, an incomplete transcript of how world historical processes (capitalism, colonialism, modernity, globalism) enabled or negated the realization of other histories. In a more archaeological register, Buchli and Lucas have discussed the "excess" in/of material culture. They show that the artifacts, buildings, and spaces of the recent past resist the pull of dominant political ideologies and reveal the scaffold of repressed pasts propping up histories of modernity, capitalism, and liberalism; B. Brown, "Reification, reanimation, and the American uncanny," *Critical Inquiry* 32: 175–207 (2006), 182–183; I. Hacking, *Historical Ontology* (Cambridge, MA: Harvard University Press, 2002); Buchli and Lucas, *Archaeologies of the Contemporary Past*. The argument about the demystification of political and economic teleologies also runs across Derrida, *Specters of Marx*.

36. See Stahl, *Making History*, for a precursor to this approach.
37. Archives, like all forms of witnessing, contain lacunae; see Agamben, *Remnants*; Trouillot, *Silencing*.
38. Stahl, *Making History*, 15–16, 31–36; also N. B. Dirks, "Is vice versa? Historical anthropologies and anthropological histories," in T. J. McDonald (ed.), *The Historic Turn in the Human Sciences*, 17–51 (Ann Arbor: University of Michigan Press, 1996).
39. On "turbulence and loss," see Guyer cited in A. Stahl, "Comparative insights into the ancient political economies of West Africa," in G. M. Feinman and L. M. Nicholas (eds.), *Archaeological Perspectives on Political Economies*, 253–270 (Salt Lake City: University of Utah Press, 2004), 258. It is accepted that archives are not mere repositories of facts and that their contents are not transparent reflections of the past. Rather, as proponents of archival ethnographies have argued, a critical engagement with archives of any sort must grapple with two facts: (1) their location in certain institutions of power whose agendas they sometimes quietly reproduce and (2) that disciplines such as history and anthropology were themselves fundamentally involved in the perpetuation of archives. Among others, see Agamben, *Remnants*; J. Derrida, *Archive Fever: A Freudian Impression* (Chicago: University of Chicago Press, 1996); C. Hamilton, V. Harris, M. Pickover, and G. Reid (eds.), *Refiguring the Archive* (New York: Springer, 2002); T. Richards, *The Imperial Archive: Knowledge and the Fantasy of Empire* (New York: Verso, 1993); and A. L. Stoler, "Colonial archives and the arts of governance," *Archival Science* 2: 87–109 (2002). To unravel archives' relationship to power, Africa-based researchers have advocated a methodology of reading sources between the lines and against the grain, attentive to the social production of past representations; e.g., D. W. Cohen, *The Combing of History* (Chicago: University of Chicago Press, 1994); J. and J. L. Comaroff, *Of Revelation and Revolution: Christianity, Colonialism, and Consciousness in South Africa* (Chicago: University of Chicago Press, 1991); J. L. and J. Comaroff, *Of Revelation and Revolution: The Dialectics of Modernity on a South African Frontier* (Chicago: University of Chicago Press, 1997). More recently, Stoler, *Along the Archival Grain*, has suggested combining against-the-grain analyses with readings that go "along the grain" of archives. Doing so not only ensures a retrieval of subaltern experiences but also enables nuanced readings of the uncertainties and fantasies animating the colonial order of things, sensitive to the fault lines of colonial reason. This two-punch method informs my analysis of archival evidence throughout this book.
40. The bodies of sources relevant to Siin's history and the background conditions informing their production are reviewed in Richard, "From cosaan to colony," 32–40. For a Senegal-specific synthesis, see C. Becker, "Histoire de la Sénégambie du XVe au XVIIIe siècle: Un bilan," *Cahiers d'Études Africaines* 25(2): 213–242 (1985). While classical treatments of oral traditions in African history tended to focus on methodological issues, recent scholarship has been more mindful of interpretive possibilities: K. Barber, *I Could Speak until Tomorrow: Oriki, Women,*

and the Past in a Yoruba Town (Edinburgh: Edinburgh University Press, 1991); Baum, *Shrines*; D. W. Cohen, S. F. Miescher, and L. White (eds.), *African Words, African Voices: Critical Practices in Oral History* (Bloomington: Indiana University Press, 2001); and P. R. Schmidt, *Historical Archaeology in Africa: Representations, Social Memory, and Oral Traditions* (Lanham, MD: Altamira, 2006).

41. On "experience-near" accounts, see C. Geertz, *Local Knowledge: Further Essays in Interpretative Anthropology* (New York: Basic Books, 1983), 55–72.

42. A common perspective is that archaeological materialities capture histories of daily, embodied habits solidified over decades, refracting aspects of Bourdieu's *habitus*, the unspoken dispositions that orient everyday human practice or what de Certeau called the details of life, the mundane tactics that carry action below the façade of reflexive thought; Bourdieu, *Outline of a Theory of Practice*; M. de Certeau, *The Practice of Everyday Life* (Berkeley: University of California Press, 1994). See M. Dietler and I. Herbich, "*Habitus*, techniques, style: An integrated approach to the social understanding of material culture and boundaries," in M. Stark (ed.), *The Archaeology of Social Boundaries*, 232–263 (Washington, DC: Smithsonian Institution Press, 1998); K. G. Lightfoot, A. Martinez, and A. M. Schiff, "Daily practice and material culture in pluralistic social settings: An archaeological study of culture change and persistence from Fort Ross, California," *American Antiquity* 63(2): 199–222 (1998); and A. B. Stahl, "Colonial entanglements and the practices of taste: An alternative to logocentric approaches," *American Anthropologist* 104(3): 827–845 (2002), for elegant examples. Since these claims often invoke *experience* as a sort of epistemological/ontological holy grail, problems of archaeological distortion also warrant a more critical discussion of what experience is archaeologically and the long kinds of experience fossilized in the archaeological record; J. Scott, "The evidence of experience," *Critical Inquiry* 17(4): 773–797 (1991), makes a similar argument about social history. Olivier, *Dark Abyss*, explores resemblances between archaeology and memory; also Schmidt, *Historical Archaeology*.

43. Trouillot, *Silencing*, 29. A third implication concerns archaeologists' suspicion toward the artifactual recovery of meaning. Trouillot's reminder cautions us against evacuating meaningfulness from material and habitual practice. As a growing body of semiotic writings in archaeology illustrates, signs have material qualities that influence processes of signification. While embodied or affective practices may not be discursive per se, they nevertheless rest on forms of meaning making; Z. Crossland, *Ancestral Encounters in Highland Madagascar: Material Signs and Traces of the Dead* (New York: Cambridge University Press, 2014); C. Gokee, "Shapen signs: Pottery techniques, indexicality, and ethnic identity in the Saalum (ca 1700–1950)," in F. G. Richard and K. MacDonald (eds.), *Ethnic Ambiguity and the African Past*, 55–86 (Walnut Creek, CA: Left Coast Press, 2015).

44. For survey and excavations conducted in 2002–2003, see Richard, "From cosaan to colony." For a summary of the 2011 survey data and outcomes,

see F. G. Richard, "Bridging the Gaps: An Archaeology of Atlantic Transitions in Siin (AD 1300–1700)" (final report, NSF no. 1015989, 2012).

45. On methodological eclecticism in African archaeology, see F. G. Richard, "Materializing colonial pasts: African archaeological perspectives," in F. G. Richard (ed.), *Materializing Colonial Encounters: Archaeologies of African Experience*, 1–38 (New York: Springer, 2015).
46. W. Benjamin, "A short history of photography," in E. Jephcott and K. Shorter (eds.), *One-Way Street and Other Writings*, 240–257 (London: New Left Books, 1979), 243, 244. See also M. Taussig, *Mimesis and Alterity: A Particular History of the Senses* (New York: Routledge, 1993), 19–32.
47. Benjamin, "A short history," 250.
48. Stahl, *Making History*.
49. Dube, *Stitches*, 1–28. This method also recalls Nietzsche's notion of untimeliness, an exhortation to think unhistorically and allow the force of sensuous experience to disrupt historicist conventions; F. Nietzsche, *On the Use and Abuse of History for Life* (Whitefish, MT: Kessinger Publishing, 2004); also Stoler, *Along the Archival Grain*, 251–253.
50. Benjamin, "Theses"; L. Barkan, *Unearthing the Past: Archaeology and Aesthetics in the Making of Renaissance Culture* (New Haven, CT: Yale University Press, 1999), ch. 3.
51. A. Tsing, *Friction: An Ethnography of Global Connection* (Princeton, NJ: Princeton University Press, 2005), 88; and A. Tsing, "On non-scalability: The living world is not amenable to precision-nested scales," *Common Knowledge* 18(3): 505–524 (2012). Echoing Tsing, González-Ruibal, "Time to destroy," 251, states that "converting archaeology into a discipline that aspires to totality and completeness robs it of its power and its essential nature, which lies in working with 'the radical undecidability of the past.'"
52. M. Steinberg (ed.), *Walter Benjamin and the Demands of History* (Ithaca, NY: Cornell University Press, 1996). This recoups the unique power of exposition that Rutherford attributes to anthropology, whose "kinky empiricism" is "always slightly off kilter, always aware of the slipperiness of its grounds and of the difficulty of adequately responding to the ethical demands spawned by its methods. Being off-kilter is a strength, not a weakness. For anthropology, it is what comes with getting real"; D. Rutherford, "Kinky empiricism," *Cultural Anthropology* 27(3): 465–479 (2012), 466. More generally, see Haraway, *Simians*, 183–201.

PART TWO INTRODUCTION

1. L. Geismar, *Recueil des coutumes civiles des races du Sénégal* (Saint-Louis: Imprimerie du Gouvernement, 1933), 23.
2. Pélissier, *Paysans*, 198, 224. For a general view on peasantries, C. Coquery-Vidrovitch, "The political economy of the African peasantry and modes of

production," in P. C. W. Gutkind and I. Wallerstein (eds.), *The Political Economy of Contemporary Africa*, 90–111 (Beverly Hills, CA: Sage, 1976), 90–93.

3. For a seminal work on tradition, see E. Hobsbawm and T. Ranger (eds.), *The Invention of Tradition* (New York: Cambridge University Press, 1983). On tradition as social production, see J. Guyer, "Traditions of invention in Equatorial Africa," *African Studies Review* 39(3): 1–28 (1996); C. Piot, *Remotely Global: Village Modernity in West Africa* (Chicago: University of Chicago Press, 1999); Feierman, *Peasant Intellectuals*; and T. Spear, "Neo-traditionalism and the limits of invention in British Africa," *Journal of African History* 44: 3–27 (2003).
4. On the construction of African peasants, see H. Labouret, *Paysans d'Afrique Occidentale* (Paris: Gallimard, 1941); L. Valensi, *Tunisian Peasants in the Eighteenth and Nineteenth Centuries* (Cambridge: Cambridge University Press, 1985); Mitchell, *Colonizing Egypt*; E. Van Hoven, "Representing social hierarchy. Administrators-ethnographers in the French Sudan: Delafosse, Monteil, and Labouret," *Cahiers d'Études Africaines* 30(2): 179–198 (1990); and Galvan, *The State*, 48–50. On colonialism as a "long conversation," see Comaroff and Comaroff, *Of Revelation*, vol. 1.
5. For related work on Seereer social transformations under the auspices of the ORSTOM Siin project, see J.-P. Dubois, "Les Serer et la question des Terres Neuves au Sénégal," *Cahiers ORSTOM* (Série Sciences Humaines) 12(1): 81–120 (1975); Dupire et al., "Résidence"; J.-M. Gastellu, "L'autonomie locale des Serer du Mbayar," in J.-L. Balans, C. Coulon, and J.-M. Gastellu (eds.), *Autonomie locale et intégration nationale au Sénégal*, 111–160 (Paris: Éditions A. Pedone, 1975); Gastellu and Delpech, *Maintenance sociale*; Lericollais, *Sob*; and P.-X. Trincaz, "Transformations sociales dans les zones nouvelles d'implantation rurales: Les Serer dans les Terres Neuves du Sénégal," *Cahiers ORSTOM* (Série Sciences Humaines) 16(1–2): 19–36 (1979). Subsequent work by Gastellu, *Égalitarisme*, and Lericollais, *Paysans sereer*, has brought greater historical sensitivity to the study of Seereer cultural economy. Pélissier's work has been picked up in discussions of precolonial societies in western Senegal; e.g., Barry, *Senegambia*; Curtin, *Economic Change*; and Klein, *Islam*.

CHAPTER THREE

1. F. Nietzsche, *The Genealogy of Morality* (New York: Cambridge University Press, 2007), 53.
2. A. Diaw and M. Diouf, "Ethnic group versus nation. Identity discourses in Senegal," in O. Nnoli (ed.), *Ethnic Conflicts in Africa*, 259–285 (Dakar: CODESRIA, 1998); M. Diouf, *Sénégal: Les ethnies et la nation* (Dakar: Nouvelles Éditions Africaines du Sénégal, 1994). On "public secrets," see M. Taussig, *Defacement: Public Secrecy and the Labor of the Negative* (Stanford, CA: Stanford University Press, 1999).

3. The Senghorian state was heavily involved in the construction of national culture in Senegal; see E. Harney, *In Senghor's Shadow: Art, Politics, and the Avant-Garde in Senegal, 1960–1995* (Durham, NC: Duke University Press, 2005). Senghor transcended ethnic pasts by building a nation-state myth on a pedestal of African and European elements. Subsequent visions of cultural politics have been more performative, decentered onto the figure of the griot, a form of journalistic clientelism, and the promotion of Wolof heritage; see Diop and Diouf, *Sénégal sous Abdou Diouf*; I. Thioub, "L'école de Dakar et la production d'une écriture académique de l'histoire," in M.-C. Diop (ed.), *Le Sénégal contemporain*, 109–153 (Paris: Karthala; Amsterdam: SEPHIS, 2002); Diouf, *Histoire du Sénégal*; I. Thiaw and I. Sarr, "Les griots journalistes du Sénégal: 'Les maîtres de la parole' wolof entre tradition et modernité," *Métamorphoses* 24: 137–144 (2008).
4. These contradictions resurface elsewhere in the multicultural politics of African liberal regimes, see J. Comaroff and J. L. Comaroff, "Reflections on liberalism, policulturalism, and ID-ology: Citizenship and difference in South Africa," *Social Identities* 9(4): 445–473 (2003).
5. On joking relationships, see F. de Jong, "A joking nation: Conflict resolution in Senegal," *Canadian Journal of African Studies* 39(2): 389–413 (2005). Diaw and Diouf, "Ethnic group," show that the black-boxing of ethnicity in Senegal has led observers to seek *ethnic* explanations to conflicts reacting to *political* marginalization, as in the Casamance independence movement; also O. Faye, "L'instrumentalisation de l'histoire et de l'ethnicité dans le discours séparatiste en Basse-Casamance (Sénégal)," *Afrika Spectrum* 29(1): 65–77 (1994).
6. An expression of the Islamo-Wolof model driving national modernity in Senegal, Wolofization has roots in the colonial era. Its shadow politics are not reducible to a definable project; rather, Wolof cultural dominance has slowly accreted *in practice* as a result of Senegal's rapid urbanization, the success of Muridism, and the growing influence of mass media (which are diffused primarily in Wolof). In towns and cities, most people unconsciously use urban Wolof (a combination of Wolof and French) in everyday interactions and in the home. While many Senegalese chafe at Wolofization, which they blame for the weakening of non-Wolof languages and cultural attachments, Wolof is becoming the cultural vernacular of urban youth, regardless of ethnic background, a phenomenon bound to gain further amplitude with expanding rates of urban migration and the increase of multiethnic households. See Cruise O'Brien et al., *La construction de l'état*, 143–155; Gellar, *Democracy in Senegal*, ch. 9; F. McLaughlin, "Dakar Wolof and the configuration of an urban identity," *Journal of African Cultural Studies* 14(2): 153–172 (2001); and I. Sarr and I. Thiaw, "Cultures, médias et diversité ethnique: La nation sénégalaise face à la Wolofisation," *Sudlangues* 18: 1–17 (2012).
7. Villalón, *Islamic Society*, 51.

8. C. Becker, M. Diouf, and M. Mbodj, "L'évolution démographique régionale du Sénégal et du bassin arachidier (Sine-Saloum) au vingtième siècle, 1904–1976," in D. Cordell and J. W. Gregory (eds.), *African Populations and Capitalism: Historical Perspectives*, 76–94 (Boulder, CO: Westview Press, 1987); Lericollais, *Paysans sereer*; and Mbodj, "Un exemple," 563–578. Demographic data from the late 1800s through the late twentieth century corroborate this picture. Lefilliâtre's 1904 census tells us that 93.5 percent of the total population in the Siin heartland, excluding the Petite Côte, was Seereer. Data for the Petite Côte collected the same year through a different methodology put the number at 67.8 percent, which reflects the area's more multicultural demography; Lefilliâtre, "Monographie du Cercle du Sine-Saloum (1904)," ANS 1G290; C. Becker and V. Martin, "Les premiers recensements au Sénégal: Le Sénégal centre-ouest et son évolution démographique (Siin–Saalum–Bawol–Pays de l'Ouest). Partie I: Présentation de documents" (unpublished manuscript, Dakar, 1978), I.10, I.78–I.79. While less systematic, Noirot's 1891 census notes Siin's homogeneity and the numeric dominance of Seereer populations, corroborated by the dominance of Seereer patronyms; E. Noirot, "Notice sur le Sine-Saloum," *Journal Officiel du Sénégal* 1892: 167–168 (1892); C. Becker and V. Martin, "Les premiers recensements au Sénégal: Le Sénégal centre-ouest et son évolution démographique (Siin–Saalum–Bawol–Pays de l'Ouest)," *Annales de Démographie Historique* 1981: 367–386 (1981), 378–381. In recent times, the Fatick region, which falls within Siin's historic boundaries, has continued to boast a majority of Seereer occupants, 55.4 percent in 1976 and 55.1 percent in 1988; Becker et al., "Évolution démographique"; and C. Becker and M. Mbodj, "La dynamique du peuplement sereer. Les Sereer du Sine," in Lericollais, *Paysans sereer*, 40–73, 43. The most recent census, compiled in 2013, does not offer a regional breakdown of ethnicity.
9. On Seereer foundational migrations, see A. Ba, *Le Takrur, des origines à la conquête par le Mali (VIe–XIIIe siècles)* (Nouakchott: CRIAA, 2002); Diouf, "Chronique"; Sarr, "Histoire du Sine-Saloum." On the formation of the Siin kingdom, see M. M. Diouf, *Lances mâles. Léopold Sédar Senghor et les traditions sérères* (Niamey: Celhto, 1996); H. Gravrand, "Le Gabou dans les traditions orales Sereer et Guélwar," *Éthiopiques* 28: 40–59 (1981); and Gravrand, *"Cosaan."* On Atlantic and colonial pasts, see Boulègue, *Grand Jolof*; and Klein, *Islam*.
10. For classic ethnographic accounts of Seereer peasants, see L. Aujas, "Les Sérères du Sénégal (moeurs et coutumes de droit privé)," *Bulletin du Comité d'Études Historiques et Scientifiques de l'A.O.F.* 14: 293–333 (1931); L.-J.-B. Bérenger-Féraud, *Les Peuplades de la Sénégambie* (Paris: Ernest Leroux, 1879); J. Bourgeau, "Note sur la coutume des Sérères du Sine et du Saloum," *Bulletin du Comité d'Études Historiques et Scientifiques de l'A.O.F.* 16: 1–65 (1933); J. Carlus, "Les Sérères de la Sénégambie," *Revue de Géographie* 6: 409–420; 7: 30–37, 98–105 (1880); A. Lasnet et al., *Une mission au Sénégal: Ethnographie—botanique—zoologie—géologie* (Paris: Augustin Challamel, 1900); M. Reynier,

"Rapport politique annuel" (1933), ANS 2G33/70; R. Rousseau, "Notes sur l'habitat rural du Sénégal" (1928), ANS 1G23/104.

11. Galvan, *The State*.
12. The notion of "space of the possibles" comes from P. Bourdieu, *The Field of Cultural Production: Essays on Art and Literature* (New York: Columbia University Press, 1993), 30. On historical production and (im)possibility, see Trouillot, *Silencing*.
13. J. Pemberton, *On the Subject of "Java"* (Ithaca, NY: Cornell University Press, 1994).
14. On savage-slotting, see Trouillot, *Global Transformations*, 7–28.
15. Bourdieu, *Outline of a Theory of Practice*, 170.
16. J.-L. Amselle, *Mestizo Logics: Anthropology of Identity in Africa and Elsewhere* (Stanford, CA: Stanford University Press, 1998); B. Anderson, *Imagined Communities: Reflections on the Origin and Spread of Nationalism* (London: Verso, 1991); C. Lentz " 'They must be Dagaba first and any other thing second . . .': The colonial and post-colonial creation of ethnic identities in north-western Ghana," *African Studies* 53(2): 57–91 (1994); T. Ranger, "The invention of tradition in precolonial Africa," in Hobsbawm and Ranger, *The Invention of Tradition*, 211–262; and L. Vail, "Introduction: Ethnicity in Southern African history," in L. Vail (ed.). *The Creation of Tribalism in Southern Africa*, 1–19 (London: James Currey, 1989).
17. C. Lentz and P. Nugent, "Ethnicity in Ghana: A comparative perspective," in C. Lentz and P. Nugent (eds.), *Ethnicity in Ghana: The Limits of Invention*, 1–28 (London: Macmillan, 2000), 5; also B. Sharpe, "Ethnography and a regional system: Mental maps and the myth of states and tribes in north-central Nigeria," *Critique of Anthropology* 6: 33–65 (1986); and D. Wright, " 'What do you mean there were no tribes in Africa?': Thoughts on boundaries—and related matters—in precolonial Africa," *History in Africa* 26: 409–426 (1999).
18. E. N. Wilmsen, *Land Filled with Flies: A Political Economic History of the Kalahari* (Chicago: University of Chicago Press, 1989).
19. J.-L. Amselle, "Ethnies et espaces: Pour une anthropologie topologique," in J.-L. Amselle and E. M'Bokolo (eds.), *Au coeur de l'ethnie: Ethnie, tribalisme, et état en Afrique*, 11–48 (Paris: La Découverte, 1985), 44; also J. Bazin, "À chacun son Bambara," in Amselle and M'Bokolo, *Au coeur de l'ethnie*, 87–127. For comments on the ethnographic crystallization of African identities, see Amselle, *Mestizo Logics*, 37–38, 56, 160; also Cohn, *Colonialism*; and N. Dirks (ed.), *Culture and Colonialism* (Ann Arbor: University of Michigan Press, 1992). Other research examined how seemingly enduring aspects of African societies, like kinship traditions and lineage structures, political boundaries, and ethnic entities might have been products of the Atlantic slave trade and colonialism: P. Ekeh, "Social anthropology and two contrasting uses of tribalism in Africa," *Comparative Studies in Society and History* 32: 660–700 (1990); Sharpe, "Ethnography"; Amselle, *Mestizo Logics*.
20. J.-L. Amselle, "*Au coeur de l'ethnie* revisité," in J.-L. Amselle and E. M'Bokolo

(eds.), *Au coeur de l'ethnie: Ethnie, tribalisme, et état en Afrique*, 2nd ed., i–x (Paris: La Découverte, 1999); J.-P. Chrétien and G. Prunier (eds.), *Les ethnies ont une histoire* (Paris: Karthala, 2003); E. N. Wilmsen and P. McAllister (eds.), *The Politics of Difference: Ethnic Premises in a World of Power* (Chicago: University of Chicago Press, 1996). See C. Young, *The Rising Tide of Cultural Pluralism: The Nation-State at Bay?* (Madison: University of Wisconsin Press, 1993), 21–25, for a discussion of primordialist and constructivist perspectives.

21. For critiques of the "invention" literature, see Lentz and Nugent, *Ethnicity in Ghana*; J. Y. D. Peel, "The cultural work of Yoruba ethnogenesis," in E. Tonkin, M. McDonald, and M. Chapman (eds.), *History and Ethnicity*, 198–215 (New York: Routledge, 1989); T. Ranger, "The invention of tradition revisited: The case of colonial Africa," in T. Ranger and O. Vaughan (eds.), *Legitimacy and the State in Twentieth-Century Africa: Essays in Honor of A. H. M. Kirk-Greene*, 62–111 (London: Macmillan, 1993); and Spear, "Neo-traditionalism." For historical analyses of African ethnicity, B. Berman and J. Lonsdale, *Unhappy Valley: Conflict in Kenya and Africa. Book Two: Violence and Ethnicity* (London: James Currey, 1992); C. Lentz, "Contested identities: The history of ethnicity in northwestern Ghana," in Lentz and Nugent, *Ethnicity in Ghana*, 137–161; and A. B. Stahl, "Ethnic style and ethnic boundaries: A diachronic case study from West-Central Ghana," *Ethnohistory* 38(3): 250–275 (1991).
22. Cohen, *Combing*; Comaroff and Comaroff, *Ethnography*; P. Geschiere, *The Perils of Belonging: Autochthony, Citizenship, and Exclusion in Africa and Europe* (Chicago: University of Chicago Press, 2009); T. C. McCaskie, *Asante Identities: History and Modernity in an African Village, 1850–1950* (Edinburgh: Edinburgh University Press, 2000); J. Y. D. Peel, *Religious Encounter and the Making of the Yoruba* (Bloomington: Indiana University Press, 1999); and Wilmsen and McAllister, *Politics of Difference*.
23. R. Brubaker and F. Cooper, "Beyond 'identity,'" *Theory and Society* 29(1): 1–47 (2000).
24. Feierman, "Colonizers"; McCaskie, *Asante Identities*.
25. Stahl, "Colonial entanglements," 830–831; also N. Thomas, *Entangled Objects: Exchange, Material Culture and Colonialism in the Pacific* (Cambridge, MA: Harvard University Press, 1991), 88.
26. Aujas, "Région," 97–98; Aujas, "Sérères," 295–298; Bourgeau, "Note," 7–9; C. Cros, *Le pays de Sine et Saloum (Sénégal)* (Vals-les-Bains: Chalvet, 1933); H. Gaden, "Légende et coutumes sénégalaises. Cahiers de Yoro Dyao," *Revue d'Ethnographie et de Sociologie* 1912: 119–137, 191–202 (1912). For reviews of Seereer migration histories, see C. Becker and V. Martin, "Notes sur les traditions orales et les sources écrites concernant le royaume du Sine," *Bulletin de l'IFAN*, B, 34(4): 732–777 (1972), 742–755, and "Essai sur l'histoire du Saloum," *Revue Sénégalaise d'Histoire* 2(1): 3–24 (1981). Some earlier sources attribute an exclusively southern origin to the Seereer in Upper Casamance (Kaabu); Bérenger-Féraud, *Peuplades*, 273–274; Pinet-Laprade, "Notice," 132–133.

27. Becker and Mbodj, "Dynamique," 50.
28. Becker and Martin, "Essai," 3–24. V. Martin and C. Becker, "Documents pouvant servir à l'histoire des îles du Saalum," *Bulletin de l'IFAN*, B, 41(4): 722–772 (1979), 726; C. Becker and V. Martin, "Vestiges, peuplements, et civilisations protohistoriques de la Sénégambie" (unpublished manuscript, Dakar, 1982). On the etymology of *Seereer*, see Galvan, *The State*, 51.
29. On Northwest Seereer, see Galvan, *The State*, 38, 40; C. Becker, "La représentation des Sereer du Nord-Ouest dans les sources européennes (XVe–XIXe siècle)," *Journal des Africanistes* 55(1–2): 165–185 (1985). For colonial accounts, "Coutumes du Sénégal" (1903), ANS 1G330; M. Dulphy, "Coutumes des Sérères Nones (1937)," in *Coutumiers juridiques de l'Afrique Occidentale Française, Tome I (Sénégal)*, 213–236 (Paris: Larose, 1939). Using linguistic data, J. L. Doneux, "Les groupes linguistiques," in R. Van Chi (ed.), *Atlas national du Sénégal*, 68–69 (Paris: IGW, 1977), questions historical connections between Siin and Northwest Seereer, and suggests the latter crystallized (linguistically, at least) through conflicted contacts with Wolof polities.
30. Becker and Martin, "Notes," 752–754; Becker et al., "Traditions villageoises." On the Soos-Seereer encounter, see Gravrand, *"Cosaan,"* 149–185; M. Klein, "Serer traditions and the development of Saalum" (unpublished manuscript, University of Toronto, Department of History, n.d.), 27; V. Martin and C. Becker, "Vestiges protohistoriques et occupation humaine au Sénégal," *Annales de Démographie Historique* 1974: 403–429 (1974); and Sarr, "Histoire du Sine-Saloum," 227.
31. Historians portray the Siin-Saalum as a sparsely settled region at the time of Seereer arrival; Galvan, *The State*, 51; Klein, "Serer traditions," 6. Martin and Becker, "Vestiges," 413, 417, 422, extrapolate higher human occupations during the first millennium AD. From the abundant record of tumuli and megaliths on the periphery of present-day demographic centers, they depict a westward sliding of populations over time as original Seereer migrants "avoided regions that were then densely settled to infiltrate more loosely populated zones, even [if it meant] settling on soils more mediocre and more difficult to work." For archaeological interpretations of Seereer-Soos cultural fusion, see Becker and Mbodj, "Dynamique," 49; S. Pradines, "Les tumulus funéraires sénégambiens (Sénégal)" Planète-Sénégal, 1996, http://www.planete-senegal.com/senegal/tumulus_funeraires_senegal.php.
32. Diouf, *Lances mâles*; Gravrand, "Gabou"; M. Mané, "Contribution à l'histoire du Kaabu, des origines au XIXe siècle," *Bulletin de l'IFAN*, B, 38(4): 87–159 (1978). Oral myths only hint at the process of Siin state formation. According to one corpus of legends, shortly after settling in Mbissel, Maisa Wali Joon, the founder of the Siin kingdom, handily resolved a dispute that had bitterly divided village residents. Recognizing this feat of leadership, the villagers unanimously handed political sovereignty to him. Maisa Wali accepted the crown on the condition that he would select one of the villagers as his great *jaraaf* (prime minister); see Diouf, "Chronique," 704–705;

Gravrand, *"Cosaan,"* 293–295. Depicted metaphorically here is a merging of political traditions built on bonds of reciprocity and checks-and-balances between migrants and aristocrats and settlers and commoners. Elsewhere, oral memory recounts that the Gelwaar organized wrestling matches upon arriving in Mbissel. These events were dominated by Buukar Biram Faay, a local Seereer champion, whose prowess so impressed Maisa Wali's sister that he married her shortly thereafter. This union between the Gelwaar princess and Seereer commoner expresses the consensual fusion of two peoples, culminating with the birth of two sons who later succeeded Maisa Wali as political rulers; Klein, "Serer traditions," 7–8. See chapter 5 for accounts of more conflicted histories.

33. C. Becker and V. Martin, "Les familles paternelles sereer. Répartitions par pays traditionnels et par castes," *Bulletin de l'IFAN*, B, 44(3/4): 321–410 (1982); and C. Becker and V. Martin, "Les familles maternelles sereer. Répartitions par pays traditionnels et par castes," *Bulletin de l'IFAN*, B, 45(3/4): 357–402 (1983); Dupire et al., "Résidence."
34. Trouillot, *Silencing*, 26–27.
35. G. Crone (ed.), *The Voyages of Cadamosto*, 54–56; V. Fernandes [1506–1510], *Description de la côte occidentale d'Afrique (Sénégal au Cap de Monte, Archipels)*, T. Monod, A. Teixeira da Mota, and R. Mauny (eds.) (Bissau: Centro de Estudos da Guiné Portuguesa, 1951), 24–27; D. Gomes [1457–1460], *De la première découverte de la Guinée*, T. Monod, R. Mauny, and G. Duval (eds.) (Bissau: Centro de Estudos da Guiné Portuguesa, 1959), 28–29. The map of Africa in Graciozo Benincasa's *Atlas* (1468) also contains the *barbacin* toponym, though it is represented some distance north of its present location (in Crone, *Voyages of Cadamosto*).
36. B. Barreira [1606], in A. Brásio (ed.), *Monumenta Missionaria Africana. Africa Ocidental*, Segunda Série, vol. 4 (Lisbon: Agência-Geral do Ultramar, 1968), 159–174; A. Donelha, *An Account of Sierra Leone and the Rivers of Guinea of Cape Verde (1625)*, A. Teixeira da Mota and P. E. H. Hair (eds.) (Lisbon: Junta de Investigações Científicas do Ultramar, 1977), 137, 286–289n223; F. de Lemos Coelho [1684], *Description of the Coast of Guinea*, P. E. H. Hair (ed.) (Liverpool: University of Liverpool, 1985), I.2, I.8–I.10, I.12; Lemaire, *Voyages*, 95–96; and Labat, *Nouvelle relation*, vol. 4, 130, 156–157. On eighteenth-century references, see J.-B. Durand, *Voyage au Sénégal* (Paris: Henri Agasse, 1802), 49–50; P. Labarthe, *Voyage au Sénégal, pendant les années 1784 et 1785, d'après les mémoires de Lajaille* (Paris: Dentu, 1802), 108–109.
37. The map is reproduced in Cultru, *Premier voyage*. Perhaps earlier, a manuscript map from the Bibliothèque Nationale attributed to La Courbe describes the Joal hinterland as occupied by the "Cereres" peoples and applies the same ethnonym to the populations living to the east of Portudal; J.-B. d'Anville, "Pays compris entre le cap Vert & les îles des sauvages près du cap Tagrin," BNF, http://gallica.bnf.fr/ark:/12148/btvlb77594998. The term *Sereres* also appears twice on d'Anville's map (1727), in R. Van Chi (ed.), *Atlas national du*

Sénégal (Paris: IGW, 1977), 55, plate 20, to label both the strip of land directly east of the Cap Vert and the "Country of the Barbecins"—that is, the Siin.

38. M. Pruneau de Pommegorge, *Description de la Nigritie* (Paris: Maradan, 1789), 126.
39. Pinet-Laprade, "Notice," 34; also Bérenger-Féraud, *Peuplades*; P.-D. Boilat, *Esquisses sénégalaises* (Paris: Bertrand, 1853); Lasnet et al., *Mission.* Some ambiguity persists in Roger's 1823 account of coastal Bawol, which explains that the seashore was inhabited by "*Sérères,*" while the interior was occupied "by another negro nation called *None*"; in J. Monteilhet, "Documents relatifs à l'histoire du Sénégal," *Bulletin du Comité d'Études Historiques et Scientifiques de l'A.O.F.* 1916: 62–119 (1916), 91. Later observers collapse these populations into a single ethnic category separate from the Seereer of Siin. While it might express local ideas of groupness, this passage also implies that the dialogue between Africans and Europeans regarding the construction of ethnic classification in the Seereer country was still ongoing in the 1820s.
40. See Crone, *Voyages of Cadamosto*, 55–56, for mentions of translators and cultural informants and a *reprise* in Fernandes, *Description*, 27.
41. Galvan, *The State*; J. Searing, "No kings, no lords, no slaves: Ethnicity and religion among the Sereer-Safèn of western Bawol, 1700–1914," *Journal of African History* 43: 407–429 (2002), 411–412. On processes of identity making, see Brubaker and Cooper, "Beyond 'identity.'"
42. Cf. Y. Fall, "Les Wolof au miroir de leur langue: Quelques observations," in Chrétien and Prunier, *Les ethnies ont une histoire*, 117–123, 120. Also I. Kopytoff (ed.), *The African Frontier: The Reproduction of Traditional African Societies* (Bloomington: Indiana University Press, 1987).
43. Toponyms were often used loosely to refer to entire populations or kingdoms well into the eighteenth century. The same accounts, for instance, couple the noun *Joal* with a person, people, or an area to denote the village itself, the river, the kingdom of Siin and its ruler, an independent region with its own chief, or the Seereer population of Siin! See A. A. Almada [ca. 1594], *Brief Treatise on the Rivers of Guinea*, P. E. H. Hair (ed.) (Liverpool: University of Liverpool, 1984); G. Thilmans, "Le Sénégal dans l'oeuvre d'Olfried Dapper," *Bulletin de l'IFAN*, B, 33(3): 508–563 (1971); map in F. Moore, *Travels into the Inland Parts of Africa* (London: Edward Cave, 1738).
44. Cultru, *Premier voyage*, 189, astutely comments on the origins of *Barbacin/Barbecin.* On the Noon, see C. Becker and V. Martin, "Mémoire inédit de Doumet: Le Kayor et les pays voisins au cours de la seconde moitié du XVIIIe siècle," *Bulletin de l'IFAN*, B, 36(1): 25–92 (1974), 36–37; I. Ciss, "Les Seereer du Nord-Ouest (Sénégal) face à la traite négrière," *Revue Sénégalaise d'Histoire* 6: 115–132 (2004).
45. E.g., J. Glasman, "Le Sénégal imaginé: Évolution d'une classification ethnique de 1816 aux années 1920," *Afrique & Histoire* 2: 111–139 (2004);

E. Sibeud, "La naissance de l'ethnographie africaniste en France avant 1914," *Cahiers d'Études Africaines* 34(4): 639–658 (1994).

46. Louis Faidherbe, who governed Senegal from 1854 to 1861 and 1863 to 1865, played a key role in fashioning the racial typologies and ethnological agendas employed by subsequent generations of colonial administrators; A. Bathily, "Aux origines de l'Africanisme: Le rôle de l'oeuvre ethno-historique de Faidherbe dans la conquête du Sénégal," in P. Bourdieu (ed.), *Le mal de voir*, 77–105 (Paris: Union Générales d'Éditions, 1976); J.-L. Amselle, *Affirmative Exclusion: Cultural Pluralism and the Role of Custom in France* (Ithaca, NY: Cornell University Press, 2003), 77–99.

47. On state terrorism in Siin, see Pinet-Laprade, "Notice"; "Excursion militaire et géographique à l'est de Gorée dans les pays de Sine et de Saloum (1859)," *Le Tour du Monde*: 33–38 (1859); Carlus, "Sérères"; V. Martin, C. Becker, and M. Mbodj, "Trois documents d'Ernest Noirot sur l'histoire des royaumes du Siin et du Saloum," *Bulletin de l'IFAN*, B, 42(1): 37–85 (1980), 68. For comments on alcoholism, see Faidherbe, Lettre au Ministre (no. 261) (Jun. 14, 1859), ANS 1B32; Pinet-Laprade, Lettre No. 42 ("Service Militaire") (Jun. 18, 1864), ANS 13G300bis.

48. On the conflation of different Seereer groups, see "Notice sur le Cayor (1870)," ANS 1G36; Bérenger-Féraud, *Peuplades*; Pinet-Laprade, "Notice."

49. Galvan, *The State*, 43. For more general accounts, see Amselle, *Affirmative Exclusion*; J. Fabian, *Time and the Other: How Anthropology Makes Its Object* (New York: Columbia University Press, 1983), and M.-L. Pratt, *Imperial Eyes: Writing and Transculturation* (London: Routledge, 1991).

50. Bérenger-Féraud, *Peuplades*, 274.

51. Aujas, "Sérères," 293–294.

52. Colonial authors drew a fundamental distinction between Seereer and Wolof populations, based on the Wolof country's apparent lack of agricultural structures akin to those found further south. The resulting contrast perceived between Wolof and neighboring peasant populations has drawn researchers' attention to the most fluid characteristics of Wolof society and emphasize cultural mobility, the historicity of Wolof ethnicity, hierarchy and state structures in the realm of politics, and Islam; e.g., Pélissier, *Paysans*, 101; G. Rocheteau, "Société Wolof et mobilité," *Cahiers ORSTOM* (Série Sciences Humaines) 12(1): 3–18 (1975); Diop, *Société wolof*. Rooting ethnic difference in natural culture also precluded the consideration that Wolof societies' weak agrarian traditions, mobility, and commercial proclivities may have been results of the socioeconomic turmoil that escalated during the Atlantic era and the years leading up to formal colonization. The historical record suggests as much when it describes the Wolof kingdom of Kajoor as the "granary" for French coastal settlements in the seventeenth and eighteenth centuries; e.g., Lemaire, *Voyages*; Pruneau de Pommegorge, *Description*. Sauvigny's account of southern Kajoor describes

an agrarian landscape similar to that of Siin save for the cattle husbandry; P. Marty, "La mission de Sauvigny dans le Sin-Saloun en 1822," in *Études sénégalaises (1725–1826)*, 27–51 (Paris: Éditions Leroux, n.d.), 37–41.

53. Bérenger-Féraud, *Peuplades*, 273–284; A. Corre, "Les Sérères de Joal et de Portudal (côte occidentale d'Afrique): Esquisse ethnographique," *Revue d'Ethnographie* 2: 1–20 (1883); C. Guy, "Le Sine-Saloum," *La Géographie* 18: 297–314 (1908), 305; Lasnet et al., *Mission*, 142; Lefilliâtre [1901], in Klein, *Islam*, 202. See also "Coutumes sérères—Région du Sine" (1936), ANS 1G26/104, 9; Rousseau, "Notes" (1928), ANS 1G23/104, 38–39.

54. Guy, "Sine-Saloum," 304. The cultivation of a geography of bounded ethnic entities was an explicit component of Governor William Ponty's [1908–1915] "politique des races," which discouraged mixing between ethnocultural groups (called "races") and sought to conserve their autonomous evolution and unique particularism; "Circulaire aux lieutenants-gouverneurs" (Sept. 22, 1909), ANS 13G72. Recent anthropological literature has convincingly argued that imperial categories were made and remade in the engagement "between the metropole and colony." Colonial modernity required the creation of an other, an inversion of itself, which it conveniently discovered in the colonies. This alter-ego made the idea of Europe possible, just as its own existence was premised on that of Europe; Trouillot, *Global Transformations*, 7–28; Stoler and Cooper, *Tensions of Empire*. The French borrowed images of domestic others—European peasants, impoverished masses, the underclass—to make sense of their African counterparts. Colonial observers drew frequent analogies between African and European peasants—as when administrators equated the Seereer with "good old Provençal peasants" (Galvan, *The State*, 49), when Bérenger-Féraud (*Peuplades*, 27–28) compared the Wolof to Italians, Corsicans, or people from southern France, or when Faidherbe likened the Bambara to the rustic Auvergnats (in Bazin, "À chacun son Bambara," 89, 100). Their encounter with Africa's "natural man" also informed perceptions of the "savage" at home, who had to be disciplined in the name of progress, modernity, and the nation-state; see Comaroff and Comaroff, *Ethnography*, 265–295.

55. S. A. MacEachern, "Scale, style, and cultural variation: Technological traditions in the northern Mandara mountains," in Stark, *Archaeology of Social Boundaries*, 107–131, 130.

56. S. Jones, *The Archaeology of Ethnicity: Constructing Identities in the Past and Present* (London: Routledge, 1997); Dietler and Herbich, "*Habitus*"; and Stahl, "Ethnic style."

57. For research on the Mandara Mountains, see N. David, K. Gavua, S. MacEachern, and J. Sterner, "Ethnicity and material culture in North Cameroon," *Canadian Journal of Archaeology* 15: 171–177 (1991); and MacEachern, "Scale." Research in Mali, Cameroon, and Senegal has endorsed a less skeptical position. The argument is that, while fluid categories like decorative grammars and vessel forms do not always permit segregation among

cultural identities, more conservative categories like manufacturing techniques and paste preparation are more reliable indicators of social and ethnic boundaries because they index enduring dispositions (*habitus*) inscribed in motor habits: O. Gosselain, "Materializing identities: An African perspective," *Journal of Archaeological Method and Theory* 7(3): 187–217 (2000); A. Mayor, É. Huysecom, A. Gallay, M. Rasse, and A. Ballouche, "Population dynamics and paleoclimate over the past 3,000 years in the Dogon Country, Mali," *Journal of Anthropological Archaeology* 24: 25–61 (2005); N. S. Guèye, "Poteries et peuplements de la Moyenne Vallée du Fleuve Sénégal du XVIe au XXe siècle: Approche ethnoarchéologique et ethnohistorique" (PhD diss., Université de Paris X, 1998); and M. Sall, *Traditions céramiques, identities et peuplement en Sénégambie* (Cambridge: BAR International Series, 2005). Recent work in Niger has modulated arguments about the conservatism of manufacturing techniques; O. Gosselain, "Thoughts and adjustments in the potter's backyard," in I. Berg (ed.), *Breaking the Mold: Challenging the Past through Pottery*, 67–79 (Oxford: Archaeopress, 2008).

58. A. T. Smith, "The end of the essential archaeological subject," *Archaeological Dialogues* 11(1): 1–20 (2004); cf. L. Meskell, "The intersection of identity and politics in archaeology," *Annual Review of Anthropology* 31: 279–301 (2002). For useful archaeological case studies, see J. Denbow, "Material culture and the dialectics of identity in the Kalahari, 700–1700," in S. K. McIntosh (ed.), *Beyond Chiefdoms: Pathways to Complexity in Africa*, 110–123 (New York: Cambridge University Press, 1999); Voss, *Archaeology of Ethnogenesis*; and Wilmsen, *Land Filled with Flies*.
59. Richard, "From cosaan to colony," 645–649.
60. S. Dieng, "Contribution à l'étude des amas coquilliers de Joal-Fadiout" (master's thesis, Université Cheikh Anta Diop de Dakar, 1980); O. Linares de Sapir, "Shell middens of Lower Casamance and problems of Diola prehistory," *West African Journal of Archaeology* 1: 23–54 (1970); G. Thilmans and C. Descamps, "Amas et tumulus coquilliers du delta du Saloum," in *Recherches scientifiques dans les parcs nationaux du Sénégal*, 31–50 (Dakar: IFAN, 1982). Terms like *neolithic, Iron Age*, and *protohistory* have long been used to periodize Senegal's past. Their application to Senegal is as problematic as elsewhere in Africa, given the inconsistency, imprecision, and questionable assumptions informing these terms. For critiques, see S. Deschamps, "Les groupes culturels du Néolithique et de l'Âge de Fer des régions de Louga, Thiès et Saint Louis, Sénégal (du VIe millénaire avant J.-C. au VIe siècle après J.-C.). Approche taphonomique et archéologique" (PhD diss., Université de Paris I, 2013); and A. Stahl, "Introduction: Changing perspectives on Africa's past," in A. Stahl (ed.), *African Archaeology: A Critical Introduction*, 1–23 (Malden, MA: Blackwell, 2005).
61. Richard, "From cosaan to colony," 354–357. But see developing work on pottery making and communities of practice, J. Habicht-Mauche, S. L. Eckert and D. L. Huntley (eds.), *The Social Life of Pots: Glaze Wares and Cultural*

Dynamics in the Southwest, AD 1250–1680 (Tucson: University of Arizona Press, 2006); L. Cordell and J. Habicht-Mauche (eds.), *Potters and Communities of Practice: Glaze Paint and Polychrome Pottery in the American Southwest, A.D. 1250 to 1700* (Tucson: University of Arizona Press, 2012); more generally, A. Roddick and A. Stahl (eds.), *Knowledge in Motion: Constellations of Learning across Time and Place* (Tucson: University of Arizona Press, 2016).

62. Richard, "From cosaan to colony," 578–579.
63. Boulègue, *Grand Jolof*; Brooks, *Landlords*.
64. Richard, "Historical and dialectical perspectives."
65. D. Wright, "Beyond migration and conquest: Oral traditions and Mandinka ethnicity in Senegambia," *History in Africa* 12: 335–348 (1985), 342.
66. Richard, "From cosaan to colony," 563–565.
67. G. Thilmans, "Sur les objets de parure trouvés à Podor (Sénégal) en 1958," *Bulletin de l'IFAN*, B, 39(4): 669–694 (1977); L. Garenne-Marot, "Archéologie d'un métal: Le cuivre en Sénégambie entre le Xe et le XIVe siècle" (PhD diss., Université de Paris I, 1993), 228–230, 343–346.
68. MacEachern. "Symbolic reservoirs."
69. S. K. and R. McIntosh, "Field survey in the tumulus zone of Senegal," *African Archaeological Review* 11: 73–107 (1993). On possible influences from the Mande world, see. I. Thiaw, "An archaeological investigation of long-term culture change in the Lower Falemmé (upper Senegal region), A.D. 500–1900" (PhD diss., Rice University, 1999); A. Gallay, G. Pignat, and P. Curdy, "Mbolop Tobé (Santhiou Kohel, Sénégal): Contribution à la connaissance du mégalithisme sénégambien," *Archives Suisses d'Anthropologie Générale* 46(2): 217–259 (1982).
70. Diouf, *Lances mâles*, 63–64; Gravrand, *"Cosaan,"* 160–161.
71. Martin and Becker, "Vestiges," 283ff.; Pradines, "Tumulus," 31; Gravrand, *"Cosaan,"* ch. 7; Pélissier, *Paysans*.
72. Lentz and Nugent, "Ethnicity in Ghana"; Stahl, "Ethnic style."
73. Taussig, *Defacement*, ii.

CHAPTER FOUR

1. Reynier, "Rapport," 1.
2. Dirks, "Is vice versa?"; Comaroff and Comaroff, *Ethnography*; Cooper and Stoler, *Tensions of Empire*.
3. Becker and Martin, "Familles paternelles" and "Familles maternelles." On the challenges of historical kinship studies, see S. R. Wooten, "Colonial administration and the ethnography of the family in the French Soudan," *Cahiers d'Études Africaines* 33(3): 419–446 (1993); and M. Vaughan, "Which family? Problems in the reconstruction of the history of the family as an economic and cultural unit," *Journal of African History* 24(2): 275–283 (1983).
4. On the codification of customs, see B. Maupoil, "L'étude des coutumes juridiques de l'A.O.F. (Étude administrative)," in *Coutumiers juridiques de l'Afrique*

Occidentale Française, Tome I (Sénégal), 1–54 (Paris: Larose, 1939); Geismar, *Recueil*. For Seereer ethnographies, see Aujas, "Sérères"; Bourgeau, "Note"; M. Dulphy, "Étude sur les coutumes sérères de la Petite Côte (Cercle de Thiès—Sénégal)," *L'Ethnographie* 37: 3–70; Dupire et al., "Résidence"; H. Gravrand, "Dynamisme interne de la famille serer," *Afrique Documents* 85–86: 95–122 (1966); B. Guigou, "Les changements du système familial et matrimonial: Les Sérères du Sine (Sénégal)" (PhD diss., École des Hautes Études en Sciences Sociales, 1992); Lericollais, *Sob*; Pélissier, *Paysans*, 209–212, 221–224.

5. Gravrand, "Dynamisme"; Dupire et al., "Résidence," 444–446.
6. Guigou, "Changements."
7. On patriliny's growing role, see Dupire et al., "Résidence"; Gravrand, "Dynamisme." On the decline of matrilineal influence, see Lericollais, *Sob*, 50–51; Lericollais, *Paysans sereer*; Pélissier, *Paysans*, 221–224. Cf. Aujas, "Sérères," who does not mention patrilineal inheritance; also Bourgeau, "Note"; Dulphy, "Étude"; and Geismar, *Recueil*.
8. P. Abelin, "Domaine national et développement au Sénégal," *Bulletin de l'IFAN*, B, 41(3): 508–538 (1979); Galvan, *The State*, 131–163; J.-M. Gastellu, "Politique coloniale et organisation économique des pays serer, Sénégal, 1910–1950," in Becker et al., *AOF: Réalités et héritages*, vol. 1, 564–576; and H. Gravrand, *Visage africain de l'Église* (Paris: Éditions de l'Orante, 1961).
9. Aujas, "Sérères," 298–302; Bourgeau, "Note," 27–31; Corre, "Sérères," 11; Martin et al., "Trois documents," 67–69; Pinet-Laprade, "Notice," 138–139. One of the most confused aspects of Senegambian social systems has been the institution of caste and whether it structures the entire social body or refers only to endogamous specialist groups, a confusion compounded by analytical formalism, which has downplayed regional variability and fluidity between casted groups; Diop, *Société wolof*; Diouf, *Kajoor*, 43–73; Becker and Martin, "Familles paternelles," 393–394; and M. Diouf, "Le problème des castes dans la société wolof," *Revue Sénégalaise d'Histoire* 2: 25–37 (1981). I avoid caste/order terminologies to focus on social groups grounded in Siin's precolonial social division of labor and reflecting their position in wider political and economic fields; Klein, *Islam*, 8.
10. On Seereer social organization, see Becker and Martin, "Familles paternelles," 327–330; L. Crétois, *Dictionnaire sereer-français*, 6 vols. (Dakar: CLAD, 1972–1977); Klein, *Islam*, 8–11; Noirot, "Notice," 167–168. *Ceddo* is an ambiguous term referring to enslaved soldiers and the military aristocracy but sometimes applied to the entire Gelwaar ruling body (in contrast with Seereer commoners). Because of the *ceddo*'s intemperance and aversion to Islam, the label also came to describe non-Muslim pagans; cf. Searing, *"God Alone Is King,"* 4–9.
11. Local farmers refer to themselves as *Sinig* (resident of the Siin; *Siin-Siin* in Wolof) or *Seereer refo rekk* (simple Seereer); Becker and Martin, "Familles paternelles," 327; Crétois, *Dictionnaire*, vol. 5, 615. In the latter case, the ethnic label is not extended to the nobility or casted groups. On enslaved groups, see Aujas, "Sérères," 309–311, and Crétois, *Dictionnaire*, vol. 5,

280–281. Servility, aristocratic institutions, and warrior classes were absent among the decentralized Seereer communities of the Bawol and Niominka villages of the Saalum Islands; M. Dupire, "Classes et échelons d'âge dans une société dysharmonique," *Journal des Africanistes* 61(2): 5–42 (1991). When they existed, low-status occupational caste groups were generally recently settled migrants, who found greater social acceptance into these less differentiated societies.

12. Galvan, *The State*, 58. See also Diagne, *Pouvoir*, 56–94; Klein, *Islam*, 11–17; Mbodj, "Un exemple," 28–44; Pélissier, *Paysans*, 199–203; Sarr, "Histoire du Sine-Saloum," 347–351.
13. Diagne, *Pouvoir*, 62. See also Aujas, "Sérères," 298–302; Carlus, "Sérères," 98–104, 412–415; Corre, "Sérères," 11; Guy, "Sine-Saloum," 308–310; Noirot, "Notice," 176; Pinet-Laprade, "Notice," 138–139. See also "Coutumes sérères," ANS 1G26/104, 1–9.
14. Martin et al., "Trois documents," 67–75; Aujas, "Sérères," 308.
15. G. Duchemin, "L'organisation religieuse et son rôle politique dans le royaume sérère du Sine (Sénégal)," *Conferencia Internacional dos Africanistas Occidentais* 5: 369–376 (1952); Gastellu, "Autonomie," 133; Klein, *Islam*, 11, 18.
16. Aujas, "Sérères," 300; Diagne, *Pouvoir*, 73–80. Galvan, *The State*, 57, coins the term "king-in-council."
17. Bourgeau, "Note," 18–19; Guy, "Sine-Saloum," 308–309.
18. On *lamaan*, see A. B. Diop, "La tenue foncière en milieu rural Wolof (Sénégal): Historique et actualité," *Notes Africaines* 118: 48–52 (1968), 49; Pélissier, *Paysans*, 215–218. On federalism, see Galvan, *The State*, 55.
19. Factionalism is captured in correspondence between military officials in Joal and Kaolack, and the Governor of Gorée: see ANS 13G314 (1861–1883 period) and ANS 13G321 (1871–1893 period).
20. See Klein, *Islam*, 17–18, for a perspective on the precolonial state. For colonial descriptions, see Aujas, "Sérères," 300–301; Bourgeau, "Note," 19. For postindependence accounts, see Diagne, *Pouvoir*; L. S. Senghor, *Liberté I: Négritude et humanisme* (Paris: Le Seuil, 1964). See Galvan, *The State*, 72–103, on how the Gelwaar regime is variably remembered in the present.
21. Bourgeau, "Note," 18; Klein, *Islam*, 19.
22. Aujas, "Région"; Guy, "Sine-Saloum," 308; Gastellu, "Politique coloniale," 571.
23. Galvan, *The State*, 59–71.
24. For comments on *ceddo*, see Guy, "Sine-Saloum," 309; Klein, *Islam*, 172; and Noirot, "Notice," 176. D. Galvan, "Freehold becomes pawning: Adapting colonial property relations in the Siin region of Senegal," in Becker et al., *AOF: Réalités et héritages*, vol. 2, 907–942, provides an account of the demise of lamanal influence.
25. Barry, *Senegambia*, 3–4, 10–17; Curtin, *Economic Change*, 6, 13–29. Much remains to be learned about agricultural history in Senegambia. Researchers disagree on whether Seereer agropastoralism and land management practices

(like *lamanat*) originated in Fuuta Tooro or were developed in contact with Wolof farmers after the Seereer exodus; Diop, "Tenue foncière"; Galvan, *The State*, 52, 238n49; Pélissier, *Paysans*, 180–203. Archaeological research is beginning to provide time depth to these discussions with evidence of African rice cultivation (*Oryza glaberrima*) in Casamance for as long as two thousand years and millet (*Pennisetum*) along the Senegal River Valley for nearly as long; Linares de Sapir, "Shell middens"; S. K. McIntosh and H. Bocoum, "New perspectives on Sincu Bara, a first millennium site in the Senegal Valley," *African Archaeological Review* 17(1): 1–43 (2000), 32.

26. Pélissier, *Paysans*, 87, 89; "Paysans sérères," 112. As early as the mid-eighteenth century, sources mention the cultivation of small millet (*mac*, *pod*) and sorghum; Becker and Martin, "Mémoire," 47; Pruneau de Pommegorge, *Description*, 31. All millet types were well-adapted to local climatic conditions, with complementary soil preferences and vegetational cycles. Sorghum could be grown on heavier soils and matured later than small millet, which gave peasants flexibility with rainfall fluctuations.

27. Curtin, *Economic Change*, 28. On the socioreligious foundations of Seereer agriculture, see Dupire, *Sagesse sereer: Essais sur la pensée sereer Ndut* (Paris: Karthala, 1994), 97–125; Lericollais, *Sob*; Lericollais, *Paysans sereer*; Pélissier, *Paysans*; V. Martin and C. Becker, "Lieux de culte et emplacements célèbres dans les pays sereer (Sénégal)," *Bulletin de l'IFAN*, B, 41(1): 133–189 (1979). Land is central to sociopolitical relations in many African agrarian societies, e.g., P. Shipton, "Land and culture in tropical Africa: Soils, symbols, and the metaphysics of the mundane," *Annual Review of Anthropology* 23: 347–377 (1994).

28. For an early reference, see Brüe [late seventeenth century] in Corre, "Sérères," 3. Colonial sources on Seereer agriculture include G. Debien, "Journal du docteur Corre en pays Sérère (Décembre 1876–Janvier 1877)," *Bulletin de l'IFAN*, B, 26(3/4): 532–599 (1964), 598; Guy, "Sine-Saloum," 302; T. Lecard, "Notice sur les états Sérères et leurs productions," *Moniteur du Sénégal et Dépendances* 534: 393–395 (1866); Pinet-Laprade, "Notice," 152–153.

29. Bourgeau, "Note," 36; Corre, "Sérères," 7–8. Reynier, "Rapport," 18–19 contends that Seereer farmers, "unlike the Wolof, also know how to respect trees and enliven (*faire vivre*) the countryside"; also Rousseau, "Notes," 7. In effect, the focus placed by Murids on intensive cultivation lessened the commitment to soil regeneration and integrated landscape management; Galvan, *The State*, 67; Pélissier, *Paysans*, 336–362.

30. A. Lericollais, "La détérioration d'un terroir: Sob, en pays Sérèr (Sénégal)," *Études Rurales* 37–39: 113–128 (1970); Lericollais, *Paysans sereer*; Pélissier, *Paysans*, 225–299.

31. My description underscores features common to the Seereer agrarian landscape despite regional variation. For example, the enclosures, fallows, and tree conservation commonly found inland were much less developed on the coast, especially where salt flats prevailed; Pélissier, *Paysans*, 276–296.

32. On field configuration, see Pélissier, *Paysans*, 240–243, 258–259. Mentions of cotton and rice farming can be found in Lecard, "Notice," 393; Pélissier, "Paysans sérères," 115; Pinet-Laprade, "Notice," 152–153; and B. Reinwald, "'Though the Earth does not lie': Agriculture transitions in Siin (Senegal) during colonial rule," *Paideuma* 43: 143–169 (1997), 149. The *iler* has been a part of agricultural practices since at least the mid-fifteenth century; Crone, *Voyages of Cadamosto*, 42; Becker and Martin, "Mémoire," 47, 90–91n92.
33. Pélissier, *Paysans*, 252–260. See Roger [1823] in Monteilhet, "Documents," 89, for an early mention of the Seereer park. The fertilizing properties of *Faidherbia albida* (*sas* in Seereer) are recognized in local knowledge and captured in the old Seereer proverb, "five *sas* fill a granary with millet"; Pélissier, *Paysans*, 270–274; Lericollais, "Dégradation," 128–129.
34. Abelin, "Domaine," 517–521; Dupire et al., "Résidence," 338–342; Galvan, "Freehold," 910–924; Lericollais, *Sob*, 15–23; Pélissier, *Paysans*, 215–224. See also Becker et al., "Traditions villageoises"; Diouf, "Chronique"; Geismar, *Recueil*, 139–143.
35. D. Galvan, "The market meets sacred fire: Land pawning as institutional syncretism in inter-war Senegal," *African Economic History* 25: 9–41 (1997), 15; Diop, "Tenue foncière," 51.
36. Geismar, *Recueil*, 137–141, on this confusion. On ownership/stewardship, see J.-M. Gastellu, "Droit d'usage et propriété privée," in E. Le Bris, E. Le Roy, and F. Leimdorfer (eds.), *Enjeux fonciers en Afrique Noire*, 269–279 (Paris: Karthala, 1982), for a general discussion. Aujas, "Sérères," 323, for instance, describes the king as the proprietor of all the land in the kingdom, while his subjects only possessed use-rights. Bourgeau, "Notes," 58–59, qualifies this interpretation by adding that before the Gelwaar monarchy land was owned by the *lamaan* but that the latter were gradually dispossessed of their estates as a result of royal encroachment on lamanal territories. Yoro Dyao (in Gaden, "Légende," 130), by contrast, opines that *lamaan* were the actual proprietors of the land, while Geismar (*Recueil*, 147–148, 157–158) is emphatic that no one in Siin owned the land, and his description of the *lamaan* is consonant with a role of caretakers and resource managers; also Dulphy, "Étude," 39–41. In addition to revealing the difficulties that colonial observers had in grappling with alternative ideas of property, these disparities likely reflected local power struggles over land claims. These are visible, for example, in competing narratives of village founding that variously play up royal authority over land by anachronistically writing the king into origin stories or play down the significance of the state and founding lineages by omitting them from foundation tales; Galvan, "Freehold," 911.
37. Noirot, "Lettre à l'Administrateur de Dakar-Thiès" (Mar. 20, 1895), ANS 13G325.
38. Diop, "Tenue foncière," 49; Galvan, "Market," 13; Pélissier, *Paysans*, 134–136.

39. For a description of firstcomers and subsequent migrants, see Galvan, "Market"; also Brooks, *Landlords*; and Kopytoff, *African Frontier*, for analogous West African examples.
40. Galvan, *The State*; Guigou, "Changements," 271.
41. J.-M. Gastellu, "L'organisation du travail en milieu Serer Ol," in Gastellu and Delpech, *Maintenance sociale*, 11–104, 56; Lericollais, *Sob*, 78–79, 307–310; Mbodj, "Un exemple," 303–308; Pélissier, *Paysans*, 246–250. On colonial cash cropping, see Klein, "Colonial rule."
42. Lericollais, "Détérioration."
43. Bourgeau, "Note," 49–51; Dulphy, "Étude," 39–40. For contemporary reflections, see Dupire et al., "Résidence"; Galvan, "Freehold," 920n33; Gastellu, "Organisation"; Lericollais, *Sob*; and G. Pontié, B. Guigou, and A. Lericollais, "La gestion de la terre dans le Sine," in Lericollais, *Paysans sereer*, 145–194.
44. See maps in Martin and Becker, "Vestiges," 415, 417; Pélissier, "Paysans sérères," 106–107. From early twentieth-century census figures, Lericollais, *Sob*, 12, estimates regional densities to have been around fifty inhabitants per square kilometer. These dovetail with 1928 figures in Rousseau, "Notes," 39, 48, 52–53, 59, which shows that Siin-Saalum had a much higher proportion of larger villages than any other *cercle*. Becker and Martin, "Premiers recensements," I.15–I.19, shows much canton-to-canton consistency between demographic figures listed by Noirot in 1891 and Lefilliâtre in 1904.
45. For colonial accounts, see Aujas, "Sérères," 307; Bourgeau, "Note," 22, 42; Corre, "Sérères," 5–6; and Lecard, "Notice," 393. For descriptions shortly before and after independence, see Pélissier, *Paysans*, 231–233; Lericollais, *Sob*, 11; Gastellu, "Organisation," 27.
46. Reynier, "Rapport," 2–3; see also "Coutumes sérères," ANS 1G26/104, 10.
47. Noirot, "Notice," 168.
48. For example, Louveau [1936] in Dubois, "Serer," 86–87, 115; Pélissier, *Paysans*, 228; Reynier, "Rapport," 2–4; Rousseau, "Notes," 38.
49. Galvan, "Freehold," 916n25.
50. Bourgeau, "Note," 22. On the village park/village center dynamic, see Lericollais, *Sob*, 11.
51. Noirot, "Notice," 168.
52. Monteilhet, "Documents," 87; Debien, "Journal," 545, 547–548, 562, 593. Martin et al., "Trois documents," 65–66, note that familial concessions (*mbind*) were larger on the coast, while inland compounds were generally smaller with fewer residents. V. Martin, "Structure de la famille chez les Serer et les Wolof au Sénégal," *Population* 125(4): 771–796 (1970), 377, argues that larger familial densities and concessions correspond with areas that were loosely subjected to the kingdom's political rule or escaped it altogether. Using Noirot's 1891 census figures, Becker and Martin, "Premiers recensements," I.11–I.14, further shows that the largest villages were found in the north and northeast of Siin (ten villages with over eight hundred

residents) and that settlement size declined moving west, with four important localities in central Siin and four along the coast.

53. Aujas, "Sérères," 309; Bourgeau, "Note," 23; Carlus, "Sérères," 100. Noirot's 1891 census figures suggest that frontier areas had modest demographies, particularly in the region of Marout that defended the border with Saalum. Rousseau, "Notes," ANS 1G26/104, 39, points outs that in 1928 the smallest villages stood along the border with Bawol; cf. Becker and Martin, "Premiers recensements," I.15–I.19.

54. Gastellu, "Organisation"; Gastellu, *Égalitarisme*.

55. Aujas, "Sérères," 307; Bourgeau, "Note," 42. On the dynamics of accumulation, see J.-M. Gastellu, "Petit traité de matrilinéarité: L'accumulation dans deux sociétés rurales d'Afrique de l'Ouest," *Cahiers ORSTOM* (Série Sciences Humaines) 21(4): 413–432 (1985); B. Reinwald, "Changing family strategies as a response to colonial challenge: Microanalytic observations on Siin/Senegal 1890–1960," *History of the Family* 2(2): 183–195 (1997), 185–187. Gravrand, "Dynamisme," postulated that the *ngak* emerged as the principal unit of domestic economy in response to the introduction of cash crops; *ngak* are seen as offshoots of an original unpartitioned *mbind*, a single economic unit where households and social interests would have been more internally cohesive. Yet, Gastellu, *Égalitarisme*, 88–89, draws on testimonies by elderly informants to show that kitchens were already local centers of production-consumption before the arrival of the railway in 1908 and, thus, before the impact of peanuts began to be felt in Siin. The dual economic spheres described below would have stretched at least back into the nineteenth century.

56. C. Coquery-Vidrovitch, "Les paysans africains: Permanences et mutations," in C. Coquery-Vidrovitch (ed.), *Sociétés paysannes du Tiers-Monde*, 25–40 (Lille: Presses Universitaires de Lille, 1980); Klein, *Peasants in Africa*. In Siin, see Bourgeau, "Note," 36; Guy, "Sine-Saloum," 305; Martin et al., "Trois documents," 53; and Reynier, "Rapport," 5–6. On risk management strategies in peasant agriculture, see A. Chayanov, *The Theory of Peasant Economy* (Madison: University of Wisconsin Press, 1986); J. Scott, *The Moral Economy of Peasants: Rebellion and Subsistence in South Asia* (New Haven, CT: Yale University Press, 1976), 5–6, 13–55, 157–192; and E. Wolf, *Peasants* (New York: Prentice Hall, 1966), 1–59.

57. Gastellu, "Organisation," 29, 39; Gastellu, *Égalitarisme*, 130. See Aujas, "Sérères," 307–308.

58. The Seereer agricultural economy—with its intricate organization of production; division, prestations, and sharing of labor; allocation and use of foodstuffs; and management of crop revenues within kitchens and sublineages—cannot be reviewed in detail here but is exhaustively examined in Gastellu, *Égalitarisme*; Guigou, "Changements." Gastellu and Delpech, *Maintenance sociale*; and Gastellu, "Organisation," 63–72, 84, stress the importance of solidarity, reciprocity, and honor (*a sim*) in the Seereer economy. These

principles helped to cement relations, ensure subsistence in lean years, and ward off reliance on external credit, thus pursuing the twin principles of subsistence and collective saving. They also entwined less successful maternal groups in dense webs of symbolic debt and reciprocity and created uneven buildups of wealth and power among lineages. Reinwald, "Though the earth," and Reinwald, "Changing family strategies," analyze changes in sexual division of labor spurred by the introduction of peanut agriculture by mapping the decline of women's rice cultivation and the devaluation of female contributions to the household economy.

59. Bourgeau, "Note," 36; Gastellu, "Organisation," 49, 89.
60. For colonial references to cattle, see Guy, "Sine-Saloum," 303, 306; P. Lemire, "Notes sur les enterrements sérères," *Bulletin de l'IFAN*, B, 17: 330–332 (1955); and Pinet-Laprade, "Notice," 150. Modern analyses can be found in Gastellu, "Organisation," 29, 130; Guigou, "Changements," 189, 419; M. Dupire, "Funérailles et relations entre lignages dans une société bilinéaire: Les Serer (Sénégal)," *Anthropos* 72(1–2): 376–400 (1977); and Lericollais, *Paysans sereer*. See also Gastellu, "Petit traité," 426, on the symbolic properties of cattle in Seereer economy before and after colonialism, which dovetails with classic exposés of symbolic capital; e.g., Bourdieu, *Outline of a Theory of Practice*, 171–183; also J. Comaroff, *Body of Power, Spirit of Resistance* (Chicago: University of Chicago Press, 1985), 72–74ff.; J. Ferguson, "The bovine mystique: Power, property, and livestock in rural Lesotho," *Man* 20: 647–674 (1985); S. Hutchinson, *Nuer Dilemmas: Coping with Money, War, and the State* (Berkeley: University of California Press, 1996).
61. Corre, "Sérères," 14; Lasnet et al., *Mission*, 150; P. Vuillot, "Notes sur le Baol," *Renseignements Coloniaux* 6: 157–164 (1898), 160. Colonial debates over whether pottery was manufactured by commoners or casted specialists continue today. For instance, all the Seereer potters examined in Sall, *Traditions céramiques*, were exclusively griot women, but his sample for the Siin was quite small. Conversely, some of the male and female elders I informally interviewed in 2003 on the Petite Côte revealed that not all potters were casted artisans; also M. Diouf, "Forgerons Wolof du Kajoor; Forgerons Sereer du Siin et du Jegem: De l'époque coloniale à nos jours" (PhD diss., École des Hautes Études en Sciences Sociales, 1983), 266–267. These differences could reflect historical/regional variations in crafts production or recent changes in ceramic manufacture.
62. On ironworking, see Carlus "Sérères," 412, 414; Lasnet et al., *Mission*, 150. Cf. Diouf, "Forgerons," 265–293, which hypothesizes a transformation from an original Seereer forge, centered on the production of agricultural tools, to a metallurgical industry dominated by casted artisans manufacturing weapons for the aristocracy. On cotton production, see Gastellu, *Égalitarisme*, 107; Mbodj, "Un exemple," 48–49; Reinwald, "Though the earth," 150–151. Sources disagree as to whether textile production was a female or male craft, whether it was the product of specialist labor (by a

caste of griot weavers) or a domestic activity, or whether the handcrafted cloth industry was centrally controlled or local in expression; Becker and Martin, "Mémoire," 46; C. Becker and V. Martin, "Détails historiques et politiques, mémoire inédit de J. A. le Brasseur (1778)," *Bulletin de l'IFAN*, B, 39: 81–132 (1977), 112; Boilat, *Esquisses*, plate II; Pinet-Laprade, "Notice," 155; Guy, "Sine-Saloum," 305; Diouf, "Forgerons," 262. We can imagine a dual system on the eve of colonization combining a sphere controlled by the king with cloth produced in royal workshops used in long-distance commerce and a household-based system designed to meet local consumptions demands and exchanged on local markets—with some geographic and temporal variation. The historical record is silent about changes in the organization of precolonial or even colonial textile production; cf. R. Roberts, "Women's work and women's property: Household social relations in the Maraka textile industry of the nineteenth century," *Comparative Studies in Society and History* 26(2): 229–250 (1984).

63. Gastellu, *Égalitarisme*, 31–39. For a less optimistic assessment, see Guigou, "Changements," 91ff., 130–132, 144–145, 216–217, which correctly suggests that while labor relationships may appear relatively equal within the sublineage, social exchanges at different levels of analysis—within kitchens, between lineages, and among individuals—reveal hierarchical imbalances in decision making, access to resources, and economic power that benefit family heads, elders, and men. Guigou persuasively argues that the moral veneer of cooperation obscures how traditional Seereer institutions have been put at risk and reshaped by contradictions in the social fabric itself—between internal and external economic challenges, different communities of interest, subsistence- and sale-centered agriculture, and the spheres of production and accumulation. The tendency to disguise social tensions within economic spheres and the new forms of organization associated with their incorporation into larger structures is common to functionalist readings; see J. I. Guyer, "Household and community in African studies," *African Studies Review* 24(2/3): 87–137 (1981).
64. Reinwald, "Though the earth," 151–152.
65. Mbodj, "Un exemple," 333–334.
66. Aujas, "Sérères," 326, 328.
67. Mbodj, "Un exemple," 53–55, 336; M. Mbodj and C. Becker, "De la traite à la crise agricole. Historique des échanges commerciaux dans le Sine," in Lericollais, *Paysans sereer*, 96–116, 97, 99, 102; Noirot, "Notice," 176; also Brooks, *Landlords*, 23, 50, 55–56.
68. Pichard in Bérenger-Féraud, *Peuplades*, 19, also 18, 20, 279; Pinet-Laprade, "Notice," 154; Guy, "Sine-Saloum," 305; also Guy, "Rapport" (Nov. 18, 1888), ANS 13G321. See Carlus, "Sérères," 105, 411, on the moral turpitude of French commerce.
69. Boilat, *Esquisses*, 106–107ff.; Corre [1876–1877] in Debien, "Journal," 549, 598–599.

70. Diouf, "Forgerons"; Klein, "Colonial rule," 90–93; Sall, *Traditions céramiques*, 350–393; Trincaz, "Transformations," 33, documents a brief upswing in cotton weaving during the 1970s. See Roberts, *Two Worlds*, on the resilience of cloth production in Mali between colonial economic policy, artisanal industries, and local markets.
71. Lericollais, "Détérioration," 117.
72. Debien, "Journal," 585, 595–596, 548.
73. Pinet-Laprade, "Notice," 148–149; Bérenger-Féraud, *Peuplades*, 275–278; Carlus, "Sérères," 417–418, 419–420, 34–37; Aujas, "Sérères," 303.
74. Bourgeau, "Note," 62; Corre, "Sérères," 18–19; R.-P. Duby, "Notes géographiques. La Sénégambie (Afrique Occidentale)," *Les Missions Catholiques* 9: 303–307 (1877), 304–305; Geismar, *Recueil*, 127.
75. Corre in Debien, "Journal," 550.
76. L. Diouf, "Une excursion dans le Sine et le Saloum," *Les Missions Catholiques* 11: 371–373 (1879); Duby, "Notes"; R.-P. Ezanno, "Fadiout," *Bulletin du Comité d'Études Historiques et Scientifiques de l'A.O.F.* 4: 68–74 (1919), 70.
77. Duby, "Notes," 305–306. For colonial descriptions of fetishes in Siin, see Corre, "Sérères," 18–19; Diouf, "Excursion," 317. For earlier accounts, see Becker and Martin, "Détails," 102; A. de Sainct-Lô, *Relation du voyage du Cap-Verd* (Paris: François Targa, 1637), 126–136ff.
78. Bourgeau, "Note," 61, 62–65; also Vuillot, "Notes," 163.
79. Gravrand, *Visage*, 40.
80. Aujas, "Sérères," 304–305; Crétois, *Dictionnaire*, vol. 2, 261–262; Duby, "Notes," 305–306; Ezanno, "Fadiout," 73. More synthetically, see Martin and Becker, "Lieux," 142–143; M. Dupire, "Chasse rituelle, divination, et reconduction de l'ordre socio-politique chez les Serer du Sine (Sénégal)," *L'Homme* 16(1): 5–32 (1976); and Pélissier, *Paysans*, 213–214.
81. The most extensive ethnographic corpus on Seereer religion was compiled by Father Gravrand over a nearly forty-year missionary career: H. Gravrand, "Rites d'initiation et vie en société chez les Sérères du Sénégal," *Afrique-Documents* 52: 129–144 (1960); Gravrand, *Visage*, 36–51; Gravrand, *"Cosaan,"* 217–228; and Gravrand, *"Pangool."* Gravrand's oeuvre is sometimes criticized for its tendency to produce deeply "Christianized" readings of Seereer religion; Martin and Becker, "Lieux," 141. For helpful treatments of Seereer religious/ritual philosophy, see Dupire "Chasse"; Faye, *Thème de la mort*; and Reinwald, "Though the earth," 145–147.
82. Gravrand, *"Cosaan,"* 40–44; Pélissier, *Paysans*, 213. Trincaz, "Transformations," captures the malaise fostered by the *Terres Neuves* relocation program to eastern Saalum from the 1930s to the 1970s.
83. Galvan, "Market," 13; also Becker et al., "Traditions villageoises"; Diouf, "Chronique"; Gravrand, *"Cosaan"*; Sarr, "Histoire du Sine-Saloum."
84. On funerary practices, see L. Aujas, "Funérailles royales et ordre de succession chez les Sérères du Sine," *Bulletin du Comité d'Études Historiques et Scientifiques de l'A.O.F.* 8: 501–508 (1927); Boilat, *Esquisses*, 99–100, 177;

Bourgeau, "Note," 62–63; Corre, "Sérères," 2, 18; Ezanno, "Fadiout," 71; Pinet-Laprade, "Notice," 149–150. For a synopsis of continuities in burial practices, see C. Becker and V. Martin, "Rites de sépulture préislamiques au Sénégal et vestiges protohistoriques," *Archives Suisses d'Anthropologie Générale* 46: 261–293 (1982), 267, 275, 280–282. For a recent archaeological synthesis, see J.-P. Cros, L. Laporte, and A. Gallay, "Pratiques funéraires dans le mégalithisme sénégambien; Décryptages et révisions," *Afrique: Archéologie & Arts* 9: 67–84 (2013).

85. On France's pragmatic Islamic diplomacy, see M. Klein, "Social and economic factors in the Muslim revolutions in Senegambia," *Journal of African History* 13: 419–441 (1972), 440–441; Cruise O'Brien, *Saints and Politicians*, 87–111; and D. Robinson, *Paths of Accommodation: Muslim Societies and French Colonial Authorities in Senegal and Mauritania, 1880–1920* (Athens: Ohio University Press, 2000).

86. Roger [1823] in Monteilhet, "Documents," 87, writes that of the three quarters making up Joal at the time of his visit, "two are inhabited by Mahometan Sérères; the third one by negroes claiming to be Christians and descendants of the Portuguese who once occupied the coast." The presence of a sizable Muslim community could denote Roger's passing knowledge of Joal, but it also underscores the cultural and religious diversity of the Seereer coast.

87. On these confrontations, see Aujas, "Sérères," 303; Boilat, *Esquisses*, 79–80ff.; Corre, "Sérères," 19–20; Duby, "Notes"; and Lamoise, "Excursion au royaume sérère," *Les Missions Catholiques* 10: 292–293 (1878). The history of nineteenth-century Christian missionization is reviewed in M. Klein, *Islam*, 43–62; and E. Foster, *Faith in Empire: Religion, Politics, and Colonial Rule in French Senegal, 1880–1940* (Stanford, CA: Stanford University Press, 2013).

88. E.g., Gastellu, "Organisation," 9; Ezanno, "Fadiout"; and Gravrand, *Visage*. For religious statistics postindependence, see Martin and Becker, "Lieux," 134–135; and Becker and Mbodj, "Dynamique," 69–72. According to Cruise O'Brien, *Mourides*, 77, the Murid population in the Siin-Saalum region grew almost seventyfold in forty years, from one thousand disciples in 1912 to 69,995 in the 1950s.

89. Boilat, *Esquisses*; and Sainct-Lô, *Relation*. See also D. H. Jones, "The Catholic mission and some aspects of assimilation in Senegal, 1817–1852," *Journal of African History* 21: 323–340 (1980); Searing, "No kings"; and J. Searing, "Conversion to Islam: Military recruitment and generational conflict in a Sereer-Safèn village (Bandia), 1920–38," *Journal of African History* 44: 7394 (2003). For broader analyses of religious dynamism, see inter alia J. Fernandez, *Bwiti: An Ethnography of the Religious Imagination* (Princeton, NJ: Princeton University Press, 1982); C. Stewart and R. Shaw, *Syncretism/Anti-Syncretism: The Politics of Religious Synthesis* (New York: Routledge, 1994); Peel, *Religious Encounter*; and A. Masquelier, *Prayer Has Spoiled Everything* (Durham, NC: Duke University Press, 2001).

90. Mbodj, "Un exemple," 131; also Galvan, *The State*, 20–32, ch. 3; Gravrand,

Visage; and Martin and Becker, "Lieux," 136–137. On religious syncretism in Siin, see Aujas, "Sérères," 303; Corre, "Sérères," 11; Diouf, "Excursion," 371–372; and Guy, "Sine-Saloum," 306. See Boilat, *Esquisses*, 20–21, 99–117; and J. Boulègue, *Les Luso-Africains de Sénégambie* (Lisbon: Gráfica Imperial, LDA, 1989), on Luso-African settlements.

91. Guigou, "Changements," 27.
92. Mitchell, "Imperial landscape." Also P. Carter, *The Road to Botany Bay: An Exploration of Landscape and History* (Minneapolis: University of Minnesota Press, 2010); and Moore et al., *Race*, on the poetics of landscape, nature, and fantasies of imperial power.
93. P. Landau, "Amazing distance: Pictures and people in Africa," in P. Landau and D. Kapin (eds.), *Images and Empires: Visuality in Colonial and Postcolonial Africa*, 1–40 (Berkeley: University of California Press, 2002), 16ff.; also R. Barthes, *Mythologies* (London: Paladin, 1972), 110. On "argument of images," see Fernandez, *Bwiti*, xix–xx, 531, 546–564. That said, ethnic vignettes in Senegal present an ambiguous genealogy, at once indebted to Orientalist representations and rooted in an earlier tradition of ethnic stereotypy in Senegal, perhaps best captured by the watercolor plates adorning Boilat's *Esquisses sénégalaises*; see M. Hinchman, "When stereotypes go left: An African priest in 19th-century Senegal," *Mots Pluriels* 10 (1999), on the co-constitution of Boilat's imagery.
94. On photographic images, see R. Barthes, *Camera Lucida* (New York: Wang and Hill, 1982); Benjamin, "A short history"; S. Sontag, *On Photography* (New York: Anchor Books, 1990). On visuality and imperial power, see Landau and Kaspin, *Images and Empires*; D. Prochaska, "Fantasia of the photothèque: French postcard views of colonial Senegal," *African Arts* 24: 40–47 (1991); and N. Bancel, P. Blanchard, and L. Gervereau (eds.), *Images et colonies; Iconographie et propagande coloniale sur l'Afrique française de 1880 à 1960* (Paris: La Découverte, 1993). See also C. Hodeir, "Decentering the gaze at French colonial expeditions," in Landau and Kaspin, *Images and Empires*, 233–252; and J.-M. Beurgougniou, R. Clignet, and P. David, *"Villages noirs" et visiteurs africains et malgaches en France et en Europe (1870–1940)* (Paris: Karthala, 2001), on discourses and performances of African identity in French colonial exhibitions. We should not overstate the objectifying magic of photography. By virtue of their indexicality, pictures allow visual details—colonial commodities, among others—to leak back into the frame, pointing to a world beyond and the modernity of peasants; see J. L. Comaroff, J. Comaroff, and D. Thomas, *Picturing a Colonial Past: The African Photographs of Isaac Schapera* (Chicago: University of Chicago Press, 2007), 6; Buck-Morss, *Dialectics of Seeing*. While descriptions of rural Senegal are often depictions *of* that evacuate the agency of those they depict, there existed a tradition of indigenous portraiture in Dakar, where African women purposefully deployed staged photography as a technology of self-making; H. N. Mustafa, "Portraits of modernity: Fashioning selves in

Dakarois popular photography," in Landau and Kaspin, *Images and Empires*, 172–192; cf. C. Pinney, *Camera Indica: The Social Life of Indian Photographs* (Chicago: University of Chicago Press, 1997), on colonial and postcolonial India.

95. Galvan, *The State*, 50, 71; Guigou, "Changements," 88–89.
96. On the interlacing of change/continuity, see M. Oland, S. Hart, and L. Frink (eds.), *Decolonizing Indigenous Histories: Exploring Prehistoric/Colonial Transitions in Archaeology* (Tucson: University of Arizona Press, 2012).

PART THREE INTRODUCTION

1. Becker and Martin, "Détails," 111.
2. Becker and Martin, "Mémoire," 42; Pruneau de Pommegorge, *Description*, 262–263; T. Clarkson, *Letters on the Slave Trade* (London, 1791); Lamiral, *L'Affrique et le peuple affriquain* (Paris: Dessenne, 1789).
3. Palmié, "Taste."
4. J. Guyer (ed.), "Jane Guyer's 'Marginal Gains: Monetary Transactions in Atlantic Africa,'" special issue, *African Studies Review* 50(2) (2007).
5. For synthetic accounts of politics and trade in Great Jolof, see Boulègue, *Grand Jolof*; Boulègue, *Royaumes wolof*, 21–24; and Brooks, *Landlords*, 61, 79–96. Some early Portuguese sources describe Jolof rulers as embattled, exiled or under the control of powerful noble families; e.g., Crone, *Voyages of Cadamosto*, 29–30; Gomes, *De la première découverte*, 52. Others comment on their awe-inspiring military might: e.g., Fernandes, *Description*, 7; D. P. Pereira [ca. 1506–1508], *Esmeraldo de situ orbis: Côte occidentale d'Afrique du sud Marocain au Gabon*, R. Mauny (ed.) (Bissau: Centro de Estudos da Guiné Portuguesa, 1956), 51; Donelha, *Account*, 128–137, 157–159. For oral traditions on Jolof, see F. Brigaud, *Histoire traditionnelle du Sénégal* (Saint-Louis: CRDS, 1962), 69–72; Cros, *Pays*, 43–51; V. Bomba, "Traditions about Ndiadiane Ndiaye, first *Buurba Djolof*," *Bulletin de l'IFAN*, B, 39(1): 1–35 (1977); and Gaden, "Légende," 16.
6. Boulègue, *Grand Jolof*, 153; Boulègue, *Royaumes wolof*, ch. 3. On economic reconfigurations following the opening of ocean routes, see Barry, *Royaume*, 70; Boulègue, *Grand Jolof*, 101.
7. Boulègue, *Grand Jolof*, 100, 141; Brooks, *Landlords*, 56–57; Thornton, *Africa and Africans*, 45, 53.
8. On dynamics of commerce, Crone, *Voyages of Cadamosto*; H. Münzer [1494], "Itinerarium," in Brásio, *Monumenta Missionaria Africana*, vol. 1, 214–253, 235–236; Almada, *Brief Treatise*, 78, 247, 263, 276, 281, 318, 367; J. Boulègue, "Relation de Francisco d'Andrade (1582)," *Bulletin de l'IFAN*, B, 29: 67–87 (1967), 83–85, 87; Gomes, *De la première découverte*, 50–54; Jobson, *Golden Trade*. Pereira, *Esmeraldo*, 47, 91, estimated that, in a heavy year, the Atlantic commerce drained as many as thirty-five hundred captives between the Senegal River and Sierra Leone. Slave exports to Portugal

appeared to slump in the late fifteenth century, which was accompanied by price inflation and a drop in exchange rates; Boulègue, *Grand Jolof,* 136. On the trans-Saharan commerce, see Austen, *Trans-Saharan Africa;* Webb, *Desert Frontier.*

9. Between 1651 and 1700, slave exports to the British and French West Indies increased from about one hundred thousand to three hundred thousand captives; Curtin, *Economic Change,* 101. On Senegambia's insertion into the South Atlantic system, see P. D. Curtin, *The Rise and Fall of the Plantation Complex: Essays in Atlantic History* (New York: Cambridge University Press, 1990).
10. Barry, *Senegambia,* 46–50; Curtin, *Economic Change,* 100–105; Wright, *The World,* 99–104, 105–106, 115–121. For accounts of French companies, see P. Cultru, *Histoire du Sénégal du XVe siècle à 1870* (Paris: Émile Larose, 1910); A. Delcourt, *La France et les établissements français au Sénégal entre 1713 et 1763* (Dakar: Mémoires IFAN No. 17, 1952); L. Jore, *Les établissements français sur la côte occidentale d'Afrique de 1758 à 1809* (Paris: Maisonneuve et Larose, 1965); and Ly, *La Compagnie du Sénégal* (Paris: Karthala, 1993).
11. The political history of European activities during the seventeenth and eighteenth centuries is detailed in Cultru, *Histoire;* A. Villard, *Histoire du Sénégal* (Dakar: Maurice Viale, 1943), 53–76; and Curtin, *Economic Change,* 92–152.
12. Searing, *West African Slavery,* 66–68. For accounts of chronic problems faced by Europeans, see anonymous letter (Aug. 15, 1706), ANSOM, $C^6 3$; de Saint-Robert, "Lettre à la Compagnie" (May 24, 1721), ANSOM $C^6 6$; de Saint-Robert, "Lettre à la Compagnie" (Dec. 28, 1722), ANSOM $C^6 7$; and letters from Blanchot and Aigremont to the Minister in January and February 1788, ANSOM $C^6 19$.
13. Following the unification of the kingdoms of Kajoor and Bawol, the Conseil de Gorée, "Lettre à la Compagnie" (May 31, 1727), ANSOM $C^6 11$, suggested deposing the new ruler, who now could bypass the French and trade directly with the English by arming his rivals with weapons and ammunitions. Similarly, Labat, *Nouvelle relation,* 4: 250–251, evokes the need to "[preserve] the equilibrium between these little princes" so that the Company can stay "in a position to impose them the law, prevent them to innovate anything either on customs." More generally, see Ly, *Compagnie,* 367; Barry, *Senegambia,* 112; C. Becker and V. Martin, "Kayor et Baol: Royaumes sénégalais et traite des esclaves au XVIIIe siècle," *Revue Française d'Histoire d'Outre-Mer* 62: 270–300 (1975), 283–290; and Searing, *West African Slavery,* ch. 5.
14. Curtin, *Economic Change,* 328; also R. Austen, *African Economic History* (Portsmouth, NH: Heinemann, 1987), 85.
15. Lemaire, *Voyages,* 72–73, reports 800 percent profits on slave transactions; D. Eltis, "The relative importance of slaves and commodities in the Atlantic trade of seventeenth-century Africa," *Journal of African History* 35(2): 237–249 (1994). For general accounts of eighteenth-century Atlantic slavery, see R. Blackburn, *The Overthrow of Colonial Slavery, 1776–1848* (London: Verso,

1989), 1–31; R. Stein, *The French Slave Trade in the Eighteenth Century: An Old Regime Business* (Madison: University of Wisconsin Press, 1979), 3–24. On shifts in Senegambia's quantitative contributions to the slave trade, see Curtin, *Economic Change*, 102; Becker and Martin, "Mémoire," 71–79; and Searing, *West African Slavery*, 32–33, 129–130. On the transition to west-central Africa, see Lovejoy, *Transformations*, 53–62. The most comprehensive source on Atlantic slavery can be found online here: Voyages: The Trans-Atlantic Slave Trade Database, http://www.slavevoyages.org.

16. For discussions of slave *imports* in northern Senegal, see Curtin, *Economic Change*, 164; Lovejoy, *Transformations*, 54; and Searing, *West African Slavery*, 28–34, 129–130. On the limits of slave trading in Wolof kingdoms, see also Klein, "Impact," 30; Despite gaps in time, space, and data quality, Becker and Martin, "Mémoire," 74–83, demonstrates clear temporal and regional fluctuations in slave exports; also Curtin, *Economic Change*, 184–185.
17. Curtin, *Economic Change*, 164–165; Richardson, "Slave exports," 13–14, 17, 19; Searing, *West African Slavery*, 152, 154. The upswing in gum production is nicely captured in Curtin, *Economic Change*, 327, 330, 331; P. D. Curtin, *Economic Change in Precolonial Africa: Supplementary Evidence* (Madison: University of Wisconsin Press, 1975), 96–99; also Becker and Martin, "Mémoire," 69–83.
18. On the O'Hara episode, see Le Brasseur, "Lettre au Ministre" (Apr. 29, 1777), ANSOM C^{6}17; also Barry, *Royaume*, 208–211; Searing, *West African Slavery*, 153n86.
19. Searing, *West African Slavery*, 29, 144; Curtin, *Economic Change*, 177–186, 187–188; Becker and Martin, "Kayor et Baol," 283.
20. In the words of Gorée's *Conseil Supérieur*, "Lettre" (Aug. 14, 1753), ANSOM C^{6}13: "Either we have to renounce this trade, which will considerably harm our commerce, or we will have to run the risk of watching our slaves starve to death." On slavery, food scarcity, and agriculture in Atlantic Senegal, see C. Becker, "Notes sur les conditions écologiques en Sénégambie aux 17e et 18e siècles," *African Economic History* 14: 167–216 (1985); and Searing, *West African Slavery*, 79, 129–134. On the colonial roots of food crises, see A. Logan, "'Why can't people feed themselves?': Archaeology as alternative archive of food security in Banda, Ghana," *American Anthropologist* 118(3): 508–524 (2016).
21. Curtin, *Economic Change*, 314, 325, 327–328; Searing, *West African Slavery*, 86.
22. Searing, *West African Slavery*, ch. 3. On linkages between Atlantic and Saharan markets, see Searing, *West African Slavery*, 82; and Webb, *Desert Frontier*.
23. Curtin, *Economic Change*, 209–211. The geography of iron production in Atlantic Senegambia is puzzling. Written accounts describe iron furnaces in Gajaaga, Bambuk, Bundu, and Fuuta Tooro, but they are largely silent about iron production in coastal states. Although iron *smithing* is reported on the coast, authors rarely indicate where coastal smiths obtained their iron or whether they smelted it. Archaeological research has documented

a vibrant 2,500-year metallurgical tradition in the Senegal River Valley, but it has largely focused on pre-Atlantic periods; see H. Bocoum, "Stagnation économique et traite atlantique (l'exemple de la sidérurgie)," in D. Samb (ed.), *Saint-Louis et l'esclavage*, 51–66 (Dakar: IFAN–Cheikh Anta Diop, 2000), for an exception; and D. J. Killick, "Iron working in the Middle Senegal Valley," in R. J. McIntosh, S. K. McIntosh, and H. Bocoum (eds.), *The Search for Takrur: Archaeological Excavations and Reconnaissance along the Middle Senegal Valley*, 191–280 (New Haven, CT: Yale University Press, 2016).

24. Klein, "Impact," 34, 40; also Barry, *Royaume*, 173–197; Curtin, *Economic Change*, 215–217; Delcourt, *La France*, 177–346; Webb, *Desert Frontier*, 97–131.
25. Klein, "Impact," 32; Searing, *West African Slavery*, ch. 5. For similar arguments elsewhere in Africa, see K. Ekholm, *Power and Prestige: The Rise and Fall of the Kongo Kingdom* (Uppsala: Skriv Service AB, 1972); R. Law, "Slaves, trade, and taxes: The material basis of political power in precolonial West Africa," *Research in Economic Anthropology* 1: 37–52 (1978); and Roberts, *Warriors*. On Lat Sukaabe, see Boulègue, *Royaumes wolof*, 327–356.
26. Barry, *Senegambia*, 81–93; Becker and Martin, "Kayor et Baol," 294; Searing, *"God Alone Is King."*
27. Searing, *West African Slavery*, 156. C. Becker, "Les effets démographiques de la traite des esclaves en Sénégambie: Esquisse d'une histoire des peuplements du XVIIe à la fin du XIXe siècle," in S. Daget (ed.), *De la traite à l'esclavage: Actes du Colloque International sur la Traite des Noirs, Nantes 1985*, 2: 71–110 (Paris: Société Française d'Histoire d'Outre-Mer, 1988), 77. On the disruption of countrysides, see C. Jannequin de Rochefort, *Voyage de Lybie au Royaume Senega* (Paris, 1643), 86–88; Conseil Supérieur, "Lettre à la Compagnie" (Jun. 3, 1754), ANSOM C[6]14; Lamiral, *Affrique*, 163–164.
28. M. Klein, "Servitude among the Wolof and Sereer of Senegambia," in S. Miers and I. Kopytoff (eds.), *Slavery in Africa: Historical and Anthropological Perspectives*, 335–363 (Madison: University of Wisconsin Press, 1977), 358.
29. Barry, *Royaume*, 102–103, 135–159; Barry, *Senegambia*, 50–54; Curtin, *Economic Change*, 46–58; Klein, "Social and economic factors"; and Searing, *"God Alone Is King."*
30. Barry, *Senegambia*, 88; Curtin, *Economic Change*, 26–27, 186; Klein, *Islam*, 16, 19–20, 26.
31. The traces of Islamization mentioned by Fernandes in the late fifteenth century had disappeared by the time of Almada's visit. D'Estrées reported no impact of the maraboutic wars on the Petite Côte in the 1670s. Concurrently, oral traditions identify three major conflicts that opposed Waagaan Faay, Jesanu Faay, and Jogo Ñilaan Juuf to marabouts, whose assaults were eventually repelled; Almada, *Brief Treatise*; Fernandes, *Description*; G. Thilmans and N. I. de Moraes, "Le passage à la Petite Côte du vice-amiral d'Estrées (1670)," *Bulletin de l'IFAN*, B, 39(1): 36–80; Diouf, "Chronique."
32. See review in Klein, "Slave trade."

CHAPTER FIVE

1. Faye, "Littérature," 1: 836–837.
2. Villard, *Histoire*, 42.
3. L. Faidherbe, "Notice historique sur le Cayor," *Bulletin de la Société de Géographie de Paris* (1883), 527–529.
4. Lemaire, *Voyages*; G. Thilmans, "La relation de François de Paris (1682–1683)," *Bulletin de l'IFAN*, B, 38(1): 1–51 (1976), 24–25. See also Diouf, *Kajoor*, on salient characters in Senegal's recent history.
5. While cornerstones of political history, dynastic traditions are not stable sites of interpretation. They unfold as fertile grounds of disagreement between aristocratic stakeholders, who dispute the accomplishments, moral character, and even legitimacy of political personages. They also coexist with popular corpuses of orality, like village traditions, which often feature a cast of nonaristocratic actors, stage humbler concerns and events, and sometimes criticize the (mis)deeds of the state. However, village traditions are complex transcripts and not bound to single principles. In Diohine, I listened to public recollections of village foundations that insisted on a special relationship of friendship, dependence, or subordination to a particular *buur* or to the monarchy in general; Becker et al., "Traditions villageoises"; Faye, "Littérature," vol. 1; and Galvan, *The State*.
6. S. K. McIntosh, "Pathways to complexity: An African perspective," in McIntosh, *Beyond Chiefdoms*, 1–30. See N. David and J. Sterner, "Wonderful society: The Burgess Shale creatures, Mandara polities, and the nature of prehistory," in McIntosh, *Beyond Chiefdoms*, 97–109; and J. I. Guyer and S. M. Eno Belinga, "Wealth in people as wealth in knowledge: Accumulation and composition in equatorial Africa," *Journal of African History* 36: 91–120 (1995), for exceptions. See A. Anghie, *Imperialism, Sovereignty, and the Making of International Law* (New York: Cambridge University Press, 2005), for a provocative analysis of how histories of colonialism and imperialism have configured the doctrine of sovereignty and, by extension, the political lexicon of the state.
7. Jameson, *Political Unconscious*.
8. M. Foucault, *"Society Must Be Defended." Lectures at the Collège de France, 1975–1976* (New York: Picador, 2003), 168.
9. See McIntosh, "Pathways," for a thorough review of some of these problems and how they have expulsed Africa from mainstream archaeological theorizing.
10. See C. Tilly, *Coercion, Capital and European States, AD 990–1990* (Cambridge: Blackwell, 1990); and S. Sassen, *Territory, Authority, Rights: From Medieval to Global Assemblages* (Princeton, NJ: Princeton University Press, 2006).
11. J. Lonsdale, "States and social processes in Africa: A historiographical survey," *African Studies Review* 24(2/3): 139–225 (1981).

12. M. Fortes and E. E. Evans-Pritchard, *African Political Systems* (London: Oxford University Press, 1940); R. Horton, "Stateless societies in the history of West Africa," in J. F. A. Ajayi and M. Crowder (eds.), *History of West Africa*, vol. 1, 78–119 (London: Longman, 1971); W. Hawthorne, "States and statelessness," in J. Parker and R. Reid (eds.), *Oxford Handbook of African History* (Oxford: Oxford University Press, 2013); David and Sterner, "Wonderful society."
13. For instance, Lonsdale, "States," uses the word *kingdom* to mark state-like arrangements before colonialism. The ethnological chiefdom, common in Polynesia (and, contestedly, in North America), has a more checkered use in African settings. *Chieftaincies*, *chiefships*, or *chefferies* often refer to single village headships appointed by colonial officers, which have limited correspondence in African political traditions. While the term lost traction in postindependence Senegal, it has endured as a valid modern category in places like Ghana; C. Lentz, "Chieftaincy has come to stay: La chefferie dans les sociétés acéphales du Nord-Ouest Ghana," *Cahiers d'Études Africaines* 40(3): 593–613 (2000); F. Zucarelli, "De la chefferie traditionnelle au canton: Évolution du canton colonial au Sénégal 1855–1960," *Cahiers d'Études Africaines* 50: 213–238 (1973).
14. See review of classic ethnographies in English-speaking Africa (Fallers on Buganda, Forde on the Yako, Fortes on the Tallensi, Gluckmann on the Lozi, Lloyd on the Yoruba, Ottenberg on Afikpo, Southall on the Alur) in McIntosh, "Pathways."
15. McIntosh, "Pathways," 4.
16. J. Herbst, *State and Power in Africa: Comparative Lessons in Authority and Control* (Princeton, NJ: Princeton University Press, 2000); cf. J. Goody, *Technology, Tradition and the State in Africa* (Cambridge: Cambridge University Press, 1971).
17. See T. Earle, *How Chiefs Come to Power: The Political Economy in Prehistory* (Stanford, CA: Stanford University Press, 1997), for a classic materialist distillation of power's economic roots.
18. Coquery-Vidrovitch, "Political economy"; Law, "Slaves"; Guyer and Eno Belinga, "Wealth in people."
19. E.g., Kea, *Settlements*; Law, *Slave Coast*; Roberts, *Warriors*; I. Wilks, *Asante in the Nineteenth Century: The Structure and Evolution of a Political Order* (Cambridge: Cambridge University Press, 1975); I. Wilks, *Forest of Gold: Essays on the Akan and the Kingdom of Asante* (Athens: Ohio University Press, 1993). These perspectives have also enjoyed currency in African archaeology. See, for instance, studies in C. R. DeCorse (ed.), *West Africa during the Atlantic Slave Trade: Archaeological Perspectives* (New York: Continuum, 2001); J. C. Monroe and A. Ogundiran (eds.), *Power and Landscape in Atlantic West Africa: Archaeological Perspectives* (Cambridge: Cambridge University Press, 2012); also J. C. Monroe, *The Precolonial State in West Africa: Building Power in Dahomey* (New York: Cambridge University Press, 2014), for an examination of state control in Dahomey.

20. See B. Diop, "Traite négrière, désertions rurales, et occupation du sol dans l'arrière-pays de Gorée," in D. Samb (ed.), *Gorée et l'esclavage*, 137–153 (Dakar: IFAN–Cheikh Anta Diop, 1997); B. Diop, "L'impact de la traite négrière sur l'habitat en pays Wolof," in D. Samb (ed.), *Saint-Louis et l'esclavage*, 177–195 (Dakar: IFAN–Cheikh Anta Diop, 2000).
21. This argument is forwarded by T. C. McCaskie, *State and Society in Precolonial Asante* (New York: Cambridge University Press, 1995), 18, who critiques Wilks's excessive Weberianization of the Asante state.
22. E. Bay, *Wives of the Leopard: Gender, Politics, and Culture in the Kingdom of Dahomey* (Charlottesville: University of Virginia Press, 1998); S. Greene, *Gender, Ethnicity and Social Change on the Upper Slave Coast: A History of the Anlo-Ewe* (Portsmouth, NH: Heinemann, 1996); McCaskie, *State and Society*; and Peel, *Religious Encounter*. For archaeological examples, S. Dueppen, *Egalitarian Revolution in the Savanna: The Origin of a West African Political System* (Bristol: Equinox, 2012); R. McIntosh, *Ancient Middle Niger: Urbanism and the Self-Organizing Landscape* (New York: Cambridge University Press, 2005); and N. Norman, "Fluid gods within cellular landscapes: Micro-monuments, ethnic pluralism, and the political landscape of Hueda, 1650–1727," *Azania* 49(1): 2–20 (2014). For classic treatment of stateless and segmentary societies during the Atlantic era, see R. Harms, *River of Wealth, River of Sorrow: The Central Zaire Basin in the Era of the Slave and Ivory Trade, 1500–1891* (New Haven, CT: Yale University Press, 1982); Horton, "Stateless societies"; and D. Northrup, *Trade without Rulers: Pre-Colonial Economic Development in South-Eastern Nigeria* (Oxford: Clarendon, 1978). On decentralized polities in southern Senegambia, see Baum, *Shrines*; and Hawthorne, *Planting Rice*.
23. David and Sterner, "Wonderful society," 99.
24. P. Abrams, "Notes on the difficulty of studying the state," *Journal of Historical Sociology* 1: 58–89 (1988); also J. Bartelson, *The Critique of the State* (New York: Cambridge University Press, 2001); F. Coronil, *The Magical State: Nature, Money and Modernity in Venezuela* (Chicago: University of Chicago Press, 1997); M. Taussig, *The Magic of the State* (New York: Routledge, 1997). For African meditations on sovereignty and fetishism, see M. McGovern, *Unmasking the State: Making Guinea Modern* (Chicago: University of Chicago Press, 2012); J. Obarrio, *The Spirit of the Laws in Mozambique* (Chicago: University of Chicago Press, 2014).
25. Bayart, *State in Africa*; T. Mitchell, "The limits of the state: Beyond statist approaches and their critics," *American Political Science Review* 85(1): 77–96 (1991); Trouillot, *Global Transformations*, 79–96.
26. D. Howland and L. White (eds.), *The State of Sovereignty: Territories, Laws, Populations* (Bloomington: Indiana University Press, 2009); J. Bartelson, *A Genealogy of Sovereignty* (New York: Cambridge University Press, 1995).
27. On nested, plural sovereignties, see Moore, *Suffering*; Obarrio, *Spirit*; J. Roitman, *Fiscal Disobedience*; D. Rutherford, *Laughing with Leviathan: Sovereignty*

and Audience in West Papua (Chicago: University of Chicago Press, 2012); and A. Simpson, *Mohawk Interruptus: Political Life across the Borders of Settler States* (Durham, NC: Duke University Press, 2014).

28. Rutherford, *Laughing*, ch. 1, for a discussion of sovereignty's binding relationship to audiences. On the matter of performance and its uptake, see also B. Arextaga, "Maddening states," *Annual Review of Anthropology* 32: 393–410 (2003); T. Blom Hansen and F. Stepputat (eds.), *States of Imagination: Ethnographic Explorations of the Postcolonial State* (Durham, NC: Duke University Press, 2002); T. Blom Hansen and F. Stepputat (eds.), *Sovereign Bodies: Citizens, Migrants and States in the Postcolonial World* (Princeton, NJ: Princeton University Press, 2005); Navarro-Yashin, *Faces*.
29. On hegemony and domination, see A. Gramsci, *Selections from the Prison Notebooks*, Q. Hoare and G. Nowell Smith (eds.) (New York: International Publishers, 1971); also Bayart, *State in Africa*; and R. Guha, *Domination without Hegemony: History and Power in Colonial India* (Cambridge, MA: Harvard University Press, 1998).
30. P. Corrigan and D. Sayer, *The Great Arch: English State Formation as Cultural Revolution* (Oxford: Blackwell, 1985). For other works, see N. Dirks, *The Hollow Crown* (Cambridge: Cambridge University Press, 1987); C. Geertz, *Negara: The Theatre State in Nineteenth-Century Bali* (Princeton, NJ: Princeton University Press, 1980); McCaskie, *State and Society*; G. Steinmetz (ed.), *State/Culture: State Formation after the Cultural Turn* (Ithaca, NY: Cornell University Press, 1999); and J.-P. Warnier, *The Pot-King: The Body and Technologies of Power* (Leiden: Brill, 2007).
31. Lefèbvre, *Production of Space*; Moore, *Suffering*.
32. As other disciplines, archaeology is wary of projecting modern categories into the political past; A. T. Smith, "Essential archaeological subject." Another concern has targeted the tendency to reduce ancient political regimes to rough caricatures on account of their distance from modern states; see C. Cobb, "Archaeology and the 'savage slot': Displacement and emplacement in the pre-modern world," *American Anthropologist* 107(4): 563–574 (2005), and Smith, *Political Landscape*.
33. A. T. Smith, "Archaeologies of sovereignty," *Annual Review of Anthropology* 40: 415–432 (2011).
34. Smith, *Political Landscape*, 77.
35. T. Inomata and L. Coben (eds.), *Spectacle, Performance, and Power in Premodern Complex Society* (Walnut Creek, CA: Altamira, 2006); A. T. Smith, "Rendering the political aesthetic: Political legitimacy in Urartian representations of the built environment," *Journal of Anthropological Archaeology* 19: 131–163 (2000); P. G. Johansen and A. Bauer (eds.), *The Archaeology of Politics: The Materiality of Political Practice and Action in the Past* (Newcastle upon Tyne: Cambridge Scholars Publishing, 2011).
36. But see S. Kus and V. Raharijaona, "Between earth and sky there are only

a few large boulders: Sovereignty and monumentality in central Madagascar," *Journal of Anthropological Archaeology* 17: 53–79 (1998), for a prescient look at these issues.

37. On the "concrete poetics" of state power in highland Madagascar and the linkages between "mind, muscle, and sensorium" upon which it rested: S. Kus and V. Raharijaona, "House to palace, village to state: Scaling up architecture and ideology," *American Anthropologist* 102: 98–113 (2000); and S. Kus and V. Raharijaona, "Visible and vocal: Sovereigns of the early Merina (Madagascar) state," in Inomata and Coben, *Archaeology of Performance,* 303–329. More generally, see K. Kristiansen and M. Rowlands, *Social Transformations in Archaeology: Local and Global Perspectives* (New York: Routledge, 1998), 386–428; McIntosh, *Beyond Chiefdoms*; J. Cameron Monroe, "'In the belly of Dan': Space, history, and power in precolonial Dahomey," *Current Anthropology* 52(6): 769–798 (2011); Monroe, *Precolonial State*; and Norman, "Liquid gods."
38. F. G. Richard, "Comment on J. Cameron Monroe, 'In the belly of Dan,'" *Current Anthropology* 52(6): 790–791 (2011).
39. L. Althusser, "Ideology and ideological state apparatuses (notes towards an investigation)," in S. Žižek (ed.), *Mapping Ideology,* 100–140 (London: Verso, 1994); also J. Scott, *Seeing like a State: How Certain Schemes to Improve the Human Condition Have Failed* (New Haven, CT: Yale University Press, 1998), for an overplayed account of state domination. But see N. Norman, "Hueda (Whydah) country and town: Archaeological perspectives on the rise and collapse of an African kingdom," *International Journal of African Historical Studies* 42(3): 387–410 (2009); Monroe and Ogundiran, *Power and Landscape.*
40. Smith, *Political Landscape,* 110.
41. L. Althusser, *Philosophy of the Encounter: Later Writings, 1978–1987* (London: Verso, 2006), discusses aleatory materialism; Massey, *For Space.*
42. J. C. Scott, *The Art of Not Being Governed: An Anarchist History of Upland Southeast Asia* (New Haven, CT: Yale University Press, 2009); Herbst, *State and Power.*
43. A. L. Stoler, "On degrees of imperial sovereignty," *Public Culture* 18(1): 125–146 (2006), on "gradated sovereignty."
44. The pulsing of political life between centralization and decentralization is not a new idea: e.g., E. Leach, *Political Systems of Highland Burma: A Study of Kachin Social Structures* (London: London School of Economics and Political Science, 1956); S. Tambiah, "The galactic polity: The structure of traditional kingdoms in Southeast Asia," *Annals of the New York Academy of Sciences* 293: 69–97 (1977). For African exposés, see Kopytoff, *African Frontier*; Horton, "Stateless societies"; Lonsdale, "States"; and David and Sterner, "Wonderful society."
45. Diouf, "Chronique," 705.
46. Diouf, "Chronique"; Gaden, "Légende," 130–132; Gravrand, *"Cosaan."*

47. Oral traditions are here reminiscent of Derrida's and Benjamin's anxious meditations on the hollow presence of sovereignty/law; J. Derrida, "Force of law: The 'mystical foundations of authority,'" *Cardozo Law Review* 11: 921–1045 (1990); W. Benjamin, "A critique of violence," in *Reflections: Essays, Aphorisms, Autobiographical Writings* (New York: Schocken Books, 1986).
48. Cros, *Pays*, 43–51; Diouf, "Chronique"; Noirot, "Notice," 444–445; Sarr, "Histoire du Sine-Saloum." See also Becker and Martin, "Essai."
49. Cadamosto, in Crone, *Voyages of Cadamosto*; Gomes, *De la première découverte*, 52; Münzer, "Itinerarium," 235; Donelha, *Description*, 21, 119, 269n180, 271, 273n186; J. Boulègue and R. Marquet, "Le voyage de Richard Rainolds en Sénégambie (1591)," *Bulletin de l'IFAN*, B, 33(1): 1–13 (1971). Becker and Martin, "Notes," 758–759n3, 763–764, offers critical reflections on these sources.
50. Dapper, in Thilmans, "Sénégal," 533, 539, 541. Dapper's account requires caution as it is a compilation of information gleaned from various earlier authors; also Almada, *Brief Treatise*, 27–28; Fr. Diego de Guadalcanal [1647], in N. I. de Moraes, *À la découverte de la Petite Côte au XVIIe siècle*, vol. 2 (Dakar: IFAN, 1995), 366; Lemaire, *Voyages*, 171.
51. For accounts of Siin's political situation during the eighteenth century, see N. de Saint-Robert, "Lettres" (Aug. 28, 1720; May 24, 1721), ANSOM $C^6$6; Conseil Supérieur du Sénégal, "Lettre à la Compagnie" (Jul. 11, 1754), ANSOM, $C^6$14; and Becker and Martin, "Mémoire," 38–40, 44. Le Brasseur's quote is from J. Le Brasseur, "Mémoire . . ." (1776), ANSOM $C^6$17. On the slave trade in Joal, see de Repentigny, "Lettre au Ministre" (Jun. 11, 1785), ANSOM $C^6$18; "Observations sur l'isle de Gorée données par M. de Rocheblave à Boniface son successeur" (n.d., probably late 1772), ANSOM $C^6$16.
52. Le Brasseur, "Questions" (1776), ANSOM DFC Gorée, No. 100. See also de Repentigny, "Mémoire du Roi pour servir d'instruction au Chevalier de Boufflers" (Nov. 1785), both in ANSOM $C^6$18. See also "Lettre No. 24" (1787), and Blanchot and Aigremont, "Lettres au Ministre" (Jan. 10, Feb. 3, Feb. 21, 1788), all in ANSOM $C^6$19.
53. Becker and Martin, "Mémoire"; Becker and Martin, "Détails"; also Klein, "Servitude."
54. Galvan, *The State*, ch. 2.
55. For methodological reasons, I keep these datasets separated. While collected according to the same procedures, the 2011 materials showed greater temporal resolution than the 2003 data, making it possible to discriminate between nineteenth- and twentieth-century occupations. This was rarely possible with the 2003 dataset, where these types of deposits often co-occur on the same sites. While the 2011 fieldwork recovered a disproportionate number of colonial-period sites, it was weaker on earlier periods, especially for the AD 1400–1700 range. Conversely, because the clearest patterns for the Atlantic era come from the 2003 data, the latter form the centerpiece of my analysis in this chapter.

56. Fieldwork methodologies are discussed in Richard, "From cosaan to colony," ch. 7.
57. F. G. Richard, National Science Foundation Annual Project Report, no. 1015989 (2011).
58. For accounts of village foundation, see Becker et al., "Traditions villageoises"; Diouf, "Chronique"; Gravrand, *"Cosaan."* On royal capitals, see Crone, *Voyages of Cadamosto,* 38; G. Loyer, *Relation du voyage du Royaume d'Issyny* (Paris: Arnoul Seneuze, 1714), 132–135; F. Shoberl, *Africa,* vol. 3 (London: R. Ackermann, 1824), 101. While the Atlantic-era trends described here hold for most areas in the Siin, they are complicated by settlement evidence collected in 2011 around Loul Sessène about thirty-five kilometers inland, where sites were sparse and poorly consolidated—a departure from phase Va (AD 1400–1700) vestiges elsewhere. This suggests some level of regional variability in residential history in the fifteenth and sixteenth centuries; Richard, National Science Foundation Report.
59. On seventeenth- and eighteenth-century instabilities, see Becker and Martin, "Mémoire," 39–40; Labat, *Nouvelle relation,* 4: 245; Mateo de Anguiano [1646–1647] in de Moraes, *À la découverte,* 2: 352. On nineteenth-century disruptions, see Boilat, *Esquisses;* H. Deschamps, *L'Afrique occidentale vue par un explorateur français, Gaspard Théodore Mollien* (Paris: Calmann-Lévy, 1967).
60. See, e.g., S. Diouf, *Fighting the Slave Trade: West African Strategies* (Oxford: James Currey, 2003); MacEachern, "Selling the iron for their shackles"; Searing, "No kings"; A. B. Stahl, "The slave trade as practice and memory. What are the Issues for archaeologists?" in C. Cameron (ed.), *Invisible Citizens: Captives and their Consequences,* 25–56 (Salt Lake City: University of Utah Press, 2008); and N. Swanepoel, "Socio-political change on a slave-raiding frontier: War, trade and 'big men' in nineteenth century Sisalaland, northern Ghana," *Journal of Conflict Archaeology* 1: 264–293 (2005).
61. Thiaw, "Archaeological investigation"; S. K. McIntosh, "Tools for understanding transformation and continuity in Senegambian society: 1500–1900," in DeCorse, *West Africa,* 14–37; A. Lawson, "Megaliths and Mande states: Sociopolitical change in the Gambia valley over the past two millennia" (PhD diss., University of Michigan, 2003); and C. Gokee, *Assembling the Village in Medieval Bambuk: An Archaeology of Interaction at Diouboye* (Sheffield: Equinox, 2016), ch. 9 and 10.
62. M. Faye, "La résidence royale de Jaxaw Siin: Histoire et archéologie" (master's thesis, Université Cheikh Anta Diop de Dakar, 2002), 48–75; Martin et al., "Trois documents," 67n2; and Becker and Martin, "Familles paternelles," 364.
63. Olivier, *Dark Abyss.*
64. T. C. McCaskie, "Accumulation, wealth, and belief in Asante history. I. To the close of the nineteenth century," *Africa* 53(1): 23–43 (1983). On temporality in oral traditions, see Barber, *I Could Speak,* 34, which examines the

Nigerian *oriki*, a historical genre of oral narration that exhausts the divide between history as factual chronicle versus history as political production. *Orikis* are palimpsests of historical moments, mobilized to evoke particular states in people. They evoke memories of the past without reducing them to the politics of the past in the present. See also R. Shaw, *Memories*, 13; and Cohen et al., *African Words*.

65. Galvan, *The State*, 54–55; also Gravrand, *"Pangool."* See M. Godelier, "Origins and formation: Processes of formation, diversity, and bases of the state," *International Social Science Journal* 32(4): 609–620 (1980), on the exchange of services.
66. On stranger-kings, see M. W. Helms, *Ulysses' Sail: An Ethnographic Odyssey of Power, Knowledge, and Geographical Distance* (Princeton, NJ: Princeton University Press, 1988); M. Sahlins, *Islands of History* (Chicago: University of Chicago Press, 1985). See Bayart, "Africa in the world," for a structural argument about Africa's extraversion and its historical openness to the outside as a source of symbolic and material power. For analyses of the ambiguous power of the foreign, see D. Rutherford, *Raiding the Land of the Foreigners* (Princeton, NJ: Princeton University Press, 2002); V. Rafael, *The Promise of the Foreign: Nationalism and the Technics of Translation in the Spanish Philippines* (Durham, NC: Duke University Press, 2005); and J. Siegel, *Objects and Objections of Ethnography* (New York: Fordham University Press, 2010).
67. Faye, "Littérature," vol. 1, 34–39, 46–49, 193–201. On Panga Yaay Saar, see also Diouf, "Chronique"; and Gravrand, *"Cosaan."*
68. See Faye, "Littérature," 2: 984–1012, for an analysis of valences of power in Seereer traditions. Faye derives the idea of "unconditional hospitality" from J. Derrida, *On Hospitality* (Stanford, CA: Stanford University Press, 2000). As the Siin kingdom stands astride identity and alterity, the paradox of true hospitality places the question of the state under the sign of impossibility. Again, Seereer moral thought shows Derridean echoes, for example, J. Derrida, *Rogues: Two Essays on Reason* (Stanford, CA: Stanford University Press, 2005), 100.
69. Becker and Martin, "Mémoire," 38.
70. Pélissier, *Paysans*; Dupire, "Chasse."
71. See E. DeMarrais, L. J. Castillo, and T. Earle, "Ideology, materialization, and power strategies," *Current Anthropology* 37(1): 15–31 (1996); G. M. Feinman and J. Marcus (eds.), *Archaic States* (Santa Fe, NM: School of American Research Press, 1998); Monroe, *Precolonial State*; and Smith, *Political Landscape*, for examples of state-controlled landscapes. C. Pinney, "Things happen: Or, from which moment does that object come?" in Miller, *Materiality*, 256–272, 269, on Adorno's implacable demand of objects.
72. Dapper, in Thilmans, "Sénégal," 541, also notes that warring factions had no interest in capturing places but sought to torch a few towns and villages. On wealth in people, see J. I. Guyer, "Wealth in people and self-realization

in equatorial Africa," *Man* 28: 243–265 (1993); Guyer and Eno Belinga, "Wealth in people"; and N. Norman, "Surplus houses: Palace politics in the Bight of Benin West Africa, AD 1650–1727," in C. T. Morehart and K. De Lucia (eds.), *Surplus: The Politics of Production and Strategies of Everyday Life*, 203–220 (Boulder: University of Colorado Press, 2015).

73. See Hansen and Stepputat, *Sovereign Bodies*, on the relationship between sovereignty and embodiment.
74. A. Weiner, "Cultural difference and the density of objects," *American Ethnologist* 21(1): 391–403 (1994).
75. For discussions of the intersection of ritual and politics, see J. and J. L. Comaroff (eds.), *Modernity and Its Malcontents: Ritual and Power in Postcolonial Africa* (Chicago: University of Chicago Press, 1993); and D. Kertzer, *Ritual, Politics, and Power* (New Haven, CT: Yale University Press, 1988).
76. Cadamosto, in Crone, *Voyages of Cadamosto*, 37.
77. S. A. MacEachern, "What was the Wandala state?" in Richard and MacDonald, *Ethnic Ambiguity*, 172–191. See also Dirks, *Hollow Crown*; and Geertz, *Negara*.
78. Le Brasseur, in Becker and Martin, "Détails," 102, writes that while normally respecting Siin's autonomy, in 1778 Kajoor and Bawol attacked the province because "they are persuaded that [its king] no longer is protected by the devils, since he has neglected to honor the cult of his fathers." On feasting, see J. Fleisher, "Ritual consumption and the politics of feasting on the eastern African coast, AD 700–1500," *Journal of World Prehistory* 23(4): 195–217 (2010); and N. Norman, "Feasts in motion: Archaeological views of parades, ancestral pageants, and socio-political process in the Hueda Kingdom, 1650–1727 AD," *Journal of World Prehistory* 23(4): 239–254 (2010). On elite consumption strategies in Senegambia, see Klein, "Impact," 29.
79. Seereer political rituals are described in A. Faye, *Thème de la mort*; M. Faye, "Résidence royale"; M. Faye, "Étude ethnographique et archéologique du pouvoir de la lingeer de Cupaan dans la royauté de Jaxaaw Siin" (master's thesis, Université Cheikh Anta Diop de Dakar, 2003); Dupire, "Chasse"; Dupire et al., "Résidence." Oral traditions underline the mystical potency of monarchs, which is sometimes mirrored in written history; e.g., Diouf, "Chronique"; Sarr, "Histoire du Sine-Saloum"; Becker and Martin, "Détails." Great magician-kings were also depicted as apt traders, businessmen, and politicians—echoes here of contemporary political discourse on witchcraft as a power at once dangerous and coveted: e.g., Bayart, *State in Africa*; P. Geschiere, *The Modernity of Witchcraft: Politics and the Occult in Postcolonial Africa* (Charlottesville: University of Virginia Press, 1999); Shaw, *Memories*.
80. Boilat, *Esquisses*, 178–179.
81. Aujas, "Funérailles"; Becker and Martin, "Rites."
82. E.g., E. Kantorowicz, *The King's Two Bodies: Study in Medieval Political Theology* (Princeton, NJ: Princeton University Press, 1997). See also Warnier, *Pot-*

King, on the semiotic properties of the king's body in west-central Africa. Faye, "Littérature," also reminds us that, like Seereer newborns thought to be reincarnations of deceased parents, Seereer kings were believed to embody the essence of earlier monarchs.

83. Dupire, "Chasse," 26–27.
84. Aujas, "Sérères," 303–304; Bourgeau, "Note," 21; Duchemin, "Organisation," 374–376.
85. P. Clastres, *Society against the State* (London: Zone Books, 1989). Boilat, *Esquisses*, 171, reports that Fadiouth was one of Siin's most prosperous villages because its main *fangool* could cause the abrupt death of horses, which kept the *ceddo* of Kajoor or Bawol from attacking the village.
86. Thus, while acting historically as a force of maintenance in Siin, the ritual domain also promoted innovation; e.g., Baum, *Shrines*; Comaroff and Comaroff, *Modernity*; and Shaw, *Memories*.
87. De Paris, in Thilmans, "Relation," 25; S. M. X. Golberry, *Fragments d'un voyage en Afrique*, vol. 1 (Paris: Treuttel et Würtz, 1802), 111; Peyries de Jalvert, "Mémoire" (n.d., probably 1752), ANSOM $C^6$13; Gallais, in Boilat, *Esquisses*, 146–147; Demanet [1764], in J. Roger de Benoist, *Histoire de l'Église catholique au Sénégal* (Paris: Karthala, 2007), 73; and Gastellu, "Autonomie."
88. Cf. J. Brooks, C. DeCorse, and J. Walton (eds.), *Small Worlds: Method, Meaning, and Narrative in Microhistory* (Santa Fe, NM: School for Advanced Research Press, 2008), for research exploring intersections between microhistory and archaeology.
89. Faye, "Littérature," 2: 1006.
90. Elders in Diohine recounted a time—probably the late nineteenth century—when the *buur* in Diakhao tried to meddle with the election of the village chief (a process normally worked out within the village elders' council). They joked that villagers managed to delegitimize the royal representative sent to oversee the elections—and thus the king's intrusion in village affairs—by creating disparaging rumors about his mental health; interview with Biram Siga Faye (Feb. 15, 2013).
91. V. Bruzzone, "La royauté de la mer à Fadiouth: Aspect de la religion traditionnelle seereer (Sénégal)" (PhD diss., Université Cheikh Anta Diop de Dakar, 1997), 169.
92. Interviews with Biram Siga Faye (Feb. 15, 2013) and Gouré Diouf, Diale Diouf, and Bisan Diouf (Feb. 19, 2013).
93. Mbembe, *On the Postcolony*; J. and J. L. Comaroff (eds.), *Law and Disorder in the Postcolony* (Chicago: University of Chicago Press, 2006).

CHAPTER SIX

1. G. E. de Azurara [1441–1448], *The Chronicle of the Discovery and Conquest of Guinea*, vol. 2 (London: Hakluyt Society, 1899), 192.
2. Ibid., 176–183. See M. Newitt, *A History of Portuguese Overseas Expansion,*

1400–1668 (New York: Routledge, 2005), ch. 2–3, on early Portuguese explorations.

3. D. Graeber, "Fetishism as social creativity: Or, fetishes are gods in the process of construction," *Anthropological Theory* 5(4): 407–436 (2006).
4. S. Alpern, "What Africans got for their slaves? A master's list of European trade goods," *History in Africa* 22: 5–43 (1995); McCaskie, "Accumulation"; G. Metcalf, "A microcosm of why Africans sold slaves: Akan consumption patterns in the 1770s," *Journal of African History* 28: 377–394 (1987); Miller, *Way of Death*; J. Prestholdt, "On the global repercussions of East African consumerism," *American Historical Review* 109(3): 755–781 (2004); and J. Searing, *West African Slavery*. For archaeological perspectives on African cultural consumption, see A. Ogundiran, "Of small things remembered: Beads, cowries and cultural translations of the Atlantic experience in Yorubaland," *International Journal of African Historical Studies* 35(2/3): 427–457 (2002); Stahl, "Colonial entanglements"; S. Wynne-Jones, *A Material Culture: Consumption and Materiality on the Coast of Precolonial East Africa* (Oxford: Oxford University Press, 2016).
5. B. Brown, "Thing theory," *Critical Inquiry* 28(1): 1–22 (2001), 4.
6. Histories of technological resilience can be found elsewhere in West Africa: P. de Barros, "The effects of the slave trade on the Bassar ironworking society of Togo," in DeCorse, *West Africa*, 59–80; A. Logan and M. D. Cruz, "Gendered taskscapes: Food, farming, and craft production in Banda, Ghana in the eighteenth to twenty-first centuries," *African Archaeological Review* 31: 203–231 (2014).
7. Brown, "Thing theory," 5; Ly, *Compagnie*, 251.
8. A. Appadurai, "Introduction: Commodities and politics of value," in A. Appadurai (ed.), *The Social Life of Things: Commodities in Cultural Perspective*, 3–62 (New York: Cambridge University Press, 1986), 5.
9. Brown, "Thing theory," 7.
10. C. Steiner, "Another image of Africa: Toward an ethnohistory of European cloth marketed in West Africa, 1873–1960," *Ethnohistory* 32: 91–110 (1985); Prestholdt, *Domesticating*; also Stahl, "Colonial entanglements."
11. Appadurai, "Introduction," 4. In given cultural and historical milieus, regimes of value orchestrate relationships between people and things; they endow various objects with value, determine their spheres of circulation, and regulate conversion and equivalence between them; see F. Myers (ed.), *Empire of Things: Regimes of Value and Material Culture* (Santa Fe, NM: School of American Research Press, 2001); and D. Graeber, *Toward an Anthropological Theory of Value: The False Coin of Our Own Dreams* (New York: Palgrave, 2001). For general literature on object circulation and consumption, see Appadurai, *Social Life of Things*; Miller, *Material Culture*; Munn, *Fame of Gawa*; M. Sahlins, "Cosmologies of capitalism: The trans-Pacific sector of 'The World System,'" in N. Dirks, G. Eley, and S. Ortner (eds.) *Culture/Power/History: A Reader in Contemporary Social Theory*, 412–455 (Princeton, NJ: Princeton University

Press, 1994); P. Spyer, *The Memory of Trade: Modernity's Entanglements on an Eastern Indonesian Island* (Durham, NC: Duke University Press, 1997); and Thomas, *Entangled Objects*. For perspectives on Africa, see T. Burke, *Lifebuoy Men, Lux Women: Commodification, Consumption, and Cleanliness in Modern Mozambique* (Durham, NC: Duke University Press, 1996); DeCorse, *Archaeology of Elmina*; J. I. Guyer (ed.), *Money Matters: Instability, Values and Social Payments in the Modern History of West African Communities* (Portsmouth, NH: Heinemann, 1995); K. G. Kelly, "Indigenous responses to colonial encounters on the West African coast: Hueda and Dahomey from the 17th through 19th centuries," in C. L. Lyons and J. Papadopoulos (eds.), *The Archaeology of Colonialism*, 96–120 (Los Angeles: Getty Research Institute, 2002); S. Newell, *The Modernity Bluff: Crime, Consumption and Modernity in Côte d'Ivoire* (Chicago: University of Chicago Press, 2014); A. Ogundiran, "Of small things"; C. Piot, "Of persons and things: Some reflections on African spheres of exchange," *Man* 26: 405–424 (1991); Piot, "Of slaves and the gift"; Piot, *Remotely Global*; Prestholdt, *Domesticating*; Stahl, *Making History*; and Weiss, *Making and Unmaking*.

12. Appadurai, "Introduction"; also Myers, *Empire of Things*; Thomas, *Entangled Objects*; W. M. J. van Binsbergen and P. Geschiere (eds.), *Commodification: Things, Agency, and Identities (The Social Life of Things Revisited)* (Münster: Lit Verlag, 1999); and Hicks and Beaudry, *Oxford Handbook*.
13. K. Marx, *Capital: A Critical Analysis of Capitalist Production*, vol. 1 (New York: International Publishers, 1967 [1867]); G. Simmel, *The Philosophy of Money* (New York: Routledge, 2004 [1907]). For the former, value inhered in production, as an embodiment of labor and concrete action, while for the latter, it emerged at the moment of exchange, a function of how much one desires an object and is willing to give for it. Appadurai, "Introduction," is heavily influenced by Simmel; Graeber, *Anthropological Theory of Value*, esp. ch. 2 and 3, roots his account in an expanded Marxist framework.
14. J. Guyer, *Marginal Gains: Monetary Transactions in Atlantic Africa* (Chicago: University of Chicago Press, 2004); P. Spyer (ed.), *Border Fetishisms: Material Objects in Unstable Spaces* (New York: Routledge, 1998); and M. Rowlands, "The archaeology of colonialism and constituting the African peasantry," in D. Miller, M. Rowland, and C. Tilley (eds.), *Domination and Resistance*, 261–283 (London: Unwin Hyman, 1989); and Guyer, "Jane Guyer's 'Marginal Gains.'" The literature on fetishes is replete with social creativity, e.g., W. Pietz, "The problem of the fetish, I," *Res* 9: 5–17 (1985); W. Pietz, "The problem of the fetish, II: The origin of the fetish," *Res* 13: 23–45 (1987); W. Pietz, "The problem of the fetish, IIIa: Bosman's Guinea and the Enlightenment theory of fetishism," *Res* 16: 105–124 (1988); Graeber, "Fetishism."
15. P. Bourdieu, *Distinction: A Social Critique of the Judgment of Taste* (Cambridge, MA: Harvard University Press, 1984).
16. I. Kopytoff, "The cultural biography of things: Commoditization as process," in Appadurai, *Social Life of Things*, 64–91. See also C. J. Holtorf,

"Notes on the life-history of a pot sherd," *Journal of Material Culture* 7(1): 49–71 (2002); C. Gosden and Y. Marshall, "The cultural biography of objects," *World Archaeology* 31(2): 169–178 (1999); G. Lucas, *The Archaeology of Time* (New York: Routledge, 2004); L. Meskell, *Object Worlds in Ancient Egypt: Material Biographies Past and Present* (Oxford: Berg, 2004); L Meskell (ed.), *Archaeologies of Materiality* (Malden, MA: Wiley, 2005).

17. For genealogical perspectives, see T. Pauketat, "Practice and history in archaeology: An emerging paradigm," *Anthropological Theory* 1(1): 73–98 (2001); T. Pauketat and S. Alt, "Agency in a postmold? Physicality and the archaeology of culture-making," *Journal of Archaeological Method and Theory* 12(3): 213–236 (2005); B. Mills and W. Walker (eds.), *Memory Work* (Santa Fe, NM: School for Advanced Research Press, 2008); R. Joyce and J. Pollard, "Archaeological assemblages and practices of deposition," in Beaudry and Hicks, *Oxford Handbook*, 291–309; S. Wynne-Jones, "Biographies of practice and the negotiation of Swahili at nineteenth-century Vumba," in Richard, *Materializing Colonial Encounters*, 155–176; and R. Joyce and S. Gillespie (eds.), *Things in Motion: Object Itineraries in Anthropological Practice* (Santa Fe, NM: School for Advanced Research Press, 2015).
18. Appadurai, "Introduction," 13.
19. Thomas, *Entangled Objects*; L. Tsing, "The global situation," *Cultural Anthropology* 15(3): 327–360 (2000). For archaeological applications, M. Dietler, "Consumption, agency, and cultural entanglement: Theoretical implications of a Mediterranean colonial encounter," in J. C. Cusick (ed.), *Studies in Culture Contact: Interaction, Culture Change, and Archaeology*, 288–315 (Carbondale, IL: Center for Archaeological Investigations, 1998); Hicks and Beaudry, *Oxford Handbook*; Stahl, "Colonial entanglements"; A. Stahl, "Circulations through worlds apart: Georgian and Victorian England in an African mirror," in Richard, *Materializing Colonial Encounters*, 71–94.
20. Change encompasses a diverse palette of expressions, including quantitative/qualitative transformations, interruptions, reversals, and cyclical recurrence, with different implications for community histories. Changes can be discrete or generalized, distributed or wholesale, mutually amplifying or contradictory. Similar observations can be made about continuities. Processes such as the intensification of a trend, modulations of a cultural theme, and slowdowns or accelerations in consumption can be apprehended either as change or continuity—indeed, two aspects of a same historical process; S. Silliman, "Change and continuity, practice and memory: Native American persistence in colonial New England," *American Antiquity* 74(2): 211–230 (2009); M. Liebmann, *Revolt: An Archaeological History of Pueblo Resistance and Revitalization in 17th Century New Mexico* (Tucson: University of Arizona Press, 2012); F. G. Richard, "Lost in tradition, found in transition: Scales of indigenous histories in Siin, Senegal," in Oland et al., *Decolonizing Indigenous Histories*, 132–157; A. Roddick and C. Hastorf, "Traditions brought to the surface: Continuity, innovation, and change in

Late Formative Period, Taraco peninsula, Bolivia," *Cambridge Archaeological Review* 20(2): 157–178 (2010).

21. J. Comaroff and J. L. Comaroff, "Ethnography on an awkward scale: Post-colonial anthropology and the violence of abstraction," *Ethnography* 4(2): 147–179 (2003).
22. On communities of practice, see Roddick and Stahl, *Knowledge in Motion*.
23. S. Mintz, *Sweetness and Power* (New York: Penguin, 1985); B. Weiss, *Sacred Trees, Bitter Harvests: Globalizing Coffee in Northwest Tanzania* (Portsmouth, NH: Heinemann, 2003); B. Chalfin, *Shea Butter Republic: State Power, Global Markets, and the Making of an Indigenous Commodity* (New York: Routledge, 2004); Tsing, "On non-scalability"; and Stahl, "Circulations."
24. Appadurai, *Modernity*; Prestholdt, *Domesticating*.
25. Ferguson, *Global Shadows*; Tsing, *Friction*; and Trouillot, *Global Transformations*.
26. W. MacGaffey, "Dialogues of the deaf: Europeans on the coast of Africa," in S. Schwartz (ed.), *Implicit Understandings*, 249–267 (New York: Cambridge University Press, 1994); Comaroff and Comaroff, *Of Revelation*, vol. 2; Sahlins, "Cosmologies"; and Hall, *Archaeology and the Modern World*.
27. On the antiquity of Saharan exchanges, see S. Magnavita, "Initial encounters: Seeking traces of ancient trade connections between West Africa and the wider world," *Afriques* 4 (2013), http://afriques.revues.org/1145; and A Dowler and E. R. Galvin (eds.), *Money, Trade, and Trade Routes in Pre-Islamic North Africa* (London: British Museum Press, 2011).
28. Brooks, *Landlords*; Boulègue, *Royaumes wolof*, 124–128, 132–142. For observations on commerce in trading posts, see Gomes, *De la première découverte*; Pereira, *Esmeraldo*; Fernandes, *Description*; Boulègue and Marquet, "Voyage"; Almada, *Brief Treatise*, 27. Luso-Africans flourished in the 1600s, before being supplanted by other trading groups after 1730; see Boulègue, *Luso-Africains*; G. Brooks, *Eurafricans in Western Africa* (Athens: Ohio University Press, 2003); P. Mark, *"Portuguese" Style and Luso-African Identity: Precolonial Senegambia, Sixteenth-Nineteenth Centuries* (Bloomington: Indiana University Press, 2002).
29. On the hide trade, see Brooks, *Landlords*, 215; G. Thilmans, "Sur l'existence, fin XVIe siècle, de comptoirs néerlandais à Joal et Portudal," *Notes Africaines* 117: 17–18 (1968); N. I. de Moraes, "Le commerce des peaux à la Petite Côte au XVIIe siècle (Sénégal)," *Notes Africaines* 134: 37–45 (1972); and N. I. de Moraes, "Le commerce des peaux à la Petite Côte au XVIIe siècle (Sénégal) (suite et fin)," *Notes Africaines* 134: 111–116 (1972). For figures on hide exports, see Lemos Coelho, *Description*; Thilmans, "Sénégal"; G. Thilmans and N. I. de Moraes, "Les passages à la Petite Côte de Pieter van den Broecke (1606–1609)," *Bulletin de l'IFAN*, B, 39(3): 471–492 (1977); de Marees [1602], in N. I. de Moraes, *À la découverte de la Petite Côte au XVIIe siècle*, vol. 1 (Dakar: Université de Dakar–IFAN–Cheikh Anta Diop, 1993), 54; also G. Thilmans and J.-P. Rossie, "Le 'Flambeau de la Navigation' de Dierick Ruiters," *Bulletin de l'IFAN*, B, 31(1): 106–119 (1969), 112.

30. Brooks, *Landlords*, 215, 217. On the provenience of hides, see Almada, *Brief Treatise*, 14–15; G. Thilmans and N. I. de Moraes, "La description de la Côte de Guinée du père Baltasar Barreira (1606)," *Bulletin de l'IFAN*, B, 34(1): 1–50 (1972); J. Boulègue, "La relation du fleuve de João Barbosa, faite par João Baptista Lavanha (vers 1600)," *Bulletin de l'IFAN*, B, 29(3/4): 496–509 (1967); Lemos Coelho, *Description*, ch. 1, 4. On the value of cattle on the Petite Côte, see Thilmans, "Relation," 34; van Wassaener [1624], in de Moraes, *À la découverte*, 2: 241.
31. On cotton cloth circulation, see Almada, *Brief Treatise*, 78, 247, 276, 281, 318; Boulègue, "Francisco d'Andrade," 83–85, 87; also N. I. de Moraes, "Le commerce des tissus à la Petite Côte au XVIIe siècle (Sénégambie)," *Notes Africaines* 139: 71–75 (1973). On salt production/trade, see Fernandes, *Description*, 28–31; Gomes, *De la première découverte*, 42n73; Labat, *Nouvelle relation*, 2: 188, 236, 304, 5: 181; Demanet, *Nouvelle histoire*, 1: 177; Becker and Martin, "Mémoire"; Jobson, *Golden Trade*; and Thilmans, "Relation," 27. For a reproduction of the Map of the River Gambra, see T. Astley (ed.) [1745–1747], *A New General Collection of Voyages and Travels* (London: Frank Cass, 1960). The trade in dried seafood has archaeological traces. In Siin, local involvement in commercial networks is attested by the presence of finely crafted pottery slipped in glossy red colors characteristic of the Saalum delta. These ceramics are reminiscent of the red pots used by residents of the Saalum Islands to carry dried oysters and shellfish to sell to other people, as described in Fernandes, *Description*, 29.
32. Mbodj, "Un exemple," 49–52; also Diouf, "Chronique."
33. Thilmans, "Sénégal"; Thilmans and Rossie, "Flambeau," 109–110.
34. Becker and Martin, "Mémoire"; Golberry, *Fragments*, 2: 110–112; Le Brasseur, "Questions sur nos possessions de la Côte d'Afrique . . ." (Apr. 12–14, 1776), ANSOM DFC, No. 100.
35. Becker and Martin, "Détails," 101, 121–122n29. However, it is likely that Siin's external trade varied on a monarch-to-monarch basis. The 1770s, for instance, experienced a recrudescence of slave trading in Siin, possibly under the effective rule of *maad* Biram Pate. Customs payments given to coastal rulers may reflect fluctuations in commercial interactions, and during this period, the total amount of customs and gifts expended on the king of Siin comes closer to that of his more powerful coastal rivals; e.g., "État des dépenses pour 1772," ANSOM C^{6}16; "État des présens et coutumes faits par le Brasseur aux rois du Pays en 1775–1776," ANSOM C^{6}17; "Gorée—état des dépenses" (1778), ANSOM C^{6}17; cf. "Mémoire sur le commerce du Sénégal" (dated 1761 but probably earlier), ANSOM C^{6}14.
36. Devaulx, "Lettre" (May 28, 1732), ANSOM C^{6}10.
37. Conseil Supérieur de Direction, "Lettres à la Compagnie" (Apr. 15 and 28, 1744), ANSOM C^{6}12; "Observations sur l'isle de Gorée données par M. de Rocheblave à Boniface son successeur" (n.d., probably late 1772), ANSOM C^{6}16.

38. Dubellay, "Lettre au Conseil des Indes" (Dec. 18, 1723), ANSOM $C^6$7; also Estoupan, "Lettre à la Compagnie" (Oct. 20, 1754), ANSOM $C^6$14.
39. Poncet de la Rivière, "Lettre à la Compagnie" (Nov. 30, 1764), ANSOM $C^6$15; *Mémoire* (1782), ANSOM $C^6$17; and "Mémoire pour servir d'instruction au Chevalier de Boufflers" (Nov. 1785), ANSOM $C^6$18, underscore the modesty of the trade in Joal. Desmenager, "Lettre au Duc de Choiseul" (Jun. 13, 1765), ANSOM $C^6$15, stresses its economic and diplomatic centrality as a supplier of captives, cattle, rice, and millet, a bridge into interior markets, and a counterbalance lessening the colony's reliance on Bawol and the latter's influence. A similar opinion is expressed by Armény de Paradis, who captures the mutual dependence between the *buur* Siin and French merchants in a series of letters (Jan. 4, 1777; Sept. 22, 1777; and Mar. 3, 1778), ANSOM $C^6$17. These matters acquired particular salience in the 1770s when the French retook Joal from the British and when Parisian stockholders and local agents quarreled over the profitability of coastal *comptoirs*. Concerned with returns on their investments, company officials saw Joal as an unnecessary expense, while employees insisted that trading posts be maintained, given the need to diversify supply areas in case of political trouble. On both positions, see "Mémoire Gorée" (1767), ANSOM $C^6$15; "Mémoire du Roy pour servir d'instruction au S. Boniface" (May 20, 1774), ANSOM $C^6$16; Le Brasseur, "Mémoire pour servir de réponse à la lettre de Monseigneur de Sartines . . ." (1776); and Le Brasseur, "Réponses aux plaintes de M. de Paradis" (ca. 1777), all in ANSOM $C^6$17.
40. M. de Maizière, "Lettre" (Mar. 7, 1768), ANSOM $C^6$15.
41. P. D. Curtin, "The abolition of the slave trade from Senegambia," in D. Eltis and J. Walvin (eds.), *The Abolition of the Atlantic Slave Trade: Origins and Effects in Europe, Africa, and the Americas*, 83–97 (Madison: University of Wisconsin Press, 1981); R. Law (ed.), *From Slave Trade to "Legitimate" Commerce: The Commercial Transition in Nineteenth-Century West Africa* (Cambridge: Cambridge University Press, 1995).
42. De Saint-Robert, "Lettre à la Compagnie" (Aug. 28, 1720), ANSOM $C^6$6.
43. E.g., Steiner, "Another image," on the Guinea coast cloth trade; Dowler and Galvin, *Money*, on the early Saharan trade.
44. Guyer, "Traditions of invention"; Guyer and Eno Belinga, "Wealth in people." Echoing Guyer's argument of composition, *assortment* is the word used by French coastal merchants and company officials throughout the Atlantic period. See J. L. A. Webb, "Toward the comparative study of money: A reconsideration of West African currencies and neoclassical monetary concepts," *International Journal of African Historical Studies* 15(3): 455–466 (1982), 457.
45. Ruiters, in Thilmans and Rossie, "Flambeau"; Lancaster [1610], in de Moraes, *À la découverte*, 1: 143; "Correspondance générale du Sieur de La Brüe" (Apr. 30, 1720), ANSOM $C^6$6; Demanet, *Nouvelle histoire*, 1: 246–247, 250; and Le Brasseur, "Copie de la réponse de M. Lebrasseur . . ." (Dec. 17, 1776), ANSOM $C^6$17.

46. On trade assemblages, see Demanet, *Nouvelle relation*, vol. 1, 242–250; Becker and Martin, "Détails." On monetary fluctuations, see Curtin, *Economic Change*, 233–270, for a comprehensive analysis from a rational actor and market theory perspective; and Webb, "Toward the comparative study." Becker and Martin, "Mémoire," 54–56, offer a valuable analysis of shifts in the value of iron bars in Senegal during the eighteenth century. More generally, Guyer, *Marginal Gains*, analyzes the manipulation of currency exchange rates along political borders to turn a profit.
47. This also speaks to another convention of Senegambian exchange—namely, the fact that units of price measurement often varied in quality, size, and quantity. Curtin, *Economic Change*, 239, mentions that containers used for measuring grain, after a good harvest, were filled to overflowing but might be only one-third full six months later in the middle of the hungry season. Cf. discussion of the *tas* (pile) in colonial Cameroon in Roitman, *Fiscal Disobedience*.
48. On *alcool de traite* in Senegal, see Lemos Coelho, *Description*, 1.6, 1.13; Demanet, *Nouvelle histoire*; Lemaire, *Voyages*. More generally, see C. Ambler, "Alcohol and the slave trade in West Africa, 1400–1850," in W. Jankowiak and D. Bradburd (eds.), *Drugs, Labor and Colonial Expansion*, 73–88 (Tucson: University of Arizona Press, 2003); J. Curto, *Enslaving Spirits: The Portuguese-Brazilian Alcohol Trade at Luanda and Its Hinterland, c. 1550–1830* (Leiden: Brill, 2004); D. van den Bersselaar, *The King of Drinks: Schnapps Gin from Modernity to Tradition* (Leiden: Brill, 2007).
49. Quantitative estimates can be found in Curtin, *Economic Change*, 316–317, 322. Based on the same figures, Curtin estimates that in the 1830s, spirits would have made up about 7 percent of total imports, compared with 59 percent for textiles, 10 percent for tobacco, 8.8 percent for beads and semiprecious stones, 6 percent for firearms, 5.4 percent for metals, and 3.8 percent for gunpowder (ibid., 318, 326). For mentions of alcohol consumption in coastal Siin, see Lemaire [1615], in de Moraes, *À la découverte*, 1: 168; Thilmans, "Relation," 23; Thilmans and Rossie, "Flambeau," 111n4.
50. Almada, *Brief Treatise*, 37; Crone, *Voyages of Cadamosto*; Donelha, *Account*; Lemaire, *Voyages*, 102–103, 126.
51. For gin consumption in Siin, see Noirot, "Notice," 452; Mbodj, "Un exemple," 336; and Rocaché, "Monographie." Van den Bersselaar, *King of Drinks*, 6, indicates that after 1850, gin from Holland and Germany supplanted American rum, which had previously dominated spirits imports on the West African coast. On manufacturers' marks, see P. A. V. R. Vermeulen, "Dutch Geneva and its Bottles" (unpublished manuscript, n.d.), 18–20; and C. Munsey, "Gin bottles: A historical and pictorial essay" (2009), http://www.cecilmunsey.com/images/1238_GIN_BOTTLES.
52. E.g., "Rapport sur la situation politique et économique" (Nov. 18, 1888), ANS 13G321; Bérenger-Féraud, *Peuplades*; and Pinet-Laprade, "Service militaire, No. 42" (Jun. 8, 1865), ANS 13G300bis. See F. G. Richard, "Response

and responsibility (before and after the 'facts'): Postcolonial thoughts on ethical writing," *Archaeological Dialogues* 17(1): 41–63 (2010), 50–51, on the empirical complexities of assessing Atlantic-era alcoholism.

53. Before equating bottle counts with social effects, we should be mindful of the problem of bottle reuse. Containers recovered archaeologically might have initially contained trade liquor but subsequently been used to hold other substances, not necessarily ethylic in nature. Conversely, it is also likely that trade liquor, even during the second half of the nineteenth century, would have also been sold in nonglass containers (gourds, ceramics, wineskin), thus reducing their material presence. That said, the sheer enormity of bottles found in trash heaps suggests that the turnover of discard was quite fast and that bottles may not have been primarily kept for reuse.

54. Despite a paucity of quantifiable data, preliminary research at Atlantic-period sites in other parts of Senegal invites more intuitive comparisons. I analyzed several of these trade import assemblages, which are also made up of a large proportion of spirits bottles. Four seasons of extensive excavations on Gorée Island have yielded large quantities of alcoholic beverage bottles, though mostly wine rather than gin. Likewise, surface collections and test excavations at the nineteenth-century site of Thiepp, residence of the *lingeer* of Bawol, also generated large volumes of case and wine bottles, a trend echoed in Diop's survey of the same region; see B. Diop, "Les sites archéologiques du Baol. Approche ethnographique. Sites dits protohistoriques, villages désertés ou *gents*" (master's thesis, Université Cheikh Anta Diop de Dakar, 1985); A Guèye, "Les expressions matérielles du pouvoir dans l'habitat au Cayor et au Baol du XVIe au XIXe siècle. Approche ethnographique" (master's thesis, Université Cheikh Anta Diop de Dakar, 1999); and I. Thiaw, "The Gorée Archaeological Project (GAP): Preliminary results," *Nyame Akuma* 60: 27–35 (2003).

55. M. Dietler, "Alcohol: Anthropological/archaeological perspective," *Annual Review of Anthropology* 35: 229–249 (2006); also Curto, *Enslaving Spirits*.

56. A. Akyeampong, *Drink, Power, and Cultural Change: A Social History of Alcohol in Ghana, c. 1800 to Recent Times* (Portsmouth, NH: Heinemann, 1996); J. Willis, *Potent Brews: A Social History of Alcohol in East Africa, 1850–1999* (Athens: Ohio University Press, 2002); and E. Akyeampong and S. Ntewusu, "Rum, gin and maize: Deities and ritual change in the Gold Coast during the Atlantic era (16th century to 1850)," *Afriques* 5 (2014), http://afriques.revues.org/1651.

57. Examination of historic materials collected in Faye, "Résidence royale," on satellite villages attached to Diakhao did not reveal significantly more diverse glass assemblages on sites said to have been inhabited by retainers, slaves, warriors, and nobles.

58. For a theoretical primer on feasting, see M. Dietler and B. Hayden (eds.), *Feasts: Archaeological and Ethnographic Perspectives on Food, Politics, and Power*

(Washington, DC: Smithsonian Institution Press, 2001). On "diacritical feasts," see M. Dietler, "Theorizing the feast: Rituals of consumption, commensal politics, and power in African contexts," in Dietler and Hayden, *Feasts*, 65–114.

59. "Note from Buur Siin Boukar Djilas to Governor" (probably 1865), ANS 13G318. Wine was popular in elite circles in Senegal. Pruneau de Pommegorge indicates that *signares*, Gorée's landed bourgeoisie and female merchant class, liked to drink French wines. When visiting Kajoor's capital in the early 1800s, Mollien observed that the king kept French wine for himself, while he plied his favorite courtiers with eau-de-vie. Further inland, the Muslim Almamy of Bundu Boubacar Saada, who resided at Fort Senudebu in the second part of the nineteenth century, was famous for his taste for fine Bordeaux wines; G. Brooks, "The *signares* of Saint-Louis and Gorée: Women entrepreneurs in eighteenth-century Senegal," in N. Hafkin and E. Bay (eds.), *Women in Africa: Studies in Social and Economic Change*, 19–44 (Stanford, CA: Stanford University Press, 1976), 24; Deschamps, *Afrique*, 89–90; and M. Gomez, *Pragmatism in the Age of Jihad: The Precolonial State of Bundu* (New York: Cambridge University Press, 1988), 151.
60. Faye, "Étude ethnographique." Cf. Akyeampong and Ntewusu, "Rum, gin and maize," for an account of political centralization drawing on trade liquor to foster commensality between the living and the spiritual world. By contrast, Thomas, *Entangled Objects*, 107, examines the relative incommensurability of European liquor and the local kava in Fiji, the former lacking the requisite qualities to bear kava's ritual burden.
61. A. Weiner, *Inalienable Possessions: The Paradox of Keeping while Giving* (Berkeley: University of California Press, 1995).
62. *Alcool de menthe* was patented by pharmacist Henri de Ricqlès in 1838 as an all-purpose remedy, used for relieving such sundry ailments as insect bites, indigestion, colds, flus, nausea, headaches, and body aches.
63. Mbodj, "Un exemple," 2: 522–529.
64. Burke, *Lifebuoy Men*; A. Masquelier (ed.), *Dirt, Undress, and Difference: Critical Perspectives on the Body's Surface* (Bloomington: Indiana University Press, 2005).
65. Almada, *Brief Treatise*, 28, 48; Lemos Coelho, *Description*, 1.6, 2.2; Thilmans, "Sénégal," 539; Delcourt, *La France*, 382–387; Demanet, *Nouvelle histoire*, 1: 252, 256–257; de Ruyter [1664], in N. I. de Moraes, *À la découverte de la Petite Côte au XVIIe siècle*, vols. 3–4 (Dakar: Université de Dakar–IFAN–Cheikh Anta Diop, 1998), 49–50; Labarthe, *Voyage*, 182, 184, 186, 228; Lemaire, *Voyages*, 35; Pereira, *Esmeraldo*, 53, 65, 73, 77, 81, 85, 95, 139; and Thilmans and de Moraes, "Passages," 481–482. The bead trade with Mediterranean regions and beyond was not a novelty in the Sahel but a practice of considerable antiquity; e.g., Dowler and Galvin, *Money, Trade, and Trade Routes*; and S. Magnavita, L. Koté, P. Breunig, and O. Idé (eds.), *Crossroads/Carrefour Sahel. Cultural and Technological Developments in the*

First Millennium BC/AD West Africa (Frankfurt: Journal of African Archaeology Monograph Series, 2009).

66. Demanet, *Nouvelle histoire*, 1: 245–246.
67. Denbow, "Material culture"; L. Gijanto, "Personal adornment and expressions of status: Beads and the Gambia River's Atlantic trade," *International Journal of Historical Archaeology* 15(4): 637–668 (2011); D. Graeber, "Beads and money: Notes toward a theory of wealth and power," *American Ethnologist* 23(1): 4–24 (1996); J. Kinahan, *Cattle for Beads: The Archaeology of Historical Contact and Trade on the Namib Coast* (Windhoek: Namibian Archaeological Trust, 2000); Ogundiran, "Of small things"; Stahl, "Colonial entanglements."
68. H. Bocoum and S. K. McIntosh, *Fouilles à Sincu Bara, Moyenne Vallée du Sénégal. Excavations at Sincu Bara, Middle Senegal Valley (Senegal)* (Dakar: CRIAA, 2002), 104; C. Descamps and G. Thilmans, "Les tumulus coquilliers des îles du Saloum (Sénégal)," *Bulletin de l'ASEQUA* 54–55: 81–91 (1979); G. Thilmans and A. Ravisé, *Protohistoire du Sénégal. Recherches archéologiques. Tome II. Sintiou-Bara et les sites du fleuve* (Dakar: IFAN, Mémoire de l'Institut Fondamental d'Afrique Noire No 91**, 1983), 80–82; and G. Thilmans, C. Descamps, and B. Khayat, *Protohistoire du Sénégal. Recherches archéologiques. Tome I. Les sites mégalithiques* (Dakar: IFAN, Mémoire de l'Institut Fondamental d'Afrique Noire No 91*, 1980), 148. On the chronology of chevron beads, see D. Rumrill, "The Mohawk glass trade bead chronology: ca. 1560–1785," *Beads* 3: 5–45 (1991); M. Smith, "Chronology from glass beads: The Spanish period in the Southeast, ca. AD 1513–1670," in C. F. Hayes III (ed.), *Proceedings of the 1982 Glass Trade Bead Conference*, 147–158 (Rochester, MN: Rochester Museum and Science Center, 1983); and L. Turgeon, "French beads in France and northeastern North America during the sixteenth century," *Historical Archaeology* 35(4): 58–59, 61–82 (2001).
69. Almada, *Brief Treatise*, 24; Dubois [1669], in de Moraes, *À la découverte*, vols. 3–4, 145; more generally, see Ogundiran, "Of small things"; Stahl, "Colonial entanglements"; and Gijanto, "Personal adornment."
70. Curtin, *Economic Change*, 312, 318.
71. C. R. DeCorse, F. G. Richard, and I. Thiaw, "Toward a systematic bead description system: A view from the Lower Falemme, Senegal," *Journal of African Archaeology* 1(1): 77–110 (2003). For colonial sources, see Boilat, *Esquisses*, 104, 325, 371, 419, 429, 439; Lasnet et al., *Une mission*, 20, 62–63, 100, 120, 140, 157; Deschamps, *Afrique*, 61, 81, 126, 131, 134, 152–153, 170, 190, 208, 270–271; and M. Park [1799], *Travels in the Interior Districts of Africa* (Durham, NC: Duke University Press, 2000), 83, 267.
72. Curtin, *Economic Change*, 314, 316–317. On the bead assemblages of eastern Senegal, see DeCorse et al., "Bead description system."
73. Stahl, "Colonial entanglements," 839, on clay beads.
74. Academic literature generally associates pipe smoking with the post-Columbian introduction of tobacco in Africa; McIntosh, "Tools"; S. K.

McIntosh, D. Gallagher, and R. J. McIntosh, "Tobacco pipes from excavations at the Museum Site, Jenne, Mali," *Journal of African Archaeology* 1(2): 171–199 (2003); J. E. Phillips, "African smoking pipes," *Journal of African History* 24: 303–319 (1983). Claims of earlier usage have been made by J. Mvondo, "La question des pipes archéologiques en Afrique: Les nouvelles évidences," *West African Journal of Archaeology* 24: 1–19 (1994), and A. Lawson, "Megaliths and Mande states," 266–267, but see counterevidence in L. Gijanto, "Change and the era of the Atlantic trade: Commerce and interaction in the Niumi commercial center (The Gambia)" (PhD diss., Syracuse University, 2010).

75. For travelers' descriptions of smoking in Senegal, see Thilmans, "Relation," 41; Lemaire, *Voyages*, 98, 80, 157–158, 162; and Boilat, *Esquisses*. For pipe usage elsewhere in West Africa, see J Boachie-Ansah, "Smoking pipes and the dating of post-16th century in Ghana: The evidence from Ahwene Koko," *West African Journal of Archaeology* 16: 53–70 (1986); K. Kelly, "Change and continuity in coastal Bénin," in DeCorse, *West Africa*, 81–100; Stahl, "Colonial entanglements."
76. This is ironic considering that the typical Seereer women depicted in Boilat, *Esquisses*, are smoking imported white clay pipes! See Thiaw, "Archaeological investigation"; and Thiaw, "Gorée," for information on French and indigenous occupations in the Upper Senegal River and Gorée. On Bonnaud pipes, see "Pipe d'étalage by Bonnaud, Marseille, ca. 1870," http://tobaccopipeartistory.blogspot.sn/2013/03/pipe-detalage-by-bonnaud-marseille-ca.html; also M. Raphaël, *La pipe en terre, son périple à travers la France* (Vitrolles: Éditions Aztec, 1991).
77. See, for instance, DeCorse, *Archaeology of Elmina*; Kelly, "Indigenous responses."
78. In "État des présens" (1777), ANSOM $C^6$17, Le Brasseur's inventory of presents to the King of Siin lists a large faience soup tureen, alongside beads, textiles, and eau-de-vie.
79. To compare, the earliest imported pottery excavated on Gorée is white salt-glazed stoneware plate fragments datable to the first half of the eighteenth century. This phenomenon, however, can also be seen in areas further inland, such as the Falemme River, where European ceramics occur both late and in small numbers; see Thiaw, "Archaeological investigation"; Richard, "Vernacular cosmopolitanisms."
80. The late appearance of European assemblages is common in the West African hinterland—e.g., Gokee, *Assembling the Village*; and Stahl, *Making History*—just as trade imports tend to appear early on coastal areas; e.g., DeCorse, *Archaeology of Elmina*; Kelly, "Indigenous responses." Siin seems to be an exception in this regard.
81. Lemaire, *Voyages*, 138; Becker and Martin, "Mémoire," 42; R. C. Geoffroy de Villeneuve, *L'Afrique, ou histoire, moeurs, usages et coutumes des Africains*, vol. 4 (Paris: Nepveu, 1814), 140–141, 151–164, 185–186; and Rocaché,

"Monographie," for descriptions of pottery making and meals in the region.

82. Richard, "From cosaan to colony," 583–591.
83. For ethnographic accounts of food valuation in Siin, see Gastellu, *Égalitarisme*; Gastellu and Delpech *Maintenance sociale*; and Pélissier, *Paysans*. The concept of moral gastronomy is developed in Weiss, *Making and Unmaking*, ch. 5. Material assemblages from the sites of Diakhao Maak, Ndiob, Mbouma, and Ndidor, which served as residences to princely elites and slave warriors, contained practically no imported ceramics; Faye, "Résidence royale." For description of foodways on Gorée, see I. Thiaw, "Every house has a story: the archaeology of Gorée Island, Sénégal," in L. Sansone, E. Soumonni, and B. Barry (eds.), *Africa, Brazil and the Construction of Trans-Atlantic Black Identities*, 45–62 (Trenton, NJ: Africa World Press, 2008); Richard, "Vernacular cosmopolitanisms."
84. Thilmans and Rossie, "Flambeau," 108; Thilmans and de Moraes, "Passages"; de Moraes, "Commerce des tissus."
85. For references on social distinction and clothing in coastal Senegal, see de Marees, in de Moraes, *À la découverte*, 1: 54; Gaspar de Sevilla [1647], in de Moraes, *À la découverte*, 2: 363; Lemaire, *Voyages*, 131–134, More generally, see J. Allman, *Fashioning Africa: Power and the Politics of Dress* (Bloomington: Indiana University Press, 2004); J. Comaroff, "The empire's old clothes: Fashioning the colonial subject," in D. Howes (ed.), *Cross-Cultural Consumption: Global Markets, Local Realities*, 19–38 (New York: Routledge, 1996); D. DiPaolo Loren, "Social skins: Orthodoxies and practices of dressing in the early colonial lower Mississippi Valley," *Journal of Social Archaeology* 1(2): 172–189 (2001); H. Hendrickson (ed.), *Clothing and Difference: Embodied Identities in Colonial and Post-colonial Africa* (Durham, NC: Duke University Press, 1996); and Newell, *Modernity Bluff*.
86. De Moraes, "Commerce des peaux."
87. The decrease of cotton cloth *trade* over time does not entail that cloth *production* decreased as well. In fact, a threefold increase of locally made textiles in the early eighteenth century and the use of cloth as currency suggest a strong local demand. Cotton and artisanal cloth production probably picked up with the greater availability of slaves during the century; see Curtin, *Economic Change*, 211–214, and Klein, "Impact," 40.
88. Geoffroy de Villeneuve, *L'Afrique*, 179–183.
89. Roberts, "Women's work"; R. Roberts, "Guinée cloth: Linked transformations within France's empire in the nineteenth century," *Cahiers d'Études Africaines* 32(4): 597–627 (1992); and Roberts, *Two Worlds*; A. Stahl and M. D. Cruz, "Men and women in a market economy: Gender and craft production in west central Ghana, c. 1775–1995," in S. Kent (ed.), *Gender in African Prehistory*, 205–226 (Walnut Creek, CA: Altamira, 1998).
90. "Copie de la réponse de M. Lebrasseur . . ." (Dec. 17, 1776), ANSOM $C^6$17; Searing, *West African Slavery*, 51.

91. Guyer, *Marginal Gains*; Ogundiran, "Of small things," 447, 455–456; Piot, "Of slaves and the gift."
92. Klein, *Islam*, 67; Mbodj, "Un exemple," 1: 81; also Cruise O'Brien, *Saints and Politicians*.
93. Flize, "Lettre au Chef de Poste de Joal" (Apr. 14, 1866), ANS 4B43.
94. Noirot, "Notice," 457; Noirot, "Rapport politique et économique" (Apr. 10, 1896), ANS 13G327 No. 5, 54–55; cf. Stahl and Cruz, "Men and women," 209.
95. Noirot [1896], in Klein, *Islam*, 174–175.
96. S. Palmié, *Wizards and Scientists: Explorations in Afro-Cuban Modernity and Tradition* (Durham, NC: Duke University Press, 2002), 9.
97. Conseil Supérieur de la Compagnie, "Lettre aux Directeurs" (Oct. 25, 1753), and Estoupan, "Lettre à la Compagnie" (Oct. 20, 1754), both in ANSOM $C^6$14. Sources suggest that cattle were prized possessions, which villagers were loath to sell: Thilmans, "Sénégal," 529–530; Becker and Martin, "Mémoire," 47, 91n94; Moore, *Travels into the Inland Parts of Africa*, 33–35; Thilmans and Rossie, "Flambeau," 119; and Lemaire, *Voyages*, 76–80, 151, who also mentions their use as dowry.
98. Weiner, *Inalienable Possessions*; Kopytoff, "Cultural biography"; M. Godelier, *L'énigme du don* (Paris: Fayard, 1996). More generally, see C. Gregory, *Gift and Commodity* (New York: Academic Press, 1982).
99. Cf. Klein, "Servitude," 352. For an archaeological analysis of cattle in colonial context, see A. Reid, "Access to cattle resources in a Tswana capital," in A. M. Reid and P. J. Lane (eds.), *African Historical Archaeologies*, 301–324 (New York: Springer, 2004).
100. K. Marx, *Grundrisse: Foundations of the Critique of Political Economy* (New York: Penguin, 1973). In a more comparative archaeological vein, see Oland et al., *Decolonizing Indigenous Histories* (especially papers by Liebmann, Richard, Stahl, and Silliman); S. Silliman, "Archaeologies of survivance and residence: Reflections on the historical archaeology of indigenous people," in N. Ferris, R. Harrison, and M. Wilcox (eds.), *Rethinking Colonial Pasts through Archaeology*, 57–75 (Oxford: Oxford University Press, 2014); M. Liebmann, "The Mickey Mouse kachina and other 'double objects': Hybridity in the material culture of colonial encounters," *Journal of Social Archaeology* 15(3): 319–341 (2015).
101. G. Simmel, *On Individuality and Social Forms*, D. Levine (ed.) (Chicago: University of Chicago Press, 1971).
102. For example, J. and J. L. Comaroff, "Beasts, banknotes, and the color of money in colonial South Africa," *Archaeological Dialogues* 12(2): 107–132 (2006); Graeber, *Anthropological Theory of Value*; and Piot, "Of persons and things."
103. Guyer, *Marginal Gains*. On looking at artifact classes intersectionally, see Mills and Walker, *Memory Work*.
104. In this sense, since they condense different times of action and directions of change, archaeological objects perform the kind of "imaginative flight"

demanded by Glissant's posture of errancy, a stance that prefers networks to totality, that perceives entangled stories rather than single ones, that confronts vectoral time and replaces it with multiple temporalities that loop back, stretch forward, and fold into each other; I. Baucom, *Specters of the Atlantic: Finance Capital, Slavery and the Philosophy of History* (Durham, NC: Duke University Press, 2005), 312–313ff.; cf. G. Deleuze and F. Guattari, *A Thousand Plateaus* (New York: Continuum, 2004). For an archaeological look at the consequences and material expressions of the Atlantic trade, see Stahl, "Slave trade."

PART FOUR INTRODUCTION

1. David, *Navétanes*, 17.
2. K. Swindell, "Serawoolies, Tillibunkas, and strange farmers: The development of migrant groundnut farming along the Gambia River, 1848–95," *Journal of African History* 21(1): 94–103 (1980).
3. Trouillot, *Global Transformations*, 7–28. Note, of course, that imagination and management are not separate existential domains but mutually informed and entangled.

CHAPTER SEVEN

1. K. Fields, *Revival and Rebellion in Colonial Central Africa* (Portsmouth, NH: Heinemann, 1985).
2. Cooper, *Colonialism*, 197.
3. See M. Taussig, *Shamanism, Colonialism, and the Wild Man* (Chicago: University of Chicago Press, 1987), on "epistemic murk." On colonial common sense, see Stoler, *Along the Archival Grain*.
4. Herbst, *State and Power*. For perspectives on colonial despotism, see M. Mamdani, *Citizen and Subject: Contemporary Africa and the Legacy of Late Colonialism* (Princeton, NJ: Princeton University Press, 1996), and C. Young, *The African Colonial State in Comparative Perspective* (New Haven, CT: Yale University Press, 1994). On the limitations of colonial governance, see B. Berman, and J. Lonsdale, *Unhappy Valley: Conflict in Kenya and Africa. Book One: State and Class* (London: James Currey, 1992); Roberts, *Two Worlds*.
5. J. Comaroff, "Reflections on the colonial state, in South Africa and elsewhere: Factions, fragments, facts, and fictions," *Social Identities* 4(3): 321–361 (1998), 341–342; also Bayart, *State in Africa*; Cooper, *Colonialism*; and Mbembe, *On the Postcolony*. See C. Boone, *Political Topographies of the African State: Territorial Authority and Institutional Choice* (New York: Cambridge University Press, 2003), on how rural societies configured French colonial rule in heterogeneous ways.
6. On parallel spheres of power in colonial Africa, see D. Lan, *Guns and Rain: Guerillas and Spirit Mediums in Zimbabwe* (Berkeley: University of California

Press, 1985); Moore, *Suffering*; and Obarrio, *Spirit*. On African functionaries, see B. Lawrance, E. Osborn, and R. Roberts (eds.), *Intermediaries, Interpreters, and Clerks: African Employees in the Making of Colonial Africa* (Madison: University of Wisconsin Press, 2006). On African resistance, see S. Berry, *Chiefs Know Their Boundaries: Essays on Property, Power and the Past in Asante, 1896–1996* (Portsmouth, NH: Heinemann, 2000); S. Mahir and P. Royer, *West African Challenge to Empire: Culture and History in the Volta-Bani Anticolonial War* (London: James Currey, 2000); and Stoller, *Embodying Colonial Memories*. On indigenous subversions of colonial law in Senegal, see Galvan, *The State*; G. W. Johnson, *The Emergence of Black Politics in Senegal: The Struggle for Power in the Four Communes, 1900–1920* (Stanford, CA: Stanford University Press, 1971).

7. The quote is from T. B. Hansen and F. Stepputat, "Sovereignty revisited," *Annual Review of Anthropology* 35: 295–315 (2006), 302; also Stoler, "On degrees." On the microphysics of rule, see Cooper and Stoler, *Tensions of Empire*; and A. L. Stoler, *Carnal Knowledge and Imperial Power: Race and the Intimate in Colonial Rule* (Berkeley: University of California Press, 2002).
8. This literature is reviewed in Richard, "Materializing colonial pasts."
9. Buchli, *Archaeology of Socialism*; S. Croucher and L. Weiss (eds.), *The Archaeology of Capitalism in Colonial Contexts* (New York: Springer, 2011); S. Dawdy, *Building the Devil's Empire: French Colonial New Orleans* (Chicago: University of Chicago Press, 2008); Hall, *Archaeology and the Modern World*; M. Leone, *An Archaeology of Liberty in an American Capital: Excavations in Annapolis* (Berkeley: University of California Press, 2005).
10. U. Linke, "Contact zones: Rethinking the sensual life of the state," *Journal of Anthropological Theory* 6(2): 205–225 (2006). More generally, see G. Burchell, C. Gordon, and P. Miller, *The Foucault Effect: Studies in Governmentality* (Chicago: University of Chicago Press, 1991); M. Dean, *Governmentality: Power and Rule in Modern Society* (London: Sage, 1999); and B. Hindess, *Discourses of Power: From Hobbes to Foucault* (Oxford: Blackwell, 1996).
11. In his *Collège de France* lectures, Foucault distinguishes three intersecting modalities of state power. *Sovereignty* refers to the exercise of rule over a territory and its subject populations, for which law, obedience, and policy are the primary instruments. *Discipline* denotes the application of power over/through bodies with the aim of surveilling, correcting, and ordering individuals within particular institutions. Lastly, *governmentality* entails a regime of power concerned with "the population" and its optimization; it seeks to shape the conduct of people by mobilizing their desires, habits, and aspirations (through a wide array of techniques and discourses) to enlist them in the project of their own rule. Rather than operating independently, these modes of power act as each other's conditions; M. Foucault, *Security, Territory, Population. Lectures at the Collège de France, 1977–1978* (New York: Palgrave Macmillan, 1997), 35–39, 51, 87–114, 115–134; Dean, *Governmentality*.

12. Rancière, "Ten theses"; Foucault, *Security*, 98. On reading state power through its effects, see Foucault, *Power*; Trouillot, *Global Transformations*, 79–96.
13. Foucault, *Power*, 326–348. I use "subjectivity" here, following Foucault, *Power*, 331, to denote two facets of identity construction in a given power formation: (1) the process of subjugation (to control and governance), and (2) the forms of consciousness and self-knowledge that orient people's courses of action. In becoming subjects to particular regimes of authority, individuals internalize certain sensibilities that influence their deeds, dealings, and decisions; to paraphrase Foucault, they are constituted by power situations of which they are the bearers. While the full spectrum of subjective expressions stretches beyond archaeological evidence (since, after all, subjectivity involves matters of psyche, self-perception, and feelings), subject positions do have *material* dimensions: certain sets of practical dispositions with archaeological traces that may have promoted self-understanding; e.g., L. Meskell, *Archaeologies of Social Life: Age, Sex, Class, Etcetera in Ancient Egypt* (Oxford: Blackwell, 1999); Smith, "The end." For discussions of subjectivity, see J. Biehl, B. Good, and A. Kleinman (eds.), *Subjectivity: Ethnographic Investigations* (Berkeley: University of California Press, 2007); and J. Butler, *The Psychic Life of Power: Theories in Subjection* (Stanford, CA: Stanford University Press, 1997).
14. For literature on the productivity of power, see Scott, *Refashioning Futures*; and D. Scott and C. Hirschkind (eds.), *Powers of the Secular Modern: Talal Asad and His Interlocutors* (Stanford, CA: Stanford University Press, 2006).
15. On early projects of agricultural colonization, see Monteilhet, "Documents"; Barry, *Royaume*; and G. Hardy, *La mise en valeur du Sénégal de 1817 à 1854* (Paris: Larose, 1921). For a fuller account of France's shifting cotton policy in Senegal between 1817 and 1865, see Roberts, *Two Worlds*, 60–75.
16. Curtin, "Abolition," 92–93; Searing, *West African Slavery*, 167.
17. Searing, *West African Slavery*, 166.
18. J. L. A. Webb, "The trade in gum arabic: Prelude to French conquest in Senegal," *Journal of African History* 26: 149–168 (1985); and Webb, *Desert Frontier*, 100–109. Gum exports doubled during the 1830s, reaching over four thousand metric tons in 1838, and continued at an annual average of at least two thousand metric tons with considerable year-to-year fluctuations; Curtin, *Economic Change*, 217; Curtin, *Supplementary Evidence*, 64–65; Barry, "Economic anthropology," 43–44. The colony's commerce, which was worth 3.6 million francs in 1824, rose to a total value of 17 million francs in 1838, as reported in Searing, *West African Slavery*, 174.
19. These "river empire" dynamics are analyzed in Webb, *Desert Frontier*, 115–124.
20. Searing, *West African Slavery*, 169, 188; Webb, "Trade in gum Arabic," 163–168; B. Barry, "Mémoire inédit de Montsérat sur l'histoire du nord du Sénégal de 1819 à 1839," *Bulletin de l'IFAN*, B, 32(1): 1–43 (1970), 22, 24, 30, 32.
21. G. Brooks, "Peanuts and colonialism: Consequences of the commercialization of peanuts in West Africa, 1830–70," *Journal of African History* 16(1):

29–54 (1975); Curtin, *Economic Change*, 230–231; Klein, *Islam*, 36–38; B. Moitt, "Slavery and emancipation in Senegal's peanut basin: The nineteenth and twentieth centuries," *International Journal of African Historical Studies* 22(1): 27–50 (1989), 27; and Swindell, "Serawoolies."

22. Barry, "Economic anthropology," 45; Curtin, *Economic Change*, 218; Mbodj, "Un exemple," 102–104; Mbodj, "Sénégal et dépendance: Le Sine-Saloum et l'arachide, 1887–1940," in Coquery-Vidrovitch, *Sociétés paysannes*, 139–154, 140–141.
23. Curtin, "Abolition," 86.
24. L. C. Barrows, "General Faidherbe, the Maurel and Prom Company, and French expansion in Senegal" (PhD diss., UCLA, 1974). See Klein, *Islam*, 38–42, on motivations that drove the "architects of empires" to promote the expansion of the colonial enterprise; and Robinson, *Holy War*, for an analysis Umar Tal's movement in the context of France's expansion.
25. Klein, "Social and economic factors." More generally, see accounts of the French conquest in A. Sabatié, *Le Sénégal: Sa conquête et son organisation (1364–1925)* (Saint-Louis: Imprimerie du Gouvernement, 1926); A. S. Kanya-Forstner, *The Conquest of the Western Sudan: A Study in French Military Imperialism* (Cambridge: Cambridge University Press, 1969); and Y.-J. Saint-Martin, *Le Sénégal sous le second Empire* (Paris: Karthala, 1989).
26. See Klein, *Islam*, ch. 4 and 5; and Barry, *Senegambia*, 223–242, for useful overviews.
27. Barry, *Senegambia*, 205. The colonial conquest was also triggered by increasing competition in oleaginous materials worldwide, which demanded more controlled markets; see Klein, "Colonial rule." On the French penetration in southern Senegambia, see Barry, *Senegambia*, ch. 16 and 19; C. Roche, *Histoire de la Casamance: Conquête et résistance* (Paris: Karthala, 1985).
28. Curtin, *Economic Change*, 149, 191.
29. Cruise O'Brien, *Saints and Politicians*; D. Robinson, "The Murids: Surveillance and collaboration," *Journal of African History* 40: 193–213 (1999); Searing, *"God Alone Is King"*; Babou, *Fighting the Greater Jihad*.
30. Searing, *West African Slavery*, 196; Diouf, *Histoire du Sénégal*, 8–9.
31. Mbodj, "Sénégal et dépendance."
32. On the abolition of slavery and subsequent labor dynamics, see Moitt, "Slavery and emancipation"; Swindell, "Serawoolies"; Klein, *Slavery and Colonial Rule*; and F. Renault, "L'abolition de l'esclavage au Sénégal: L'attitude de l'administration française (1848–1905)," *Revue Française d'Histoire d'Outre-Mer* 58(1): 5–80 (1971).
33. C. Boone, *Merchant Capital and the Roots of State Power in Senegal, 1930–1985* (New York: Cambridge University Press, 1992); Foster, *Faith in Empire*; Klein, *Islam*; Mbodj, "Un exemple."
34. Kanya-Forstner, *Conquest of the Sudan*; C. Newbury, "The formation of the Government General of French West Africa," *Journal of African History* 1(1): 111–128 (1960); C. Newbury and A. S. Kanya-Forstner, "French policy and

the scramble for West Africa," *Journal of African History* 10(2): 253–276 (1969); Saint-Martin, *Sénégal sous le second Empire*; Roberts, *Two Worlds*.

35. The phrase "graft of the state" is borrowed from J.-F. Bayart (ed.), *La greffe de l'état* (Paris: Karthala, 1996). On the economics of French imperialism, see J. Marseille, *Empire colonial et capitalisme français: Histoire d'un divorce* (Paris: Albin Michel, 1984).
36. On the policy of "putting to use," see Hardy, *Mise en valeur*. See also R. Aldrich, "Imperial *mise en valeur* and *mise en scène*: Recent works on French colonialism," *Historical Journal* 45(4): 917–936 (2002). While the French were often hands-off with peanut agriculture, see C. Bonneuil, "Penetrating the natives: Peanut breeding, peasants and the colonial state in Senegal (1900–1950)," *Science Technology Society* 4: 273–302 (1999), for colonial experiments to improve seed varieties after World War I.
37. Pélissier, *Paysans*.
38. J. Fouquet, *La traite des arachides dans le pays de Kaolack* (Saint-Louis: Centre-IFAN-Sénégal, 1958), 55, 112; Klein, "Colonial rule," 77–78. See P. David, *Ernest Noirot: Un administrateur colonial hors normes (1851–1913)* (Paris: Karthala, 2012), 93–134, for an account of administrator Noirot's commitment to commerce-oriented infrastructure building.
39. Boone, *Merchant Capital*.
40. On the four communes, see M. Diouf, "The French colonial policy of assimilation and the civility of the originaires of the Four Communes (Senegal): A nineteenth century globalization project," *Development and Change* 29: 671–696 (1998); H. Jones, *The Métis of Senegal: Urban Life and Politics in French West Africa* (Bloomington: Indiana University Press, 2013), warns about not overstating the urban/rural divide.
41. M. A. Klein, "Chiefship in Sine-Saloum, 1887–1914," in V. Turner (ed.), *Colonialism in Africa, 1870–1960*, 3: 39–73 (Cambridge: Cambridge University Press, 1971), 57.
42. Newbury, "Formation," 124.
43. Noirot, "Lettre au Bour Saloum" (Mar. 6, 1896), ANS 13G326; Klein, "Chiefship," 56.
44. On colonial law, see R. Roberts and K. Mann, "Law in colonial Africa," in K. Mann (ed.), *Law in Colonial Africa*, 3–58 (Portsmouth, NH: Heinemann, 1991); and R. Roberts, *Litigants and Households: African Disputes and Colonial Courts in the French Soudan, 1895–1912* (Portsmouth, NH: Heinemann, 2005). On the *indigénat*, see A. I. Asiwaju, "Control through coercion: A study of the indigenat regime in French West Africa, 1887–1946," *Bulletin de l'IFAN*, B, 41(1): 35–71 (1979); G. Mann, "What was the Indigénat? The 'Empire of Law' in French West Africa," *Journal of African History* 50: 331–353 (2009); and I. Merle, "Retour sur le régime de l'indigénat: Genèse et contradictions des principes répressifs dans l'empire français," *French Politics, Culture & Society* 20(2): 77–97 (2002). For discussions of "high-modern" state hubris and its failures in French West Africa, see C. Bonneuil,

"Development as experiment: Science and state building in late colonial and postcolonial Africa, 1930–1970," *Osiris* 15: 258–281 (2000); cf. Scott, *Seeing like a State*.

45. Aujas, "Sérères"; Guy, "Sine-Saloum." See Klein, "Chiefship," for a synthetic account.
46. Directeur des Affaires Politiques, "Rapport sur la commission des frontières" (Feb. 2, 1896), ANS 1F19; Klein, "Chiefship," 63–64; also Bayart, *State in Africa*.
47. Noirot, "Lettre au Gouverneur-Général" (Apr. 10, 1896), ANS 13G326. More generally, see Lawrance et al., *Intermediaries*.
48. Lefilliâtre, "Lettre au Directeur des Affaires Étrangères" (Oct. 3, 1901), ANS 13G332; Klein, "Chiefship," 59–60, 65.
49. Klein, "Servitude," 350–351; Curtin, *Economic Change*, 191.
50. G. Wilder, *The French Imperial Nation-State: Negritude and Colonial Humanism between the Two World Wars* (Chicago: University of Chicago Press, 2005), 80. Wilder is critical of approaches locating the paradoxes of imperialism in gaps between Republican ideals and colonial practice; to him, French rule was always already colonial and humanist at once and thus consumed by internal contradictions. Cf. F. Cooper, *Decolonization and African Society: The Labor Question in French and British Africa* (New York: Cambridge University Press, 1996), and *Colonialism*, 142–148; A. L Conklin, *A Mission to Civilize: The Republican Idea of the Empire in France and West Africa, 1895–1930* (Stanford, CA: Stanford University Press, 1997). The phrase "hegemony on a shoestring" comes from S. Berry, *No Condition Is Permanent: The Social Dynamics of Agrarian Change in Sub-Saharan Africa* (Madison: University of Wisconsin Press, 1993), ch. 2.
51. See M. Foucault, *Birth of Biopolitics*, on the relationship between liberalism and governmentality; also T. Lemke, " 'The birth of biopolitics': Michel Foucault's lecture at the Collège de France on neo-liberal governmentality," *Economy and Society* 30(2): 190–207 (2001). This biopolitical rationale was at the core of programs like the *sociétés de prévoyances*, which meant to integrate farmers into agricultural markets while inculcating the virtues of savings; Mbodj, "Un exemple," 2: 433–461; A. Sow, "Les sociétés indigènes de prévoyance du Sénégal des origines à 1947" (PhD diss., Université de Dakar, 1983); G. Mann and J. Guyer, "Imposing a guide on the indigene: The fifty year experience of the sociétés de prévoyance in French West and Equatorial Africa," in E. Stiansen and J. Guyer (eds.), *Credit, Currencies and Culture*, 124–151 (Stockholm: Nordiska Afrikainstitutet, 1999).
52. Galvan, "Market"; David, *Ernest Noirot*, 112; F. Snyder, *Capitalism and Legal Change: An African Transformation* (New York: Academic Press, 1981). See W. Mwangi, "Of coins and conquest: The East African Currency Board, Rupee crisis, and the problem of colonialism in the East African protectorate," *Contemporary Studies in Society and History* 43(4): 763–787 (2001), for an

analysis of currency imposition/circulation and colonial state domination; also Roitman, *Fiscal Disobedience*; Conklin, *Mission to Civilize*, ch. 1.

53. On "politique des races," see Klein, "Chiefship," 68. For analyses of biopolitics/biopower's relationship to race, see Foucault, *"Society Must Be Defended"*; Stoler, *Carnal Knowledge*.
54. D. Robinson, "Ethnography and customary law in Senegal," *Cahiers d'Études Africaines* 32(2): 221–237 (1992). On ethnographic states, see N. Dirks, *Castes of Mind: Colonialism and the Making of Modern India* (Princeton, NJ: Princeton University Press, 2001), ch. 3; Stoler, "On degrees." For literature on peasants as targets of state-led modernization, see Scott, *Seeing like a State*; Mitchell, *Rule of Experts*; E. Weber, *Peasants into Frenchmen: The Modernization of Rural France, 1870–1914* (Stanford, CA: Stanford University Press, 1976). On France's indigenous policy, see H. Labouret, "À la recherche d'une politique indigène dans l'ouest africain," *Bulletin du Comité de l'Afrique Française* 12: 636–640 (1930). Conklin, *Mission to Civilize*, ch. 7, notes that human *mise en valeur* began in earnest in the 1920s.
55. Bérenger-Féraud, *Peuplades*, 279, 284.
56. E.g., Geismar, *Recueil*; Rousseau, "Notes."
57. Spear, "Neo-traditionalism"; Guyer, "Traditions of invention."
58. Rowlands, "Archaeology of colonialism," 261–283. Cf. Stahl, *Making History*; and Monroe, *Precolonial State*.
59. Martin et al., "Trois documents."
60. This is based on personal observation of collections housed at the Archaeology Laboratory of the Institut National d'Afrique Noire (IFAN) in Dakar.
61. E.g., Noirot [1896], in Martin et al., "Trois documents."
62. Guigou, "Changements."
63. E.g., M. Gastellu, *Égalitarisme*, 25–26; Geismar, *Recueil*, 23; Reynier, "Rapport," 13–14; and Rousseau, "Notes," 39.
64. Bourgeau, "Note," 47–51; Dulphy, "Étude," 49–52; Reinwald, "Changing family strategies." For broader literature on the African subversion of colonial law, see S. F. Moore, *Social Facts and Fabrication: "Customary" Law on Kilimanjaro 1880–1980* (New York: Cambridge University Press, 1986); and B. Shadle, " 'Changing traditions to meet current altering conditions': Customary law, African courts, and the rejection of codification in Kenya, 1930–1960," *Journal of African History* 40: 411–431 (1999).
65. Taussig, *Shamanism*, xiii. The idea of "sincere fiction" derives from P. Bourdieu, *The Logic of Practice* (Cambridge: Polity, 1990), 112.
66. On colonial anxieties, see Stoler, *Along the Archival Grain*, ch. 7; and M. Taussig, *The Nervous System* (New York: Routledge, 1991). Also A. Stoler (ed.), *Imperial Debris: On Ruins and Ruination* (Durham, NC: Duke University Press, 2013); and G. Gordillo, *Rubble: The Afterlives of Destruction* (Durham, NC: Duke University Press, 2014), on the disposition of "imperial disregard."

67. J. Suret-Canale, *French Colonialism in Tropical Africa, 1900–1945* (New York: Pica Press, 1971), 94, 155.
68. E.g., Lericollais, *Sob*; Pélissier, *Paysans*.
69. Comaroff and Comaroff, *Of Revelation*, vol. 2; Wilder, *French Imperial Nation-State*.
70. Keane, *Christian Moderns*; B. Latour, *We Have Never Been Modern* (Cambridge, MA: Harvard University Press, 1993).

CHAPTER EIGHT

1. In Klein, "Colonial rule," 73.
2. D. C. Galvan, "The social reproduction of community-based development: Syncretism and sustainability in a Senegalese farmers' association," *Journal of Modern African Studies* 45(1): 61–88 (2007). Cf. R. Fredericks, "Disorderly Dakar: The cultural politics of household waste in Senegal's capital city," *Journal of Modern African Studies* 51(3): 435–458 (2013), for an urban example.
3. Cooper and Stoler, *Tensions of Empire*; see also Cooper, *Colonialism*.
4. This literature is too vast and diverse to summarize in full. A useful entry point can be found in Becker et al., *AOF: Réalités et héritages*. For an overview of legal institutions, see G. Hesseling, *Histoire politique du Sénégal: Institutions, droit et société* (Paris: Karthala, 1985). On colonial political economy, see Gellar, *Structural Changes*; and Klein, "Colonial rule." On labor, see Klein, *Slavery and Colonial Rule*. On colonial commerce, see Boone, *Merchant Capital*. For an analysis of health policy in colonial Senegal, see M. Echenberg, *Black Death, White Medicine: Bubonic Plague and the Politics of Public Health in Colonial Senegal, 1914–1945* (Portsmouth, NH: Heinemann, 2001). A number of researchers have examined France's "Islamic policy," including D. Robinson and J.-L. Triaud (eds.), *Le temps des marabouts: Itinéraires et trajectoires islamiques en Afrique Occidentale Francaise, v. 1880–1960* (Paris: Karthala, 1997); Robinson, *Paths of Accommodation*. For studies of African struggles for power, see Johnson, *Emergence of Black Politics*; Cooper, *Decolonization*; and Lawrance et al., *Intermediaries*. For analyses of Africa and French imperialism, see G. W. Johnson (ed.), *Double Impact: France and Africa in the Age of Imperialism* (Westport, CT: Greenwood, 1985); Conklin, *Mission to Civilize*; and G. Mann, "Locating colonial histories: Between France and West Africa," *American Historical Review* 110(2): 409–434 (2005).
5. Klein, *Islam*; Klein, "Chiefship"; Klein, "Colonial rule"; and Mbodj, "Un exemple"; Mbodj, "Sénégal et dépendance." For other studies of the Senegalese countryside, see Snyder, *Capitalism*; Boone, *Political Topographies*; and O. Linares, *Power, Prayer and Production: The Jola of Casamance, Senegal* (New York: Cambridge University Press, 2007).
6. But see Cooper, "Conflict and connection"; and Cooper, *Colonialism*, for a subtle conceptual engagement with colonial power. Other exceptions,

however, can be found in Bonneuil, "Penetrating the natives"; and Bonneuil, "Development as experiment"; Galvan, "Market"; and Galvan, *The State*; Reinwald, "Changing family strategies"; J. Carney and M. Watts, "Manufacturing dissent: Work, gender, and the politics of meaning in a peasant society," *Africa* 60(2): 207–241 (1990); Snyder, *Capitalism*; and R. Baum, "Crimes of the dream world: French trials of Diola witches in colonial Senegal," *International Journal of African Historical Studies* 37(2): 201–228 (2004). Klein, *Islam*; and Klein, "Chiefship," offer astute observations about how colonialism reshaped the field of economic practices in Siin and how rural Africans learned to adapt to colonial administration but devotes less attention to reconfigurations in cultural experience.

7. Cooper, *Colonialism*, 143, 142–148, also 157.
8. Cooper, *Decolonization*; Conklin, *Mission to Civilize*.
9. See Foucault, *"Society Must Be Defended"*; and Foucault, *Security*; Wilder, *French Imperial Nation-State*.
10. As noted in Klein, *Islam*, 230–231.
11. Bonneuil, "Development as experiment," 259–260, offers a different chronology, locating the birth of the developmentalist state in Africa in the 1930s in association with post–Great Depression efforts to improve native conditions and mapping its continuities into the postindependence era. Also Wilder, *French Imperial Nation-State*, on "colonial humanism"; F. Coronil, "Smelling like a market," *American Historical Review* 106(1): 119–129 (2001), on the political force of markets; and Boone, *Political Topographies*, on regional variations in state-society articulations.
12. P. Pels, *A Politics of Presence: Contacts between Missionaries and Walugru in Late Colonial Tanganyika* (Amsterdam: Harwood Academic Publishers, 1999), 43ff.
13. M. F. Bille, F. Hastrup, and T. Sørensen (eds.), *An Anthropology of Absence* (New York: Springer, 2010); M. Engelke, *A Problem of Presence: Beyond Scripture in an African Church* (Berkeley: University of California Press, 2007); Munn, "Excluded spaces."
14. Siin's history during the first fifty years of the nineteenth century is difficult to assess, in part because of its near absence in the archival record of these decades. Between 1817 and 1850, France's attention was unilaterally focused on the Senegal Valley, and it is possible the province played a minor commercial role, possibly limited to provisioning, or reoriented toward British commerce out of the Gambia. Systematic sampling of the correspondence between the governor of Gorée and the colony yielded few references to the Siin. The Moniteur du Sénégal is equally silent prior to the 1850s; B. Grosbellet, "Le Moniteur du Sénégal et Dépendances comme source de l'histoire du Sénégal pendant le premier gouvernement de Faidherbe (1856–1861)" (master's thesis, Université Cheikh Anta Diop de Dakar, 1967); Mbodj, "Un exemple," 72; L. L. C. Faidherbe, "Notice ethnographique sur la colonie de Sénégal et dépendances," in J. Ancelle (ed.),

Les explorations au Sénégal et dans les contrées voisines depuis l'antiquité jusqu'à nos jours, ix–xl (Paris: Maisonneuve Frères et C. Leclerc, 1886).

15. Boilat, *Esquisses*. The colony signed two treaties with Siin in 1837 and 1849 to curb the exactions committed by *ceddo* on merchants and crop producers; Mbodj, "Un exemple," 95–96.
16. On the French military campaigns in Siin, see "Excursion militaire"; Pinet-Laprade, "Notice." On Ma Ba's invasion, see "Lettre au Commandant de Gorée" (May 24, 1864), ANS 13G319, No. 160; On Ma Ba's defeat, see Klein, *Islam*, ch. 4 and 5; Diouf, "Chronique."
17. Pinet-Laprade, "Rapport au Ministre" (Jun. 18, 1863), ANS 13G23; Canard, "Lettre au Commandant de Poste de Joal" (May 26, 1877), ANS 4B51; d'Etienne, "Lettre" (Apr. 5, 1882) and Cleris, "Lettre au Commandant de Poste de Joal" (Aug. 26, 1883), both in ANS 4B63.
18. Rapport du Gouverneur (Oct. 10, 1850); Aumont, "Lettre au Governeur" (Jan. 24, 1851), both in ANS 13G303.
19. Mailhetard, "Lettre au Chef de Poste" (Nov. 22, 1867), and Archambault, "Lettre au Chef de Poste" (Mar. 12, 1868), both in ANS 4B43. Father Diouf, "Excursion," 325, for instance, mentions the village of Djilas, which, having suffered the king's tyranny, sent its cattle to fadial. Resistance here was probably articulated by exploiting the channels of kinship and lineage allegiances with coastal inhabitants.
20. Noirot, "Rapport politique et économique" (Apr. 10, 1896), ANS 13G327 No. 5. Seereer oral literature also alludes to *pangool* driving away the king or enemies of the kingdom (like Ma Ba) by sending clouds of bees or causing diluvial rains to wet their assailants' powder; Faye, "Littérature," 1: 147, 153, 155, 249, and 303.
21. Dupire, "Chasse," 9.
22. Munn, "Excluded spaces," 453.
23. Mbodj, "Un exemple," 81, 497; also Klein, *Islam*, 67.
24. Klein, *Islam*, 186, ch. 8; Mbodj, "Sénégal et dépendance." In a letter to the commandant de Gorée (Mar. 1867, ANS 13G320 No. 160), de Chaunas complains that *ceddo* had begun to take to cultivation, which would leave no army against Ma Ba's soldiers. In 1896, Noirot indicated that *ceddo* were increasingly converting to agricultural labor, although the *buur*'s movements and tours of the countryside were still an occasion for pillages and ransoming villages; "Rapport," ANS 13G327.
25. Pélissier, *Paysans*, 202; Galvan, "Market," 14. Klein, *Islam*, 230–231, notes that "in Senegal [he] often asked retired chiefs just what the canton chief's job consisted of. In all cases, the first two things the chiefs listed were recruitment and the collection of taxes. Only when pressed a little did several of them talk about the chief's role as an intermediary between the people and the administration."
26. Aujas, "Sérères"; Pélissier, *Paysans*, 204–205.
27. K. Moseley, "Caravel and caravan: West Africa and the world-economies,

ca. 900–1900 AD," *Review* 15(3): 523–555 (1992), 598, shows that Senegal's dependence on the world market remained low until the late nineteenth century.

28. Klein, *Islam*, 174.
29. Noirot [1896], in Klein, *Islam*, 175; *Journal Officiel du Sénégal*, no. 1859 (Jul. 9, 1891), in David, *Ernest Noirot*, 108–109; Klein, *Islam*, 177.
30. Klein, *Islam*, 176; "Bour Sine au Directeur des Affaires Politiques" (Dec. 14, 1896), ANS 13G327; Noirot [1892], in Klein, "Chiefship," 65.
31. Roitman, *Fiscal Disobedience*, 6–9ff.
32. Noirot, "Lettre au Directeur des Affaires Politiques" (May 25 and Jun. 24, 1892), ANS 13G3222; Klein, *Islam*, 162–163.
33. Noirot, "Lettre No. 76" (Sept. 5, 1890), ANS 13G321, 4–5 (italics in the original).
34. David, *Ernest Noirot*, 104.
35. Genèbre, "Lettre au Gouverneur du Sénégal" (Jan. 17, 1889), ANS 13G321; Reinwald, "Though the earth."
36. Asiwaju, "Control through coercion." For instance, when villages refused to work on a public project, such as building a road or a bridge, they were frequently fined. See Noirot, "Lettre au Gouverneur-Général" (Mar. 28, 1896), ANS 13G325; Noirot, "Aperçu général: Travaux publics," ANS 13G327; "Administrateur au Gouverneur-Général" (Feb. 10, 1898), ANS 13G330; and *Journal Officiel du Sénégal* (Apr. 14, 1898).
37. Directeur des Affaires Politiques, "Rapport sur la commission des frontières" (Feb. 2, 1896), ANS 1F19. See Mann, "What was the Indigénat," 343, on state weakness as a point of application of arbitrary power.
38. Canard, "Lettre à Mr. Clermont" (Dec. 8, 1877), ANS 13G318.
39. Klein, *Islam*, 179; R. Delavignette, *Freedom and Authority in French West Africa* (Oxford: Oxford University Press, 1950), 42; W. B. Cohen, *Rulers of Empire: The French Colonial Service in Africa* (Palo Alto, CA: Hoover Institution Press, 1971), 63–65.
40. Cooper, "Conflict and connection," 1533.
41. E.g., "Chefs indigènes. Bulletins individuels de Notes. Sine-Saloum (Fin XIXe siècle)," ANS 13G52; also Searing, "No kings." Elders are never short of stories about the illegitimate deeds of noblemen working for the colonial administration, which included thefts, arbitrary imprisonment, or forcefully recruiting the sons of political enemies for military enlistment. Mostly, chiefs appropriated the labor of villagers and imposed days of work in their fields.
42. Galvan, *The State*, ch. 4. Cf. E. Saada, "Race and Sociological Reason in the Republic," *International Sociology* 17(2): 361–391 (2002), 377.
43. Mbodj, "Un exemple," vol. 2.
44. Myers, *Empire of Things*.
45. Mbodj, "Un exemple"; Marseille, *Empire colonial*.
46. Rocaché, "Monographie"; Martin et al., "Trois documents," 44.

47. Noirot, "Lettre au Directeur des Affaires Indigènes" (Nov. 8, 1895), ANS 13G325 No. 287.
48. Lombard, *Riz des villes*; J. McCann, *Stirring the Pot: A History of African Cuisine* (Athens: Ohio University Press, 2009).
49. Guyer, *Marginal Gains*; Guyer, *Money Matters*; Mwangi, "Of coins and conquest"; Roitman, *Fiscal Disobedience.*
50. David, *Navétanes.*
51. Interviews with Boukar Faye in Ndoffane (Jan. 17, 2011), Siga Diouf in Ndoffane-Kasnack (Jan. 21, 2011), and Aliou Sarr at Keur Mbaye Sarr (Jan. 21, 2011). See F. G. Richard, "The ruins of French imperialism: An archaeology of rural dislocations in twentieth-century Senegal," in M. Leone and J. Knaupf (eds.), *Historical Archaeologies of Capitalism*, 445–465 (New York: Springer, 2015).
52. Guigou, "Changements," 77–78.
53. Becker et al., "Traditions villageoises."
54. Dubois, "Serer"; Trincaz, "Transformations" 34. In Seereer traditional cosmology, for instance, the deceased always must find a way back to their place of birth, no matter where or how far they died, so they can aspire to eternal rest. The symbolism of the earth for the Seereer, as a metonym for land, and thus a substance materializing one's attachment to the ancestors, cultural identity, and the protection of the lineage, has been reported in other contexts. Writing in the 1950s, Gravrand mentions that a pregnant woman, when visiting nonrelatives, would discreetly scatter a bit of soil from her home over her host's bed before sitting on it, so as to shield herself and her baby from potential dangers, spells, and mystical malevolence; Gravrand, "Aux sources de la vie humaine," 292; Gravrand, "Symbolisme serer"; and Gravrand, *"Pangool."*
55. Aujas, "Région"; Klein, *Islam*, 114–116, 150–152.
56. Genèbre, "Rapport sur la situation politique et commerciale du Cercle du Sine-Saloum" (Jan. 17, 1889), ANS 13G314: Rabourdin, "Rapport politique sur le Cercle du Sine-Saloum" (May 10, 1888), ANS 13G314; Corre, "Sérères," 4; Aujas, "Sérères," 331. See also Mbodj, "Un exemple," 336; Reinwald, "Though the earth," 150–151.
57. Noirot described how the stretchiness of farming settlements and lack of infrastructure prevented French commerce from reaching the interior and enlisting new customers. Thirty years later, a representative of local business in Fatick lamented that the absence of a bridge on the Siin River reduced access to peanut producers to the east, noting that the multiplication of "savage" trading points, often to the benefit of Lebanese traders, weakened French commerce and administrative control; David, *Ernest Noirot*, 104; M. Izaure, "Discourse adressé à M. le Chef de la Colonie . . ." (1924), ANS 10D6/32.
58. Martin et al., "Trois documents"; Lericollais, *Paysans sereer.*

59. Diop and Diouf, *Sénégal sous Abdou Diouf*; S. Gellar, *Senegal: An African Nation between Islam and the West*, 2nd ed. (Boulder, CO: Westview Press, 1995). On postindependence land reforms, see Abelin, "Domaine"; and Lericollais, *Paysans seereer*. More generally, on the politics of landholding, "Debating the land question in Africa," *Comparative Studies in Society and History* 44(4): 638–668 (2002); K. Juul and C. Lund (eds.), *Negotiating Property in Africa* (Portsmouth, NH: Heinemann, 2006); C. Lentz and R. Kuba (eds.), *Land and the Politics of Belonging in West Africa* (Leiden: Brill, 2006).
60. E.g., Moore, *Suffering*; B. Chalfin, *Neoliberal Frontiers: An Ethnography of Sovereignty in West Africa* (Chicago: University of Chicago Press, 2010); Comaroff and Comaroff, *Theory from the South*; Obarrio, *Spirit*.
61. Z. Crossland, "Towards an archaeology of 'empty' space. The Efitra of the Middle West of Madagascar," *Michigan Discussions in Anthropology* 14: 18–36 (2003); M. L. Smith, "Urban empty spaces: Contentious places for consensus-building," *Archaeological Dialogues* 15(2): 216–231 (2008); also Miller, *Materiality*.
62. Lombard, *Riz des villes*.
63. McCaskie, *Asante Identities*, for a compelling example of village microhistory.
64. These manifold stories can be gleaned in Lericollais, *Paysans seereer*; and Galvan, *The State*.

CONCLUSION

1. Baucom, *Specters of the Atlantic*, 333.
2. Marx, *18th Brumaire*, 15.
3. Our interlocutor was reacting to an article by Dakar historian Mbaye Guèye, which painted an unflattering portrait of king of Siin Kumba Ndofeen and his defeat of Ma Ba in 1867. He contrasted the latter with Niokhobaye Diouf's seminal synopsis of Seereer traditions published in the journal he was carrying. Unlike Guèye—an urban, Wolof outsider—Diouf had impeccable credentials: both Seereer and a relative of our interlocutor, he was also a member of the royal family and thus a spokesperson for the official strand of historical memory. In other words, our host equated a particular kind of pedigree—grassroots *and* royal, namely—as the condition of true historical knowledge, a rhetoric embraced by the Gelwaar as their visions of the Seereer past have been challenged by others; M. Guèye, "Koumba Ndoffène, roi du Sine de 1853 à 1871," *Historiens-Géographes du Sénégal* 7: 14–22 (1999); Diouf, "Chronique"; M. Diarra, "Un village du Sénégal: Diakhao," *Sud Quotidien*, Apr. 19, 2001.
4. Interviews with members of the royal family (Apr. 2003), including Khady Diouf, the daughter of the last king of Siin, Mahecor Diouf, and one of his sisters, the then-*lingeer*; also Galvan, *The State*, 78–91.
5. G. Deleuze, *Nietzsche et la philosophie* (Paris: PUF, 1962), for an inventive take on Nietzsche's idea of eternal recurrence.

6. A. Dione, "Mbissel: À la rencontre de l'éléphant protecteur," *Le Soleil*, Oct. 24, 2012; interview with Maliam Sagne (Feb. 2015).
7. Note the rapprochement with Ferguson, *Global Shadows*.
8. A. Faye, "Performance poétique et variabilité en pays sérère: L'exemple des chants de culture (o njoom)," *Liens* 8 (2005); Faye, "Littérature"; L. S. Senghor, *La poésie de l'action: Conversations avec Mohamed Aziza* (Paris: Stock, 1980). Also Schmidt, *Historical Archaeology*.
9. Holston, *Insurgent Citizenships*, 33.
10. J. L. and J. Comaroff, *Ethnicity, Inc.* (Chicago: University of Chicago Press, 2009). In this sense, Senegal has not been immune to a zeitgeist of liberal multiculturalism, where cultural difference is positively appraised as an emblem of national richness, without ever confronting the structures of power involved in the making and perpetuating of "difference," and the concrete effects on those who inhabit that category.
11. H. Bocoum, personal communication (Jun. 2004).
12. J. Clifford, *The Predicament of Culture: Twentieth-Century Ethnography, Literature, Art* (Cambridge, MA: Harvard University Press, 1988), ch. 10.
13. S. B. Diagne, "L'avenir de la tradition," in M.-C. Diop, *Sénégal: Trajectoires d'un état*, 279–298 (Dakar: CODESRIA, 1992).
14. I. Ndoye, "Prédictions des saltigués de Fatick," *Nettali* (Jun. 8, 2009), http://www.nettali.net/Le-prochain-president-du-Senegal.html.
15. Diouf, *Histoire du Sénégal*. As Sarr and Thiaw, "Cultures," 11, remark, it is particulate ethnic others that fill ethnographic museums in Senegal, while Wolof becomes coeval with national culture.
16. Latour, *We Have Never Been Modern*.
17. B. M. Knauft (ed.), *Critically Modern: Alternatives, Alterities, Anthropologies* (Indianapolis: Indiana University Press, 2002); also Trouillot, *Global Transformations*, 45; and Palmié, *Wizards and Scientists*, for Caribbean views. Cf. Liebmann, "Mickey Mouse kachina."
18. F. Cooper, "Possibility and constraint: African independence in historical perspective," *Journal of African History* 49: 167–196 (2008), 196.
19. Galvan, "Social reproduction."
20. Obarrio, *Spirit*; Scott, *Conscripts*; Scott, "After history."
21. B. Weiss (ed.), *Producing African Futures: Ritual and Reproduction in a Neoliberal Age* (Leiden: Brill, 2004).
22. C. Piot, *Nostalgia for the Future: West Africa after the Cold War* (Chicago: University of Chicago Press, 2010); A. Diaw, "Les intellectuels entre mémoire nationaliste and interprétations de la modernité," in Diop, *Le Sénégal contemporain*, 549–574; Diagne, "Avenir de la tradition." On exhuming alternative histories of the future in Africa, see J. Roitman, "Africa, otherwise," in B. Goldstone and J. Obarrio (eds.), *African Futures: Essays on Crisis, Emergence, and Possibility*, 23–38 (Chicago: University of Chicago Press, 2017).

Index